OUR ANCESTORS OF ALBANY COUNTY NEW YORK

VOLUME 2

Sherida K. Eddlemon

HERITAGE BOOKS
2013

HERITAGE BOOKS
AN IMPRINT OF HERITAGE BOOKS, INC.

Books, CDs, and more—Worldwide

For our listing of thousands of titles see our website
at
www.HeritageBooks.com

Published 2013 by
HERITAGE BOOKS, INC.
Publishing Division
5810 Ruatan Street
Berwyn Heights, Md. 20740

Copyright © 2004 Sherida K. Eddlemon

All rights reserved. No part of this book may be reproduced or transmitted in any form or by any means, electronic or mechanical, including photocopying, recording or by any information storage and retrieval system without written permission from the author, except for the inclusion of brief quotations in a review.

International Standard Book Numbers
Paperbound: 978-0-7884-2504-2
Clothbound: 978-0-7884-6805-6

PREFACE

In 1624 the Dutch West India Company established a small settlement, Fort Orange, near what was later to become Albany, NY. When the English took over the colony they renamed the area, New York, after the Duke of York. Albany County has rich history left behind by our ancestors. These early settlers left many genealogical footprints. This work is volume two in a series devoted to finding those past footprints. This compilation contains over 6,000 entries. Albany was a center of commerce and growth very early in Colonial America.

The following abbreviations have been used in this volume:

B	Birth Date
D	Death Date
MD	Marriage Date
PRTS	Parents
PB	Place of Birth
PD	Place of Death
PMD	Place of Marriage
F	Fraternal Order
CMTS	Comments
RES	Residence
CEN	Census
NATD	Naturalization Date
I	Issue
CD	Christening Date

Hopefully, you will locate your ancestor within these pages.

OTHER HERITAGE BOOKS BY SHERIDA K. EDDLEMON:

Missouri Genealogical Records And Abstracts:
Volume 1: 1766-1839
Volume 2: 1752-1839
Volume 3: 1787-1839
Volume 4: 1741-1839
Volume 5: 1755-1839
Volume 6: 1621-1839
Volume 7: 1535-1839

Missouri Genealogical Gleanings 1840 And Beyond, Volumes 1-8

Missouri Birth and Death Records, Volumes 1-4

Butler County, Missouri, Genealogical Tidbits

Callaway County, Missouri, Marriage Records, 1821-1871

Lewis County, Missouri, Index to Circuit Court Records, Vol. 1 1833-1841

Morgan County, Missouri, Marriage Records, 1833-1893

Records of Randolph County, Missouri, 1833-1964

Ralls County, Missouri, Settlement Records, 1832-1853

Genealogical Abstracts from Missouri Church Records and Other Religious Sources, Volume 1

The "Show-Me" Guide to Missouri:
Sources for Genealogical and Historical Research

Ten Thousand Missouri Taxpayers

Genealogical Abstracts of the Cumberland Presbyterian Church, Vol. 1

Kentucky Genealogical Records and Abstracts, Volume 1: 1781-1839
Kentucky Genealogical Records and Abstracts, Volume 2: 1796-1839

A Genealogical Collection of Kentucky Birth and Death Records

Index to the Arkansas General Land Office, 1820-1907
Volumes 1-10

1890 Genealogical Census Reconstruction: Mississippi Edition, Volume 1

Genealogical Abstracts from Tennessee Newspapers, 1791-1808
Genealogical Abstracts from Tennessee Newspapers, 1803-1812
Genealogical Abstracts from Tennessee Newspapers, 1821-1828

Tennessee Genealogical Records and Abstracts

Dickson County, Tennessee, Marriage Records, 1817-1879

Our Ancestors of Albany County, New York, Volume 1

Abbey, Dorephus: (OC) Printer, (CMTS) Albany 1815 City Directory
Abbey, Seth A: (OC) Printer, (CMTS) Albany 1815 City Directory
Abbot, Asa: (CMTS) 1790 Federal Census Rensselaerville
Abbot, Asa S.: (MD) Aug. 27, 1812, (PMD) Rensselaerville, (Spouse) Eunice White
Abbot, Lorenzo E.: (RES) Home for Aged Men, (CMTS) 1889 Albany City Directory
Abbot, Samuel: (CMTS) 1790 Federal Census Rensselaerville
Abbot, William: (CMTS) 1790 Federal Census, Watervliet
Abbott, Franklin: (RES) Albany, (CMTS) 1889 Albany City Directory
Abbott, Harriet E.: (CMTS) Graduate State Normal College, Albany, NY, 1854, (RES) Syracuse, Onondage Co., NY
Abbott, Jessie B.: (CMTS) Graduate State Normal College, Albany, NY, 1882, (RES) Centre Brunswick, Rennselaer Co., NY
Abbott, Kittie F.: (CMTS) Graduate State Normal College, Albany, NY, 1879, (RES) Bath, Rensselaer Co., NY
Abeel, Christoffel: (CD) Dec. 16, 1696, (PRTS) Johannes Abeel and Catalina Schuyler
Abel, Henry: (OC) Weigher of Hay, (CMTS) Albany 1815 City Directory
Abel, Henry Van Patten: (B) Jul. 15, 1806, (PB) Albany, Albany Co., NY, (PRTS) Henry Abel and Elizabeth Van Patten
Abel, Mayra A.: (CMTS) Graduate State Normal College, Albany, NY, 1865, (RES) Bath, Steuben Co., NY
Abel, Widow Johanna: (OC), (CMTS) Albany 1815 City Directory
Able, Andrew: (CMTS) 1790 Federal Census, Watervliet
Abraham, Christian: (CMTS) 1790 Federal Census, Watervliet
Abrams, Myers: (F) Member Washington Lodge, No. 85, 1900, Albany, NY
Ackart, Margaret B.: (CMTS) Graduate State Normal College, Albany, NY, 1886, (RES) Crandall's Corners, Washington Co., WA
Acker, John J.: (F) Member Temple Lodge, No. 14, 1900, Albany, NY, (CMTS) Life Member
Acker, Richard: (OC) Laborer, (CMTS) Albany 1815 City Directory
Acker, Richard: (MD) Jul. 19, 1810, (PMD) First Lutheran Church, Albany, NY, (Spouse) Sally Artcher
Acker, Richard: (MD) Oct. 8, 1822, (Spouse) Rebecca Kennedy, (PMD) First Lutheran Church, Albany, Albany Co., NY
Acker, Samuel: (OC) Cartman, (CMTS) Albany 1815 City Directory
Acker, Thomas: (OC) Steamboat Pilot, (CMTS) Albany 1815 City Directory
Ackerman, Alfred H.: (F) Member Temple Lodge, No. 14, 1900, Albany, NY
Ackerman, Casparus: (CMTS) 1790 Federal Census Rensselaerville
Ackerman, Gilbert: (RES) 152 S. Pearl, (CMTS) Albany 1815 City Directory

Ackerman, Gilbert: (MD) Feb. 14, 1799, (Spouse) Rachel DeGarmo, (PMD) First Dutch Reformed Church, Albany, Albany Co., NY
Ackerman, Gilbert: (B) 1768, (D) Oct. 11, 1834, (DP) Albany
Ackerman, Jane C.: (CMTS) Graduate State Normal College, Albany, NY, 1855, (RES) Pillar Point, Jefferson Co., NY
Ackley, Cutlip: (CMTS) 1790 Federal Census Rensselaerville
Ackley, Lucy A.: (CMTS) Graduate State Normal College, Albany, NY, 1857, (RES) Kinderhook, Columbia Co., NY
Adams, Deborah L.: (CMTS) Graduate State Normal College, Albany, NY, 1857, (RES) Albany, Albany Co., NY
Adams, Emily R.: (CMTS) Graduate State Normal College, Albany, NY, 1861, (RES) Sherburne, Chegnango Co., NY
Adams, George J.: (F) Member Mount Vernon Lodge, No. 3, 1900, Albany, NY
Adams, Imogene: (CMTS) Graduate State Normal College, Albany, NY, 1877, (RES) Troy, Rensselaer Co., NY
Adams, Joseph: (CMTS) 1790 Federal Census Rensselaerville
Adams, Joseph: (B) May 30, 1727, (BP) Albany, NY, (D) Aug. 10, 1778
Adams, Joseph: (OC) Currier, (CMTS) Albany 1815 City Directory
Adams, Lucie: (CMTS) Graduate State Normal College, Albany, NY, 1877, (RES) Hamden, Delaware Co.
Adams, Mary L.: (CMTS) Graduate State Normal College, Albany, NY, 1892, (RES) North Spencer, Tioga Co., NY
Adams, Michael T.: (F) Member Mount Vernon Lodge, No. 3, 1900, Albany, NY
Adams, Samuel: (RES) 97 Washington, (CMTS) Albany 1815 City Directory
Adams, Sarah A.: (CMTS) Graduate State Normal College, Albany, NY, 1865, (RES) Marion, Wayne Co., NY
Adams, Thomas: (RES) 63 Maiden Lane, (CMTS) Albany 1815 City Directory
Adams, William: (OC) Merchant, (CMTS) Albany 1815 City Directory
Adams, William C.: (MD) Aug. 31, 1722, (Spouse) Maude Jones, (PMD) Albany, Albany CO., NY
Adams, William Charles: (B) Jun. 12, 1699, (D) Jun. 12, 1757, (DP) Albany, NY
Addington, George: (F) Member Temple Lodge, No. 14, 1900, Albany, NY
Addison, Otis: (OC) Embargo Alley, (CMTS) Albany 1815 City Directory
Adee, Nettie D.: (CMTS) Graduate State Normal College, Albany, NY, 1891, (RES) Davenport, Delaware Co., NY
Adler, Danie;: (F) Member Washington Lodge, No. 85, 1900, Albany, NY
Adsit, John: (OC) Grocer, (CMTS) Albany 1815 City Directory
Agnew, Anna: (CMTS) Graduate State Normal College, Albany,

NY, 1868, (RES) Ogdensburgh, St. Lawrence Co., NY
Agnew, Ida: (CMTS) Graduate State Normal College, Albany,
    NY, 1889, (RES) Tarrytown, Westcher Co., NY
Ainsworth, Kate M.: (CMTS) Graduate State Normal College, Albany,
    NY, 1888, (RES) Saratoga Springs, Saratoga Co., NY
Aitken, Margaret B.: (CMTS) Graduate State Normal College, Albany,
    NY, 1895, (RES) Johnstown, Fulton Co., NY
Akerly, Alice M.: (CMTS) Graduate State Normal College, Albany,
    NY, 1887, (RES) Green Lawn, Suffolk Co., NY
Akin, Isaac W.: (F) Member Masters Lodge, No. 5, 1900, Albany, NY
Akins, Anna B.: (CMTS) Graduate State Normal College, Albany,
    NY, 1893, (RES) Tuckahoe, Westchester Co., NY
Akins, Laura E.: (CMTS) Graduate State Normal College, Albany,
    NY, 1894, (RES) Greenbush, Rensselaer Co., NY
Albee, Amasa: (CD) May 9, 1819, Third Presbyterian Church, Albany,
    Albany Co., NY
Albreagh, Henry: (CMTS) 1790 Federal Census, Watervliet
Albreagh, John: (CMTS) 1790 Federal Census, Watervliet
Alby, Amasa: (OC) Shoemaker, (CMTS) Albany 1815 City Directory
Alden, Frances: (CMTS) Graduate State Normal College, Albany,
    NY ,1878, (RES) Smith's Basin, Washington Co.,NY
Aldrich, Zachariah: (OC) Cartman, (CMTS) Albany 1815 City Directory
Aldridge, Clara E.: (CMTS) Graduate State Normal College, Albany,
    NY, 1891, (RES) Rone, Oneida Co., NY
Alexander, Annie M.: (CMTS) Graduate State Normal College, Albany,
    NY, 1864, (RES) Albany, Albany Co., NY
Alexander, Andrew: (MD) Dec. 19, 1854, (Spouse) Mary Silliman,
    (PMD) Albany Co., NY
Alexander, Charles: (CMTS) 1790 Federal Census, Watervliet
Alexander, Hugh: (CMTS) 1790 Federal Census, Watervliet
Alexander, Joseph: (OC) Merchant, (CMTS) Albany 1815 City Directory
Alexander, Mary C.: (CMTS) Graduate State Normal College, Albany,
    NY, 1872, (RES) Cedar Hill, Albany Co., NY
Alexander, Mary W.: (CMTS) Graduate State Normal College, Albany,
    NY, 1874, (RES) Bethlehem, Albany Co., NY
Alexander, Sarah A.: (CMTS) Graduate State Normal College, Albany,
    NY, 1872, (RES) Cedar Hill, Albany Co., NY
Alexander, William B.: (CMTS) Albany 1815 City Directory
Alexander, William H.: (OC) Merchant, (CMTS) Albany 1815 City
    Directory
Alford, Helen A.: (CMTS) Graduate State Normal College, Albany,
    NY, 1865, (RES) Buffalo, Erie Co., NY
Alger, David: (CMTS) 1790 Federal Census Rensselaerville
Alger, Emma J.: (CMTS) Graduate State Normal College, Albany,
    NY, 1874, (RES) Ames. Montgomery Co., NY

Allan, Benjamin: (F) Member Washington Lodge, No. 85, 1900, Albany, NY
Allanson, James E.: (F) Member Mount Vernon Lodge, No. 3, 1900, Albany, NY, (CMTS) Past Master 1880
Allanson, Peter: (OC) Sawyer, (CMTS) Albany 1815 City Directory
Allanson, Richard: (OC) Architect, (CMTS) Albany 1815 City Directory
Allanson, Richard: (OC) Attorney, (CMTS) Albany 1815 City Directory
Allen, Asa K: (RES) 80 Beaver, (CMTS) Albany 1815 City Directory
Allen, Benjamin: (OC) Preceptor, (CMTS) Albany 1815 City Directory
Allen, Benjamin: (B) Sep. 11, 1775, (BP) Albany, Albany Co., NY
Allen, David: (CMTS) 1790 Federal Census, Watervliet
Allen, Florence E.: (CMTS) Graduate State Normal College, Albany, NY, 1892, (RES) Rose Valley, Wayne Co., NY
Allen, Huldah A.: (CMTS) Graduate State Normal College, Albany, NY, 1854, (RES) Schenectady, Schenectady Co., NY
Allen, John: (CMTS) 1790 Federal Census Rensselaerville
Allen, Kate M.: (CMTS) Graduate State Normal College, Albany, NY, 1855, (RES) Hudson, Columbia Co., NY
Allen, Peleg: (CMTS) 1790 Federal Census Rensselaerville
Allen, Pliny: (OC) Merchant, (CMTS) Albany 1815 City Directory
Allen, Solomon: (OC) Broker, (CMTS) Albany 1815 City Directory
Allen, Tilley: (OC) Merchant, (CMTS) Albany 1815 City Directory
Allen, William: (CMTS) 1790 Federal Census, Watervliet
Allicot, Thomas: (RES) 39 Columbia, (CMTS) Albany 1815 City Directory
Allshesky, Theodore F.: (F) Member Mount Vernon Lodge, No. 3, 1900, Albany, NY
Almy, Maria C.: (CMTS) Graduate State Normal College, Albany, NY, 1848, (RES) Hart's Village, Dutchess Co., NY
Alsdorf, John J.: (F) Member Temple Lodge, No. 14, 1900, Albany, NY
Alsop, Robert: (RES) 142 Washington, (CMTS) Albany 1815 City Directory
Alton, Margaret B.: (CMTS) Graduate State Normal College, Albany, NY, 1889, (RES) Troy, Rensselaer Co., NY
Ameille, John: (OC) Confectioner, (CMTS) Albany 1815 City Directory
Ames, Ezra: (OC) portrait painter, (CMTS) Albany 1815 City Directory
Ames, Judson: (F) Member Mount Vernon Lodge, No. 3, 1900, Albany, NY
Ammenheuser, Sophie: (CMTS) Graduate State Normal College, Albany, NY, 1892, (RES) Albany, Albany Co., NY
Amsdell, Theodore M.: (F) Member Temple Lodge, No. 14, 1900, Albany, NY, (CMTS) Life Member
Anable, Samuel: (F) Member Masters Lodge, No. 5, 1900, Albany, NY
Anaud, John J.: (OC) Carpenter, (CMTS) Albany 1859 City Directory

Anderson, John: (OC) Laborer, (CMTS) Albany 1815 City Directory
Anderson, R.: (OC) Merchant, (CMTS) Albany 1815 City Directory
Anderson, Robert: (OC) Laborer, (CMTS) Albany 1815 City Directory
Anderson, Robert: (OC) Merchant, (CMTS) Albany 1815 City Directory
Anderson, W.: (OC) Merchant, (CMTS) Albany 1815 City Directory
Anderson, William: (OC) Waterman, (CMTS) Albany 1815 City Directory
Anderson , S. Grace: (CMTS) Graduate State Normal College, Albany, NY, 1884, (RES) Clayville, Oneida Co., NY
Andews, Orin: (OC) Baker, (CMTS) Albany 1859 City Directory
Andrews, Daniel: (CMTS) 1790 Federal Census Rensselaerville
Andrews, Ella F.: (CMTS) Graduate State Normal College, Albany, NY, 1881, (RES) Yonkers, Westchester Co., NY
Andrews, Emelis A.: (CMTS) Graduate State Normal College, Albany, NY, 1853, (RES) Albany, Albany Co., NY
Andrews, John: (RES) Boarding House at 53 N. Pearl, (CMTS) Albany 1815 City Directory
Andrews, John: (OC) Frelinghuysen, (CMTS) Albany 1815 City Directory
Andrews, John: (OC) Merchant, (CMTS) Albany 1815 City Directory
Andrews, Mary F.: (CMTS) Graduate State Normal College, Albany, NY, 1868, (RES) Albany, Albany Co., NY
Andrews, Michl.: (OC) Moulder, (CMTS) Albany 1859 City Directory
Andrews, Orphana E.: (CMTS) Graduate State Normal College, Albany, NY, 1857, (RES) LaFayette, Onondaga Co., NY
Andrews, Parthenia L.: (OC) Widow, (CMTS) Albany 1859 City Directory
Andrews, Rapin: (OC) Clerk, (CMTS) Albany 1859 City Directory
Andrews, Samuel: (RES) House Third above Knox, (CMTS) Albany 1859 City Directory
Andrews, Truman: (OC) Printer, (CMTS) Albany 1859 City Directory
Andrews, Widow: (RES) 25 Capitol, (CMTS) Albany 1815 City Directory
Andrews, William: (OC) Teacher, (CMTS) Albany 1815 City Directory
Andrews, William: (OC) Police, (CMTS) Albany 1859 City Directory
Andrews , Orin F.: (OC) Baker, (CMTS) Albany 1859 City Directory
Ands, Frederick: (OC) Grocer, Papin & Co., (CMTS) Albany 1859 City Directory
Andserson, Charlotte M.: (CMTS) Graduate State Normal College, Albany, NY, 1853, (RES) Albany, Albany Co., NY
Angel, Thomas: (OC) Currier, (CMTS) Albany 1815 City Directory
Angell, Harriet: (CMTS) Graduate State Normal College, Albany, NY, 1877, (RES) Taberg, Oneida Co., NY
Angers, James: (CMTS) 1790 Federal Census, Watervliet
Anglein, Timothy: (OC) Laborer, (CMTS) Albany 1859 City Directory
Angus, Charles: (OC) Printer, (CMTS) Albany 1859 City Directory
Angus, Charles H.: (F) Member Temple Lodge, No. 14, 1900,

Albany, NY
Angus, David: (OC) Baker, (CMTS) Albany 1815 City Directory
Angus, George C.: (F) Member Temple Lodge, No. 14, 1900,
Albany, NY
Angus, Jacob B.: (OC) Carpenter, (CMTS) Albany 1815 City Directory
Angus, James: (OC) Carpenter, (CMTS) Albany 1815 City Directory
Angus, Jennie F.: (CMTS) Graduate State Normal College, Albany,
NY, 1892, (RES) Clyde, Wayne Co., NY
Angus, John G.: (OC) Cigarmaker, (CMTS) Albany 1859 City Directory
Angus, John H.: (OC) Police Constable, (CMTS) Albany 1815 City
Directory
Angus, Miss Maria: (OC) Boards at 146 Swan, Arbor Hill, (CMTS)
Albany 1859 City Directory
Angus, Mrs. Robert: (OC) Boarding House, (CMTS) Albany 1859 City
Directory
Angus, Stephen: (OC) Moulder, (CMTS) Albany 1859 City Directory
Angus, Thomas: (OC) Cartman, (CMTS) Albany 1815 City Directory
Annable, Joseph: (OC) Butcher, (CMTS) Albany 1815 City Directory
Annecke, Mary: (OC) Embroidering, (CMTS) Albany 1859 City Directory
Annecke, Theodore: (OC) Gasfitter, (CMTS) Albany 1859 City Directory
Annesley, Isaac: (CO) L. Annesley & Co., Looking Glasses & Picture
Frames, (CMTS) Albany 1859 City Directory
Annesley, Lawson: (CO) L. Annesley & Co., Looking Glasses & Picture
Frames, (CMTS) Albany 1859 City Directory
Annesley, Richard L.: (OC) O. S. Rice & Co., painter, (CMTS) Albany
1859 City Directory
Annesley, William: (OC) Gilder, (CMTS) Albany 1859 City Directory
Annesly, William: (OC) Gilder, (CMTS) Albany 1815 City Directory
Anniver, Widow: (OC) Flora, (CMTS) Albany 1815 City Directory
Ansboro, Peter: (OC) Porterhouse, (CMTS) Albany 1859 City Directory
Antes, Ida M.: (CMTS) Graduate State Normal College, Albany,
NY, 1880, (RES) Plank Road, Onondaga Co., NY
Anthiny, Henry A.: (OC) Machinist, (CMTS) Albany 1859 City Directory
Anthony, Charles H.: (OC) School, (CMTS) Albany 1859 City Directory
Anthony, Elizabeth: (OC) Widow, (CMTS) Albany 1859 City Directory
Anthony, Horace C.: (F) Member Temple Lodge, No. 14, 1900,
Albany, NY
Anthony, John: (CMTS) 1790 Federal Census, Watervliet
Anthony, Samuel: (CMTS) 1790 Federal Census, Watervliet
Anthony, Susan: (CMTS) Graduate State Normal College, Albany,
NY, 1868, (RES) Union Springs, Cayuga Co., NY
Anthony, Wm. H.: (OC) Barber, (CMTS) Albany 1859 City Directory
Antis, Francis: (CMTS) 1790 Federal Census, Watervliet
Apple, Henry: (CMTS) 1790 Federal Census, Watervliet
Apple, Jacob: (OC) Pedler, (CMTS) Albany 1859 City Directory

Appledown, John: (OC) Paperhanger, (CMTS) Albany 1859 City Directory
Appleton, Henry D.: (F) Member Masters Lodge, No. 5, 1900, Albany, NY
Appleton, John: (RES) 188 Washington Ave., (CMTS) Albany 1859 City Directory
Appleton, Joseph L.: (F) Member Temple Lodge, No. 14, 1900, Albany, NY
Appleton, Wm.: (OC) Produce, (CMTS) Albany 1859 City Directory
Apps, David: (OC) Engineer, (CMTS) Albany 1859 City Directory
Apps, Jacob: (OC) Fireman, (CMTS) Albany 1859 City Directory
Apps, Mr.: (OC) Laborer, (CMTS) Albany 1859 City Directory
Apps, Robert: (OC) Boilermaker, (CMTS) Albany 1859 City Directory
Apps, William H.: (OC) Laborer, (CMTS) Albany 1859 City Directory
Archer, Edmund: (CMTS) 1790 Federal Census, Watervliet
Archer, George: (OC) Teamster, (CMTS) Albany 1815 City Directory
Archer, James: (OC) Teamster, (CMTS) Albany 1815 City Directory
Archer, Widow: (OC) of George Archer, (CMTS) Albany 1815 City Directory
Archer, William: (OC) Teamster, (CMTS) Albany 1815 City Directory
Archlager, Charles: (OC) Tailor, (CMTS) Albany 1859 City Directory
Arcularius, Mehitable: (OC) Grocer, (CMTS) Albany 1815 City Directory
Argberger, John B.: (OC) Shoemaker, (CMTS) Albany 1859 City Directory
Argersinger, Cora J.: (CMTS) Graduate State Normal College, Albany, NY, 1888, (RES) Johnstown, Fulton Co., NY
Arkell, John: (OC) Arkell & Vickers, Grocer, (CMTS) Albany 1859 City Directory
Arkles, Joseph: (OC) Farmer, (CMTS) Albany 1859 City Directory
Armatage, Charles T.: (OC) Clerk, (CMTS) Albany 1859 City Directory
Armatage, J. H.: (OC) Grocer, (CMTS) Albany 1859 City Directory
Armington, Anthony R.: (F) Member Temple Lodge, No. 14, 1900, Albany, NY
Armington, Charlotte: (OC) Millinery, (CMTS) Albany 1859 City Directory
Armour, John B.: (OC) Brushmaker, (RES) House at Newtonville, (CMTS) Albany 1859 City Directory
Arms, Mary E.: (CMTS) Graduate State Normal College, Albany, NY, 1857, (RES) New York, New York Co., NY
Arms, Noahdiah L.: (OC) Tailoress, (CMTS) Albany 1859 City Directory
Armsby, James H.: (OC) Physician, (CMTS) Albany 1859 City Directory
Armstage, Charles H.: (F) Member Temple Lodge, No. 14, 1900, Albany, NY
Armstead, Mrs. Jane: (RES) House at 381 State, (CMTS) Albany 1859 City Directory

Armstrong, James: (OC) Printer, (CMTS) Albany 1859 City Directory
Armstrong, John: (OC) Machinist, (CMTS) Albany 1859 City Directory
Armstrong, Michael: (OC) Baker, (CMTS) Albany 1815 City Directory
Armstrong, Adam: (CMTS) Albany 1815 City Directory
Armstrong, Cornelius W.: (OC) Commission Merchant, (CMTS) Albany 1859 City Directory
Armstrong, Emma V.: (CMTS) Graduate State Normal College, Albany, NY, 1890, (RES) Peekskill, Putnam Co., NY
Armstrong, F. Edith: (CMTS) Graduate State Normal College, Albany, NY, 1888, (RES) Oak Corners, Ontario Co., NY
Armstrong, John: (CMTS) 1790 Federal Census Rensselaerville
Armstrong, K. Maud: (CMTS) Graduate State Normal College, Albany, NY, 1891, (RES) Oak Corners, Ontario Co., NY
Armstrong, Miss Eleanor: (OC) Steamtress, (CMTS) Albany 1859 City Directory
Armstrong, Robert: (OC) Printer, (CMTS) Albany 1859 City Directory
Arnhout, Jacob: (CMTS) 1790 Federal Census, Watervliet
Arnold, Amos: (OC) Carman, (CMTS) Albany 1859 City Directory
Arnold, Benj. W.: (OC) Arnold, Folsom & Co., Lumber, (CMTS) Albany 1859 City Directory
Arnold, Freeman S.: (F) Member Temple Lodge, No. 14, 1900, Albany, NY
Arnold, Helen C.: (CMTS) Graduate State Normal College, Albany, NY, 1893, (RES) Palmyra, Wayne Co., NY
Arnold, Henry: (O) Carpenter, (CMTS) Albany 1859 City Directory
Arnold, Hugh A.: (F) Member Masters Lodge, No. 5, 1900, Albany, NY
Arnold, James I.: (RES) House at 4 Park Place, (CMTS) Albany 1859 City Directory
Arnold, John: (OC) Cartman, (CMTS) Albany 1815 City Directory
Arnold, Moses: (OC) Tailor, (CMTS) Albany 1859 City Directory
Arnold, Rose M.: (CMTS) Graduate State Normal College, Albany, NY, 1889, (RES) Albany, Albany Co., NY
Arnold, S. Elizabeth: (CMTS) Graduate State Normal College, Albany, NY, 1872, (RES) Hartford, Washington Co., NY
Arnold, William D.: (F) Member Masters Lodge, No. 5, 1900, Albany, NY
Arnold, J. Newton: (OC) Clerk N.Y.C.R.R., (CMTS) Albany 1859 City Directory
Arnott, James B.: (OC) Tailor, (CMTS) Albany 1859 City Directory
Arnott, Jr., James: (OC) Tailor, (CMTS) Albany 1859 City Directory
Arnout, Margaret S.: (CMTS) Graduate State Normal College, Albany, NY, 1847, (RES) New York, New York Co., NY
Arrison, Jennie L.: (CMTS) Graduate State Normal College, Albany, NY, 1895, (RES) Oxford, Chenango Co., NY
Arrowsmith, J. W.: (OC) Drygoods, (CMTS) Albany 1859 City Directory

Arshowe, Oong: (OC) Tea Dealer, Arshowe & Berry, (CMTS) Albany 1859 City Directory
Artcher, Ann: (OC) Widow, (CMTS) Albany 1859 City Directory
Artcher, John: (OC) Brickmaker, (CMTS) Albany 1859 City Directory
Artcher, Laura A.: (CMTS) Graduate State Normal College, Albany, NY, 1885, (RES) Albany, Albany Co., NY
Artcher, Michael: (OC) Artcher & Lyman,Flour, (CMTS) Albany 1859 City Directory
Arthur, Peter: (OC) Engineer, (CMTS) Albany 1859 City Directory
Artle, George: (OC) Laborer, (CMTS) Albany 1859 City Directory
Ash, Alfred S.: (OC) Clerk, (CMTS) Albany 1859 City Directory
Ash, John: (CMTS) 1790 Federal Census, Watervliet
Ashton, Emily R.: (CMTS) Graduate State Normal College, Albany, NY, 1880, (RES) East Albany, Rensselaer Co., NY
Ashton, Joseph: (OC) Patternmaker, (CMTS) Albany 1859 City Directory
Ashton, Josephine: (CMTS) Graduate State Normal College, Albany, NY, 1883, (RES) East Albany, Rensselaer Co., NY
Ashwell, Joseph: (CMTS) 1790 Federal Census, Watervliet
Aspinall, Robert: (OC) Mason, (CMTS) Albany 1859 City Directory
Aspinwall, Lewis: (OC) Brass Founder, (CMTS) Albany 1815 City Directory
Asprion, John: (OC) Mason, (CMTS) Albany 1859 City Directory
Assaleona, Leon: (OC) Fruit, (CMTS) Albany 1859 City Directory
Aston, Thomas: (CMTS) 1790 Federal Census, Watervliet
Atchinson, Atlanta: (CMTS) Graduate State Normal College, Albany, NY, 1872, (RES) Schoharie Corners, Schoharie Co., NY
Atchinson, Harriet L.: (CMTS) Graduate State Normal College, Albany, NY, 1880, (RES) Jefferson, Schoharie Co., NY
Atherton, George W.: (OC) Teacher, (CMTS) Albany 1859 City Directory
Atkins, Ester E.: (CMTS) Graduate State Normal College, Albany, NY, 1860, (RES) Esopus, Ulster Co., NY
Atkins, Francis: (OC) Teamster, (CMTS) Albany 1859 City Directory
Atkins, James: (OC) Cutter, (CMTS) Albany 1859 City Directory
Atkinson, Caroline G.: (CMTS) Graduate State Normal College, Albany, NY, 1885, (RES) Albany, Albany Co., NY
Atkinson, Edward J.: (OC) Waiter, (CMTS) Albany 1859 City Directory
Atkinson, James: (OC) Grocer, (CMTS) Albany 1859 City Directory
Atkinson, James: (RES) 51 Union, (CMTS) Albany 1815 City Directory
Atkinson, Mary: (OC) Tailoress, (CMTS) Albany 1859 City Directory
Atkinson, Robert: (OC) Baker, (CMTS) Albany 1859 City Directory
Atter, John: (CMTS) 1790 Federal Census, Watervliet
Attridge, Patrick: (OC) Washington Garden, (CMTS) Albany 1815 City Directory
Attwood, Isaac: (CMTS) 1790 Federal Census Rensselaerville
Atwell, M. Eudora: (CMTS) Graduate State Normal College, Albany,

NY, 1889, (RES) Gulf Summit, Broome Co., NY
Atwood, John: (OC) Clerk in the Dept. of Public Instruction, (CMTS) Albany 1859 City Directory
Atwood, M. Elizabeth: (CMTS) Graduate State Normal College, Albany, NY, 1854, (RES) Albany, Albany Co., NY
Aubin, Napeoleon: (OC) Gas Works, (CMTS) Albany 1859 City Directory
Auer, Alois: (OC) Gardner, (CMTS) Albany 1859 City Directory
Auer, Louis C.: (F) Member Washington Lodge, No. 85, 1900, Albany, NY
Aufasser, Moses: (OC) Pedler, (CMTS) Albany 1859 City Directory
Augusty, Samuel C: (OC) Cooper, (CMTS) Albany 1815 City Directory
Aussen, Jacob: (OC) Cooper, (CMTS) Albany 1859 City Directory
Austin, Abraham: (OC) Carman, (CMTS) Albany 1859 City Directory
Austin, Anna E.: (CMTS) Graduate State Normal College, Albany, NY, 1886, (RES) West Exeter, Otsego Co., NY
Austin, Arthur C.: (F) Member Temple Lodge, No. 14, 1900, Albany, NY
Austin, Benjamin: (OC) Cartman, (CMTS) Albany 1815 City Directory
Austin, Charles L.: (OC) Attorney, (CMTS) Albany 1859 City Directory
Austin, David P.: (OC) Teacher, (CMTS) Albany 1859 City Directory
Austin, J. C.: (OC) Dentist, (CMTS) Albany 1859 City Directory
Austin, J. Louise: (CMTS) Graduate State Normal College, Albany, NY, 1891, (RES) Mahopac Falls, Putnam Co., NY
Austin, James M.: (OC) Butcher, (CMTS) Albany 1859 City Directory
Austin, Jeremiah: (OC) Bookkeeper, (CMTS) Albany 1859 City Directory
Austin, Jeremiah J.: (OC) Austin & Co., Agents for Albany & Canal Line, (CMTS) Albany 1859 City Directory
Austin, Matthew: (CMTS) 1790 Federal Census Rensselaerville
Austin, Mathias: (MD) Feb. 7, 1813, (Spouse) Elizabeth Weymir, (PMD) Albany, Albany Co., NY
Austin, Matthias: (B) Apr. 1, 1790, (BP) Albany, Albany Co., NY
Austin, Matthias: (OC) Carpenter, (CMTS) Albany 1859 City Directory
Austin, Minnie I.: (CMTS) Graduate State Normal College, Albany, NY, 1890, (RES) Watertown, Jefferson Co., NY
Austin, Robert: (OC) Laborer, (CMTS) Albany 1859 City Directory
Austin, Robert F.: (RES) Boards at the Dunlop House, (CMTS) Albany 1859 City Directory
Austin, Sarah F.: (CMTS) Graduate State Normal College, Albany, NY, 1882, (RES) Peekskill, Westchester Co., NY
Austin, Thomas: (OC) Meat Stall, (CMTS) Albany 1859 City Directory
Austin, Valentine: (OC) Cooper, (CMTS) Albany 1815 City Directory
Austin, William: (OC) Tin Plate Worker, (CMTS) Albany 1815 City Directory
Austin, William L.: (F) Member Masters Lodge, No. 5, 1900, Albany, NY

Auty, Alexander: (OC) Liquors, (CMTS) Albany 1859 City Directory
Avann, James W.: (OC) Shoemaker, (CMTS) Albany 1859 City Directory
Avann, Olivia A.: (CMTS) Graduate State Normal College, Albany, NY, 1889, (RES) Fultonville, Montgomery Co., NY
Avann, Thomas: (RES) Boards at 96 Bradford, (CMTS) Albany 1859 City Directory
Averill, Horace: (OC) Averill & Ruggles, Flour and Grain, (CMTS) Albany 1859 City Directory
Averill, William F.: (OC) Washington Cont., (CMTS) Albany 1815 City Directory
Avery, Archibald: (RES) House at 85 Hudson, (CMTS) Albany 1859 City Directory
Avery, Elias: (OC) Broker, (CMTS) Albany 1859 City Directory
Avery, Lee: (MD) Dec. 10, 1808, (Spouse) Eliza Hooker, (PMD) First Dutch Reformed Church, Albany, Albany Co., NY
Avery, Mrs. Amos: (RES) House at 21 Ten Broeck, (CMTS) Albany 1859 City Directory
Avery, Sarah C.: (CMTS) Graduate State Normal College, Albany, NY, 1867, (RES) Minaville, Montgomery CO., NY
Avery, Sophie L.: (CMTS) Graduate State Normal College, Albany, NY, 1870, (RES) Windham, Greene Co., NY
Avery, Widow of Lee Avery: (RES) 9 Liberty, (CMTS) Albany 1815 City Directory
Ayer, Abbie: (CMTS) Graduate State Normal College, Albany, NY, 1872, (RES) North Greenbush, Rensselaer Co., NY
Ayer, Daniel: (OC) Land Agent, (CMTS) Albany 1859 City Directory
Ayers, Alfred: (OC) Carpenter, (CMTS) Albany 1859 City Directory
Ayers, William: (OC) Tailor, (CMTS) Albany 1859 City Directory
Babb, William: (OC) Merchant, (CMTS) Albany 1815 City Directory
Babbet, Ira: (OC) Brickmaker, (CMTS) Albany 1815 City Directory
Babbitt, Ellen B.: (CMTS) Graduate State Normal College, Albany, NY, 1853, (RES) Syracuse, Onondage Co., NY
Babbitt, Mary E.: (CMTS) Graduate State Normal College, Albany, NY, 1894, (RES) Warren, OH
Babcock, A. Allen: (OC) Agent, (CMTS) Albany 1859 City Directory
Babcock, Anna L.: (CMTS) Graduate State Normal College, Albany, NY, 1865, (RES) South Hampton, Suffolk Co., NY
Babcock, Benjamin: (OC) Painter, (CMTS) Albany 1859 City Directory
Babcock, Beulah E.: (CMTS) Graduate State Normal College, Albany, NY, 1889, (RES) Mount Vernon, Westchester Co., NY
Babcock, Cordtland S.: (F) Member Temple Lodge, No. 14, 1900, Albany, NY
Babcock, Daniel L.: (OC) Captain, Steamboat, Young America, (CMTS) Albany 1859 City Directory
Babcock, Darius: (CMTS) 1790 Federal Census Rensselaerville

Babcock, Edith M.: (CMTS) Graduate State Normal College, Albany, NY, 1887, (RES) Mt. Vernon, Westchester Co., NY
Babcock, Edward: (OC) Insurance Agent, (CMTS) Albany 1859 City Directory
Babcock, Elisha: (OC) Shoemaker, (CMTS) Albany 1859 City Directory
Babcock, Fanny A.: (CMTS) Graduate State Normal College, Albany, NY, 1852, (RES) Westford, Otesgo Co., NY
Babcock, Horace H.: (OC) Boston and Harlem Railroad Office, (CMTS) Albany 1859 City Directory
Babcock, Ida M.: (CMTS) Graduate State Normal College, Albany, NY, 1884, (RES) Laurens, Otesgo Co., NY
Babcock, James L.: (OC) Physician, (CMTS) Albany 1859 City Directory
Babcock, John M.: (OC) Carman, (CMTS) Albany 1859 City Directory
Babcock, Joseph M.: (OC) Tinsmith, (CMTS) Albany 1859 City Directory
Babcock, Julia A.: (CMTS) Graduate State Normal College, Albany, NY, 1892, (RES) Ogdensburgh, St. Lawrence Co., NY
Babcock, Mena: (CMTS) Graduate State Normal College, Albany, NY, 1883, (RES) Haverstraw, Rockland Co., NY
Babcock, Meriba A.: (CMTS) Graduate State Normal College, Albany, NY, 1854, (RES) DeKalb, St. Lawrence Co., NY
Babcock, Minnie: (CMTS) Graduate State Normal College, Albany, NY, 1884, (RES) Troy, Rensselaer Co., NY
Babcock, Robert: (OC) County Clerk, City Hall, (CMTS) Albany 1859 City Directory
Babcock, Timothy: (OC) Shoemaker, (CMTS) Albany 1859 City Directory
Babington, Daniel: (OC) Butcher, (CMTS) Albany 1859 City Directory
Babst, Adam: (CMTS) 1790 Federal Census, Watervliet
Babst, Rudolph: (CMTS) 1790 Federal Census, Watervliet
Bach, Jacob: (OC) Pedler, (CMTS) Albany 1859 City Directory
Bach, Joseph: (OC) Butcher, (CMTS) Albany 1859 City Directory
Bach, Simon: (OC) Pedler, (CMTS) Albany 1859 City Directory
Bacheller, Benj. F.: (OC) Harnessmaker, (CMTS) Albany 1859 City Directory
Bacheller, Dwight: (OC) Harnessmaker, (CMTS) Albany 1859 City Directory
Bachman, B.: (OC) Cigarmaker, (CMTS) Albany 1859 City Directory
Bachman, Renatus: (RES) House at 113 Dove, (CMTS) Albany 1859 City Directory
Backer, Aaron B.: (CMTS) 1790 Federal Census, Watervliet
Backer, James F.: (F) Member Temple Lodge, No. 14, 1900, Albany, NY
Backman, Henry A.: (OC) Resident, (CMTS) Albany 1859 City Directory
Backus, E. F.: (OC) Bookseller, (CMTS) Albany 1815 City Directory
Bacon, Adelia S.: (CMTS) Graduate State Normal College, Albany,

NY, 1883, (RES) Batchellerville, Saratoga Co., NY
Bacon, Frances A.: (CMTS) Graduate State Normal College, Albany, NY, 1855, (RES) Albany, Albany Co., NY
Bacon, George: (OC) Saddler, (CMTS) Albany 1815 City Directory
Bacon, John F.: (OC) Attorney, (CMTS) Albany 1815 City Directory
Bacon, Patrick: (OC) Coal Heaver, (CMTS) Albany 1859 City Directory
Bacon, Samuel N.: (OC) Coffe & Spice Manufacturers, Bacon & Stickneys, (CMTS) Albany 1859 City Directory
Bacon, William: (OC) Merchant, (CMTS) Albany 1815 City Directory
Bacon, William H.: (RES) House at Blooming Grove, (CMTS) Albany 1859 City Directory
Bader, Philip: (CMTS) 1790 Federal Census Rensselaerville
Badgely, John: (CMTS) 1790 Federal Census, Watervliet
Badger, Walter: (OC) Innkeeper, (CMTS) Albany 1815 City Directory
Badgley, Anthony: (CMTS) 1790 Federal Census, Watervliet
Badgley, Claude M.: (F) Member Masters Lodge, No. 5, 1900, Albany, NY
Badgley, Joseph D.: (OC) Monteath & Badgley, Wholesale Grocer, (CMTS) Albany 1859 City Directory
Bagg, Hattie C.: (CMTS) Graduate State Normal College, Albany, NY, 1878, (RES) Greenbush, Rensselaer Co., NY
Baggs, John: (OC) Engineer at Thomas Young's, (CMTS) Albany 1859 City Directory
Bagley, Mrs. Elizabeth: (RES) House at 48 Orange, (CMTS) Albany 1859 City Directory
Bagley, Thomas: (OC) Clerk, (CMTS) Albany 1859 City Directory
Bagnell, Wm.: (OC) Painter, (CMTS) Albany 1859 City Directory
Bahan, John: (RES) Boards at 22 Van Woert, (CMTS) Albany 1859 City Directory
Bahner, John: (OC) Cigarmaker, (CMTS) Albany 1859 City Directory
Bailey, Charles: (OC) Charcoalmaker, (CMTS) Albany 1859 City Directory
Bailey, Charles: (OC) Laborer, (CMTS) Albany 1859 City Directory
Bailey, Charles A.: (F) Member Masters Lodge, No. 5, 1900, Albany, NY
Bailey, David: (CMTS) 1790 Federal Census Rensselaerville
Bailey, Edith A.: (CMTS) Graduate State Normal College, Albany, NY, 1892, (RES) Croton Falls, Westchester Co., NY
Bailey, Edward: (OC) Bailey & Joralemon, Stoves, (CMTS) Albany 1859 City Directory
Bailey, Edward: (OC) Clerk, (CMTS) Albany 1859 City Directory
Bailey, Elisha: (OC) Bailey & Brothers, Dry Goods, (CMTS) Albany 1859 City Directory
Bailey, Emily: (CMTS) Graduate State Normal College, Albany, NY, 1847, (RES) Utica, Oneida Co., NY

Bailey, Emma L.: (CMTS) Graduate State Normal College, Albany,
   NY, 1881, (RES) Coeymans, Albany Co., NY
Bailey, Isaac: (OC) Bailey & Brothers, Dry Goods, (CMTS) Albany 1859
   City Directory
Bailey, James: (OC) Porterhouse, (CMTS) Albany 1859 City Directory
Bailey, James: (OC) Potato Merchant, (CMTS) Albany 1859 City
   Directory
Bailey, John: (OC) Carpenter, (CMTS) Albany 1815 City Directory
Bailey, John: (OC) Pedler, (CMTS) Albany 1859 City Directory
Bailey, John E.: (OC) Clerk, (CMTS) Albany 1859 City Directory
Bailey, John V.: (OC) Printer, (CMTS) Albany 1859 City Directory
Bailey, Joseph: (OC) Cooper, (CMTS) Albany 1859 City Directory
Bailey, Joseph: (OC) Paver, (CMTS) Albany 1859 City Directory
Bailey, Lemuel: (OC) Furrier, (CMTS) Albany 1859 City Directory
Bailey, Mary A.: (CMTS) Graduate State Normal College, Albany,
   NY, 1891, (RES) New Hampton, Orange CO., NY
Bailey, Nelson: (OC) Bailey & Brothers, Dry Goods, (CMTS) Albany
   1859 City Directory
Bailey, Theodore P.: (F) Member Mount Vernon Lodge, No. 3, 1900,
   Albany, NY
Bailey, W. H.: (OC) Physician, (CMTS) Albany 1859 City Directory
Bailly, John P.: (F) Member Mount Vernon Lodge, No. 3, 1900,
   Albany, NY
Bain, Isabella M.: (CMTS) Graduate State Normal College, Albany,
   NY, 1879, (RES) Galway, Saratoga Co., NY
Bain, Julia C.: (CMTS) Graduate State Normal College, Albany,
   NY, 1891, (RES) Belcer, Washington Co., NY
Bain, Mrs John: (RES) House at 68 Swan, Arbor Hill, (CMTS) Albany
   1859 City Directory
Bain, Peter: (OC) Laborer, (CMTS) Albany 1859 City Directory
Bain, Peter: (RES) 53 State, (CMTS) Albany 1815 City Directory
Bain, Peter C.: (OC) Bookbinder, (CMTS) Albany 1859 City Directory
Bain, Peter W.: (OC) Carman, (CMTS) Albany 1859 City Directory
Bain, Thomas: (OC) Laborer, (CMTS) Albany 1859 City Directory
Bain, William H.: (F) Member Temple Lodge, No. 14, 1900,
   Albany, NY
Baird, John: (OC) Eagle Tavern, (CMTS) Albany 1815 City Directory
Baird, Mary: (OC) Millener, (CMTS) Albany 1815 City Directory
Bake, Elizabeth J.: (CMTS) Graduate State Normal College, Albany,
   NY, 1880, (RES) Spencertown, Columbia Co., NY
Bake, M. Alice: (CMTS) Graduate State Normal College, Albany,
   NY, 1880, (RES) Spencertown, Columbia Co., NY
Baker, Adam: (OC) Cooper, (CMTS) Albany 1859 City Directory
Baker, Amanda M.: (CMTS) Graduate State Normal College, Albany,
   NY, 1866, (RES) Corning, Stueben Co., NY

Baker, Andrew: (CMTS) 1790 Federal Census, Watervliet
Baker, Benjamin: (CMTS) 1790 Federal Census, Watervliet
Baker, C. A.: (OC) Stoves, (CMTS) Albany 1859 City Directory
Baker, Catherine: (OC) Widow, (CMTS) Albany 1859 City Directory
Baker, Charles A.: (F) Member Masters Lodge, No. 5, 1900, Albany, NY
Baker, Charles C.: (OC) Painter, (CMTS) Albany 1859 City Directory
Baker, Charles N.: (F) Member Temple Lodge, No. 14, 1900, Albany, NY
Baker, Charlotte A.: (CMTS) Graduate State Normal College, Albany, NY, 1890, (RES) Troy, Rensselaer Co., NY
Baker, George: (CMTS) 1790 Federal Census Rensselaerville
Baker, George C.: (F) Member Masters Lodge, No. 5, 1900, Albany, NY
Baker, George E.: (OC) Deputy Clerk, Court of Appeals, (CMTS) Albany 1859 City Directory
Baker, George F.: (OC) Clerk, Bank Department, State Hall, (CMTS) Albany 1859 City Directory
Baker, George W.: (OC) Clerk, (RES) 92 Swan St, Arbor Hill, (CMTS) Albany 1859 City Directory
Baker, Helen M.: (CMTS) Graduate State Normal College, Albany, NY, 1849, (RES) Albany, Albany Co., NY
Baker, Henry E.: (OC) Clerk, Canal Department, State Hall, (CMTS) Albany 1859 City Directory
Baker, Jacob: (OC) Basketmaker, (CMTS) Albany 1859 City Directory
Baker, Jacob: (OC) Flour & Grain, (CMTS) Albany 1859 City Directory
Baker, James: (CMTS) 1790 Federal Census Rensselaerville
Baker, James A.: (F) Member Masters Lodge, No. 5, 1900, Albany, NY
Baker, James F.: (F) Member Masters Lodge, No. 5, 1900, Albany, NY (CMTS) Past Master
Baker, Jas. L.: (OC) Stoves, (CMTS) Albany 1859 City Directory
Baker, John: (OC) Bootlastmaker, (CMTS) Albany 1859 City Directory
Baker, John A.: (OC) Clerk, (CMTS) Albany 1859 City Directory
Baker, John C.: (OC) Coachmaker, (CMTS) Albany 1859 City Directory
Baker, Jos. W.: (OC) Rockefellar & Bros., Carpenter, (CMTS) Albany 1859 City Directory
Baker, Josiah: (CMTS) 1790 Federal Census Rensselaerville
Baker, Leonard: (RES) 18 Van Schaick, (CMTS) Albany 1815 City Directory
Baker, Leonard: (OC) Hairdresser, (CMTS) Albany 1815 City Directory
Baker, Libbie A.: (CMTS) Graduate State Normal College, Albany, NY, 1887, (RES) Dean's Corners, Saratoga Co., NY
Baker, Margaret C.: (CMTS) Graduate State Normal College, Albany, NY, 1860, (RES) Elmira, Chemung Co., NY
Baker, Mary J.: (CMTS) Graduate State Normal College, Albany, NY, 1889, (RES) Gloversville, Fulton Co., NY
Baker, Mrs. Sophia: (RES) House at 118 Hawk St., (CMTS) Albany 1859

Baker, Patience A.: (RES) House at 55 Colonie, (CMTS) Albany 1859 City Directory
Baker, Peter: (CMTS) 1790 Federal Census Rensselaerville
Baker, Pierce: (OC) Livery Stable, (CMTS) Albany 1815 City Directory
Baker, Princess A.: (CMTS) Graduate State Normal College, Albany, NY, 1891, (RES) Gloversville, Fulton Co., NY
Baker, Samuel: (CMTS) 1790 Federal Census Rensselaerville
Baker, Samuel: (OC) Stoves at 16 Green St. and Confectionary at 43 South Pearl St., (CMTS) Albany 1859 City Directory
Baker, Sarah L.: (CMTS) Graduate State Normal College, Albany, NY, 1890, (RES) Lansingburgh, Rensselaer Co., NY
Baker, Silas: (CMTS) 1790 Federal Census Rensselaerville
Baker, Solomon: (OC) Printer, (CMTS) Albany 1859 City Directory
Baker, Thomas: (OC) Saddler, (CMTS) Albany 1815 City Directory
Baker, William: (OC) Sexton, St. Pauls, (CMTS) Albany 1859 City Directory
Baker, Wm.: (OC) Laborer, (CMTS) Albany 1859 City Directory
Baker, Wm.: (OC) Switchman, N.Y.C.R.R., (CMTS) Albany 1859 City Directory
Bakie, Thomas J.: (F) Member Mount Vernon Lodge, No. 3, 1900, Albany, NY
Balcom, Carrie C.: (CMTS) Graduate State Normal College, Albany, NY, 1895, (RES) Oxford, Chenango Co., NY
Baldridge, H.: (F) Member Mount Vernon Lodge, No. 3, 1900, Albany, NY
Baldwin, Amanda P.: (CMTS) Graduate State Normal College, Albany, NY, 1855, (RES) New York, New York Co., NY
Baldwin, Andrew J.: (OC) Clerk, (CMTS) Albany 1859 City Directory
Baldwin, Anna M.: (CMTS) Graduate State Normal College, Albany, NY, 1894, (RES) Prattsburgh, Stueben Co., NY
Baldwin, Bronson A.: (OC) Carman, (CMTS) Albany 1859 City Directory
Baldwin, Clara L.: (CMTS) Graduate State Normal College, Albany, NY, 1854, (RES) Syracuse, Onondage Co., NY
Baldwin, Ebenezer: (OC) Counsellor, (CMTS) Albany 1815 City Directory
Baldwin, Enos: (OC) Plane Maker, (CMTS) Albany 1815 City Directory
Baldwin, Jeremiah: (OC) Engineer, (CMTS) Albany 1859 City Directory
Baldwin, John L.: (RES) Boards at Dunlop House, (CMTS) Albany 1859 City Directory
Baldwin, Michael: (OC) Porter, (CMTS) Albany 1859 City Directory
Baldwin, Jr., Henry: (OC) Over the Bank of Albany, (CMTS) Albany 1859 City Directory
Balister, Mary: (OC) Widow, (CMTS) Albany 1859 City Directory
Ball, Charles A.: (F) Member Temple Lodge, No. 14, 1900,

Albany, NY
Ball, Frederick: (CMTS) 1790 Federal Census Rensselaerville
Ball, George: (CMTS) 1790 Federal Census Rensselaerville
Ball, George: (OC) Compositor, (CMTS) Albany 1859 City Directory
Ball, Harriet E.: (CMTS) Graduate State Normal College, Albany, NY, 1890-1894, (RES) Troy, Rensselaer Co., NY
Ball, Henry: (CMTS) 1790 Federal Census Rensselaerville
Ball, Henry D.: (F) Member Temple Lodge, No. 14, 1900, Albany, NY
Ball, John: (OC) Carpenter, (CMTS) Albany 1859 City Directory
Ball, Magdalen: (OC) Nurse, (CMTS) Albany 1859 City Directory
Ball, Mary: (OC) Boarding House, (CMTS) Albany 1859 City Directory
Ball, Mary: (RES) Boarding House at 9 Union, (CMTS) Albany 1815 City Directory
Ball, Paul: (OC) Mason, (CMTS) Albany 1859 City Directory
Ball, Widow Jane: (OC), (CMTS) Albany 1815 City Directory
Ball, William Henry: (F) Member Temple Lodge, No. 14, 1900, Albany, NY
Ballantine, Wm.: (OC) Pianomaker, (CMTS) Albany 1859 City Directory
Ballard, Ambrose: (OC) Carpenter, (CMTS) Albany 1859 City Directory
Ballard, John: (OC) Stair Builder, (CMTS) Albany 1859 City Directory
Ballard, John H.: (OC) Machinist, (CMTS) Albany 1859 City Directory
Ballard, Julia M.: (CMTS) Graduate State Normal College, Albany, NY, 1887, (RES) Brewster, Putnam Co., NY
Ballas, Joseph: (OC) Moulder, (CMTS) Albany 1859 City Directory
Ballentine, Alex: (OC) Machinist, (CMTS) Albany 1859 City Directory
Ballentine, James: (OC) Mason, (CMTS) Albany 1859 City Directory
Ballin, Louis: (OC) Shoemaker, (CMTS) Albany 1859 City Directory
Ballin, Silas: (F) Member Washington Lodge, No. 85, 1900, Albany, NY
Ballin, Simon: (OC) Clothing, (CMTS) Albany 1859 City Directory
Ballin, Simon L.: (F) Member Washington Lodge, No. 85, 1900, Albany, NY
Ballou, Jr., Ransom: (OC) Gordon & Ballou, Dry Goods, (CMTS) Albany 1859 City Directory
Balthes, Frederick P.: (OC) Tailor, (CMTS) Albany 1859 City Directory
Bamberg, Isaac: (OC) Laces and Ribbons, (CMTS) Albany 1859 City Directory
Bamberg, William: (OC) Harnessmaker, (CMTS) Albany 1859 City Directory
Bamer, Jr., William: (F) Member Mount Vernon Lodge, No. 3, 1900, Albany, NY
Bamm, Mrs. Catherine: (RES) House at Sycamore Cottage, (CMTS) Albany 1859 City Directory
Banan, Ann: (OC) Eating House, (CMTS) Albany 1859 City Directory

Banan, James: (OC) Laborer, (CMTS) Albany 1859 City Directory
Banard, Alex: (RES) 114 Third, (CMTS) Albany 1859 City Directory
Bancroft, Henrietta A.: (CMTS) Graduate State Normal College, Albany, NY, 1878, (RES) Troy, Rensselaer Co., NY
Bancroft, Jennie M.: (CMTS) Graduate State Normal College, Albany, NY, 1872, (RES) Troy, Rensselaer Co., NY
Bancroft, John: (OC) Builder, (CMTS) Albany 1859 City Directory
Bancroft, Joseph: (OC) Builder, (CMTS) Albany 1859 City Directory
Bancroft, LeGrand: (OC) Attorney, (CMTS) Albany 1859 City Directory
Bancroft, Martha B.: (CMTS) Graduate State Normal College, Albany, NY, 1849, (RES) Weathersfield, Wyoming CO., NY
Bancroft, Royal: (OC) Wood Dealer, (CMTS) Albany 1859 City Directory
Bancroft, Wm. H.: (OC) Architect, (CMTS) Albany 1859 City Directory
Banhimer, Abram: (OC) Pedler, (CMTS) Albany 1859 City Directory
Banker, Fred.: (OC) Sailmaker, (CMTS) Albany 1859 City Directory
Banker, Garret: (CMTS) 1790 Federal Census, Watervliet
Banker, Gershom: (OC) Chief Clerk Freight and Passenger Dept., N.Y.C.R.R., (CMTS) Albany 1859 City Directory
Banker, John: (OC) Clerk N.Y.C.R.R., (CMTS) Albany 1859 City Directory
Banks, A. Bleecker: (F) Member Masters Lodge, No. 5, 1900, Albany, NY
Banks, A. Bleecker: (OC) Law Book Publisher, (CMTS) Albany 1859 City Directory
Banks, Herman: (OC) Painter, (CMTS) Albany 1859 City Directory
Banks, Louisa: (OC) Widow, (CMTS) Albany 1859 City Directory
Banks, Jr., Robert L.: (F) Member Masters Lodge, No. 5, 1900, Albany, NY
Bantam, Christina: (OC) Widow, (CMTS) Albany 1859 City Directory
Bantam, John S.: (OC) Carpenter, (CMTS) Albany 1859 City Directory
Bantam, Summarland T.: (OC) Painter, (CMTS) Albany 1859 City Directory
Bantham, Andrew J.: (OC) Clerk, (CMTS) Albany 1859 City Directory
Bantham, John: (OC) Blacksmith, (CMTS) Albany 1815 City Directory
Bantham, John G.: (OC) Goldbeater, (CMTS) Albany 1859 City Directory
Banyer, Goldsbrow: (RES) 62 N. Pearl, (CMTS) Albany 1815 City Directory
Baragar, Mrs. Harriet: (OC) Nurse, (CMTS) Albany 1859 City Directory
Barben, Henry: (OC) Painter, (CMTS) Albany 1859 City Directory
Barben, Mattias: (OC) Porter, (CMTS) Albany 1859 City Directory
Barber, Edgar A.: (OC) Clerk in Comptroller's Office, (CMTS) Albany 1859 City Directory
Barber, Elijah: (CMTS) 1790 Federal Census Rensselaerville
Barber, Fletcher: (OC) Clerk, (CMTS) Albany 1859 City Directory
Barber, Jeremiah: (OC) Waiter, (CMTS) Albany 1859 City Directory
Barbin, Edwd.: (OC) Shoemaker, (CMTS) Albany 1859 City Directory

Barclay, Widow: (CMTS) 1790 Federal Census, Watervliet
Barclay, Fannie: (CMTS) Graduate State Normal College, Albany, NY, 1868, (RES) Nyack, Rockland Co., NY
Barclay, William: (OC) Accountant, (CMTS) Albany 1815 City Directory
Bardell, Alfred W.: (OC) Tinplater, (CMTS) Albany 1859 City Directory
Barden, Michael: (OC) Laborer, (CMTS) Albany 1859 City Directory
Bardwell, Jane: (OC) Widow, (CMTS) Albany 1859 City Directory
Bardwell, Margaret L.: (CMTS) Graduate State Normal College, Albany, NY, 1864, (RES) Albany, Albany Co., NY
Bargan, Patrick: (OC) Cooper, (CMTS) Albany 1859 City Directory
Barguet, Bissett: (OC) Tailor, (CMTS) Albany 1859 City Directory
Barhouf, Michael: (OC) Brass Worker, (CMTS) Albany 1859 City Directory
Barhydt, Richard: (OC) Pianoware Room, (CMTS) Albany 1859 City Directory
Barjait, Michael: (OC) Furnaceman, (CMTS) Albany 1859 City Directory
Barker, Ann: (OC) Widow, (CMTS) Albany 1859 City Directory
Barker, Catherine: (OC) Widow of Jas. D., (CMTS) Albany 1859 City Directory
Barker, H. V. B.: (OC) Resident Engineer of Champlain Canal, (CMTS) Albany 1859 City Directory
Barker, Mattie E.: (CMTS) Graduate State Normal College, Albany, NY, 1885, (RES) Albany, Albany Co., NY
Barker, Miss Elizabeth: (RES) House at 33 Grand, (CMTS) Albany 1859 City Directory
Barker, Miss Jane: (RES) House at 33 Grand, (CMTS) Albany 1859 City Directory
Barker, Thomas: (OC) Moulder, (CMTS) Albany 1859 City Directory
Barnard, Cornelius C.: (OC) Baker, (CMTS) Albany 1859 City Directory
Barnard, Daniel D.: (OC) Attorney, (CMTS) Albany 1859 City Directory
Barnard, Frances S.: (CMTS) Graduate State Normal College, Albany, NY, 1889, (RES) Westmoreland, Oneida Co., NY
Barnard, Frederick J.: (RES) 724 Elk, (CMTS) Albany 1859 City Directory
Barnard, John B.: (OC) Boots and Shoes, (CMTS) Albany 1859 City Directory
Barnard, John B. F.: (OC) F. Agent Merchants Dispatch, (CMTS) Albany 1859 City Directory
Barnard, Joseph: (OC) Blacksmith, (CMTS) Albany 1815 City Directory
Barnard, Phoebe A.: (CMTS) Graduate State Normal College, Albany, NY, 1847, (RES) Union Village, Washington Co., NY
Barnard, Robert: (OC) Hatter, (CMTS) Albany 1815 City Directory
Barnard, Samuel W.: (RES) 111 Washington Ave., (CMTS) Albany 1859 City Directory
Barnes, David M.: (OC) Barnes & Godfrey, Morning Times, (CMTS)

Albany 1859 City Directory
Barnes, Eva J.: (CMTS) Graduate State Normal College, Albany,
   NY, 1871, (RES) Newark Valley, Tioga Co., NY
Barnes, G W.: (OC) Wheelwright, (CMTS) Albany 1815 City Directory
Barnes, Grace E.: (CMTS) Graduate State Normal College, Albany,
   NY, 1888, (RES) Rhinebeck, Dutchess Co., NY
Barnes, Harriet E.: (CMTS) Graduate State Normal College, Albany,
   NY, 1857, (RES) Galen, Wayne Co., NY
Barnes, Helen S.: (CMTS) Graduate State Normal College, Albany,
   NY, 1863, (RES) Munnsville, Madison Co., NY
Barnes, J. S.: (RES) Boards at Congress Hall, (CMTS) Albany 1859 City
   Directory
Barnes, John Sanford: (OC) Attorney, (CMTS) Albany 1859 City
   Directory
Barnes, Joseph C.: (OC) Clerk, (CMTS) Albany 1859 City Directory
Barnes, Lemuel: (CMTS) 1790 Federal Census Rensselaerville
Barnes, Phenias: (CMTS) 1790 Federal Census Rensselaerville
Barnes, Roswell: (CMTS) 1790 Federal Census Rensselaerville
Barnes, Samuel S.: (OC) printer, (CMTS) Albany 1859 City Directory
Barnes, Simmons S.: (OC) Furnaceman, (CMTS) Albany 1859 City
   Directory
Barnes, Susan M.: (OC) Teacher, (CMTS) Albany 1859 City Directory
Barnes, Theresa A.: (CMTS) Graduate State Normal College, Albany,
   NY, 1850, (RES) Evans' Mills, Jefferson Co., NY
Barnes, William: (OC) Attorney, (CMTS) Albany 1859 City Directory
Barnet, Jonas S.: (F) Member Mount Vernon Lodge, No. 3, 1900,
   Albany, NY
Barnet, Valentine: (CMTS) 1790 Federal Census Rensselaerville
Barnet, William: (F) Member Washington Lodge, No. 85, 1900,
   Albany, NY
Barnett, Abram: (OC) Livery, (CMTS) Albany 1859 City Directory
Barnett, Charity: (CMTS) Graduate State Normal College, Albany,
   NY, 1856, (RES) Stamford, Delaware Co., NY
Barnett, Hattie M.: (CMTS) Graduate State Normal College, Albany,
   NY, 1887, (RES) Schroon Lake, Essex Co., NY
Barney, Benj: (OC) Chandler, (CMTS) Albany 1815 City Directory
Barney, Jacob: (OC) Lumber Merchant, (CMTS) Albany 1815 City
   Directory
Barney, Jos.: (OC) P, (CMTS) Albany 1815 City Directory
Barney, Paul C.: (OC) Clerk at Post Office, (CMTS) Albany 1859 City
   Directory
Barnhart, Cornelius: (OC) Baker, (CMTS) Albany 1859 City Directory
Barnum, Noah: (CMTS) 1790 Federal Census Rensselaerville
Barr, Hugh: (CMTS) 1790 Federal Census, Watervliet
Barr, Joseph: (OC) Porter, (CMTS) Albany 1859 City Directory

Barragar, Mrs. Harriet: (OC) Nurse, (CMTS) Albany 1859 City Directory
Barret, Christopher: (OC) Morocco Dresser, (CMTS) Albany 1815 City Directory
Barret, Matthew: (OC) Laborer, (CMTS) Albany 1815 City Directory
Barret, Ann: (OC) Widow, (CMTS) Albany 1889 City Directory
Barrett, Catherine: (OC) Widow, (CMTS) Albany 1889 City Directory
Barrett, Edward: (OC) Laborer, (CMTS) Albany 1889 City Directory
Barrett, Edward F.: (OC) Shipping Clerk, (CMTS) Albany 1889 City Directoy
Barrett, Ellen: (OC) Widow, (CMTS) Albany 1859 City Directory
Barret, George: (OC) Collector, A.S. & W. W. R. R., Collector, (CMTS) Albany 1889 City Directory
Barrett, George: (OC) Plumber, (RES) Greenbush, (CMTS) Albany 1889 City Directory
Barret, Henry J.: (OC) Pressman, (CMTS) Albany 1889 City Directory
Barrett, Isaac B.: (F) Member Masters Lodge, No. 5, 1900, Albany, NY
Barrett, J. Edward: (OC) Barrett & Co., Tin Roofer, (CMTS) Albany 1859 City Directory
Barrett, James: (OC) Mason, (CMTS) Albany 1859 City Directory
Barrett, John: (OC) Moulder, (CMTS) Albany 1859 City Directory
Barrett, John: (OC) Butcher, (CMTS) Albany 1859 City Directory
Barrett, John H.: (OC) Laborer, (CMTS) Albany 1859 City Directory
Barrett, Mary: (OC) Widow, (CMTS) Albany 1859 City Directory
Barrett, Mattie L.: (CMTS) Graduate State Normal College, Albany, NY, 1873, (RES) Fort Ann, Washington Co., NY
Barrett, Patrick: (OC) Moulder, (CMTS) Albany 1859 City Directory
Barrett, Patrick: (OC) Prop. Ferry House, Greenbush, (CMTS) Albany 1859 City Directory
Barrett, Richard: (OC) Butcher, (RES) House at 168 Sand, (CMTS) Albany 1859 City Directory
Barrett, Richard: (RES) 154 Jay, (CMTS) Albany 1859 City Directory
Barrett, Robert: (OC) Plumber, (CMTS) Albany 1859 City Directory
Barrett, Thomas: (CD) Nov. 7, 1742, (PB) Albany, Albany Co., NY
Barrett, Thomas: (OC) Tailor, (CMTS) Albany 1859 City Directory
Barrett, Thomas: (OC) Currier, Greenbush, (CMTS) Albany 1859 City Directory
Barrett, William: (OC) Goldbeater, (CMTS) Albany 1859 City Directory
Barrett, Wyman R.: (OC) Produce, (CMTS) Albany 1859 City Directory
Barry, Angel: (OC) Laborer, (CMTS) Albany 1859 City Directory
Barry, George: (OC) Laborer, (CMTS) Albany 1859 City Directory
Barry, Michael: (OC) Grocer, (CMTS) Albany 1859 City Directory
Barry, Thomas: (OC) Porter, (CMTS) Albany 1859 City Directory
Barry, Thomas: (OC) Watchman, (CMTS) Albany 1859 City Directory
Barston, C. Louisa: (CMTS) Graduate State Normal College, Albany, NY, 1853, (RES) Hannibal, Oswego Co., NY

Barth, Henry: (OC) Joiner, (CMTS) Albany 1859 City Directory
Bartholf, Bertha: (CMTS) Graduate State Normal College, Albany, NY, 1883, (RES) Visscher's Ferr, Saratoga Co., NY
Bartholomew, A: (OC) Capt. Steamboat Richmond, (CMTS) Albany 1815 City Directory
Bartholomew, Charles: (OC) Grocer, (CMTS) Albany 1859 City Directory
Bartholomew, Riley: (RES) House at 63 Lumber, (CMTS) Albany 1859 City Directory
Bartlett, Dennis N.: (OC) Teamster, (CMTS) Albany 1859 City Directory
Bartlett, Elijah: (OC) Shoemaker, (CMTS) Albany 1815 City Directory
Bartlett, Julia M.: (OC) Teacher, (CMTS) Albany 1859 City Directory
Bartlett, Mary: (OC) Widow, (CMTS) Albany 1859 City Directory
Bartlett, Mary E.: (CMTS) Graduate State Normal College, Albany, NY, 1887, (RES) Albany, Albany Co., NY
Bartlett, Nellie: (CMTS) Graduate State Normal College, Albany, NY, 1887, (RES) Albany, Albany Co., NY
Bartley, Abraham: (CMTS) 1790 Federal Census, Watervliet
Bartley, Bridget: (OC) Widow, (CMTS) Albany 1859 City Directory
Bartley, Catherine: (RES) 39 Third, Arbor Hill, (CMTS) Albany 1859 City Directory
Bartley, Helen J.: (CMTS) Graduate State Normal College, Albany, NY, 1865, (RES) Albany, Albany Co., NY
Bartley, James: (OC) Grocer, (CMTS) Albany 1859 City Directory
Bartley, John: (OC) Moulder, (CMTS) Albany 1859 City Directory
Bartley, Mrs. James: (RES) 24 1/2 Canal, (CMTS) Albany 1859 City Directory
Bartley, William: (OC) Tailor, (CMTS) Albany 1859 City Directory
Barton, David B.: (OC) Clerk, (CMTS) Albany 1859 City Directory
Barton, Dennis: (OC) Laborer, (CMTS) Albany 1859 City Directory
Barton, Dora L.: (CMTS) Graduate State Normal College, Albany, NY, 1892, (RES) Clyde, Wayne Co., NY
Barton, Silas: (OC) Mason, (CMTS) Albany 1859 City Directory
Barton, Thomas: (OC) Moulder, (CMTS) Albany 1859 City Directory
Barton, Thomas: (OC) Laborer, (CMTS) Albany 1859 City Directory
Barton, William J.: (OC) Clerk, (CMTS) Albany 1859 City Directory
Bartoo, Mary J.: (CMTS) Graduate State Normal College, Albany, NY, 1848, (RES) Water Valey, Erie Co., NY
Bartram, Chas.: (OC) Clerk, (CMTS) Albany 1859 City Directory
Basckum, Matthias: (OC) Machinist, (CMTS) Albany 1859 City Directory
Bascomb, H.: (OC) Surgeon-Dentist, (CMTS) Albany 1815 City Directory
Basinger, Ella D.: (CMTS) Graduate State Normal College, Albany, NY, 1887, (RES) East Springfield, Otsego Co., NY
Bass, Farnsworth: (OC) Printer, (CMTS) Albany 1859 City Directory
Basset, Michael: (CMTS) 1790 Federal Census, Watervliet
Bassett, Caroline A.: (CMTS) Graduate State Normal College, Albany,

NY, 1862, (RES) Gowanda, Cattaraugus Co., NY
Bassett, Daniel E.: (OC) Brickyard, (CMTS) Albany 1859 City Directory
Bassett, Helen J.: (CMTS) Graduate State Normal College, Albany,
    NY, 1870, (RES) Albany, Albany Co., NY
Bassett, N. B.: (OC) Watchmaker, (CMTS) Albany 1815 City Directory
Bassett, Richard O.: (F) Member Temple Lodge, No. 14, 1900,
    Albany, NY
Bassler, Frederick: (CMTS) 1790 Federal Census Rensselaerville
Bassler, Hendrick: (CMTS) 1790 Federal Census Rensselaerville
Bastian, Peter: (CMTS) 1790 Federal Census Rensselaerville
Batchelder, Walter W.: (F) Member Masters Lodge, No. 5, 1900,
    Albany, NY
Batcheldor, Benjamin: (RES) 49 Washington, (CMTS) Albany 1815 City
    Directory
Batcheldor, Galen: (OC) Merchant, (CMTS) Albany 1815 City Directory
Batchelor, Benjamin: (CMTS) 1790 Federal Census Rensselaerville
Bates, Jeremiah H.: (OC) Cooper, (CMTS) Albany 1815 City Directory
Bates, Minnie: (CMTS) Graduate State Normal College, Albany,
    NY, 1883, (RES) East Albany, Rensselaer Co., NY
Bates, Samuel: (OC) Cooper, (CMTS) Albany 1815 City Directory
Batterman, John: (CMTS) 1790 Federal Census, Watervliet
Battersby, John: (F) Member Temple Lodge, No. 14, 1900,
    Albany, NY
Baum, Mary E.: (CMTS) Graduate State Normal College, Albany,
    NY, 1848, (RES) Central Square, Oswego Co., NY
Baumes, Della C.: (CMTS) Graduate State Normal College, Albany,
    NY, 1889, (RES) Cedar Hill, Albany C., NY
Baxter, Duncan: (F) Member Temple Lodge, No. 14, 1900,
    Albany, NY
Baxter, Duncan: (CMTS) 1790 Federal Census, Watervliet
Baxter, Fanny: (CMTS) Graduate State Normal College, Albany,
    NY, 1857, (RES) Buffalo, Erie Co., NY
Baxter, Mary A.: (CMTS) Graduate State Normal College, Albany,
    NY, 1890, (RES) Port Washington, Queens Co., NY
Baxter, Samuel: (RES) 155 S. Market, (CMTS) Albany 1815 City
    Directory
Baxter, Sidney F.: (F) Member Temple Lodge, No. 14, 1900,
    Albany, NY
Bay, William: (OC) Physician, (CMTS) Albany 1815 City Directory
Bayles, Annie E.: (CMTS) Graduate State Normal College, Albany,
    NY, 1889, (RES) Newburgh, Orange Co., NY
Beach, Amanda S.: (CMTS) Graduate State Normal College, Albany,
    NY, 1854, (RES) Albany, Albany Co., NY
Beach, Jessie A.: (CMTS) Graduate State Normal College, Albany,
    NY, 1886, (RES) Little Falls, Herkimer Co., NY

Beach, Mary M.: (CMTS) Graduate State Normal College, Albany,
   NY, 1856, (RES) Cheektowaga, Erie Co., NY
Beach, Widow Sarah: (RES) 83 Washington, (CMTS) Albany 1815
   City Directory
Beale, Mary L.: (CMTS) Graduate State Normal College, Albany,
   NY, 1846, (RES) Kinderhook, Columbia Co., NY
Beals, Mary E. H.: (CMTS) Graduate State Normal College, Albany,
   NY, 1871, (RES) Mt. Vision, Otsego Co., NY
Beard, Francis: (CMTS) 1790 Federal Census, Watervliet
Beasley, Samuel: (OC) Laborer, (CMTS) Albany 1815 City Directory
Beattie, Sarah L.: (CMTS) Graduate State Normal College, Albany,
   NY, 1887, (RES) Salem, Washington Co., NY
Beatty, John: (OC) Laborer, (CMTS) Albany 1815 City Directory
Beaty, Abby A.: (CMTS) Graduate State Normal College, Albany,
   NY, 1868, (RES) Salem, Washington Co., NY
Beaty, Carrie A.: (CMTS) Graduate State Normal College, Albany,
   NY, 1879, (RES) Salem, Washington Co., NY
Beaty, Mary L.: (CMTS) Graduate State Normal College, Albany,
   NY, 1853, (RES) Greenwich, Washington Co., NY
Beaudry, Maude N.: (CMTS) Graduate State Normal College, Albany,
   NY, 1895, (RES) Westchester, Westchester Co., NY
Beaudry, Pearl E.: (CMTS) Graduate State Normal College, Albany,
   NY, 1886, (RES) Mayfield, Fulton Co., NY
Beauman, Charles: (CMTS) 1790 Federal Census, Watervliet
Beaver, Thomas: (CMTS) 1790 Federal Census, Watervliet
Bechsted, John: (CMTS) 1790 Federal Census Rensselaerville
Bechtel, John: (F) Member Mount Vernon Lodge, No. 3, 1900,
   Albany, NY
Beck, T. Romeyn: (OC) Physician, (CMTS) Albany 1815 City Directory
Becker, Aaron: (CMTS) 1790 Federal Census, Watervliet
Becker, Christian: (CMTS) 1790 Federal Census Rensselaerville
Becker, Direck: (CMTS) 1790 Federal Census, Watervliet
Becker, Emma J.: (CMTS) Graduate State Normal College, Albany,
   NY, 1871, (RES) Cobleskill, Schoharie Co., NY
Becker, John A.: (F) Member Masters Lodge, No. 5, 1900, Albany, NY
Becker, Maggie: (CMTS) Graduate State Normal College, Albany,
   NY, 1885, (RES) Knowersville, Albany Co., NY
Becker, Wm.: (RES) 42 Washington, (CMTS) Albany 1815 City
   Directory
Beckley, Frances S.: (CMTS) Graduate State Normal College, Albany,
   NY, 1892, (RES) Ravenna, OH
Beckman, George F.: (F) Member Mount Vernon Lodge, No. 3, 1900,
   Albany, NY
Beckman, Johannes: (CMTS) 1790 Federal Census, Watervliet
Beckwith, Emma: (CMTS) Graduate State Normal College, Albany,

NY, 1872, (RES) Stissing, Dutchess Co., NY
Beckwith, Mary T.: (CMTS) Graduate State Normal College, Albany, NY, 1874, (RES) Stissing, Dutchess Co., NY
Bedell, Annie C.: (CMTS) Graduate State Normal College, Albany, NY, 1892, (RES) East Schodack, Rensselaer Co., NY
Bedell, Ida L.: (CMTS) Graduate State Normal College, Albany, NY, 1885, (RES) Coxsackie, Greene CO., NY
Bedell, Sarah A.: (CMTS) Graduate State Normal College, Albany, NY, 1887, (RES) Coeymans Junction, Albany Co., NY
Bedell, Sarah B.: (CMTS) Graduate State Normal College, Albany, NY, 1855, (RES) Grand Island, Erie Co., NY
Bedford, Mary F.: (CMTS) Graduate State Normal College, Albany, NY, 1887, (RES) N. Harpersfield, Delaware Co., NY
Bedford, Rachel: (CMTS) Graduate State Normal College, Albany, NY, 1863, (RES) Monticello, Sullivan Co., NY
Beebe, Carrie A.: (CMTS) Graduate State Normal College, Albany, NY, 1882, (RES) New Concord, Columbia Co., NY
Beebe, Mirah H.: (CMTS) Graduate State Normal College, Albany, NY, 1875, (RES) Canaan, Columbia Co., NY
Beebe, Nellie A.: (CMTS) Graduate State Normal College, Albany, NY, 1875, (RES) Canaan, Columbia Co., NY
Beebe, William H.: (F) Member Washington Lodge, No. 85, 1900, Albany, NY
Beeby, Joseph: (OC) Grocer, (CMTS) Albany 1815 City Directory
Beech, Josiah: (CMTS) 1790 Federal Census Rensselaerville
Beecher, Laura F.: (CMTS) Graduate State Normal College, Albany, NY, 1857, (RES) N. Broadalbin, Fulton Co., NY
Beecher, Martha C.: (CMTS) Graduate State Normal College, Albany, NY, 1872, (RES) West Granville, Washington Co., NY
Beecher, Susan E.: (CMTS) Graduate State Normal College, Albany, NY, 1849, (RES) Batavia, Genesse Co., NY
Beeckman, Anna: (RES) 30 Van Schaick, (CMTS) Albany 1815 City Directory
Beeckman, John S.: (RES) 52 N. Pearl, (CMTS) Albany 1815 City Directory
Beeckman, Peter D.: (RES) 21 Van Schaick, (CMTS) Albany 1815 City Directory
Beekman, Christina: (CMTS) 1790 Federal Census, Watervliet
Beers, Rozilla: (CMTS) Graduate State Normal College, Albany, NY, 1875, (RES) Chaseville, Otsego Co., NY
Beers, Sarah A.: (CMTS) Graduate State Normal College, Albany, NY, 1885, (RES) Rome, Oneida Co., NY
Begraft, Francis: (CMTS) 1790 Federal Census Rensselaerville
Beker, Alexander R.: (F) Member Temple Lodge, No. 14, 1900, Albany, NY, (CMTS) Life Member

Belding, Samuel B.: (F) Member Mount Vernon Lodge, No. 3, 1900,
 Albany, NY
Bell, Bessie: (CMTS) Graduate State Normal College, Albany,
 NY, 1891, (RES) Port Chester, Westchester Co., NY
Bell, Cora: (CMTS) Graduate State Normal College, Albany,
 NY, 1885, (RES) Knowersville, Albany Co., NY
Bell, Frances E.: (CMTS) Graduate State Normal College, Albany,
 NY, 1872, (RES) Bloonburgh, Sullivan Co., NY
Bell, Grace D.: (CMTS) Graduate State Normal College, Albany,
 NY, 1892, (RES) Schodack Depot, Rensselaer Co., NY
Bell, James: (OC) Brewer, (CMTS) Albany 1815 City Directory
Bell, Mary F.: (CMTS) Graduate State Normal College, Albany,
 NY, 1886, (RES) Port Chester, Westchester Co., NY
Bell, Samuel: (OC) Shoemaker, (CMTS) Albany 1815 City Directory
Bell, Sarah: (CMTS) Graduate State Normal College, Albany,
 NY, 1889, (RES) Bath-on-Hudson, Rensselaer Co., NY
Bell, Stephen: (CMTS) 1790 Federal Census, Watervliet
Bellamy, Simon: (RES) 18 Beaver, (CMTS) Albany 1815 City Directory
Beller, Adrian: (OC) Grocer, (CMTS) Albany 1815 City Directory
Bellows, Edgar: (F) Member Temple Lodge, No. 14, 1900,
 Albany, NY
Bellows, Roswell: (RES) 135 Washington, (CMTS) Albany 1815 City
 Directory
Belton, Jonathan: (OC) Shoemaker, (CMTS) Albany 1815 City Directory
Beman, Amelia E.: (CMTS) Graduate State Normal College, Albany,
 NY, 1859, (RES) Alden, Erie Co., NY
Bement, Caleb N.: (OC) Merchant, (CMTS) Albany 1815 City Directory
Bemis, Mehetabell W.: (CMTS) Graduate State Normal College, Albany,
 NY, 1860, (RES) Auburn, Cayuga Co., NY
Bemus, David: (CMTS) 1790 Federal Census Rensselaerville
Bendell, Herman: (F) Member Washington Lodge, No. 85, 1900,
 Albany, NY, (CMTS) Past Members
Bendell, Moses: (F) Member Washington Lodge, No. 85, 1900,
 Albany, NY, (CMTS) Past Members
Bender, John: (OC) Laborer, (CMTS) Albany 1815 City Directory
Bender, Matthew: (F) Member Masters Lodge, No. 5, 1900, Albany, NY
Bender, Sarah E.: (CMTS) Graduate State Normal College, Albany,
 NY, 1853, (RES) Bethlehem Centre, Albany Co., NY
Bendict, Emma L.: (CMTS) Graduate State Normal College, Albany,
 NY, 1879, (RES) Clifton Park, Saratoga Co., NY
Bendict, Polly M.: (CMTS) Graduate State Normal College, Albany,
 NY, 1856, (RES) Victory, Cayuga Co., NY
Benedict, Ezra G.: (F) Member Masters Lodge, No. 5, 1900, Albany, NY
Benedict, Lewis: (OC) Merchant, (CMTS) Albany 1815 City Directory
Benedict, M. Elizabeth: (CMTS) Graduate State Normal College, Albany,

NY, 1883, (RES) Johnsonville, Pensselaer
Benedict, Minnie E.: (CMTS) Graduate State Normal College, Albany, NY, 1883, (RES) Johnsonville, Pensselaer
Benedict, Stephen: (CMTS) 1790 Federal Census, Watervliet
Benham, Ellen J.: (CMTS) Graduate State Normal College, Albany, NY, 1857, (RES) Byron, Genesee Co., NY
Benham, James: (OC) Merchant, (CMTS) Albany 1815 City Directory
Benjamin, Caleb: (CMTS) Albany 1815 City Directory
Benjamin, Frances M.: (CMTS) Graduate State Normal College, Albany, NY, 1868, (RES) South Otselie, Chenango Co., NY
Benjamin, George H.: (F) Member Masters Lodge, No. 5, 1900, Albany, NY, (CMTS) Past Master
Benjamin, Abraham T.: (F) Member Temple Lodge, No. 14, 1900, Albany, NY
Benne, Henry F.: (OC) Confectioner, (CMTS) Albany 1815 City Directory
Bennet, Aaron: (OC) Nailer, (CMTS) Albany 1815 City Directory
Bennet, Joseph: (CMTS) 1790 Federal Census Rensselaerville
Bennet, Robert: (RES) 2 Van Schaick, (CMTS) Albany 1815 City Directory
Bennett, Ann E.: (CMTS) Graduate State Normal College, Albany, NY, 1859, (RES) South Danby, Tompkins Co., NY
Bennett, Carrie C.: (CMTS) Graduate State Normal College, Albany, NY, 1871, (RES) Albany, Albany Co., NY
Bennett, Daniel C.: (F) Member Masters Lodge, No. 5, 1900, Albany, NY
Bennett, Emma L.: (CMTS) Graduate State Normal College, Albany, NY, 1880, (RES) Auburn, Cayuga Co., NY
Bennett, Esther: (CMTS) Graduate State Normal College, Albany, NY, 1855, (RES) South Danby, Tompkins Co., NY
Bennett, Jennie E.: (CMTS) Graduate State Normal College, Albany, NY, 1886, (RES) Fort Edward, Washington Co., NY
Bennett, Lilia M.: (CMTS) Graduate State Normal College, Albany, NY, 1892, (RES) Fort Miller, Washington Co., NY
Bennett, Lucy E.: (CMTS) Graduate State Normal College, Albany, NY, 1887, (RES) Canandaigua, Ontario Co., NY
Bennett, Marion L.: (CMTS) Graduate State Normal College, Albany, NY, 1878, (RES) Newark, Wayne Co., NY
Bennett, Mary C.: (CMTS) Graduate State Normal College, Albany, NY, 1855, (RES) Veteran, Chemung Co., NY
Bensen, Albert V.: (F) Member Mount Vernon Lodge, No. 3, 1900, Albany, NY
Benson, Abbie C.: (CMTS) Graduate State Normal College, Albany, NY, 1884, (RES) Albany, Albany Co., NY
Benson, Abraham: (OC) Carpenter, (CMTS) Albany 1815 City Directory
Benson, Dirick: (CMTS) 1790 Federal Census, Watervliet

Benson, John: (F) Member Temple Lodge, No. 14, 1900,
    Albany, NY
Benson, John: (CMTS) 1790 Federal Census, Watervliet
Benson, John: (OC) Grocer, (CMTS) Albany 1815 City Directory
Benson, Maira: (RES) 9 N. Market, (CMTS) Albany 1815 City Directory
Benson, Richard: (OC) Mill Wright, (CMTS) Albany 1815 City Directory
Bentley, John: (OC) Shoemaker, (CMTS) Albany 1815 City Directory
Bentley, Randel: (OC) Skipper, (CMTS) Albany 1815 City Directory
Benton, Wright: (OC) Nailer, (CMTS) Albany 1815 City Directory
Berckley, Christian: (CMTS) 1790 Federal Census Rensselaerville
Berckley, Henry: (CMTS) 1790 Federal Census Rensselaerville
Berckley, Joachum: (CMTS) 1790 Federal Census Rensselaerville
Berckley, Peter: (CMTS) 1790 Federal Census Rensselaerville
Berger, Andress: (CMTS) 1790 Federal Census, Watervliet
Berger, Andress: (CMTS) 1790 Federal Census, Watervliet
Berger, William: (CMTS) 1790 Federal Census, Watervliet
Bergh, Hattie: (CMTS) Graduate State Normal College, Albany,
    NY, 1874, (RES) Breakabeen, Schoharie Co., NY
Berkeley, Eberhart: (CMTS) 1790 Federal Census Rensselaerville
Berlin, Jr., Fred C.: (F) Member Temple Lodge, No. 14, 1900,
    Albany, NY
Bernard, John: (OC) manager theatre, (CMTS) Albany 1815 City
    Directory
Bernheimer, Henry: (F) Member Washington Lodge, No. 85, 1900,
    Albany, NY
Berns, Mary E.: (CMTS) Graduate State Normal College, Albany,
    NY, 1884, (RES) Albany, Albany Co., NY
Berry, G. W.: (OC) Tea Dealer, Arshowe & Berry, (CMTS) Albany 1859
    City Directory
Berry, N. W.: (OC) Tea Dealer, Arshowe & Berry, (CMTS) Albany 1859
    City Directory
Berseau, Peter: (CMTS) 1790 Federal Census, Watervliet
Bessmer, Katherine: (CMTS) Graduate State Normal College, Albany,
    NY, 1888, (RES) New York, New York Co., NY
Best, Fannie E.: (CMTS) Graduate State Normal College, Albany,
    NY, 1877, (RES) Niverville, Columbia Co., NY
Best, Jacob: (OC) Merchant Taylor, (CMTS) Albany 1815 City Directory
Best, John: (F) Member Washington Lodge, No. 85, 1900,
    Albany, NY, (CMTS) Past Members
Best, Mary E.: (CMTS) Graduate State Normal College, Albany,
    NY, 1854, (RES) Kinderhook, Columbia Co., NY
Betger, Andrew: (CMTS) 1790 Federal Census Rensselaerville
Betts, Mary: (CMTS) Graduate State Normal College, Albany,
    NY, 1875, (RES) West Laurens, Otsego Co., NY
Betzholtz, George: (CMTS) 1790 Federal Census Rensselaerville

Bewel, Christopher: (CMTS) 1790 Federal Census, Watervliet
Bibie, Thomas: (CMTS) 1790 Federal Census, Watervliet
Bicker, Walter: (CMTS) 1790 Federal Census, Watervliet
Biddell, Louise D.: (CMTS) Graduate State Normal College, Albany, NY, 1885, (RES) Hunter, Greene Co., NY
Bigelow, Ella F.: (CMTS) Graduate State Normal College, Albany, NY, 1870, (RES) Dannemora, Clinton Co., NY
Bigelow, John M.: (F) Member Masters Lodge, No. 5, 1900, Albany, NY
Bignel, Japhat: (CMTS) 1790 Federal Census, Watervliet
Bilderbeck, Ida M.: (CMTS) Graduate State Normal College, Albany, NY, 1889, (RES) South Hartwick, Otsego Co., NY
Billson, C. A.: (F) Member Washington Lodge, No. 85, 1900, Albany, NY
Bingham, George H.: (F) Member Temple Lodge, No. 14, 1900, Albany, NY
Bingham, L. Maria: (CMTS) Graduate State Normal College, Albany, NY, 1851, (RES) Van Buren, Onondoga Co., NY
Bingham, Sarah A.: (CMTS) Graduate State Normal College, Albany, NY, 1852, (RES) Albany, Albany Co., NY
Binley, George W.: (F) Member Temple Lodge, No. 14, 1900, Albany, NY
Birch, Sarah M.: (CMTS) Graduate State Normal College, Albany, NY, 1857, (RES) Amsterdam, Montogmery CO., NY
Birdsall, Maj Benjamin: (RES) 22 Pine, (CMTS) Albany 1815 City Directory
Birdsall, Sarah M.: (CMTS) Graduate State Normal College, Albany, NY, 1852, (RES) Schenectady, Schenectady Co., NY
Birdsall, Theophilus: (OC) Shoemaker, (CMTS) Albany 1815 City Directory
Bishop, Caroline: (CMTS) Graduate State Normal College, Albany, NY, 1873, (RES) Castile, Wyoming Co., NY
Bishop, Carrie K.: (CMTS) Graduate State Normal College, Albany, NY, 1881, (RES) Worchester, Otsego Co., NY
Bishop, Electra R.: (CMTS) Graduate State Normal College, Albany, NY, 1860, (RES) Oswego, Oswego Co., NY
Bishop, Elihu: (OC) Laborer, (CMTS) Albany 1815 City Directory
Bishop, Ellen: (CMTS) Graduate State Normal College, Albany, NY, 1875, (RES) Castile, Wyoming Co., NY
Bishop, Ettie E.: (CMTS) Graduate State Normal College, Albany, NY, 1866, (RES) Warsaw, Wyoming Co., NY
Bishop, George C.: (F) Member Temple Lodge, No. 14, 1900, Albany, NY
Bishop, James: (OC) Blacksmith, (CMTS) Albany 1815 City Directory
Bishop, Thomas J.: (F) Member Temple Lodge, No. 14, 1900, Albany, NY, (CMTS) Life Member

Blach, Lewis L.: (F) Member Masters Lodge, No. 5, 1900, Albany, NY
Black, Elizabeth: (CMTS) Graduate State Normal College, Albany, NY, 1889, (RES) Schodack Depot, Rensselaer Co., NY
Black, James: (OC) Grocer, (CMTS) Albany 1815 City Directory
Black, Widow Mary: (RES) 22 Union, (CMTS) Albany 1815 City Directory
Blackall, John: (OC) Laborer, (CMTS) Albany 1815 City Directory
Blackall, Wm.: (OC) Laborer, (CMTS) Albany 1815 City Directory
Blackburn, John: (F) Member Masters Lodge, No. 5, 1900, Albany, NY
Blain, Peter: (CMTS) 1790 Federal Census, Watervliet
Blair, Arthur: (F) Member Mount Vernon Lodge, No. 3, 1900, Albany, NY
Blair, Louis E.: (F) Member Mount Vernon Lodge, No. 3, 1900, Albany, NY
Blair, Mabel: (CMTS) Graduate State Normal College, Albany, NY, 1891, (RES) Putnam, Washington Co., NY
Blair, Simeon: (OC) Teacher, (CMTS) Albany 1815 City Directory
Blake, Henry: (OC) Carpenter, (CMTS) Albany 1815 City Directory
Blake, Jacob: (OC) Shoemaker, (CMTS) Albany 1815 City Directory
Blake, James: (OC) Cartman, (CMTS) Albany 1815 City Directory
Blake, Mary D.: (CMTS) Graduate State Normal College, Albany, NY, 1892, (RES) Great Bend, Jefferson Co., NY
Blakely, Agnes: (CMTS) Graduate State Normal College, Albany, NY, 1892, (RES) White Plains, Westchester Co., NY
Blakely, Julia E.: (CMTS) Graduate State Normal College, Albany, NY, 1880, (RES) North Bennington, VT
Blakeman, David: (RES) 103 Beaver, (CMTS) Albany 1815 City Directory
Blakeman, Ella A.: (CMTS) Graduate State Normal College, Albany, NY, 1866, (RES) Greenbush, Rensselaer Co., NY
Blakeman, Luther: (OC) Teamster, (CMTS) Albany 1815 City Directory
Blakeman, S.: (OC) Midwife, (CMTS) Albany 1815 City Directory
Blakeney, David: (CMTS) 1790 Federal Census, Watervliet
Blakeslee, George H.: (F) Member Masters Lodge, No. 5, 1900, Albany, NY
Blakey, Widow: (RES) 43 Hudson, (CMTS) Albany 1815 City Directory
Blakley, Widow Lucy: (OC) Grocer, (CMTS) Albany 1815 City Directory
Blanchard, Wm.: (OC) Grocer, (CMTS) Albany 1815 City Directory
Blasie, William: (F) Member Washington Lodge, No. 85, 1900, Albany, NY, (CMTS) Past Members
Blatner, Jacob M.: (F) Member Mount Vernon Lodge, No. 3, 1900, Albany, NY
Blatner, Joseph H.: (F) Member Masters Lodge, No. 5, 1900, Albany, NY
Blatner, Sol. H.: (F) Member Washington Lodge, No. 85, 1900, Albany, NY

Blauvekt, Isaac: (F) Member Masters Lodge, No. 5, 1900, Albany, NY
Blauvelt, Catharine E.: (CMTS) Graduate State Normal College, Albany, NY, 1860, (RES) Blauveltville, Rockland Co., NY
Blazdel, Levy: (CMTS) 1790 Federal Census, Watervliet
Bleakeley, Clarissa: (CMTS) Graduate State Normal College, Albany, NY, 1860, (RES) Cohoes, Albany Co., NY
Bleecker, B.: (OC) Merchant, (CMTS) Albany 1815 City Directory
Bleecker, Barent: (OC) Merchant, (CMTS) Albany 1815 City Directory
Bleecker, Garret Van Zandt: (RES) 87 do., (CMTS) Albany 1815 City Directory
Bleecker, Harmanus: (OC) Counsellor, (CMTS) Albany 1815 City Directory
Bleecker, Henry: (OC) Merchant, (CMTS) Albany 1815 City Directory
Bleecker, James: (RES) 82 S. Pearl, (CMTS) Albany 1815 City Directory
Bleecker, Jr., John R.: (RES) 354 N. Market, (CMTS) Albany 1815 City Directory
Bleecker, Nicholas: (OC) Merchant, (CMTS) Albany 1815 City Directory
Bleecker, Widow Elizabeth: (RES) 32 Steuben, (CMTS) Albany 1815 City Directory
Blessing, Elmer A.: (F) Member Temple Lodge, No. 14, 1900, Albany, NY
Blessing, Frederick: (CMTS) 1790 Federal Census, Watervliet
Blessing, Ira H.: (F) Member Temple Lodge, No. 14, 1900, Albany, NY
Blessing, Martinus: (CMTS) 1790 Federal Census, Watervliet
Blewer, J. Willard: (F) Member Mount Vernon Lodge, No. 3, 1900, Albany, NY
Bliss, Edna A.: (CMTS) Graduate State Normal College, Albany, NY, 1895, (RES) Alfred, Allegany Co., NY
Bliss, George W.: (F) Member Temple Lodge, No. 14, 1900, Albany, NY
Bliss, Ida M.: (CMTS) Graduate State Normal College, Albany, NY, 1890, (RES) Clyde, Wayne Co., NY
Bliven, Charles R.: (OC) Foreman, (CMTS) Albany 1889 City Directory
Bliven, Geo. L.: (OC) Engineer, (CMTS) Albany 1889 City Directory
Bliven, John M.: (OC) Switchman, (CMTS) Albany 1889 City Directory
Bliven, M. Caroline: (CMTS) Graduate State Normal College, Albany, NY, 1892, (RES) Crystal Run, Orange Co., NY
Blodget, John: (CMTS) 1790 Federal Census, Watervliet
Blood, Nellie H.: (CMTS) Graduate State Normal College, Albany, NY, 1893 (RE)S Mill Point, Montgomery CO., NY
Bloodgood, Fr.: (OC) Clerk, (CMTS) Albany 1815 City Directory
Bloodgood, James A: (OC), (CMTS) Albany 1815 City Directory
Bloodgood, Lynot: (RES) 86 N. Pearl and 46 Quay, (CMTS) Albany 1815 City Directory

Bloomendall, John M: (CMTS) 1790 Federal Census, Watervliet
Bloomer, Joseph: (OC) Ship Carpenter, (CMTS) Albany 1815 City
    Directory
Bloomingdale, Jacob: (RES) 46 Hudson, (CMTS) Albany 1815 City
    Directory
Boardman, Annie C.: (CMTS) Graduate State Normal College, Albany,
    NY, 1891, (RES) Lyons, Wayne Co., NY
Boardman, John: (OC) Builder, (CMTS) Albany 1815 City Directory
Boardman, Wm.: (OC) Sexton, (CMTS) Albany 1815 City Directory
Bocking, John: (OC) Baker, (CMTS) Albany 1815 City Directory
Bodley, Edith: (CMTS) Graduate State Normal College, Albany,
    NY, 1886, (RES) High Falls, Ulster Co., NY
Bodwell, Mary L.: (CMTS) Graduate State Normal College, Albany,
    NY, 1855, (RES) Inverness, Livingston Co., NY
Bogardus, Ephraim P.: (CMTS) 1790 Federal Census, Watervliet
Bogart, Barent: (OC) Sexton Dutch Church, (CMTS) Albany 1815 City
    Directory
Bogart, Garret: (OC) Counsellor, (CMTS) Albany 1815 City Directory
Bogart, Henry I.: (RES) 181 N. Market, (CMTS) Albany 1815 City
    Directory
Bogart, Isaac: (RES) 455 S. Market, (CMTS) Albany 1815 City Directory
Bogart, John: (OC) Chamberlain, (CMTS) Albany 1815 City Directory
Bogert, Christopher: (CMTS) 1790 Federal Census, Watervliet
Bogert, Peter: (CMTS) 1790 Federal Census, Watervliet
Bogert, Peter: (CMTS) 1790 Federal Census, Watervliet
Bohanon, Wm.: (OC) Laborer, (CMTS) Albany 1815 City Directory
Boldemann, John D.: (OC) Merchant, (CMTS) Albany 1815 City
    Directory
Boldry, Ella: (CMTS) Graduate State Normal College, Albany,
    NY, 1879, (RES) Green Island, Albany Co., NY
Bolenbaker, Luella C.: (CMTS) Graduate State Normal College, Albany,
    NY, 1893, (RES) Red Hook, Duchess Co., NY
Boltenhouse, John: (CMTS) 1790 Federal Census, Watervliet
Bolton, David: (CMTS) 1790 Federal Census Rensselaerville
Bolton, Margaret T.: (CMTS) Graduate State Normal College, Albany,
    NY, 1892, (RES) Richfield Springs, Otsego Co., NY
Bond, Edward: (OC) Shoemaker, (CMTS) Albany 1815 City Directory
Bond, L. V.: (F) Member Temple Lodge, No. 14, 1900,
    Albany, NY
Bond, Newton R.: (F) Member Temple Lodge, No. 14, 1900,
    Albany, NY
Bond, Robert: (NATD) Oct. 25, 1878, (RES) Cohoes, (CMTS) Ireland
Bond, William: (OC) Cooper, (CMTS) Albany 1815 City Directory
Bonney, Laurentine L.: (CMTS) Graduate State Normal College, Albany,
    NY, 1862, (RES) Brownvillw, Jefferson Co. NY

Bonsee, Henry Z.: (CMTS) 1790 Federal Census Rensselaerville
Bony, Job: (OC) Grocer, (CMTS) Albany 1815 City Directory
Bookheim, Levi: (F) Member Washington Lodge, No. 85, 1900, Albany, NY
Bookheim, Louis W.: (F) Member Washington Lodge, No. 85, 1900, Albany, NY
Boom, Leonard F.: (F) Member Temple Lodge, No. 14, 1900, Albany, NY
Boon, Nicholas: (OC) Taylor, (CMTS) Albany 1815 City Directory
Boos, John: (F) Member Temple Lodge, No. 14, 1900, Albany, NY
Booth, Harriet: (CMTS) Graduate State Normal College, Albany, NY, 1850, (RES) Goshen, Orange Co., NY
Booth, Isaac: (CMTS) 1790 Federal Census, Watervliet
Booth, William H.: (F) Member Temple Lodge, No. 14, 1900, Albany, NY
Boothby, Nellie M.: (CMTS) Graduate State Normal College, Albany, NY, 1883, (RES) Greenbush, Rensselaer Co., NY
Bordman, Timothy: (CMTS) 1790 Federal Census Rensselaerville
Boright, Edna L.: (CMTS) Graduate State Normal College, Albany, NY, 1888, (RES) Chatham. Columbia Co., NY
Bork, Christian: (OC) Grocer, (CMTS) Albany 1815 City Directory
Borst, Warren R.: (F) Member Temple Lodge, No. 14, 1900, Albany, NY
Borthwick, Edwin: (F) Member Washington Lodge, No. 85, 1900, Albany, NY
Bostwick, Flora M.: (CMTS) Graduate State Normal College, Albany, NY, 1892, (RES) Stillwater, Saratoga Co., NY
Bostwick, Theodora H.: (CMTS) Graduate State Normal College, Albany, NY, 1861, (RES) Sandy Hill, Washington Co., NY
Bostwick, William: (CMTS) 1790 Federal Census, Watervliet
Bothamly, William B.: (F) Member Temple Lodge, No. 14, 1900, Albany, NY
Bothwell, Alice G.: (CMTS) Graduate State Normal College, Albany, NY, 1891, (RES) Albany, Albany Co., NY
Botman, John: (OC) Plater: (RES) 23 & 26 Church, (CMTS) Albany 1815 City Directory
Bouck, Peter C.: (F) Member Mount Vernon Lodge, No. 3, 1900, Albany, NY
Boughton, John W.: (F) Member Mount Vernon Lodge, No. 3, 1900, Albany, NY
Bourn, Alonzo: (OC) Grocer, (CMTS) Albany 1815 City Directory
Bourn, John: (OC) Merchant, (CMTS) Albany 1815 City Directory
Bovee, Matthew: (CMTS) 1790 Federal Census, Watervliet
Bowden, Robert S.: (NATD) Oct. 23, 1886, (RES) Cohoes, (CMTS)

Ireland
Bowen, Adelaide J.: (CMTS) Graduate State Normal College, Albany,
  NY, 1860, (RES) Newport, Herkimer Co., NY
Bowen, Helen M.: (CMTS) Graduate State Normal College, Albany,
  NY, 1866, (RES) Aurora, Cayuga Co., NY
Bowen, Mary A.: (CMTS) Graduate State Normal College, Albany,
  NY, 1887, (RES) Oneomta, Otsego Co., NY
Bowen, Olive E.: (CMTS) Graduate State Normal College, Albany,
  NY, 1885, (RES) Hartford, Washington Co., NY
Bower, Lucia M.: (CMTS) Graduate State Normal College, Albany,
  NY, 1888, (RES) Stony Point, Rockland Co., NY
Bowers, Augustus: (F) Member Mount Vernon Lodge, No. 3, 1900,
  Albany, NY, (CMTS) Past Master 1863
Bowers, Georgia A.: (CMTS) Graduate State Normal College, Albany,
  NY, 1890, (RES) Johnston, Fulton Co., NY
Bowers, James: (CMTS) 1790 Federal Census, Watervliet
Bowers, Jonas: (OC) Printer, (CMTS) Albany 1815 City Directory
Bowers, Robert J.: (F) Member Temple Lodge, No. 14, 1900,
  Albany, NY
Bowers, Sarah T.: (CMTS) Graduate State Normal College, Albany,
  NY, 1854, (RES) New York, New York Co., NY
Bowhay, Catharine A.: (CMTS) Graduate State Normal College, Albany,
  NY, 1860, (RES) Troy, Rensselaer Co., NY
Bowie, James: (OC) Shoemaker, (CMTS) Albany 1815 City Directory
Bowman, John: (OC) Western Turnpike, (CMTS) Albany 1815 City
  Directory
Bowman, Nelson C.: (F) Member Temple Lodge, No. 14, 1900,
  Albany, NY
Bowne, Gabriel: (RES) 29 Pine, (CMTS) Albany 1815 City Directory
Bowne, John: (OC) Carpenter, (CMTS) Albany 1815 City Directory
Bowne, W. H. D. W.: (F) Member Temple Lodge, No. 14, 1900,
  Albany, NY
Bowyer, Pattie E.: (CMTS) Graduate State Normal College, Albany,
  NY, 1877, (RES) Chestertown, Warren Co., NY
Boyce, Henrietta: (CMTS) Graduate State Normal College, Albany,
  NY, 1866, (RES) Dover Plains, Dutchess Co., NY
Boyce, Nicholas: (OC) Paver, (CMTS) Albany 1815 City Directory
Boyd, Hamilton: (OC) Merchant, (CMTS) Albany 1815 City Directory
Boyd, Hattie E.: (CMTS) Graduate State Normal College, Albany,
  NY, 1888, (RES) Wallington, Wayne Co., NY
Boyd, James: (CMTS) 1790 Federal Census, Watervliet
Boyd, James: (OC), (CMTS) Albany 1815 City Directory
Boyd, Mary A.: (CMTS) Graduate State Normal College, Albany,
  NY, 1863, (RES) Albany, Albany Co., NY
Boyd, Peter & John I.: (OC) Merchant, (CMTS) Albany 1815 City

Directory
Boyd, Robert: (OC) Brewer, (CMTS) Albany 1815 City Directory
Boyd, William: (F) Member Mount Vernon Lodge, No. 3, 1900, Albany, NY
Boyd, Wm.: (OC) Jeweller, (CMTS) Albany 1815 City Directory
Boynton, Calvin: (OC) Merchant, (CMTS) Albany 1815 City Directory
Boynton, Johan: (OC) Grocer, (CMTS) Albany 1815 City Directory
Boynton, Nathan: (OC) Carpenter, (CMTS) Albany 1815 City Directory
Boynton, Sarah E.: (CMTS) Graduate State Normal College, Albany, NY, 1860, (RES) McLean, Tompkins Co., NY
Brace, Caroline A.: (CMTS) Graduate State Normal College, Albany, NY, 1856, (RES) Salina, Onondaga Co. NY
Brace, Emma M.: (CMTS) Graduate State Normal College, Albany, NY, 1856, (RES) Salina, Onondaga Co. NY
Bradford, Harriet C.: (CMTS) Graduate State Normal College, Albany, NY, 1869, (RES) Crown Point, Essex Co., NY
Bradford, John M: (OC) Pastor Dutch church, (CMTS) Albany 1815 City Directory
Bradley, Daniel G.: (F) Member Temple Lodge, No. 14, 1900, Albany, NY
Bradley, Henry: (NATD) Oct. 24, 1876, (RES) Cohoes, (CMTS) Ireland
Bradley, Jennie: (CMTS) Graduate State Normal College, Albany, NY, 1886, (RES) Walton, Delaware Co., NY
Bradley, S. Minnie: (CMTS) Graduate State Normal College, Albany, NY, 1871, (RES) Castile, Wyoming Co., NY
Bradt, Adrian: (CMTS) 1790 Federal Census, Watervliet
Bradt, Albert: (CMTS) 1790 Federal Census, Watervliet
Bradt, Albert: (OC) Innkeeper, (CMTS) Albany 1815 City Directory
Bradt, Anthony: (CMTS) 1790 Federal Census, Watervliet
Bradt, Baltus: (CMTS) 1790 Federal Census, Watervliet
Bradt, Daniel: (OC) Bricklayer, (CMTS) Albany 1815 City Directory
Bradt, David: (CMTS) 1790 Federal Census, Watervliet
Bradt, Francis B.: (RES) 176 N. Market, (CMTS) Albany 1815 City Directory
Bradt, Garret: (CMTS) 1790 Federal Census, Watervliet
Bradt, Garret: (OC) Ferry, (CMTS) Albany 1815 City Directory
Bradt, Henry: (CMTS) 1790 Federal Census, Watervliet
Bradt, Henry: (RES) 683 S. Market, (CMTS) Albany 1815 City Directory
Bradt, Jr., Henry: (OC) Manson, (CMTS) Albany 1815 City Directory
Bradt, Isaac: (OC) Cartman, (CMTS) Albany 1815 City Directory
Bradt, John: (CMTS) 1790 Federal Census, Watervliet
Bradt, John B.: (CMTS) 1790 Federal Census, Watervliet
Bradt, John F.: (RES) 176 N. Market, (CMTS) Albany 1815 City Directory
Bradt, John S.: (CMTS) 1790 Federal Census, Watervliet

Bradt, John V: (RES) 203 N. Market, (CMTS) Albany 1815 City
   Directory
Bradt, Laura: (CMTS) Graduate State Normal College, Albany,
   NY, 1886, (RES) Walton, Delaware Co., NY
Bradt, Peter: (RES) 79 N. Market, (CMTS) Albany 1815 City Directory
Bradt, Peter A: (CMTS) 1790 Federal Census, Watervliet
Bradt, Peter J: (CMTS) 1790 Federal Census, Watervliet
Bradt, Staats: (CMTS) 1790 Federal Census, Watervliet
Bradt, Storm A: (CMTS) 1790 Federal Census, Watervliet
Bradt, Widow C: (OC) Lumber st, (CMTS) Albany 1815 City Directory
Bradt, Widow Mary: (RES) 149 N. Market, (CMTS) Albany 1815 City
   Directory
Bradt, William: (CMTS) 1790 Federal Census, Watervliet
Brady, Philip: (NATD) Oct. 27, 1877, (RES) Cohoes, (CMTS) Ireland
Brainard, Albert E.: (F) Member Masters Lodge, No. 5, 1900, Albany, NY
Brainard, Elijah: (OC) Pumpmaker, (CMTS) Albany 1815 City Directory
Brainard, John: (OC) Teacher, (CMTS) Albany 1815 City Directory
Brainard, Morris F.: (F) Member Temple Lodge, No. 14, 1900,
   Albany, NY
Brainard, William H.: (F) Member Masters Lodge, No. 5, 1900,
   Albany, NY
Brainerd, Florence A.: (CMTS) Graduate State Normal College, Albany,
   NY, 1892, (RES) Nyack, Rockland Co., NY
Brambly, William: (CMTS) 1790 Federal Census, Watervliet
Brand, Harriet N.: (CMTS) Graduate State Normal College, Albany,
   NY, 1854, (RES) Van Buren, Onondaga Co., NY
Brand, Mary L.: (CMTS) Graduate State Normal College, Albany,
   NY, 1852, (RES) Belle Isle, Onondaga Co., NY
Brand, Jr., Adam: (F) Member Temple Lodge, No. 14, 1900,
   Albany, NY
Brandner, Caroline D.: (CMTS) Graduate State Normal College, Albany,
   NY, 1891, (RES) Warwick, Orange Co., NY
Brandt, Aaron: (OC) Cartman, (CMTS) Albany 1815 City Directory
Brandt, Edmund: (CMTS) 1790 Federal Census, Watervliet
Brant, Michael: (CMTS) 1790 Federal Census Rensselaerville
Bratt, Jacob: (CMTS) 1790 Federal Census, Watervliet
Brattig, Adolph: (F) Member Temple Lodge, No. 14, 1900,
   Albany, NY
Bray, Sarah: (CMTS) Graduate State Normal College, Albany,
   NY, 1857, (RES) Kinderhook, Columbia CO., NY
Brayton, Eunice E.: (CMTS) Graduate State Normal College, Albany,
   NY, 1872, (RES) Hartford, Washington Co., NY
Breakenridge, Geo. T.: (F) Member Masters Lodge, No. 5, 1900,
   Albany, NY
Breckinridge, Mary G.: (CMTS) Graduate State Normal College, Albany,

NY, 1894, (RES) Binghamton, Broome Co., NY
Breen, Ella M.: (CMTS) Graduate State Normal College, Albany,
  NY, 1891, (RES) Poughkeepsie, Dutchess Co., NY
Breen, Michael: (NATD) Oct. 11, 1881, (RES) Cohoes, (CMTS) Ireland
Breen, Michael: (NATD) Oct. 24, 1860, (RES) Cohoes, (CMTS) Ireland
Breese, Mary A.: (CMTS) Graduate State Normal College, Albany,
  NY, 1863, (RES) Horseheads, Chemung Co., NY
Brennan, Peter: (NATD) Mar. 22, 1890, (RES) Cohoes, (CMTS) Ireland
Bresler, Frederick U.: (F) Member Temple Lodge, No. 14, 1900,
  Albany, NY
Breszee, Adella: (CMTS) Graduate State Normal College, Albany,
  NY, 1891, (RES) Poughkeepsie, Dutchess Co., NY
Brett, Elizabeth M.: (CMTS) Graduate State Normal College, Albany,
  NY, 1879, (RES) Albany, Albany Co., NY
Brett, Martin: (NATD) Oct. 17, 1888, (RES) Cohoes, (CMTS) Ireland
Brett, S. Anna: (CMTS) Graduate State Normal College, Albany,
  NY, 1893, (RES) Galway, Saratoga Co., NY
Brett, Virginia I.: (CMTS) Graduate State Normal College, Albany,
  NY, 1883, (RES) Albany, Albany Co., NY
Brewer, Anna T.: (CMTS) Graduate State Normal College, Albany,
  NY, 1890, (RES) Tarrytown, Westchester Co., NY
Brewer, George: (CMTS) 1790 Federal Census, Watervliet
Brewer, Ulrick: (CMTS) 1790 Federal Census, Watervliet
Brewster, H. Elizabeth: (CMTS) Graduate State Normal College, Albany,
  NY, 1869, (RES) Westchester, Otsego Co., NY
Brice, James: (CMTS) 1790 Federal Census Rensselaerville
Bridge, Carrie Foreman: (CMTS) Graduate State Normal College, Albany,
  NY, 1873, (RES) Leroy, Genesee Co., NY
Bridge, Nathan: (RES) 210 Washington, (CMTS) Albany 1815 City
  Directory
Bridgen, Earl: (OC) Shoemaker, (CMTS) Albany 1815 City Directory
Brigden, Thomas: (OC) Master in Chancery, (CMTS) Albany 1815
  City Directory
Brigden, Timothy: (OC) Silversmith, (CMTS) Albany 1815 City Directory
Briggs, Benjamin: (CMTS) 1790 Federal Census Rensselaerville
Briggs, Clara M.: (CMTS) Graduate State Normal College, Albany,
  NY, 1882, (RES) Laurens, Otsego Co., NY
Briggs, Ella M.: (CMTS) Graduate State Normal College, Albany,
  NY, 1883, (RES) Laurens, Otsego Co., NY
Briggs, Frances L.: (CMTS) Graduate State Normal College, Albany,
  NY, 1863, (RES) Coeymans, Albany Co., NY
Briggs, Lameul: (OC) Laborer, (CMTS) Albany 1815 City Directory
Briggs, Nancy E.: (CMTS) Graduate State Normal College, Albany,
  NY, 1857, (RES) Honeoye, Ontario Co., NY
Briggs, Rowland: (CMTS) 1790 Federal Census Rensselaerville

Briggs, Sara F.: (CMTS) Graduate State Normal College, Albany,
　　NY, 1895, (RES) Rochester, Monroe Co., NY
Brigham, Antibus: (OC) Steamboat Pilot, (CMTS) Albany 1815
　　City Directory
Brigham, Ella M.: (CMTS) Graduate State Normal College, Albany,
　　NY, 1895, (RES) Fairport, Monroe Co., NY
Brigham, Mary: (RES) 51 Hudson, (CMTS) Albany 1815 City Directory
Brigham, Wm.: (RES) 51 Hudson, (CMTS) Albany 1815 City Directory
Bright, Philip: (OC) Mason, (CMTS) Albany 1815 City Directory
Brilleman, Isaac: (F) Member Washington Lodge, No. 85, 1900,
　　Albany, NY
Brimahll, Horace F.: (F) Member Temple Lodge, No. 14, 1900,
　　Albany, NY
Brimmer, Ida: (CMTS) Graduate State Normal College, Albany,
　　NY, 1884, (RES) Painted Post, Steuben Co., NY
Brinckerhoff, John: (RES) 3 Dock, (CMTS) Albany 1815 City Directory
Brinckerhoff, Widow Eliza: (RES) 39 N. Pearl, (CMTS) Albany
　　1815 City Directory
Brinckley, W.: (RES) 31 Union, (CMTS) Albany 1815 City Directory
Brink, Alfred D.: (F) Member Washington Lodge, No. 85, 1900,
　　Albany, NY, (CMTS) Past Members
Brisbin, William: (F) Member Mount Vernon Lodge, No. 3, 1900,
　　Albany, NY
Bristol, Carrie L.: (CMTS) Graduate State Normal College, Albany,
　　NY, 1880, (RES) W. Sandlake, Rensselaer Co., NY
Bristol, Delia A.: (CMTS) Graduate State Normal College, Albany,
　　NY, 1855, (RES) Macedon, Wayne Co., NY
Bristol, Phinette K.: (CMTS) Graduate State Normal College, Albany,
　　NY, 1885, (RES) W. Sandlake, Rensselar Co., NY
Bristol, Tamma: (CMTS) Graduate State Normal College, Albany,
　　NY, 1874, (RES) Amenia, Dutchess Co., NY
Britain, J. Thespian: (OC) Hotel, (CMTS) Albany 1815 City Directory
Briton, William: (CMTS) 1790 Federal Census Rensselaerville
Britt, Frederick: (CMTS) 1790 Federal Census, Watervliet
Broadstreet, Samuel: (RES) 26 Washington, (CMTS) Albany 1815 City
　　Directory
Brockway, Able: (CMTS) 1790 Federal Census Rensselaerville
Brome, Cora F.: (CMTS) Graduate State Normal College, Albany,
　　NY, 1888, (RES) New Hampton, Orange Co., NY
Bromlee, David: (OC) Grocer, (CMTS) Albany 1815 City Directory
Bromlee, Robert: (OC) Grocer, (CMTS) Albany 1815 City Directory
Bromlee, Samuel: (OC) Innkeeper, (CMTS) Albany 1815 City Directory
Bromley, Agnes L.: (CMTS) Graduate State Normal College, Albany,
　　NY, 1872, (RES) Albany, Albany Co., NY
Bromley, Frances M.: (CMTS) Graduate State Normal College, Albany,

NY, 1866, (RES) Medina, Orleans Co., NY
Bronck, Nicholas: (CMTS) 1790 Federal Census, Watervliet
Bronell, George: (CMTS) 1790 Federal Census Rensselaerville
Bronk, Jonas: (CMTS) 1790 Federal Census, Watervliet
Bronk, Peter: (CMTS) 1790 Federal Census, Watervliet
Brook, Ernest C.: (F) Member Mount Vernon Lodge, No. 3, 1900, Albany, NY
Brooks, Alida W.: (CMTS) Graduate State Normal College, Albany, NY, 1889, (RES) Montgomery, Orange Co., NY
Brooks, Anthony: (OC) Carpenter, (CMTS) Albany 1815 City Directory
Brooks, Emma E.: (CMTS) Graduate State Normal College, Albany, NY, 1852, (RES) Churchville, Monroe Co., NY
Brooks, Henry: (OC) Mason, (CMTS) Albany 1815 City Directory
Brooks, Jesse: (OC) Grocer, (CMTS) Albany 1815 City Directory
Brooks, Jonas H.: (F) Member Masters Lodge, No. 5, 1900, Albany, NY
Brooks, John: (OC) Painter, (CMTS) Albany 1815 City Directory
Brooks, Jonathan: (OC), (CMTS) Albany 1815 City Directory
Brooks, Jr., Jonathan: (OC), (CMTS) Albany 1815 City Directory
Brooks, Peter: (CMTS) 1790 Federal Census, Watervliet
Brooks, Peter: (OC) Carpenter, (CMTS) Albany 1815 City Directory
Brooks, Ruth A.: (CMTS) Graduate State Normal College, Albany, NY, 1863, (RES) Moscow, Livingston Co., NY
Broon, Patrick: (NATD) Jan. 26, 1869, (RES) Cohoes, (CMTS) Ireland
Brotherton, Isaac: (OC) Shoemaker, (CMTS) Albany 1815 City Directory
Brougham, Joseph H.: (F) Member Mount Vernon Lodge, No. 3, 1900, Albany, NY
Brower, Alice: (CMTS) Graduate State Normal College, Albany, NY, 1884, (RES) Clove Junction, Dutchess Co., NY
Brower, Cornelius: (RES) 69 N. Pearl, (CMTS) Albany 1815 City Directory
Brower, H. L.: (OC) Skipper, (CMTS) Albany 1815 City Directory
Brower, John: (OC) Painter, (CMTS) Albany 1815 City Directory
Brower, Nancy: (OC) N, (CMTS) Albany 1815 City Directory
Brower, Wm.: (OC) Shoemaker, (CMTS) Albany 1815 City Directory
Brown, Adaline M.: (CMTS) Graduate State Normal College, Albany, NY, 1854, (RES) Rutland, Jefferson Co., NY
Brown, Agnes L.: (CMTS) Graduate State Normal College, Albany, NY, 1854, (RES) Albany, Albany Co., NY
Brown, Agnes M.: (CMTS) Graduate State Normal College, Albany, NY, 1874, (RES) Corinth, Saratoga Co., NY
Brown, Alice A.: (CMTS) Graduate State Normal College, Albany, NY, 1889, (RES) Hoosick, Rensselaer Co., NY
Brown, Allen: (OC) Merchant, (CMTS) Albany 1815 City Directory
Brown, Andrew: (CMTS) 1790 Federal Census Rensselaerville
Brown, Asaph B.: (F) Member Temple Lodge, No. 14, 1900,

Albany, NY
Brown, Carrie F.: (CMTS) Graduate State Normal College, Albany,
NY, 1873, (RES) Butternuts, Otsego Co., NY
Brown, Coquelico: (OC) Gold and Eagle Fancy Chairs, (CMTS) Albany
1815 City Directory
Brown, Daniel: (CMTS) 1790 Federal Census Rensselaerville
Brown, Daniel C.: (F) Member Masters Lodge, No. 5, 1900, Albany, NY
Brown, David: (CMTS) 1790 Federal Census Rensselaerville
Brown, Edward: (OC) Merchant, (CMTS) Albany 1815 City Directory
Brown, Emily C.: (CMTS) Graduate State Normal College, Albany,
NY, 1891, (RES) Deposit, Broome Co., NY
Brown, Euretta E.: (CMTS) Graduate State Normal College, Albany,
NY, 1890, (RES) Kinderhool, Columbia Co., NY
Brown, George: (CMTS) 1790 Federal Census, Watervliet
Brown, Goodwin: (F) Member Masters Lodge, No. 5, 1900, Albany, NY
Brown, Harriet A.: (CMTS) Graduate State Normal College, Albany,
NY, 1860, (RES) Miller's Place, Suffolk Co., NY
Brown, Helen S.: (CMTS) Graduate State Normal College, Albany,
NY, 1864, (RES) Ludlowville, Tompkins Co., NY
Brown, Jacob: (CMTS) 1790 Federal Census, Watervliet
Brown, James: (F) Member Washington Lodge, No. 85, 1900,
Albany, NY
Brown, James: (OC) Grocer, (CMTS) Albany 1815 City Directory
Brown, James: (OC) Taylor, (CMTS) Albany 1815 City Directory
Brown, Jennie S.: (CMTS) Graduate State Normal College, Albany,
NY, 1877, (RES) Shushan, Washington Co., NY
Brown, John: (CMTS) 1790 Federal Census, Watervliet
Brown, John: (OC) Mason, (CMTS) Albany 1815 City Directory
Brown, John: (OC) Tobacconist, (CMTS) Albany 1815 City Directory
Brown, Julia E.: (CMTS) Graduate State Normal College, Albany,
NY, 1875, (RES) South Schodack, Rensselaer Co., NY
Brown, Lilly: (CMTS) Graduate State Normal College, Albany,
NY, 1857, (RES) Albany, Albany Co., NY
Brown, Luther: (CMTS) 1790 Federal Census Rensselaerville
Brown, Lydia H.: (CMTS) Graduate State Normal College, Albany,
NY, 1870, (RES) Schenectady, Schenactady Co., NY
Brown, Lyman P.: (F) Member Mount Vernon Lodge, No. 3, 1900,
Albany, NY
Brown, Margaret J.: (CMTS) Graduate State Normal College, Albany,
NY, 1855, (RES) Henwood, Albany Co., NY
Brown, Mary: (CMTS) Graduate State Normal College, Albany,
NY 1849, (RES) Manchester, Ontario Co., NY
Brown, Mary A.: (CMTS) Graduate State Normal College, Albany,
NY, 1878, (RES) Lkingsboro, Fulton Co., NY
Brown, Matilda A.: (CMTS) Graduate State Normal College, Albany,

NY, 1856, (RES) Conquest, Cayuga Co., NY
Brown, May E.: (CMTS) Graduate State Normal College, Albany,
   NY, 1891, (RES) Bridgewater, Oneida Co., NY
Brown, Mordecai: (CMTS) 1790 Federal Census, Watervliet
Brown, Oliver: (CMTS) 1790 Federal Census, Watervliet
Brown, Ophelia: (CMTS) Graduate State Normal College, Albany,
   NY, 1848, (RES) Oppenheim Fulton Co., NY
Brown, Peter: (OC) Cartman, (CMTS) Albany 1815 City Directory
Brown, Phoebe: (CMTS) Graduate State Normal College, Albany,
   NY, 1862, (RES) Corinth, Saratoga Co., NY
Brown, Rufus: (OC) Merchant, (CMTS) Albany 1815 City Directory
Brown, S.: (OC) Plater, (CMTS) Albany 1815 City Directory
Brown, Samuel: (CMTS) 1790 Federal Census, Watervliet
Brown, Samuel W.: (F) Member Masters Lodge, No. 5, 1900, Albany, NY
Brown, Sarah A.: (CMTS) Graduate State Normal College, Albany,
   NY, 1854, (RES) Nunda, Livington Co., NY
Brown, Sarah F.: (CMTS) Graduate State Normal College, Albany,
   NY, 1877, (RES) Albany, Albany Co., NY
Brown, Sarah P.: (CMTS) Graduate State Normal College, Albany,
   NY, 1861, (RES) Albany, Albany Co., NY
Brown, Sophia E.: (CMTS) Graduate State Normal College, Albany,
   NY, 1865, (RES) Canajoharie, Montogomery Co., NY
Brown, Stephen: (CMTS) 1790 Federal Census, Watervliet
Brown, Stephen: (CMTS) 1790 Federal Census Rensselaerville
Brown, Thomas: (CMTS) 1790 Federal Census Rensselaerville
Brown, W. Howard: (F) Member Masters Lodge, No. 5, 1900,
   Albany, NY
Brown, Widow Betsey: (RES) 11 Chapel, (CMTS) Albany 1815
   City Directory
Brown, Widow Mary: (RES) 40 Fox, (CMTS) Albany 1815
   City Directory
Brown, William: (CMTS) 1790 Federal Census Rensselaerville
Brown, William: (OC) Blacksmith, (CMTS) Albany 1815 City Directory
Brown, William: (OC) Merchant, (CMTS) Albany 1815 City Directory
Brown, Widow Martha: (OC) Grocer, (CMTS) Albany 1815 City
   Directory
Brown, Wm.: (OC) Blacksmith, (CMTS) Albany 1815 City Directory
Browne, Florence E.: (CMTS) Graduate State Normal College, Albany,
   NY, 1869, (RES) Bangall, Duchess Co., NY
Browne, Florence G.: (CMTS) Graduate State Normal College, Albany,
   NY, 1870, (RES) Troy, Rensselaer Co., NY
Browne, Walter A.: (F) Member Mount Vernon Lodge, No. 3, 1900,
   Albany, NY
Brownell, Catherine M.: (CMTS) Graduate State Normal College, Albany,
   NY, 1851, (RES) Schoharie, Schoharie Co., NY

Brownell, Elvena C.: (CMTS) Graduate State Normal College, Albany, NY, 1858, (RES) Shutter's Corners, Schoharie Co., NY
Brownell, Ezra: (RES) 67 Eagle, (CMTS) Albany 1815 City Directory
Browning, Benjamin: (OC) Blacksmith, (CMTS) Albany 1815 City Directory
Brownlow, William: (F) Member Temple Lodge, No. 14, 1900, Albany, NY
Bruce, Michael: (CMTS) 1790 Federal Census, Watervliet
Bruce, William: (F) Member Masters Lodge, No. 5, 1900, Albany, NY
Brumaghim, Edward C.: (F) Member Temple Lodge, No. 14, 1900, Albany, NY, (CMTS) Life Member
Brunson, Allen: (RES) 19 Washington, (CMTS) Albany 1815 City Directory
Brust, Luara J.: (CMTS) Graduate State Normal College, Albany, NY, 1882, (RES) Centre Brunswick, Rensselaer CO., NY
Bryan, Clement: (RES) 35 Church, (CMTS) Albany 1815 City Directory
Bryan, John: (OC) Furrier, (CMTS) Albany 1815 City Directory
Bryan, John O.: (OC) Laborer, (CMTS) Albany 1815 City Directory
Bryan, William J.: (F) Member Temple Lodge, No. 14, 1900, Albany, NY, (CMTS) Past Master 1896
Bryant, Emily J.: (CMTS) Graduate State Normal College, Albany, NY, 1866, (RES) New York, New York Co., NY
Bryant, John: (OC) Brickmaker, (CMTS) Albany 1815 City Directory
Bryard, Peter: (OC) Confectioner, (CMTS) Albany 1815 City Directory
Bryce, Belle: (CMTS) Graduate State Normal College, Albany, NY, 1877, (RES) De Lansey, Delaware Co., NY
Buch, Baltis: (CMTS) 1790 Federal Census Rensselaerville
Buchanan, Charles J.: (F) Member Temple Lodge, No. 14, 1900, Albany, NY, (CMTS) Life Member
Buchanan, George: (NATD) Mar. 30, 1886, (RES) Cohoes, (CMTS) Ireland
Buchanan, James: (NATD) Mar. 30, 1888, (RES) Cohoes, (CMTS) Ireland
Buchanan, John: (NATD) Oct. 23, 1860, (RES) Cohoes, (CMTS) Ireland
Buchanan, Jr., John: (NATD) Oct. 23, 1886, (RES) Cohoes, (CMTS) Ireland
Buchanan, Sr., John: (NATD) Mar. 30, 1886, (RES) Cohoes, (CMTS) Ireland
Buchanan, Sarah A.: (CMTS) Graduate State Normal College, Albany, NY, 1877, (RES) Troy, Rensselaer Co., NY
Buck, Effie R.: (CMTS) Graduate State Normal College, Albany, NY, 1882, (RES) Crown Point, Essex Co., NY
Buck, Margaret A.: (CMTS) Graduate State Normal College, Albany, NY, 1859, (RES) Chemung. Chemung Co., NY
Buck, Media M.: (CMTS) Graduate State Normal College, Albany,

NY, 1891, (RES) Crown Point, Essex Co., NY
Buck, S. Eugenia: (CMTS) Graduate State Normal College, Albany, NY, 1891, (RES) West Troy, Albany Co., NY
Buck, Viva A.: (CMTS) Graduate State Normal College, Albany, NY, 1882, (RES) Crown Point, Essex Co., NY
Buckbee, John: (OC) Grocer, (CMTS) Albany 1815 City Directory
Buckbee, Sophia: (OC) Seamstress, (CMTS) Albany 1815 City Directory
Buckelew, Mary: (CMTS) Graduate State Normal College, Albany, NY, 1856, (RES) Brooklyn. Kings Co., NY
Buckelew, Sarah F.: (CMTS) Graduate State Normal College, Albany, NY, 1854, (RES) Brooklyn. Kings Co., NY
Buckingham, Gideon: (CMTS) 1790 Federal Census Rensselaerville
Buckley, Billy: (OC) Justice of the Peace, (CMTS) Albany 1815 City Directory
Buckley, Charles S.: (F) Member Temple Lodge, No. 14, 1900, Albany, NY
Buckley, Ellen G.: (CMTS) Graduate State Normal College, Albany, NY, 1890, (RES) Irvington-on-Hudson, Westchester CO., NY
Buckley, James P.: (F) Member Temple Lodge, No. 14, 1900, Albany, NY
Buckly, John: (OC) Merchant, (CMTS) Albany 1815 City Directory
Buel, Jesse: (OC) Printer, (CMTS) Albany 1815 City Directory
Buell, Lansing M.: (F) Member Masters Lodge, No. 5, 1900, Albany, NY
Bugbee, Silas: (CMTS) 1790 Federal Census, Watervliet
Bugden, Herbert E.: (F) Member Temple Lodge, No. 14, 1900, Albany, NY
Buhl, Gertel J.: (F) Member Temple Lodge, No. 14, 1900, Albany, NY
Bulger, Charles E.: (F) Member Mount Vernon Lodge, No. 3, 1900, Albany, NY
Bulkely, Chester: (OC) Merchant, (CMTS) Albany 1815 City Directory
Bull, Jeremiah: (CMTS) 1790 Federal Census Rensselaerville
Bullock, John: (CMTS) 1790 Federal Census, Watervliet
Bullock, William: (OC) Merchant, (CMTS) Albany 1815 City Directory
Bulsing, Benjamin: (CMTS) 1790 Federal Census, Watervliet
Bulsing, Cornelius: (CMTS) 1790 Federal Census, Watervliet
Bulsing, Solomon: (CMTS) 1790 Federal Census, Watervliet
Bumpus, Frederick: (CMTS) 1790 Federal Census Rensselaerville
Bunder, Christian: (CMTS) 1790 Federal Census, Watervliet
Bunnel, Nathaniel: (RES) Boarding House at 33 Hudson, (CMTS) Albany 1815 City Directory
Burch, George S.: (F) Member Temple Lodge, No. 14, 1900, Albany, NY
Burdick, Linneus H.: (F) Member Temple Lodge, No. 14, 1900, Albany, NY

Burger, Phlip G.: (F) Member Temple Lodge, No. 14, 1900,
    Albany, NY
Burgess, William L.: (F) Member Mount Vernon Lodge, No. 3, 1900,
    Albany, NY
Burham, William F.: (F) Member Temple Lodge, No. 14, 1900,
    Albany, NY
Burham, Edward P.: (F) Member Temple Lodge, No. 14, 1900,
    Albany, NY
Burhams, George M.: (F) Member Temple Lodge, No. 14, 1900,
    Albany, NY
Burhans, Henry: (CMTS) 1790 Federal Census, Watervliet
Burhans, John: (CMTS) 1790 Federal Census, Watervliet
Burke, Adams J.: (F) Member Mount Vernon Lodge, No. 3, 1900,
    Albany, NY
Burke, Joshua A.: (OC) Merchant, (CMTS) Albany 1815 City Directory
Burn, Henry W.: (F) Member Temple Lodge, No. 14, 1900,
    Albany, NY
Burnap, George: (OC) Grocer, (CMTS) Albany 1815 City Directory
Burnison, James: (NATD) Mar. 28, 1890, (RES) Cohoes, (CMTS) Ireland
Burnop, Philip: (OC) Baker, (CMTS) Albany 1815 City Directory
Burns, James: (NATD) Oct. 30, 1886, (RES) Cohoes, (CMTS) Ireland
Burns, John: (OC) Laborer, (CMTS) Albany 1815 City Directory
Burns, Peter: (OC) Laborer, (CMTS) Albany 1815 City Directory
Burnside, John: (CMTS) 1790 Federal Census, Watervliet
Burnside, Thomas: (CMTS) 1790 Federal Census, Watervliet
Burnside, William: (CMTS) 1790 Federal Census, Watervliet
Burr, Mrs. Ann: (OC) Artificial florist, (CMTS) Albany 1815 City
    Directory
Burr, Robert: (NATD) Feb. 19, 1874, (RES) Cohoes, (CMTS) Ireland
Burrel, William: (RES) 79 N. Market, (CMTS) Albany 1815 City
    Directory
Burt, John: (OC) Carpenter, (CMTS) Albany 1815 City Directory
Burtle, Elizabeth: (CMTS) 1790 Federal Census, Watervliet
Burton, Isaac: (OC) Blacksmith, (CMTS) Albany 1815 City Directory
Burton, Joseph: (OC) Painter, (CMTS) Albany 1815 City Directory
Burton, Matthew: (OC) Carpenter, (CMTS) Albany 1815 City Directory
Burtwick, James: (CMTS) 1790 Federal Census Rensselaerville
Busie, Matthew: (CMTS) 1790 Federal Census, Watervliet
Busseter, Charles: (CMTS) 1790 Federal Census, Watervliet
Bussing, Henry: (CMTS) 1790 Federal Census, Watervliet
Bussing, John H.: (CMTS) 1790 Federal Census, Watervliet
Butler, Ira: (OC) Teamster, (CMTS) Albany 1815 City Directory
Butler, W. Burdett: (F) Member Temple Lodge, No. 14, 1900,
    Albany, NY
Butler, William Henry: (F) Member Mount Vernon Lodge, No. 3, 1900,

Albany, NY
Butman, John: (OC) Silver Plater, (CMTS) Albany 1815 City Directory
Byckman, Widow Elizabeth: (RES) 10 Beaver, (CMTS) Albany 1815 City Directory
Byrne, Michael: (NATD) Feb. 5, 1875, (RES) Cohoes, (CMTS) Ireland
Byrne, Widow Rosetta: (RES) 53 Orange, (CMTS) Albany 1815 City Directory
Cables, John: (RES) Boarding House at 5 Mark Lane, (CMTS) Albany 1815 City Directory
Cadwell, Able: (CMTS) 1790 Federal Census Rensselaerville
Cagger, William: (OC) Morocco Dresser, (CMTS) Albany 1815 City Directory
Cahalmers, Robert: (F) Member Temple Lodge, No. 14, 1900, Albany, NY
Cahill, Joseph: (NATD) Oct. 18, 1884, (RES) Cohoes, (CMTS) Ireland
Cahill, Patrick: (NATD) Oct. 25, 1864, (RES) Cohoes, (CMTS) Ireland
Cahill, Patrick: (NATD) Oct. 17, 1860, (RES) Cohoes, (CMTS) Ireland
Cain, Michael: (NATD) Feb. 7, 1877, (RES) Cohoes, (CMTS) Ireland
Caldwell, E: (OC) City Hotel, (CMTS) Albany 1815 City Directory
Caldwell, Joseph: (CMTS) 1790 Federal Census, Watervliet
Caldwell, Walter Lee: (F) Member Temple Lodge, No. 14, 1900, Albany, NY
Caldwell, William: (OC) Merchant, (CMTS) Albany 1815 City Directory
Caldwell, William J: (RES) 55 Sand, (CMTS) Albany 1815 City Directory
Calkins, Matthew: (CMTS) 1790 Federal Census Rensselaerville
Callaghan, Maurice: (NATD) Feb. 23, 1871, (RES) Cohoes, (CMTS) Ireland
Callahan, Patrick: (NATD) Mar. 28, 1870, (RES) Cohoes, (CMTS) Ireland
Callahan, Thomas: (NATD) Mar. 31, 1892, (RES) Cohoes, (CMTS) Ireland
Callen, Peter J.: (F) Member Temple Lodge, No. 14, 1900, Albany, NY
Caly, Christian: (CMTS) 1790 Federal Census, Watervliet
Cameron, Allen: (OC) Shoemaker, (CMTS) Albany 1815 City Directory
Cameron, Edward M.: (F) Member Masters Lodge, No. 5, 1900, Albany, NY
Cameron, Frderick W.: (F) Member Temple Lodge, No. 14, 1900, Albany, NY
Cameron, James: (OC) Carpenter, (CMTS) Albany 1815 City Directory
Cameron, Robert: (OC) Tailor, (CMTS) Albany 1815 City Directory
Cammeron, Alexander: (OC) Silversmith, (CMTS) Albany 1815 City Directory
Camp, Philo: (CMTS) 1790 Federal Census Rensselaerville
Campain, John: (OC) Shoemaker, (CMTS) Albany 1815 City Directory
Campbell, Alexander: (CMTS) 1790 Federal Census, Watervliet

Campbell, Archibald: (OC) Deputy Secretary, (CMTS) Albany 1815 City Directory
Campbell, Charles C.: (F) Member Mount Vernon Lodge, No. 3, 1900, Albany, NY
Campbell, Daniel: (OC) potter, (CMTS) Albany 1815 City Directory
Campbell, Jesse: (RES) 16 Green, (CMTS) Albany 1815 City Directory
Campbell, John: (OC) Flour Store, (CMTS) Albany 1815 City Directory
Campbell, John: (OC) Laborer, (CMTS) Albany 1815 City Directory
Campbell, Lewis: (OC) Leather Store, (CMTS) Albany 1815 City Directory
Campbell, Robert: (NATD) Feb. 21, 1874, (RES) Cohoes, (CMTS) Ireland
Campbell, Thomas: (RES) 213 S. Market, (CMTS) Albany 1815 City Directory
Campbell, William: (CMTS) 1790 Federal Census Rensselaerville
Campbell, William: (OC) Merchant, (CMTS) Albany 1815 City Directory
Campbell, William H.: (F) Member Mount Vernon Lodge, No. 3, 1900, Albany, NY
Cande, Medad: (OC) Innkeeper, (CMTS) Albany 1815 City Directory
Cande, William L.: (OC) Merchant, (CMTS) Albany 1815 City Directory
Canfield, Francis: (OC) Laborer, (CMTS) Albany 1815 City Directory
Canfield, William C.: (OC) Washington, (CMTS) Albany 1815 City Directory
Canners, James: (NATD) Oct. 28, 1887, (RES) Cohoes, (CMTS) Ireland
Cannon, James: (NATD) Aug. 4, 1896, (RES) Cohoes, (CMTS) Ireland
Cantine, Edward B.: (F) Member Temple Lodge, No. 14, 1900, Albany, NY
Capron, Benjamin: (OC) Carpenter, (CMTS) Albany 1815 City Directory
Capron, Marthiah: (OC) Carpenter, (CMTS) Albany 1815 City Directory
Capron, Oliver: (CMTS) 1790 Federal Census, Watervliet
Capron, William N.: (OC) Merchant, (CMTS) Albany 1815 City Directory
Carey, Henry: (OC) Barrett & Co., Tin Roofer, (CMTS) Albany 1859 City Directory
Carey, William: (OC) Teamster, (CMTS) Albany 1815 City Directory
Carey, Zenas: (OC) Physician, (CMTS) Albany 1815 City Directory
Clark, Abraham: (OC) Mason, (CMTS) Albany 1815 City Directory
Carlisle, William: (RES) Boarding House at 50 Liberty, (CMTS) Albany 1815 City Directory
Carlow, Patrick: (NATD) Oct. 22, 1874, (RES) Cohoes, (CMTS) Ireland
Carlow, Sylvanus: (OC) Grocer, (CMTS) Albany 1815 City Directory
Carmen, Elijah: (CMTS) 1790 Federal Census, Watervliet
Carmichael, Daniel: (OC) Baker, (CMTS) Albany 1815 City Directory
Carmichael, James: (OC) Baker, (CMTS) Albany 1815 City Directory
Carmichael, John: (RES) 10 Mark Lane, (CMTS) Albany 1815 City Directory

Carmichael, William: (OC) Skipper, (CMTS) Albany 1815 City Directory
Carmody, John: (NATD) Oct. 17, 1860, (RES) Cohoes, (CMTS) Ireland
Carpenter, Henry: (OC) Carpenter, (CMTS) Albany 1815 City Directory
Carpenter, Philip: (RES) 48 Chapel, (CMTS) Albany 1815 City Directory
Carpenter, William: (OC) Tailor, (CMTS) Albany 1815 City Directory
Carpenter, Jr., George W.: (F) Member Masters Lodge, No. 5, 1900, Albany, NY
Carr, John: (CMTS) 1790 Federal Census, Watervliet
Carr, Samuel: (OC) Carpenter, (CMTS) Albany 1815 City Directory
Carr, William: (CMTS) 1790 Federal Census, Watervliet
Carriere, Jr., John B.: (F) Member Temple Lodge, No. 14, 1900, Albany, NY
Carrigan, William: (CMTS) 1790 Federal Census, Watervliet
Carrol, William D.: (OC) Cartman, (CMTS) Albany 1815 City Directory
Carson, Thomas: (OC) Jeweller, (CMTS) Albany 1815 City Directory
Carter, John: (RES) 50 Church, (CMTS) Albany 1815 City Directory
Carter, William H.: (F) Member Mount Vernon Lodge, No. 3, 1900, Albany, NY
Carty, Frank: (F) Member Temple Lodge, No. 14, 1900, Albany, NY
Cary, Samuel: (CMTS) 1790 Federal Census, Watervliet
Casburg, James: (NATD) Feb. 24, 1874, (RES) Cohoes, (CMTS) Ireland
Case, Justus: (OC) Nailer, (CMTS) Albany 1815 City Directory
Case, Spencer T.: (F) Member Mount Vernon Lodge, No. 3, 1900, Albany, NY
Casey, James: (NATD) Oct. 19, 1870, (RES) Cohoes, (CMTS) Ireland
Casey, John: (NATD) Oct. 27, 1893, (RES) Cohoes, (CMTS) Ireland
Casey, Patrick: (NATD) Oct. 25, 1860, (RES) Cohoes, (CMTS) Ireland
Casmore, William: (OC) Laborer, (CMTS) Albany 1815 City Directory
Cass, Conradt: (CMTS) 1790 Federal Census, Watervliet
Cassiday, William: (NATD) Oct. 23, 1866, (RES) Cohoes, (CMTS) Ireland
Cassidy, Patrick: (OC) Butcher, (CMTS) Albany 1815 City Directory
Cassils, George: (NATD) Oct. 14, 1872, (RES) Cohoes, (CMTS) Ireland
Cassin, Ruford: (NATD) Oct. 24, 1877, (RES) Cohoes, (CMTS) Ireland
Cassin, William: (NATD) Oct. 24, 1877, (RES) Cohoes, (CMTS) Ireland
Cassman, Jonathan: (CMTS) 1790 Federal Census Rensselaerville
Castle, Thomas S.: (F) Member Mount Vernon Lodge, No. 3, 1900, Albany, NY
Caswell, Asa: (RES) 61 State cont., (CMTS) Albany 1815 City Directory
Caswell, John M: (OC) Gunsmith, (CMTS) Albany 1815 City Directory
Cator, Wilhelmus: (CMTS) 1790 Federal Census, Watervliet
Cave, Thomas: (OC) Distiller, (CMTS) Albany 1815 City Directory
Center, Asa H.: (OC) Merchant, (CMTS) Albany 1815 City Directory
Center, Luther: (OC) Teamster, (CMTS) Albany 1815 City Directory

Chamberlain, Frank F.: (F) Member Masters Lodge, No. 5, 1900,
    Albany, NY, (CMTS) Past Master
Chamberlain, Joseph: (OC) Gunsmith, (CMTS) Albany 1815 City
    Directory
Chamberlain, Timothy: (OC) Grocer, (CMTS) Albany 1815 City
    Directory
Chambers, Elizabeth: (OC) Widow, (CMTS) Albany 1815 City Directory
Chambers, James: (OC) Mason, (CMTS) Albany 1815 City Directory
Chanberlain, E. T.: (F) Member Masters Lodge, No. 5, 1900,
    Albany, NY
Chapin, William: (OC) Laborer, (CMTS) Albany 1815 City Directory
Chapman, Clarence C.: (F) Member Masters Lodge, No. 5, 1900,
    Albany, NY
Chapman, Eleazer: (CMTS) 1790 Federal Census Rensselaerville
Chapman, John: (OC) Weaver, (CMTS) Albany 1815 City Directory
Chapman, Napoleon B.: (F) Member Temple Lodge, No. 14, 1900,
    Albany, NY
Chapman, Norman: (OC) Blacksmith, (CMTS) Albany 1815 City
    Directory
Chapman, Rueben: (OC) Flour Store, (CMTS) Albany 1815 City
    Directory
Chapman, William: (OC) Merchant, (CMTS) Albany 1815 City Directory
Charles, George: (OC) Tanner & Inspector of Leather, (CMTS) Albany
    1815 City Directory
Charles, Nathaniel: (OC) Carpenter, (CMTS) Albany 1815 City Directory
Charnock, Charles: (OC) Comedian, (CMTS) Albany 1815 City Directory
Chase, Isaac: (CMTS) 1790 Federal Census Rensselaerville
Cheesborough, B. A.: (OC) Merchant, (CMTS) Albany 1815 City
    Directory
Cheesbrough, Elijah: (CMTS) 1790 Federal Census Rensselaerville
Chemishere, Dennis: (RES) 579 S. Market, (CMTS) Albany 1815 City
    Directory
Chemmency, John: (RES) 33 Quay, (CMTS) Albany 1815 City Directory
Chesney, Alexander: (CMTS) 1790 Federal Census, Watervliet
Chesney, William: (CMTS) 1790 Federal Census, Watervliet
Chesnut, William: (OC) Cartman, (CMTS) Albany 1815 City Directory
Chestney, James: (OC) Chair Maker, (CMTS) Albany 1815 City Directory
Chinn, Widow Margaret: (RES) 26 Maiden Lane, (CMTS) Albany 1815
    City Directory
Chism, George M.: (F) Member Temple Lodge, No. 14, 1900,
    Albany, NY
Chism, Jr., John Davis: (F) Member Temple Lodge, No. 14, 1900,
    Albany, NY
Christian, David: (OC) Shoemaker, (CMTS) Albany 1815 City
    Directory

Churchill, George: (OC) Printer, (CMTS) Albany 1815 City Directory
Circuit, Travel: (OC) Gardener, (CMTS) Albany 1815 City Directory
Clacker, William: (OC) Shoemaker, (CMTS) Albany 1815 City Directory
Clairmont, Henry B.: (F) Member Temple Lodge, No. 14, 1900,
    Albany, NY
Clan, Lawrence: (CMTS) 1790 Federal Census, Watervliet
Clancy, Bernard: (NATD) Oct. 24, 1892, (RES) Cohoes, (CMTS) Ireland
Clancy, John: (NATD) Oct. 19, 1887, (RES) Cohoes, (CMTS) Ireland
Clar, Reuben: (OC) Shoemaker, (CMTS) Albany 1815 City Directory
Clar, Terrins: (OC) Grocer, (CMTS) Albany 1815 City Directory
Clark, Aaron: (OC) Attorney, (CMTS) Albany 1815 City Directory
Clark, Abraham: (CMTS) 1790 Federal Census Rensselaerville
Clark, Alexander: (NATD) Oct. 24, 1888, (RES) Cohoes, (CMTS) Ireland
Clark, Capt William: (RES) 18 Store Lane, (CMTS) Albany 1815 City
    Directory
Clark, D. P.: (OC) Merchant, (CMTS) Albany 1815 City Directory
Clark, Daniel P.: (OC) Cabinetmaker, (CMTS) Albany 1815 City
    Directory
Clark, Deborah: (OC) Millener, (CMTS) Albany 1815 City Directory
Clark, Eli Clinton: (F) Member Masters Lodge, No. 5, 1900,
    Albany, NY, (CMTS) Past Master
Clark, Henry: (F) Member Temple Lodge, No. 14, 1900,
    Albany, NY
Clark, Henry: (OC) Gardener, (CMTS) Albany 1815 City Directory
Clark, John: (CMTS) 1790 Federal Census, Watervliet
Clark, John: (OC) Tin-Plate Worker, (CMTS) Albany 1815 City Directory
Clark, John F.: (OC) Coach Painter, (CMTS) Albany 1815 City Directory
Clark, Lewis: (OC) Deputy Wagon Master, (CMTS) Albany 1815 City
    Directory
Clark, Nathaniel: (CMTS) 1790 Federal Census, Watervliet
Clark, Nathan: (CMTS) 1790 Federal Census Rensselaerville
Clark, Paul: (RES) Lydius cont., (CMTS) Albany 1815 City Directory
Clark, Rachel: (CMTS) 1790 Federal Census, Watervliet
Clark, Samuel: (OC) Carpenter, (CMTS) Albany 1815 City Directory
Clark, Thomas: (OC) Innkeeper, (CMTS) Albany 1815 City Directory
Clark, Walter: (OC) Merchant, (CMTS) Albany 1815 City Directory
Clark, Widow Nancy: (RES) 63 Eagle, (CMTS) Albany 1815 City
    Directory
Clark, William A.: (OC) Merchant, (CMTS) Albany 1815 City Directory
Clarke, George: (RES) 140 State, (CMTS) Albany 1815 City Directory
Clarl, James: (OC) Merchant, (CMTS) Albany 1815 City Directory
Class, Peter: (CMTS) 1790 Federal Census, Watervliet
Cleary, Patrick: (NATD) Oct. 28, 1887, (RES) Cohoes, (CMTS) Ireland
Clemmashere, Henry: (OC) Cooper, (CMTS) Albany 1815 City Directory
Clench, Benjamin V: (OC) Auctioneer, (CMTS) Albany 1815 City

Directory
Clerk, Walter: (CMTS) 1790 Federal Census, Watervliet
Cleveland, Baltis: (CMTS) 1790 Federal Census Rensselaerville
Cleveland, Chester: (CMTS) 1790 Federal Census Rensselaerville
Clifford, John: (OC) Merchant, (CMTS) Albany 1815 City Directory
Cline, Matthew: (OC) Tobacconist, (CMTS) Albany 1815 City Directory
Clink, Johannes: (CMTS) 1790 Federal Census Rensselaerville
Clinton, Joseph: (CMTS) 1790 Federal Census, Watervliet
Clinton, Patrick: (NATD) Feb. 22, 1879, (RES) Cohoes, (CMTS) Ireland
Clowes, Timothy: (OC) Rector St Peter's Church, (CMTS) Albany 1815 City Directory
Cludius, Widow Mary: (RES) 32 Orange, (CMTS) Albany 1815 City Directory
Cluet, Elizabeth: (RES) 144 N. Market, (CMTS) Albany 1815 City Directory
Clute, Abraham: (CMTS) 1790 Federal Census, Watervliet
Clute, Derick: (CMTS) 1790 Federal Census, Watervliet
Clute, Frederick: (CMTS) 1790 Federal Census, Watervliet
Clute, Garret: (CMTS) 1790 Federal Census, Watervliet
Clute, Gerardus: (CMTS) 1790 Federal Census, Watervliet
Clute, Jacob: (CMTS) 1790 Federal Census, Watervliet
Clute, John: (CMTS) 1790 Federal Census, Watervliet
Clute, Nicholas: (CMTS) 1790 Federal Census, Watervliet
Clute, Jr., John: (CMTS) 1790 Federal Census, Watervliet
Coates, William: (OC) Merchant, (CMTS) Albany 1815 City Directory
Cobb, James N.: (OC) Merchant, (CMTS) Albany 1815 City Directory
Cobb, Zenas: (RES) 81 Washington, (CMTS) Albany 1815 City Directory
Coberry, James: (NATD) Oct. 21, 1875, (RES) Cohoes, (CMTS) Ireland
Coborn, Enoch: (OC) Mason, (CMTS) Albany 1815 City Directory
Coburn, Theodore: (OC) Mason, (CMTS) Albany 1815 City Directory
Cocklin, John: (OC) Mason, (CMTS) Albany 1815 City Directory
Code, Patrick: (OC) Morocco Dresser, (CMTS) Albany 1815 City Directory
Cody, Joseph: (CMTS) 1790 Federal Census Rensselaerville
Coey, James: (NATD) Oct. 26, 1887, (RES) Cohoes, (CMTS) Ireland
Coey, Patrick: (NATD) Oct. 23, 1885, (RES) Cohoes, (CMTS) Ireland
Coffee, James: (OC) Gardener, (CMTS) Albany 1815 City Directory
Cognat, Peter: (CMTS) 1790 Federal Census, Watervliet
Cogswell, Smith: (OC) Merchant, (CMTS) Albany 1815 City Directory
Cogswell, Widow: (OC) Boarding House, (CMTS) Albany 1815 City Directory
Colbern, Joshua: (OC) Shoe Store, (CMTS) Albany 1815 City Directory
Colbert, James: (NATD) Mar. 29, 1892, (RES) Cohoes, (CMTS) Ireland
Colbert, Maurice: (NATD) Oct. 27, 1871, (RES) Cohoes, (CMTS) Ireland
Cole, Charles W.: (F) Member Temple Lodge, No. 14, 1900,

Albany, NY
Cole, Edward H.: (F) Member Temple Lodge, No. 14, 1900, Albany, NY
Cole, Francis: (OC) Cooper, (CMTS) Albany 1815 City Directory
Cole, Frederick W.: (F) Member Temple Lodge, No. 14, 1900, Albany, NY
Cole, Jaob: (OC) Brewer, (CMTS) Albany 1815 City Directory
Cole, John: (CMTS) 1790 Federal Census, Watervliet
Cole, Philip: (OC) Ferryman, (CMTS) Albany 1815 City Directory
Cole, Royal: (CMTS) 1790 Federal Census Rensselaerville
Cole, Simon: (OC) Ferryman, (CMTS) Albany 1815 City Directory
Cole, Harry E.: (F) Member Temple Lodge, No. 14, 1900, Albany, NY
Collier, Thomas: (OC) Tobacconist, (CMTS) Albany 1815 City Directory
Colligan, Edward: (NATD) Oct. 23, 1885, (RES) Cohoes, (CMTS) Ireland
Collin, James: (NATD) Feb. 9, 1874, (RES) Cohoes, (CMTS) Ireland
Collins, Albert E.: (F) Member Temple Lodge, No. 14, 1900, Albany, NY
Collins, James: (OC) Butcher, (CMTS) Albany 1815 City Directory
Collins, Mrs. Patty: (OC) School Teacher, (CMTS) Albany 1815 City Directory
Colvin, John: (CMTS) 1790 Federal Census, Watervliet
Combs, Frank B.: (F) Member Temple Lodge, No. 14, 1900, Albany, NY
Combs, Lewis B.: (F) Member Temple Lodge, No. 14, 1900, Albany, NY
Comstock, Andrew: (OC) Shoemaker, (CMTS) Albany 1815 City Directory
Conant, Francis: (OC) Merchant, (CMTS) Albany 1815 City Directory
Conant, F.: (OC) Merchant, (CMTS) Albany 1815 City Directory
Conant, P.: (OC) Merchant, (CMTS) Albany 1815 City Directory
Conder, James: (CMTS) 1790 Federal Census Rensselaerville
Condon, William: (NATD) Oct. 24, 1892, (RES) Cohoes, (CMTS) Ireland
Conger, Reuben: (CMTS) 1790 Federal Census Rensselaerville
Conger, Uzziah: (CMTS) 1790 Federal Census, Watervliet
Conkey, Isaac A: (OC) Grocer, (CMTS) Albany 1815 City Directory
Conkey, William J.: (F) Member Temple Lodge, No. 14, 1900, Albany, NY
Conley, Walter H.: (F) Member Masters Lodge, No. 5, 1900, Albany, NY
Connel, Daniel: (OC) Cartman, (CMTS) Albany 1815 City Directory
Connel, Robert: (CMTS) 1790 Federal Census, Watervliet
Connell, Hugh: (NATD) Feb. 5, 1875, (RES) Cohoes, (CMTS) Ireland
Connell, John: (NATD) Apr. 3, 1886, (RES) Cohoes, (CMTS) Ireland
Connell, Patrick: (NATD) Mar. 25, 1886, (RES) Cohoes, (CMTS) Ireland

Connelly, James: (NATD) Mar. 29, 1894, (RES) Cohoes, (CMTS) Ireland
Conner, Andrew: (CMTS) 1790 Federal Census, Watervliet
Conner, Edward: (CMTS) 1790 Federal Census, Watervliet
Conner, Francis: (CMTS) 1790 Federal Census, Watervliet
Connolly, Solomon: (CMTS) 1790 Federal Census, Watervliet
Connoly, Patrick: (OC) Cartman, (CMTS) Albany 1815 City Directory
Connor, Francis: (OC) Shoe Black, (CMTS) Albany 1815 City Directory
Connor, James: (NATD) Oct. 23, 1885, (RES) Cohoes, (CMTS) Ireland
Connor, Michael: (NATD) Oct. 25, 1878, (RES) Cohoes, (CMTS) Ireland
Connors, Danial: (NATD) Sep. 25, 1889, (RES) Cohoes, (CMTS) Ireland
Conroy, Patrick: (NATD) Oct. 18, 1865, (RES) Cohoes, (CMTS) Ireland
Constick, Franklin: (F) Member Temple Lodge, No. 14, 1900, Albany, NY
Constock, Andrew: (OC) Shoemaker, (CMTS) Albany 1815 City Directory
Converse, Henry T.: (F) Member Masters Lodge, No. 5, 1900, Albany, NY
Conway, John: (NATD) Sep. 24, 1868, (RES) Cohoes, (CMTS) Ireland
Conway, John: (NATD) Oct. 27, 1860, (RES) Cohoes, (CMTS) Ireland
Coogan, William C.: (F) Member Temple Lodge, No. 14, 1900, Albany, NY
Cook, George: (CMTS) 1790 Federal Census Rensselaerville
Cook, John: (RES) 33 Church, (CMTS) Albany 1815 City Directory
Cook, John: (OC) Brickmaker, (CMTS) Albany 1815 City Directory
Cook, John T.: (F) Member Mount Vernon Lodge, No. 3, 1900, Albany, NY, (CMTS) Past Master 1898
Cook, Robert P.: (F) Member Temple Lodge, No. 14, 1900, Albany, NY
Cook, Seth P.: (F) Member Temple Lodge, No. 14, 1900, Albany, NY
Cookingham, M. F.: (F) Member Temple Lodge, No. 14, 1900, Albany, NY
Cooley, Adenijah: (CMTS) 1790 Federal Census Rensselaerville
Cooley, Joseph: (CMTS) 1790 Federal Census Rensselaerville
Cooley, Mrs.: (OC) Milliner, (CMTS) Albany 1815 City Directory
Coon, Conradt: (CMTS) 1790 Federal Census, Watervliet
Coon, John: (RES) 99 N. Market, (CMTS) Albany 1815 City Directory
Coonly, Frederick: (CMTS) 1790 Federal Census, Watervliet
Coonly, George: (CMTS) 1790 Federal Census, Watervliet
Coonly, Solomon: (CMTS) 1790 Federal Census, Watervliet
Coons, Adam: (CMTS) 1790 Federal Census Rensselaerville
Coons, John: (CMTS) 1790 Federal Census Rensselaerville
Cooper, Andrew: (OC) Innkeeper, (CMTS) Albany 1815 City Directory
Cooper, Charles D.: (RES) 50 State, (CMTS) Albany 1815 City Directory
Cooper, Jacob: (CMTS) 1790 Federal Census, Watervliet

Cooper, Jacob: (CMTS) 1790 Federal Census Rensselaerville
Cooper, John L.: (F) Member Masters Lodge, No. 5, 1900,
    Albany, NY
Cooper, Obediah: (CMTS) 1790 Federal Census, Watervliet
Cooper, Philip: (OC) Grocer, (CMTS) Albany 1815 City Directory
Cooper, Philip: (OC) Grocer, (CMTS) Albany 1815 City Directory
Cooper, Thomas: (CMTS) 1790 Federal Census, Watervliet
Copeland, John: (CMTS) 1790 Federal Census, Watervliet
Corey, Charles H.: (F) Member Temple Lodge, No. 14, 1900,
    Albany, NY
Corlip, James: (NATD) Oct. 25, 1882, (RES) Cohoes, (CMTS) Ireland
Corliss, Stephen P.: (F) Member Temple Lodge, No. 14, 1900,
    Albany, NY
Cornell, Fenimore L.: (F) Member Temple Lodge, No. 14, 1900,
    Albany, NY
Corning, Erastus: (RES) 10 Green, (CMTS) Albany 1815 City Directory
Cornwaell, Levi: (OC) Laborer, (CMTS) Albany 1815 City Directory
Cortmill, William: (NATD) Oct. 24, 1891, (RES) Cohoes, (CMTS)
    Ireland
Cosgraves, John: (OC) Glover, (CMTS) Albany 1815 City Directory
Costigan, Francis: (OC) Carpenter, (CMTS) Albany 1815 City Directory
Cottam, Shubel: (OC) Pewterer, (CMTS) Albany 1815 City Directory
Cottam, William C: (OC) Baker, (CMTS) Albany 1815 City Directory
Coufhlin, Patrick: (NATD) Oct. 22, 1886, (RES) Cohoes, (CMTS) Ireland
Coughlin, John: (NATD) Oct. 28, 1871, (RES) Cohoes, (CMTS) Ireland
Coughlin, Timothy: (NATD) Mar. 30, 1888, (RES) Cohoes, (CMTS)
    Ireland
Counel, James: (OC) Carpenter, (CMTS) Albany 1815 City Directory
Countryman, Nicholas: (CMTS) 1790 Federal Census, Watervliet
Courtney, George L.: (F) Member Temple Lodge, No. 14, 1900,
    Albany, NY
Courtney, Widow Bridget: (RES) 35 Maiden Lane, (CMTS) Albany 1815
    City Directory
Couse, Andrew: (F) Member Masters Lodge, No. 5, 1900,
    Albany, NY
Couture, Joseph: (NATD) Mar. 21, 1894, (RES) Cohoes, (CMTS) Ireland
Covenhoven, Samuel: (CMTS) 1790 Federal Census, Watervliet
Covert, Abraham: (OC) Grocer, (CMTS) Albany 1815 City Directory
Covert, Elisha: (CMTS) 1790 Federal Census, Watervliet
Covert, Stephen: (CMTS) 1790 Federal Census, Watervliet
Cowdry, Resolved: (OC) Blacksmith, (CMTS) Albany 1815 City
    Directory
Cowell, John: (CMTS) 1790 Federal Census, Watervliet
Cowell, Joseph: (RES) Arbor-hill, (CMTS) Albany 1815 City Directory
Cowell, Samuel: (OC) Grocer, (CMTS) Albany 1815 City Directory

Cowell, Thomas J.: (F) Member Washington Lodge, No. 85, 1900, Albany, NY, (CMTS) Past Members
Cowlbeck, Hiram W.: (F) Member Masters Lodge, No. 5, 1900, Albany, NY
Cowlbeck, Thomas: (F) Member Masters Lodge, No. 5, 1900, Albany, NY
Cowles, Isaac: (CMTS) 1790 Federal Census Rensselaerville
Cowles, William: (CMTS) 1790 Federal Census Rensselaerville
Cows, John: (CMTS) 1790 Federal Census, Watervliet
Cox, Edward G.: (F) Member Masters Lodge, No. 5, 1900, Albany, NY
Cox, Rodman D.: (F) Member Mount Vernon Lodge, No. 3, 1900, Albany, NY
Crabb, David: (OC) Laborer, (CMTS) Albany 1815 City Directory
Crabb, John: (OC) Teacher, (CMTS) Albany 1815 City Directory
Craig, Joseph D.: (F) Member Masters Lodge, No. 5, 1900, Albany, NY, (CMTS) Past Master
Craig, Samuel: (OC) Laborer, (CMTS) Albany 1815 City Directory
Craley, Franklin S.: (F) Member Temple Lodge, No. 14, 1900, Albany, NY
Cram, Robert: (OC) Merchant, (CMTS) Albany 1815 City Directory
Cramp, Ralph W.: (F) Member Temple Lodge, No. 14, 1900, Albany, NY
Crane, Rhodolphus: (RES) 1 Hudson, (CMTS) Albany 1815 City Directory
Crannel, Matthew: (OC) Baker, (CMTS) Albany 1815 City Directory
Crannel, William W.: (OC) Barber, (CMTS) Albany 1815 City Directory
Crannell, Charles R.: (F) Member Temple Lodge, No. 14, 1900, Albany, NY
Crannell, William Windslow: (CMTS) 1790 Federal Census, Watervliet
Crannell, Jr., F. F.: (F) Member Temple Lodge, No. 14, 1900, Albany, NY
Crary, Jonathan: (OC) Laborer, (CMTS) Albany 1815 City Directory
Craven, Christopher J.: (F) Member Temple Lodge, No. 14, 1900, Albany, NY
Craver, Moses: (F) Member Temple Lodge, No. 14, 1900, Albany, NY
Craw, Elijah: (OC) Mason, (CMTS) Albany 1815 City Directory
Crawford, Charles H.: (F) Member Temple Lodge, No. 14, 1900, Albany, NY
Crawford, Eugene: (F) Member Mount Vernon Lodge, No. 3, 1900, Albany, NY
Crawford, Ezex (sic) McI.: (F) Member Masters Lodge, No. 5, 1900, Albany, NY
Crawford, John: (OC) Merchant, (CMTS) Albany 1815 City Directory

Crawman, John: (OC) Paver, (CMTS) Albany 1815 City Directory
Crenningham, Andrew: (OC) Laborer, (CMTS) Albany 1815 City
 Directory
Cress, Bastian: (CMTS) 1790 Federal Census Rensselaerville
Cress, Michael: (CMTS) 1790 Federal Census Rensselaerville
Cressler, Philip: (CMTS) 1790 Federal Census, Watervliet
Cressler, Silvester: (CMTS) 1790 Federal Census, Watervliet
Cribbet, Francis: (CMTS) 1790 Federal Census, Watervliet
Crippen, Charles S.: (F) Member Masters Lodge, No. 5, 1900,
 Albany, NY
Crippen, Ichabod: (CMTS) 1790 Federal Census Rensselaerville
Cristy, James: (OC) Ship Carpenter, (CMTS) Albany 1815 City Directory
Crocker, David: (CMTS) 1790 Federal Census Rensselaerville
Crocker, Enock: (CMTS) 1790 Federal Census Rensselaerville
Crocker, Jonathan: (CMTS) 1790 Federal Census Rensselaerville
Crocker, Unknown: (CMTS) 1790 Federal Census Rensselaerville
Crocker, Jr., Jonathan: (CMTS) 1790 Federal Census Rensselaerville
Croissant, Charles: (F) Member Mount Vernon Lodge, No. 3, 1900,
 Albany, NY
Croissant, John: (F) Member Mount Vernon Lodge, No. 3, 1900,
 Albany, NY
Cronkite, Casper: (CMTS) 1790 Federal Census, Watervliet
Cronkite, Gilbert: (CMTS) 1790 Federal Census, Watervliet
Cronkite, Jessie: (CMTS) 1790 Federal Census, Watervliet
Crosby, Elkanah: (OC) Mason, (CMTS) Albany 1815 City Directory
Crountz, Frederick: (CMTS) 1790 Federal Census, Watervliet
Crowley, Dennis: (NATD) Feb. 21, 1874, (RES) Cohoes, (CMTS) Ireland
Cruttenden, Leverett: (OC) Public Square, (CMTS) Albany 1815 City
 Directory
Cujay, Widow of Fortune: (RES) 208 S. Pearl, (CMTS) Albany 1815 City
 Directory
Culligan, John: (NATD) Oct. 25, 1872, (RES) Cohoes, (CMTS) Ireland
Cullings, James: (CMTS) 1790 Federal Census, Watervliet
Culver, Ashbel: (CMTS) 1790 Federal Census Rensselaerville
Culver, Roger: (CMTS) 1790 Federal Census Rensselaerville
Cumming, Widow Mary: (OC) Grocer, (CMTS) Albany 1815 City
 Directory
Cummings, Daniel: (CMTS) 1790 Federal Census, Watervliet
Cummings, Gilbert: (OC) Merchant, (CMTS) Albany 1815 City Directory
Cummings, James: (OC) Grocer, (CMTS) Albany 1815 City Directory
Cummings, Jane: (RES) 33 Union, (CMTS) Albany 1815 City Directory
Cummings, John: (CMTS) 1790 Federal Census, Watervliet
Cummings, John: (NATD) Apr. 3, 1891, (RES) Cohoes, (CMTS) Ireland
Cundall, Henry E.: (F) Member Temple Lodge, No. 14, 1900,
 Albany, NY

Cunniff, Bernard: (NATD) Oct. 25, 1872, (RES) Cohoes, (CMTS) Ireland
Cunniff, James: (NATD) Feb. 21, 1874, (RES) Cohoes, (CMTS) Ireland
Cunningham, A. C.: (F) Member Masters Lodge, No. 5, 1900,
    Albany, NY
Cunningham, Daniel: (NATD) Oct. 26, 1893, (RES) Cohoes, (CMTS)
    Ireland
Cunningham, Hugh: (F) Member Mount Vernon Lodge, No. 3, 1900,
    Albany, NY
Cunningham, John: (NATD) Oct. 20, 1874, (RES) Cohoes, (CMTS)
    Ireland
Cunningham, Louis: (NATD) Sep. 21, 1868, (RES) Cohoes, (CMTS)
    Ireland
Cure, Peter: (OC) Shoemaker, (CMTS) Albany 1815 City Directory
Cureton, Charles O.: (F) Member Temple Lodge, No. 14, 1900,
    Albany, NY
Cureton, John: (RES) 9 Fox, (CMTS) Albany 1815 City Directory
Curley, Christopher: (NATD) Mar. 29, 1892, (RES) Cohoes, (CMTS)
    Ireland
Curley, John: (NATD) Mar. 29, 1892, (RES) Cohoes, (CMTS) Ireland
Curran, Mathias: (NATD) Oct. 12, 1876, (RES) Cohoes, (CMTS) Ireland
Curreen, Thomas: (OC) Mariner, (CMTS) Albany 1815 City Directory
Curry, John: (CMTS) 1790 Federal Census, Watervliet
Curtis, Jatham: (CMTS) 1790 Federal Census Rensselaerville
Curtis, Levi: (OC) Grocer, (CMTS) Albany 1815 City Directory
Cushman, Harry C.: (F) Member Masters Lodge, No. 5, 1900,
    Albany, NY
Cushman, Paul: (OC) Potter, (CMTS) Albany 1815 City Directory
Cutler, John: (CMTS) 1790 Federal Census, Watervliet
Cutler, John: (RES) 16 S. Pearl, (CMTS) Albany 1815 City Directory
Cutler, Lorenzo: (F) Member Temple Lodge, No. 14, 1900,
    Albany, NY
Cutler, Walter P.: (F) Member Masters Lodge, No. 5, 1900,
    Albany, NY
Cutter, Jonathan: (CMTS) 1790 Federal Census, Watervliet
Cuyler, Abraham: (CMTS) 1790 Federal Census, Watervliet
Cuyler, Jacob C: (OC) Overseer of Poor, (CMTS) Albany 1815 City
    Directory
Cuyler, John: (CMTS) 1790 Federal Census, Watervliet
Cuyler, Widow Elizabeth: (RES) 171 S. Pearl, (CMTS) Albany 1815 City
    Directory
Dailey, Ansel: (F) Member Temple Lodge, No. 14, 1900,
    Albany, NY
Dale, Henry: (CMTS) 1790 Federal Census Rensselaerville
Dale, William A: (OC) Tweed, (CMTS) Albany 1815 City Directory
Daley, Michael: (NATD) Oct. 24, 1874, (RES) Cohoes, (CMTS) Ireland

Daley, Michael: (NATD) Oct. 17, 1874, (RES) Cohoes, (CMTS) Ireland
Daley, Patrick: (NATD) Oct. 16, 1880, (RES) Cohoes, (CMTS) Ireland
Dalton, William: (CMTS) 1790 Federal Census, Watervliet
Damp, Frederick: (CMTS) 1790 Federal Census, Watervliet
Dana, D.: (OC) Grocers: (RES) 93 Washington, (CMTS) Albany 1815
   City Directory
Dana, J. W.: (OC) Grocers: (RES) 93 Washington, (CMTS) Albany 1815
   City Directory
Daniel, James: (OC) Earthenware House, (CMTS) Albany 1815 City
   Directory
Daniel, James: (OC) Hatter, (CMTS) Albany 1815 City Directory
Daniel, John: (CMTS) 1790 Federal Census, Watervliet
Daniels, Jonas D.: (OC) Grocer, (CMTS) Albany 1815 City Directory
Daniels, Warner: (OC) Furnace, (CMTS) Albany 1815 City Directory
Danohue, John: (NATD) Sep. 27, 1864, (RES) Cohoes, (CMTS) Ireland
Davenport, Franklin R.: (F) Member Temple Lodge, No. 14, 1900,
   Albany, NY
Davenport, Samuel J.: (F) Member Temple Lodge, No. 14, 1900,
   Albany, NY
Davey, George W.: (F) Member Mount Vernon Lodge, No. 3, 1900,
   Albany, NY
Davidson, George G.: (F) Member Masters Lodge, No. 5, 1900,
   Albany, NY
Davidson, Wm.: (NATD) Oct. 18, 1860, (RES) Cohoes, (CMTS) Ireland
Davidson, Robert: (F) Member Temple Lodge, No. 14, 1900,
   Albany, NY
Davis, Alias: (OC) Teamster, (CMTS) Albany 1815 City Directory
Davis, Charles E.: (F) Member Masters Lodge, No. 5, 1900,
   Albany, NY
Davis, Charles G.: (F) Member Temple Lodge, No. 14, 1900,
   Albany, NY
Davis, Charles J.: (F) Member Temple Lodge, No. 14, 1900,
   Albany, NY
Davis, Edward: (CMTS) 1790 Federal Census, Watervliet
Davis, Edward: (RES) 32 N. Market, (CMTS) Albany 1815 City Directory
Davis, Evan: (CMTS) 1790 Federal Census, Watervliet
Davis, Ezekil: (CMTS) 1790 Federal Census, Watervliet
Davis, Henry B.: (RES) 367 N. Market, (CMTS) Albany 1815 City
   Directory
Davis, Jedediah: (CMTS) 1790 Federal Census, Watervliet
Davis, Jeremiah: (CMTS) 1790 Federal Census, Watervliet
Davis, John: (CMTS) 1790 Federal Census, Watervliet
Davis, John: (CMTS) 1790 Federal Census Rensselaerville
Davis, Louis: (OC) Barber, (CMTS) Albany 1815 City Directory
Davis, Nathaniel: (OC) Merchant, (CMTS) Albany 1815 City Directory

Davis, Richard: (CMTS) 1790 Federal Census, Watervliet
Davis, Robert: (OC) Baker, (CMTS) Albany 1815 City Directory
Davis, Samuel: (CMTS) 1790 Federal Census, Watervliet
Davis, Thadeus: (CMTS) 1790 Federal Census, Watervliet
Davis, Thomas: (NATD) Oct. 22, 1860, (RES) Cohoes, (CMTS) Ireland
Davis, William: (CMTS) 1790 Federal Census, Watervliet
Davison, James: (CMTS) 1790 Federal Census, Watervliet
Davison, Patrick: (OC) Cartman, (CMTS) Albany 1815 City Directory
Davison, Peter: (OC) Cancer Doctor, (CMTS) Albany 1815 City Directory
Dawson, Richard: (OC) Carpenter, (CMTS) Albany 1815 City Directory
Dawson, Thomas: (OC) Grocer, (CMTS) Albany 1815 City Directory
Dawson, William: (OC) Teamster, (CMTS) Albany 1815 City Directory
Day, Adrian: (RES) Schecectady Turnpike, (CMTS) Albany 1815 City Directory
Day, John: (CMTS) 1790 Federal Census, Watervliet
Day, John O: (NATD) Oct. 22, 1860, (RES) Cohoes, (CMTS) Ireland
Day, Noah: (CMTS) 1790 Federal Census Rensselaerville
Day, Simon: (NATD) Oct. 22, 1860, (RES) Cohoes, (CMTS) Ireland
Day, Thomas: (OC) Carpenter, (CMTS) Albany 1815 City Directory
Daymon, Francis: (OC) Teacher, (CMTS) Albany 1815 City Directory
Daymond, wodow: (OC) Sturgeon, (CMTS) Albany 1815 City Directory
DeCamp, Titus: (CMTS) 1790 Federal Census, Watervliet
DeForest, Curtis: (OC) Merchant, (CMTS) Albany 1815 City Directory
DeForest, Derick: (OC) Shoemaker, (CMTS) Albany 1815 City Directory
DeFreest, Jessee: (CMTS) 1790 Federal Census, Watervliet
DeGarmo, Widow Cornelia: (RES) 150 S. Pearl, (CMTS) Albany 1815 City Directory
DeLund, Francis: (OC) Laborer, (CMTS) Albany 1815 City Directory
DeRuso, Joseph: (CMTS) 1915, Census, District No. 3 Ward No. 18
DeRuso, Mary: (CMTS) 1915, Census, District No. 3 Ward No. 18
DeVoe, Christopher: (OC) Grocer, (CMTS) Albany 1815 City Directory
DeVoe, Frederick: (RES) Arbor Hill, (CMTS) Albany 1815 City Directory
DeVoe, William: (OC) Shoemaker, (CMTS) Albany 1815 City Directory
DeWitt, Andrew H.: (OC) Weigher of Hay, (CMTS) Albany 1815 City Directory
DeWitt, Ephraim: (OC) Superintendant Ferry, (CMTS) Albany 1815 City Directory
DeWitt, Rev. John: (OC) Pastor Dutch church, (CMTS) Albany 1815 City Directory
DeWitt, Simeon: (OC) Surveyor General, (CMTS) Albany 1815 City Directory
Dean, Capt.: (OC) Stewart, (CMTS) Albany 1815 City Directory
Dean, Charles B.: (OC) Teamster, (CMTS) Albany 1815 City Directory

Dean, Frederick A.: (F) Member Temple Lodge, No. 14, 1900, Albany, NY
Dearstyne, Chester F.: (F) Member Masters Lodge, No. 5, 1900, Albany, NY
Dearstyne, Edmund C.: (F) Member Temple Lodge, No. 14, 1900, Albany, NY
Dearstyne, Frank S.: (F) Member Temple Lodge, No. 14, 1900, Albany, NY
DeBarthe, William E.: (F) Member Temple Lodge, No. 14, 1900, Albany, NY
Decker, Benjamin: (CMTS) 1790 Federal Census Rensselaerville
Deer, George: (OC) Laborer, (CMTS) Albany 1815 City Directory
DeGroot, Peter J.: (F) Member Temple Lodge, No. 14, 1900, Albany, NY
Delamater, John: (OC) Physician & Surgeon, (CMTS) Albany 1815 City Directory
Delany, Richard: (NATD) Oct. 28, 1872, (RES) Cohoes, (CMTS) Ireland
Delemans, Andrew: (OC) Segar Maker, (CMTS) Albany 1815 City Directory
Delevan, Henry W.: (OC) Hardware, (CMTS) Albany 1815 City Directory
Delong, David: (CMTS) 1790 Federal Census, Watervliet
Delong, Henry: (CMTS) 1790 Federal Census Rensselaerville
Demars, Edgar: (NATD) Oct. 18, 1887, (RES) Cohoes, (CMTS) Ireland
Demit, Jr., Isaac: (OC) Whip Maker, (CMTS) Albany 1815 City Directory
Demun, Augustus: (OC) Tin Smith, (CMTS) Albany 1815 City Directory
Denison, Frank: (F) Member Mount Vernon Lodge, No. 3, 1900, Albany, NY
Denison, Fred P.: (F) Member Masters Lodge, No. 5, 1900, Albany, NY
Dennis, John D.: (OC), (CMTS) Albany 1815 City Directory
Dennison, Albert: (CMTS) 1790 Federal Census Rensselaerville
Dennison, Jr., Daniel: (CMTS) 1790 Federal Census Rensselaerville
Dennison, Ebenezer: (CMTS) 1790 Federal Census Rensselaerville
Dennison, Joseph: (CMTS) 1790 Federal Census, Watervliet
Dennison, Joseph: (OC) Grocer, (CMTS) Albany 1815 City Directory
Denniston, Garret V: (OC) Attorney, (CMTS) Albany 1815 City Directory
Denny, John: (OC) Dyer, (CMTS) Albany 1815 City Directory
Denny, Penelope: (OC) Widow, (CMTS) Albany 1815 City Directory
Dentz, John: (CMTS) 1790 Federal Census, Watervliet
Dereraux, Patrick: (NATD) Feb. 14, 1881, (RES) Cohoes, (CMTS) Ireland
Desmond, Patrick: (NATD) Mar. 29, 1894, (RES) Cohoes, (CMTS) Ireland
Desobe, Joseph O.: (F) Member Masters Lodge, No. 5, 1900, Albany, NY

Devlin, Patrick: (NATD) Oct. 24, 1876, (RES) Cohoes, (CMTS) Ireland
Devo, David: (OC) Carpenter, (CMTS) Albany 1815 City Directory
Devoe, David: (CMTS) 1790 Federal Census Rensselaerville
Devoe, John: (CMTS) 1790 Federal Census, Watervliet
Devoe, John: (CMTS) 1790 Federal Census Rensselaerville
Dewey, Timothy: (OC) Merchant, (CMTS) Albany 1815 City Directory
Dexter, Samuel: (OC) Druggist, (CMTS) Albany 1815 City Directory
Dexter, Thomas: (OC) Innkeeper, (CMTS) Albany 1815 City Directory
Deyermand, John: (OC) Grocer, (CMTS) Albany 1815 City Directory
Deyermand, William: (OC) Mason, (CMTS) Albany 1815 City Directory
Deyermond, James: (OC) Cartman, (CMTS) Albany 1815 City Directory
Deyo, David: (OC) Carpenter, (CMTS) Albany 1815 City Directory
Diamond, John: (NATD) Oct. 7, 1865, (RES) Cohoes, (CMTS) Ireland
Diamond, Widow Mary: (RES) 109 Lydius, (CMTS) Albany 1815 City Directory
Dickinson, Everett M.: (F) Member Temple Lodge, No. 14, 1900, Albany, NY
Dickson, Daniel: (CMTS) 1790 Federal Census Rensselaerville
Dietz, Adam: (CMTS) 1790 Federal Census Rensselaerville
Dietz, Jacobus: (CMTS) 1790 Federal Census Rensselaerville
Dietz, John J.: (CMTS) 1790 Federal Census Rensselaerville
Dietz, Jr., Adam: (CMTS) 1790 Federal Census Rensselaerville
Dillon, Michael: (NATD) Feb. 20, 1879, (RES) Cohoes, (CMTS) Ireland
Dillow, Jr., Richard: (F) Member Temple Lodge, No. 14, 1900, Albany, NY
Dimmick, Francis: (RES) 4 Dock, (CMTS) Albany 1815 City Directory
Dismond, Timothy: (NATD) Aug. 4, 1896, (RES) Cohoes, (CMTS) Ireland
Diveney, Thomas: (NATD) Oct. 26, 1889, (RES) Cohoes, (CMTS) Ireland
Divol, Adam: (OC) Cutler, (CMTS) Albany 1815 City Directory
Dixon, Jr., Adam: (OC) Tin Plate Worker, (CMTS) Albany 1815 City Directory
Dixon, Frederick: (F) Member Mount Vernon Lodge, No. 3, 1900, Albany, NY
Doag, Peter: (OC) Tailor, (CMTS) Albany 1815 City Directory
Dobson, John: (OC) Shoemaker, (CMTS) Albany 1815 City Directory
Dodds, John: (CMTS) 1790 Federal Census, Watervliet
Dodge, David S.: (OC) Carpenter, (CMTS) Albany 1815 City Directory
Dodge, Emund: (CMTS) 1790 Federal Census, Watervliet
Dodge, Henry: (CMTS) 1790 Federal Census, Watervliet
Dodge, Hezekiah: (CMTS) 1790 Federal Census, Watervliet
Dodge, John: (OC) Carpenter, (CMTS) Albany 1815 City Directory
Doeg, Peter: (CMTS) 1790 Federal Census, Watervliet
Doige, Thomas: (OC) porter house, (CMTS) Albany 1815 City Directory
Dole, John: (OC) Carpenter, (CMTS) Albany 1815 City Directory

Dole, Widow Ann: (OC) Beaver, (CMTS) Albany 1815 City Directory
Don, Alexander: (OC) Watchmaker, (CMTS) Albany 1815 City Directory
Donahoe, Dennis: (NATD) Feb. 20, 1878, (RES) Cohoes, (CMTS) Ireland
Donahoe, Richard: (NATD) Oct. 16, 1872, (RES) Cohoes, (CMTS) Ireland
Donahoe, Thomas: (NATD) Oct. 26, 1876, (RES) Cohoes, (CMTS) Ireland
Done, Joshua: (CMTS) 1790 Federal Census Rensselaerville
Done, Widow Fanny: (OC), (CMTS) Albany 1815 City Directory
Donnelly, Andrew: (OC) Last Maker, (CMTS) Albany 1815 City Directory
Donnelly, James: (NATD) Feb. 25, 1880, (RES) Cohoes, (CMTS) Ireland
Donnelly, John: (NATD) Feb. 21, 1874, (RES) Cohoes, (CMTS) Ireland
Donnelly, Peter: (OC) Skipper, (CMTS) Albany 1815 City Directory
Donnelly, Thomas: (OC) Sargent at Arms for the Assembly, (CMTS) Albany 1815 City Directory
Donnelly, Thomas: (NATD) Oct. 22, 1860, (RES) Cohoes, (CMTS) Ireland
Doras, Sarah: (RES) 40 Church, (CMTS) Albany 1815 City Directory
Dore, James: (NATD) Oct. 7, 1865, (RES) Cohoes, (CMTS) Ireland
Dore, John: (NATD) Oct. 16, 1860, (RES) Cohoes, (CMTS) Ireland
Dorenbergh, Adam: (CMTS) 1790 Federal Census, Watervliet
Dorman, Jarid: (CMTS) 1790 Federal Census Rensselaerville
Dorman, Jeremiah: (CMTS) 1790 Federal Census, Watervliet
Dorman, Thomas: (CMTS) 1790 Federal Census, Watervliet
Dorr, Elisha: (RES) 51 Division, (CMTS) Albany 1815 City Directory
Dorr, John: (OC) Laborer, (CMTS) Albany 1815 City Directory
Dorsey, Edward: (NATD) Feb. 21, 1874, (RES) Cohoes, (CMTS) Ireland
Doty, J. F.: (OC) Watch Maker, (CMTS) Albany 1815 City Directory
Doubleday, Ulysses: (OC) Printer, (CMTS) Albany 1815 City Directory
Doud, Mrs: (RES) 51 Beaver, (CMTS) Albany 1815 City Directory
Doughty, Widow Mary: (RES) 71 Maiden Lane, (CMTS) Albany 1815 City Directory
Douglas, Duncan: (F) Member Masters Lodge, No. 5, 1900, Albany, NY
Douglas, Kenneth R.: (F) Member Masters Lodge, No. 5, 1900, Albany, NY
Douglass, Alexander: (CMTS) 1790 Federal Census, Watervliet
Douglass, James B.: (OC) Merchant, (CMTS) Albany 1815 City Directory
Douglass, Nathaniel: (CMTS) 1790 Federal Census Rensselaerville
Douglass, Sally: (RES) Boarding House at rear of 3 Hamilton, (CMTS) Albany 1815 City Directory
Douglas, Weeter: (CMTS) 1790 Federal Census, Watervliet
Douglass, Widow Sarah: (RES) 561 S. Market, (CMTS) Albany 1815 City Directory

Douw, John D. P.: (OC) Merchant, (CMTS) Albany 1815 City Directory
Douw, Widow Catherine: (RES) 12 Orange, (CMTS) Albany 1815 City
    Directory
Dowd, Philip: (NATD) Oct. 26, 1887, (RES) Cohoes, (CMTS) Ireland
Dowd, William: (NATD) Oct. 22, 1881, (RES) Cohoes, (CMTS) Ireland
Dox, Peter: (CMTS) 1790 Federal Census, Watervliet
Dox, Peter: (OC) Alderman, (CMTS) Albany 1815 City Directory
Dox, Peter: (OC) Mason, (CMTS) Albany 1815 City Directory
Dox, Peter P.: (OC) Post Office, (CMTS) Albany 1815 City Directory
Doyle, Dennis: (OC) Frelinghuysen, (CMTS) Albany 1815 City Directory
Drake, Mary: (RES) 214 S. Pearl, (CMTS) Albany 1815 City Directory
Drake, Peter: (OC) Tiger, (CMTS) Albany 1815 City Directory
Draper, Harry G.: (F) Member Temple Lodge, No. 14, 1900,
    Albany, NY
Draper, Thomas: (CMTS) 1790 Federal Census, Watervliet
Driggs, Joshua D.: (OC) Grocer, (CMTS) Albany 1815 City Directory
Driscoll, James: (NATD) Mar. 16, 1870, (RES) Cohoes, (CMTS) Ireland
Driscoll, James: (NATD) Oct. 21, 1874, (RES) Cohoes, (CMTS) Ireland
Driscoll, Michael: (NATD) Feb. 10, 1874, (RES) Cohoes, (CMTS) Ireland
Driscoll, Simon: (NATD) Oct. 21, 1874, (RES) Cohoes, (CMTS) Ireland
Drislane, William E.: (F) Member Temple Lodge, No. 14, 1900,
    Albany, NY
Drury, James: (NATD) Sep. 21, 1868, (RES) Cohoes, (CMTS) Ireland
Druy, Benjamin: (OC) Hair Dresser, (CMTS) Albany 1815 City Directory
Ducan, Richard: (OC) Builder, (CMTS) Albany 1815 City Directory
Ducan, Thomas: (OC) Builder, (CMTS) Albany 1815 City Directory
Dudley, Charles E: (RES) 54 N. Pearl, (CMTS) Albany 1815 City
    Directory
Duesenbury, Richard: (OC) Lumberyard, (CMTS) Albany 1815 City
    Directory
Duff, Thomas: (NATD) Mar. 28, 1890, (RES) Cohoes, (CMTS) Ireland
Duffaw, John: (OC) Patroon, (CMTS) Albany 1815 City Directory
Duffey, William: (RES) 516 S. Market, (CMTS) Albany 1815 City
    Directory
Duhig, John: (NATD) Oct. 18, 1887, (RES) Cohoes, (CMTS) Ireland
Dumary, T. Henry: (F) Member Temple Lodge, No. 14, 1900,
    Albany, NY
Dunbar, John: (CMTS) 1790 Federal Census, Watervliet
Dunbar, Levinus: (CMTS) 1790 Federal Census, Watervliet
Dunbar, Levinus: (RES) 13 Van Tromp, (CMTS) Albany 1815 City
    Directory
Dunbar, Robert: (CMTS) 1790 Federal Census Rensselaerville
Dunbar, Robert W.: (OC) Grocer, (CMTS) Albany 1815 City Directory
Dunbau, Robert: (CMTS) 1790 Federal Census, Watervliet
Duncan, William: (OC) Ferryman, (CMTS) Albany 1815 City Directory

Dunham, John: (CMTS) 1790 Federal Census Rensselaerville
Dunham, Josiah: (OC) Shoemaker, (CMTS) Albany 1815 City Directory
Dunkley, William: (OC) Glover, (CMTS) Albany 1815 City Directory
Dunlap, James: (OC) Carpenter, (CMTS) Albany 1815 City Directory
Dunlap, Robert: (OC) Brewer, (CMTS) Albany 1815 City Directory
Dunleavy, Mary: (RES) 21 Chapel, (CMTS) Albany 1815 City Directory
Dunn, Christopher: (OC) Innkeeper, (CMTS) Albany 1815 City Directory
Dunn, Edward: (OC) Merchant, (CMTS) Albany 1815 City Directory
Dunn, Richard: (OC) Merchant, (CMTS) Albany 1815 City Directory
Dunn, Robert: (OC) Skipper, (CMTS) Albany 1815 City Directory
Dunn, Widow of Cornelius M: (OC) Grocer, (CMTS) Albany 1815 City Directory
Dunnegan, John: (NATD) Oct. 23, 1886, (RES) Cohoes, (CMTS) Ireland
Dupong, Peter J.: (CMTS) 1790 Federal Census Rensselaerville
Durant, Anthony: (OC) Shoemaker, (CMTS) Albany 1815 City Directory
Durant, Marary: (OC) Carpenter, (CMTS) Albany 1815 City Directory
Durant, William: (RES) 445 S. Market, (CMTS) Albany 1815 City Directory
Dutcher, Calvin: (RES) 69 Eagle, (CMTS) Albany 1815 City Directory
Dutcher, Salem: (OC) Skipper, (CMTS) Albany 1815 City Directory
Duvepack, John: (CMTS) 1790 Federal Census, Watervliet
Dwight, Jacob: (OC) Leather Dresser, (CMTS) Albany 1815 City Directory
Dwyer, Thomas: (NATD) Feb. 20, 1879, (RES) Cohoes, (CMTS) Ireland
Dye, Asa: (CMTS) 1790 Federal Census Rensselaerville
Dyer, Elizabeth: (OC) Widow, (CMTS) Albany 1815 City Directory
Dyer, Wiliam S.: (F) Member Masters Lodge, No. 5, 1900, Albany, NY
Dyer, William: (OC) Frelinghuysen, (CMTS) Albany 1815 City Directory
Eagan, Charles: (NATD) Oct. 23, 1860, (RES) Cohoes, (CMTS) Ireland
Eagon, Kearon: (NATD) Sep. 30, 1865, (RES) Cohoes, (CMTS) Ireland
Earing, Christian: (CMTS) 1790 Federal Census, Watervliet
Easterly, Martin: (OC) Shoemaker, (CMTS) Albany 1815 City Directory
Easton, Frederick: (F) Member Masters Lodge, No. 5, 1900, Albany, NY
Easton, William: (F) Member Masters Lodge, No. 5, 1900, Albany, NY
Easton, William: (OC) Shoemaker, (CMTS) Albany 1815 City Directory
Eaton, Calvin W.: (F) Member Masters Lodge, No. 5, 1900, Albany, NY, (CMTS) Past Master
Eaton, Jacob: (OC) Cooper, (CMTS) Albany 1815 City Directory
Eaton, James W.: (F) Member Masters Lodge, No. 5, 1900, Albany, NY
Eaton, Origin: (CMTS) 1790 Federal Census Rensselaerville

Eaton, Reuben: (OC) Shoemaker, (CMTS) Albany 1815 City Directory
Eaton, Samuel: (CMTS) 1790 Federal Census Rensselaerville
Eaton, Stephen: (CMTS) 1790 Federal Census Rensselaerville
Eaton, Theophilus: (OC) Printer, (CMTS) Albany 1815 City Directory
Eaton, William: (OC), (CMTS) Albany 1815 City Directory
Ebel, William G.: (F) Member Temple Lodge, No. 14, 1900, Albany, NY
Ebert, John: (CMTS) 1790 Federal Census Rensselaerville
Ecker, Jacob: (CMTS) 1790 Federal Census, Watervliet
Ecker, John: (CMTS) 1790 Federal Census, Watervliet
Eckerson, Teunis: (CMTS) 1790 Federal Census, Watervliet
Eddy, John: (OC) Carpenter, (CMTS) Albany 1815 City Directory
Edge, Samuel: (OC) Shoemaker, (CMTS) Albany 1815 City Directory
Edgerton, Ebenezer: (OC) Shoemaker, (CMTS) Albany 1815 City Directory
Edgerton, Frederick W.: (F) Member Temple Lodge, No. 14, 1900, Albany, NY
Edgerton, Giles: (OC) Carpenter, (CMTS) Albany 1815 City Directory
Edmunds, John: (CMTS) 1790 Federal Census Rensselaerville
Edwards, Charles: (CMTS) 1790 Federal Census Rensselaerville
Edwards, John: (OC) Barber, (CMTS) Albany 1815 City Directory
Edwards, Joshua: (RES) 50 Van Schaick, (CMTS) Albany 1815 City Directory
Edwards, Leand: (F) Member Temple Lodge, No. 14, 1900, Albany, NY
Egan, Cornelia: (RES) Boarding House at 38 Hudson, (CMTS) Albany 1815 City Directory
Egan, John L.: (NATD) Feb. 28, 1872, (RES) Cohoes, (CMTS) Ireland
Egberts, Anthony: (CMTS) 1790 Federal Census, Watervliet
Egerton, Asa: (OC) Merchant, (CMTS) Albany 1815 City Directory
Egerton, William S.: (F) Member Masters Lodge, No. 5, 1900, Albany, NY
Egglinton, Eliah: (CMTS) 1790 Federal Census, Watervliet
Egner, William: (CMTS) 1790 Federal Census Rensselaerville
Ehlers, August: (F) Member Temple Lodge, No. 14, 1900, Albany, NY
Eights, Abraham: (OC) Dockmaster, (CMTS) Albany 1815 City Directory
Eights, Jonathan: (OC) Physician, (CMTS) Albany 1815 City Directory
Ekins, Andrew: (NATD) Oct. 24, 1862, (RES) Cohoes, (CMTS) Ireland
Eldridge, Herbert C.: (F) Member Masters Lodge, No. 5, 1900, Albany, NY
Elemndorf, Peter E.: (RES) 66 N. Pearl, (CMTS) Albany 1815 City Directory
Elgie, Augustus: (F) Member Mount Vernon Lodge, No. 3, 1900,

Albany, NY
Eli, Worthington: (CMTS) 1790 Federal Census, Watervliet
Eliot, Robert: (B) Feb. 20, 1781, (BP) Albany, NY
Ellers, Charles E.: (F) Member Mount Vernon Lodge, No. 3, 1900, Albany, NY
Ellianham, John: (OC) Chair Maker, (CMTS) Albany 1815 City Directory
Elliott, Andrew: (OC) Sawyer, (CMTS) Albany 1815 City Directory
Elliott, James: (RES) 29 S. Pearl, (CMTS) Albany 1815 City Directory
Elliott, Nathan: (CMTS) 1790 Federal Census Rensselaerville
Elliott, Robert: (B) Jan. 14, 1830, (BP) Albany, NY, (PRTS) Robert Elliott and Rachel Denniston
Elliott, Robert: (RES) 13 Beaver, (CMTS) Albany 1815 City Directory
Ellison, Danual: (NATD) Mar. 29, 1892, (RES) Cohoes, (CMTS) Ireland
Ellison, Widow Elizabeth: (RES) 34 Montgomery, (CMTS) Albany 1815 City Directory
Ely, John: (OC) Physicians & Surgeon, (CMTS) Albany 1815 City Directory
Ely, Jr., John: (OC) Deputy, (CMTS) Albany 1815 City Directory
Embrick, Peter: (CMTS) 1790 Federal Census Rensselaerville
Emerson, Samuel: (OC) Painter & Glaizer, (CMTS) Albany 1815 City Directory
Enders, Solomon: (OC) Cabinet Maker, (CMTS) Albany 1815 City Directory
Enders, Solomon: (MD) Aug. 29, 1813, (Spouse) Catherine Young, (PMD) First Dutch Reformed Church, Albany, NY
Engel, Daniel: (B) Apr. 20, 1794, (CD) May 4, 1794, (BP) Berne, Albany, Beaver Dam Dutch Reformed Church, (PRTS) Daniel Engel and Catharina Becker
Engel, Henrich: (B) Apr. 15, 1787, (CD) May 18, 1787, (BP) Berne, Albany Co., NY, (PRTS) Peter Engel and Sara Werner
Engel, Jacob: (B) Sep. 13, 1831, (CD) Nov. 2, 1831, (BP) Berne, Albany, NY, (PRTS) David Engel and Katharine ????
Engel, Peter: (B) Mar. 9, 1803, (CD) May 13, 1803, (BP) Berne, Albany Co., NY St. Paul Lutheran Evangelical Church, Daniel Engel and Catherine Becker
Engell, Jacob: (CD) Sep. 13, 1789, (BP) Berne, Albany, Beaver Dam Dutch Reformed Church, (PRTS) Daniel Engell and Catharina Becker.
Engels, Peter Henry: (B) Mar. 29, 1819, (CD) Apr. 20, 1819, (BP) Berne, Albany, NY, St. Paul Evangelical Church, (PRTS) Henry Engels
Engle, Daniel: (CMTS) 1790 Federal Census Rensselaerville
Engle, Jacob: (CMTS) 1790 Federal Census Rensselaerville
Engle, Jacob: (B) Feb. 8, 1827, (CD) Aug. 11, 1827, (BP) Berne, Albany, NY, Christopher Engle and Judith ????.
Engle, Peter: (CMTS) 1790 Federal Census Rensselaerville

English, John: (OC) Laborer, (CMTS) Albany 1815 City Directory
English, Margaret: (CEN) 1880 Cohoes, Albany Co., NY, (CMTS)
    Widow, (A) 61, (BP) Ireland, (OC) Housekeeper, Listed with
    William English, son, 27, NY
English, William: (CEN) 1880 12th Ward, Albany, Albany Co., NY,
    (CMTS) Single, (A) 60, (BP) NY, (OC) Shoemaker, Listed
    with Jane A. Morgan, sister, widow, 56, NY
English, William: (NATD) Oct. 26, 1876, (RES) Cohoes, (CMTS) Ireland
English, William: (CEN) 1880 Cohoes, Albany Co., NY, (CMTS)
    Married, (A) 45, (BP) Ireland, (OC) Laborer, Listed with Ellen, 45,
    Ireland, Keeping House, Mary A., 19, Ireland, Cotton Mill Worker,
    Elizabeth, 14, Ireland, Cotton Mill Worker, Ellen, 13, Ireland,
    Cotton Mill Worker, Kate, 11, NY, Cotton Mill Worker, Joseph, 9,
    NY, William, 5, NY, Alice, 2 NY
Enlish, William I.: (CEN) 1880, Cohoes, Albany, NY, (CMTS) Married,
    (A) 38, (BP) England, (OC) Tin Smith, Listed with Catharine, 28,
    England, Keeping House, Charles, 9, England, George, 5, Rhode
    Island, William, 3, England
Ennis, Thomas: (OC) Teacher, (CMTS) Albany 1815 City Directory
Enright, Patrick: (NATD) Oct. 23, 1884, (RES) Cohoes, (CMTS) Ireland
Epes, John: (OC) Harness Maker, (CMTS) Albany 1815 City Directory
Epes, William: (OC) Coach Maker, (CMTS) Albany 1815 City Directory
Erdmann, Wm. G. B.: (F) Member Temple Lodge, No. 14, 1900,
    Albany, NY
Ernst, Joseph A.: (F) Member Temple Lodge, No. 14, 1900,
    Albany, NY
Ertzbergen, Daniel: (OC) Fisherman, (CMTS) Albany 1815 City Directory
Ertzbergen, Jacob: (OC) Lumber, (CMTS) Albany 1815 City Directory
Ertzbergen, John: (OC) Barber, (CMTS) Albany 1815 City Directory
Ertzberger, Archibald S.: (F) Member Temple Lodge, No. 14, 1900,
    Albany, NY
Ertzberger, David: (CEN) 1880 7th Ward, Albany, NY, (CMTS)
    Single, (A) 25, (BP) NY, (OC) Cigar Maker
Ertzberger, Edmon J.: (CEN) 1880 7th Ward, Albany, NY, (A) 23, (BP)
    NY, (OC) Collar Factory Work
Ertzberger, Lewis: (CEN) 1880 7th Ward, Albany, NY, (CMTS)
    Widowed, (A) 58, (OC) Cigar Maker, (BP) NY, Listed with
    Lewis, 11, son, Henry S., 47, brother, Laborer, NY, Ann Eliza,
    Sister, 44, NY, Emmaline Wood, 70, NY, Tailoress, other
Ertzberger, Wm. G.: (CEN) 1880 17th Ward, Albany, NY, (CMTS)
    Married, (A) 63, (BP) NY, (OC) Cigar Maker, Listed with
    Martha, 43, wife, Archibald R., son, 20, Bookkeeper, Clara H.,
    18. duaghter, Shirt Maker, Grace, 15, daughter, milliner, Alviari,
    12, daughter, John, 7, son
Ervine, David: (RES) 53 Fox, (CMTS) Albany 1815 City Directory

Ervine, Theophilus: (OC) Painter, (CMTS) Albany 1815 City Directory
Erwin, John: (RES) 374 N. Market, (CMTS) Albany 1815 City Directory
Esmay, Thomas: (CMTS) 1790 Federal Census, Watervliet
Evans, Edward R.: (F) Member Masters Lodge, No. 5, 1900, Albany, NY
Evans, Jonathan: (CMTS) 1790 Federal Census, Watervliet
Evans, Platt: (OC) Tailor, (CMTS) Albany 1815 City Directory
Evans, Samuel: (OC) Ship Carpenter, (CMTS) Albany 1815 City Directory
Everest, Noah: (OC) Grocer, (CMTS) Albany 1815 City Directory
Everett, Jesse: (OC), (CMTS) Albany 1815 City Directory
Eversen, Every: (OC) Cooper, (CMTS) Albany 1815 City Directory
Everton, John: (OC) Silversmith, (CMTS) Albany 1815 City Directory
Everston, Albert: (CEN) 1880 14th Ward, Albany, NY, (CMTS) Married, (A) 64, (OC) Grain Dealer, (BP) NY, Sarah M., 49, wife, Carrie, 21, daughter, Mary A., 18, daughter, Charles A., son, 16, Gurdon G., 13, son
Evertson, Jacob: (RES) 22 Fox, (CMTS) Albany 1815 City Directory
Evertson, John: (OC) Tanner, (CMTS) Albany 1815 City Directory
Evertson, Widow Rebecca: (RES) 34 Montgonery, (CMTS) Albany 1815 City Directory
Evertson, Widow of Henry: (RES) 33 Hudson, (CMTS) Albany 1815 City Directory
Every, Nicholas: (CMTS) 1790 Federal Census, Watervliet
Evits, Solomon: (CMTS) 1790 Federal Census Rensselaerville
Ewings, John: (CMTS) 1790 Federal Census, Watervliet
Fagan, Andrew: (OC) Justice of the Peace, (CMTS) Albany 1815 City Directory
Fahey, Martin: (NATD) Mar. 28, 1890, (RES) Cohoes, (CMTS) Ireland
Fairfield, John: (NATD) Oct. 24, 1862, (RES) Cohoes, (CMTS) Ireland
Fairlie, Joseph: (CMTS) 1790 Federal Census, Watervliet
Falls, Richard W.: (RES) 24 Green, (CMTS) Albany 1815 City Directory
Fanlin, Abastatia: (RES) 65 Beaver, (CMTS) Albany 1815 City Directory
Fannery, Wm.: (NATD) Oct. 26, 1876, (RES) Cohoes, (CMTS) Ireland
Fanning, Elisha: (OC) Mason, (CMTS) Albany 1815 City Directory
Fargo, Zebediah: (CMTS) 1790 Federal Census, Watervliet
Farnham, Henry: (OC) Carver, (CMTS) Albany 1815 City Directory
Farnham, Lewis: (OC) Builder, (CMTS) Albany 1815 City Directory
Farnham, Rufus: (OC) Carpenter, (CMTS) Albany 1815 City Directory
Faro, Christian: (CMTS) 1790 Federal Census, Watervliet
Faro, David: (CMTS) 1790 Federal Census, Watervliet
Faro, Henry: (CMTS) 1790 Federal Census, Watervliet
Faro, Peter: (CMTS) 1790 Federal Census, Watervliet
Farrelly, Robert: (NATD) Oct. 23, 1876, (RES) Cohoes, (CMTS) Ireland
Farrrel, Philip: (OC) Chandler, (CMTS) Albany 1815 City Directory

Fasoldt, Otto H.: (F) Member Masters Lodge, No. 5, 1900, Albany, NY
Fasset, Benjamin: (OC) Cartman, (CMTS) Albany 1815 City Directory
Fasset, Timothy: (OC) Builder, (CMTS) Albany 1815 City Directory
Fay, John: (OC) Merchant, (CMTS) Albany 1815 City Directory
Feagler, Casper: (CMTS) 1790 Federal Census, Watervliet
Feehary, Lawrence: (OC) Laborer, (CMTS) Albany 1815 City Directory
Feeley, Michael: (NATD) Jul. 25, 1871, (RES) Cohoes, (CMTS) Ireland
Felt, Asa: (OC) Teamster, (CMTS) Albany 1815 City Directory
Felter, Peter: (CMTS) 1790 Federal Census, Watervliet
Felter, Philip: (CMTS) 1790 Federal Census, Watervliet
Felter, Jr., Philip: (CMTS) 1790 Federal Census, Watervliet
Feltman, John: (RES) 94 Beaver, (CMTS) Albany 1815 City Directory
Felts, Cleanthus: (OC) Teacher, (CMTS) Albany 1815 City Directory
Fenn, Jacob: (OC) Grocer, (CMTS) Albany 1815 City Directory
Ferguson, Duncan: (CMTS) 1790 Federal Census, Watervliet
Ferguson, George: (CMTS) 1790 Federal Census, Watervliet
Fero, David: (B) Jun. 12, 1771, (BP) Albany, (PRTS) Christian Fero and Catharine Leverse
Ferrington, March: (CMTS) 1790 Federal Census Rensselaerville
Fetherly, John: (OC) Laborer, (CMTS) Albany 1815 City Directory
Fetter, John: (CMTS) 1790 Federal Census Rensselaerville
Fiddler, Lancelot: (RES) 70 Pearl, (CMTS) Albany 1815 City Directory
Field, William: (OC) Coachmaker, (CMTS) Albany 1815 City Directory
Field, William G.: (F) Member Temple Lodge, No. 14, 1900, Albany, NY
Fields, Widow Catherine: (RES) 39 Union, (CMTS) Albany 1815 City Directory
Fiffany, William: (OC) Painter, (CMTS) Albany 1815 City Directory
Finch, Charles C.: (F) Member Masters Lodge, No. 5, 1900, Albany, NY
Finch, Wellington: (F) Member Mount Vernon Lodge, No. 3, 1900, Albany, NY
Finehout, Peter: (CMTS) 1790 Federal Census, Watervliet
Finkel, Albert D.: (F) Member Temple Lodge, No. 14, 1900, Albany, NY
Finnegan, Thomas: (NATD) Oct 25, 1878, (RES) Cohoes, (CMTS) Ireland
Fish, John: (OC) Grocer, (CMTS) Albany 1815 City Directory
Fish, Phenias: (CMTS) 1790 Federal Census Rensselaerville
Fisher, Johannes: (CMTS) 1790 Federal Census Rensselaerville
Fisher, John B.: (RES) 34 Columbia, (CMTS) Albany 1815 City Directory
Fisher, John D.: (RES) 110 S. Pearl, (CMTS) Albany 1815 City Directory
Fisher, Widow: (RES) 197 N. Market, (CMTS) Albany 1815 City Directory

Fisher, William: (OC) Sawyer, (CMTS) Albany 1815 City Directory
Fisher, Widow Sarah: (RES) 41 Columbia, (CMTS) Albany 1815 City Directory
Fisk, Frank H.: (F) Member Temple Lodge, No. 14, 1900, Albany, NY
Fisk, Henry: (OC) Merchant, (CMTS) Albany 1815 City Directory
Fisk, Horace: (OC) Merchant, (CMTS) Albany 1815 City Directory
Fisk, Widow Dorothy: (RES) 68 Washington, (CMTS) Albany 1815 City Directory
Fitzgerald, James: (NATD) Feb. 10, 1874, (RES) Cohoes, (CMTS) Ireland
Fitzgerald, James: (NATD) Oct. 25, 1860, (RES) Cohoes, (CMTS) Ireland
Fitzgerald, James: (NATD) Oct. 25, 1860, (RES) Cohoes, (CMTS) Ireland
Fitzgerald, John: (NATD) Aug. 12, 1873, (RES) Cohoes, (CMTS) Ireland
Fitzpatrick, John: (NATD) Oct. 28, 1871, (RES) Cohoes, (CMTS) Ireland
Flag, Widow of John: (OC) Innkeeper, (CMTS) Albany 1815 City Directory
Flansburgh, Daniel: (CMTS) 1790 Federal Census, Watervliet
Flansburgh, David: (CMTS) 1790 Federal Census, Watervliet
Flansburgh, Peter: (CMTS) 1790 Federal Census, Watervliet
Flansburgh, William: (CMTS) 1790 Federal Census, Watervliet
Flatley, Patrick: (NATD) Oct. 25, 1872, (RES) Cohoes, (CMTS) Ireland
Flatt, Phineas: (OC) Ferryman, (CMTS) Albany 1815 City Directory
Fleming, Andress: (CMTS) 1790 Federal Census, Watervliet
Fleming, John: (NATD) Oct. 18, 1887, (RES) Cohoes, (CMTS) Ireland
Fletcher, Timothy: (OC) Grocer, (CMTS) Albany 1815 City Directory
Flinn, John: (CMTS) 1790 Federal Census, Watervliet
Flint, Squire: (OC) porter, (CMTS) Albany 1815 City Directory
Floger, Isaiah: (OC) Whitewasher, (CMTS) Albany 1815 City Directory
Floyd, Albion Ward: (F) Member Temple Lodge, No. 14, 1900, Albany, NY
Flumnow, John: (CMTS) 1790 Federal Census, Watervliet
Flynn, Hugh: (OC) Grocer, (CMTS) Albany 1815 City Directory
Flynn, Michael: (NATD) Mar. 30, 1886, (RES) Cohoes, (CMTS) Ireland
Flynn, William: (NATD) Mar. 29, 1893, (RES) Cohoes, (CMTS) Ireland
Fobes, Philander: (OC) Innkeeper, (CMTS) Albany 1815 City Directory
Foley, David: (NATD) Oct. 27, 1871, (RES) Cohoes, (CMTS) Ireland
Foley, Dennis: (NATD) Oct. 24, 1872, (RES) Cohoes, (CMTS) Ireland
Foley, Dennis: (NATD) Oct. 18, 1887, (RES) Cohoes, (CMTS) Ireland
Foley, James: (NATD) Oct. 18, 1887, (RES) Cohoes, (CMTS) Ireland
Foley, Michael: (NATD) Oct. 18, 1887, (RES) Cohoes, (CMTS) Ireland
Foley, Patrick: (NATD) Oct. 25, 1889, (RES) Cohoes, (CMTS) Ireland
Folicott, John: (CMTS) 1790 Federal Census, Watervliet
Folsom, Alexander: (OC) Arnold, Folsom & Co., Lumber, (CMTS) Albany 1859 City Directory
Fonda, Abraham: (CMTS) 1790 Federal Census, Watervliet

Fonda, Douw (sic) H.: (F) Member Temple Lodge, No. 14, 1900,
    Albany, NY
Fonda, Hendrick: (CMTS) 1790 Federal Census, Watervliet
Fonda, Isaac: (CMTS) 1790 Federal Census, Watervliet
Fonda, Isaac: (RES) 4 Van Tromp, (CMTS) Albany 1815 City Directory
Fonda, Jacob: (CMTS) 1790 Federal Census, Watervliet
Fonda, John: (F) Member Mount Vernon Lodge, No. 3, 1900,
    Albany, NY, (CMTS) Life Member, Past Master 1866
Fonda, John: (CMTS) 1790 Federal Census, Watervliet
Fonda, Widow Willimpy: (RES) 324 N. Market, (CMTS) Albany 1815
City Directory
Fondey, Widow of John Jr: (OC) N. Mark, (CMTS) Albany 1815 City
    Directory
Fookes, Henry H.: (F) Member Temple Lodge, No. 14, 1900,
    Albany, NY
Foot, James: (CMTS) 1790 Federal Census, Watervliet
Foot, Samuel A: (OC) Counsellor, (CMTS) Albany 1815 City Directory
Foote, Elisha: (OC) Ordinary, (CMTS) Albany 1815 City Directory
Forbes, Alexander: (OC) Carpenter, (CMTS) Albany 1815 City Directory
Forbes, George G: (OC) Bookbinder, (CMTS) Albany 1815 City
    Directory
Forbes, Nathaniel: (OC) Carpenter, (CMTS) Albany 1815 City Directory
Forbey, John: (OC) Sawyer, (CMTS) Albany 1815 City Directory
Forby , George: (OC) Innkeeper, (CMTS) Albany 1815 City Directory
Ford, Benjamin: (RES) 10 Green, (CMTS) Albany 1815 City Directory
Ford, Eliakim: (OC) Boatman, (CMTS) Albany 1815 City Directory
Ford, Philip: (RES) 173 N. Market, (CMTS) Albany 1815 City Directory
Ford, Thomas W.: (OC) Merchant, (CMTS) Albany 1815 City Directory
Forest, Widow Agnes: (RES) 42 Sand, (CMTS) Albany 1815 City
    Directory
Forgey, Philip: (OC) Fisherman, (CMTS) Albany 1815 City Directory
Forman, Benoni B.: (OC) Silversmith, (CMTS) Albany 1815 City
    Directory
Forman, William: (OC) Saddler, (CMTS) Albany 1815 City Directory
Forrister, Robert W.: (F) Member Temple Lodge, No. 14, 1900,
    Albany, NY
Forsyth, Alexander: (RES) 65 Chapel, (CMTS) Albany 1815 City
    Directory
Forsyth, George: (RES) 62 Lydius, (CMTS) Albany 1815 City Directory
Forsyth, Russel: (OC) Ferry, (CMTS) Albany 1815 City Directory
Fort, Anocha: (CMTS) 1790 Federal Census, Watervliet
Fort, Charles N.: (F) Member Masters Lodge, No. 5, 1900,
    Albany, NY
Fort, Nicholas: (CMTS) 1790 Federal Census, Watervliet
Fort, Sophia: (OC) Seamstress, (CMTS) Albany 1815 City Directory

Fort, Thomas: (OC) Butcher, (CMTS) Albany 1815 City Directory
Foster, Caleb: (CMTS) 1790 Federal Census, Watervliet
Foster, Cesar: (OC) Butcher, (CMTS) Albany 1815 City Directory
Foster, Harry S.: (F) Member Temple Lodge, No. 14, 1900,
    Albany, NY
Foster, Jacob: (CMTS) 1790 Federal Census, Watervliet
Foster, James: (CMTS) 1790 Federal Census, Watervliet
Foster, Watson: (CMTS) 1790 Federal Census, Watervliet
Fowler, Isaac: (OC) Carpenter, (CMTS) Albany 1815 City Directory
Fowler, Jonathan: (CMTS) 1790 Federal Census Rensselaerville
Fowler, Wm.: (OC) Merchant, (CMTS) Albany 1815 City Directory
Fox, Bristol: (OC) Carpenter, (CMTS) Albany 1815 City Directory
Franks, John: (OC) Waterman, (CMTS) Albany 1815 City Directory
Fraser, George: (OC) Stonecutter, (CMTS) Albany 1815 City Directory
Fraser, Hugh: (OC) Grocer, (CMTS) Albany 1815 City Directory
Fraser, John: (OC) Carpenter, (CMTS) Albany 1815 City Directory
Fraser, Margaret: (OC) Millener, (CMTS) Albany 1815 City Directory
Fraser, Robert: (OC) Cartman, (CMTS) Albany 1815 City Directory
Frat, Casper: (OC) Grocer, (CMTS) Albany 1815 City Directory
Frazer, Mr.: (OC) Gardener: (RES) Arbor Hill, (CMTS) Albany 1815 City
    Directory
Fredenrich, Jr., John C.: (RES) 84 S. Pearl, (CMTS) Albany 1815 City
    Directory
Frederick, Michael: (CMTS) 1790 Federal Census, Watervliet
Frederick, Stephen: (CMTS) 1790 Federal Census, Watervliet
Frederick, Tebalt: (CMTS) 1790 Federal Census, Watervliet
Fredrick, Charles F.: (F) Member Mount Vernon Lodge, No. 3, 1900,
    Albany, NY
Fredrick, John E.: (F) Member Mount Vernon Lodge, No. 3, 1900,
    Albany, NY
Freeland, John: (OC) Carpenter, (CMTS) Albany 1815 City
    Directory
Freeman, Ira I.: (OC) Chair Maker, (CMTS) Albany 1815 City Directory
Freeman, John: (CMTS) 1790 Federal Census, Watervliet
Freeman, Silas: (CMTS) 1790 Federal Census, Watervliet
Freest, Philip: (CMTS) 1790 Federal Census, Watervliet
Freest, William: (CMTS) 1790 Federal Census, Watervliet
Fretts, Nicholas: (CMTS) 1790 Federal Census, Watervliet
Friday, Abraham B.: (OC) Blacksmith, (CMTS) Albany 1815 City
    Directory
Friday, Conradt: (CMTS) 1790 Federal Census, Watervliet
Fridendall, Frederick: (CMTS) 1790 Federal Census, Watervliet
Friedman, Jr., Jacob S.: (F) Member Temple Lodge, No. 14, 1900,
    Albany, NY, (CMTS) Life Member
Frisbee, Luther: (F) Member Temple Lodge, No. 14, 1900,

Frisby, Benjamin: (CMTS) 1790 Federal Census Rensselaerville Albany, NY
Frisby, Jr., Benjamin: (CMTS) 1790 Federal Census Rensselaerville
Frisby, Reuben: (CMTS) 1790 Federal Census Rensselaerville
Frisby, Thomas: (CMTS) 1790 Federal Census Rensselaerville
Frost, Frank L.: (F) Member Masters Lodge, No. 5, 1900, Albany, NY
Frost, William K.: (F) Member Masters Lodge, No. 5, 1900, Albany, NY
Fry, Joseph: (RES) 61 Chapel and 99 State, (CMTS) Albany 1815 City Directory
Fryer, Barent: (CMTS) 1790 Federal Census Rensselaerville
Fryer, Isaac: (CMTS) 1790 Federal Census, Watervliet
Fryer, Isaac I.: (OC) Alderman, (CMTS) Albany 1815 City Directory
Fryer, Isaac J: (CMTS) 1790 Federal Census, Watervliet
Fryer, Jacob: (CMTS) 1790 Federal Census, Watervliet
Fryer, John: (CMTS) 1790 Federal Census, Watervliet
Fryer, John W.: (OC) Silversmith, (CMTS) Albany 1815 City Directory
Fryer, Jr., John: (CMTS) 1790 Federal Census, Watervliet
Fryer, Widow Ellinor: (RES) 126 N. Market, (CMTS) Albany 1815 City Directory
Fryer, William: (OC) Painter, (CMTS) Albany 1815 City Directory
Fryer, John: (OC) painters, (CMTS) Albany 1815 City Directory
Fshuyler, David: (RES) 38 N. Pearl, (CMTS) Albany 1815 City Directory
Fuir, William: (OC) Shoemaker, (CMTS) Albany 1815 City Directory
Fuller, Benjamin H.: (F) Member Temple Lodge, No. 14, 1900, Albany, NY
Fuller, Gersham: (CMTS) 1790 Federal Census, Watervliet
Fuller, Howard N.: (F) Member Temple Lodge, No. 14, 1900, Albany, NY
Fuller, Jonas: (OC) Brickmaker, (CMTS) Albany 1815 City Directory
Fuller, Joseph W.: (F) Member Mount Vernon Lodge, No. 3, 1900, Albany, NY
Fuller, Rueben: (OC) Carpenter, (CMTS) Albany 1815 City Directory
Fuller, Samuel: (OC) Innkeeper, (CMTS) Albany 1815 City Directory
Fuller, Samuel: (OC) Wheelwright, (CMTS) Albany 1815 City Directory
Fulton, Francis: (CMTS) 1790 Federal Census, Watervliet
Furlong, Peter: (OC) Whitesmith, (CMTS) Albany 1815 City Directory
Fursman, Jesse W.: (F) Member Temple Lodge, No. 14, 1900, Albany, NY
Gaffers, Henry H.: (OC) Cartman, (CMTS) Albany 1815 City Directory
Gaffney, Thomas: (NATD) Feb. 24, 1877, (RES) Cohoes, (CMTS) Ireland
Gaffney, Thomas A.: (NATD) Apr. 19, 1869, (RES) Cohoes, (CMTS) Ireland
Gager, John: (OC) Coroner, (CMTS) Albany 1815 City Directory

Galaffaro, Charles: (F) Member Temple Lodge, No. 14, 1900, Albany, NY
Gallagher, James: (NATD) Feb. 16, 1876, (RES) Cohoes, (CMTS) Ireland
Gallahan, Mrs. Bridget: (RES) 65 Maiden Lane, (CMTS) Albany 1815 City Directory
Gallien, Henry T.: (F) Member Masters Lodge, No. 5, 1900, Albany, NY
Galoway, Wm.: (OC) Brush Factory, (CMTS) Albany 1815 City Directory
Galusha, Zachariah: (OC) Grocer, (CMTS) Albany 1815 City Directory
Galvin, John: (NATD) Mar. 28, 1870, (RES) Cohoes, (CMTS) Ireland
Gansevoort, Coenradt: (RES) 14 Montgomery, (CMTS) Albany 1815 City Directory
Gansevoort, Jr., Leonard: (RES) 386 N. Market, (CMTS) Albany 1815 City Directory
Gansevoort, Peter: (OC) Counsellor, (CMTS) Albany 1815 City Directory
Gansevoort, Widow Catherine: (RES) 316 N. Market, (CMTS) Albany 1815 City Directory
Gansey, Nathaniel: (CMTS) 1790 Federal Census, Watervliet
Garahan, Patrick: (NATD) Feb. 26, 1877, (RES) Cohoes, (CMTS) Ireland
Garbrance, Widow Jane: (RES) 128 S. Pearl, (CMTS) Albany 1815 City Directory
Gardeneer, Sarah: (CMTS) 1790 Federal Census, Watervliet
Gardiner, Charles E.: (F) Member Temple Lodge, No. 14, 1900, Albany, NY
Gardinier, Henry: (OC) Carpenter, (CMTS) Albany 1815 City Directory
Gardinier, Widow: (OC) Patroon, (CMTS) Albany 1815 City Directory
Gardner, Christian: (CMTS) 1790 Federal Census, Watervliet
Gardner, Daniel: (CMTS) 1790 Federal Census Rensselaerville
Gardner, Elizabeth: (RES) 1 Chapel, (CMTS) Albany 1815 City Directory
Garey, John: (OC) Shoemaker, (CMTS) Albany 1815 City Directory
Garling, Bernhard: (OC) Tailor, (CMTS) Albany 1815 City Directory
Garner, Christiana: (RES) 40 Fox, (CMTS) Albany 1815 City Directory
Garrahan, Martin: (NATD) Mar. 30, 1863, (RES) Cohoes, (CMTS) Ireland
Garrison, Garrit: (CMTS) 1790 Federal Census, Watervliet
Garrison, John: (CMTS) 1790 Federal Census Rensselaerville
Garrison, Widow: (RES) 412 N. Market, (CMTS) Albany 1815 City Directory
Garrison, Widow Caty: (OC) Ferry, (CMTS) Albany 1815 City Directory
Garrison, Widow Hannah: (OC) Rensselaer, (CMTS) Albany 1815 City Directory
Garvey, John: (OC) Currier, (CMTS) Albany 1815 City Directory
Garvey, Thomas J.: (F) Member Temple Lodge, No. 14, 1900, Albany, NY
Gates, Garret: (OC) Merchant, (CMTS) Albany 1815 City Directory

Gates, John: (RES) 5 Van Tromp, (CMTS) Albany 1815 City Directory
Gates, Stephen: (CMTS) 1790 Federal Census, Watervliet
Gaus, Louis H.: (F) Member Masters Lodge, No. 5, 1900,
 Albany, NY
Gavigan, James: (NATD) Oct. 23, 1860, (RES) Cohoes, (CMTS) Ireland
Gay, Eugene A.: (F) Member Temple Lodge, No. 14, 1900,
 Albany, NY
Gay, Gilbert H.: (F) Member Mount Vernon Lodge, No. 3, 1900,
 Albany, NY
Gay, Stephen: (OC) Shoemaker, (CMTS) Albany 1815 City Directory
Gaylor, John H.: (F) Member Mount Vernon Lodge, No. 3, 1900,
 Albany, NY
Gaylor, William J.: (F) Member Mount Vernon Lodge, No. 3, 1900,
 Albany, NY
Geary, A. Lincoln: (F) Member Mount Vernon Lodge, No. 3, 1900,
 Albany, NY
Gebhard, John G.: (F) Member Temple Lodge, No. 14, 1900,
 Albany, NY
Geddes, John: (OC) Grocer, (CMTS) Albany 1815 City Directory
Gee, Stephen: (CMTS) 1790 Federal Census, Watervliet
Geer, Arthur H.: (F) Member Masters Lodge, No. 5, 1900,
 Albany, NY
Geer, Darius: (OC) Carpenter, (CMTS) Albany 1815 City Directory
Geer, Frederick L.: (F) Member Temple Lodge, No. 14, 1900,
 Albany, NY
Geer, Robert: (F) Member Temple Lodge, No. 14, 1900,
 Albany, NY
Geer, Seth: (OC) Carpenter, (CMTS) Albany 1815 City Directory
Geller, Charles C.: (F) Member Mount Vernon Lodge, No. 3, 1900,
 Albany, NY
Genay, Louis: (RES) 1 Chapel, (CMTS) Albany 1815 City Directory
Genoe, Lewis: (CMTS) 1790 Federal Census, Watervliet
George, Henry: (F) Member Mount Vernon Lodge, No. 3, 1900,
 Albany, NY
Geowey, Philip D. F.: (F) Member Temple Lodge, No. 14, 1900,
 Albany, NY
Geowey, William D.: (F) Member Temple Lodge, No. 14, 1900,
 Albany, NY
Gibbany, Robert: (OC) Cartman, (CMTS) Albany 1815 City Directory
Gibbeny, A: (OC) Manteau Maker, (CMTS) Albany 1815 City Directory
Gibbeny, Robert: (CMTS) 1790 Federal Census, Watervliet
Gibbons, Edward: (NATD) Oct. 17, 1884, (RES) Cohoes, (CMTS) Ireland
Gibbons, James: (OC) Butcher, (CMTS) Albany 1815 City Directory
Gibbs, Lyman S.: (F) Member Masters Lodge, No. 5, 1900,
 Albany, NY

Gibbs, William: (CMTS) 1790 Federal Census, Watervliet
Gibson, David: (OC) Grocer, (CMTS) Albany 1815 City Directory
Gibson, James: (OC) Cartman, (CMTS) Albany 1815 City Directory
Gibson, James M.: (RES) 247 Washington, (CMTS) Albany 1815 City
    Directory
Gibson, Robert W.: (F) Member Masters Lodge, No. 5, 1900,
    Albany, NY
Gibson, William: (OC) Chair Maker, (CMTS) Albany 1815 City Directory
Gibson, Wm.: (OC) Butcher, (CMTS) Albany 1815 City Directory
Gifford, William: (CMTS) 1790 Federal Census, Watervliet
Gilbert, Frank R.: (F) Member Masters Lodge, No. 5, 1900,
    Albany, NY
Gilbert, George W.: (F) Member Mount Vernon Lodge, No. 3, 1900,
    Albany, NY
Gilbert, Joseph: (F) Member Washington Lodge, No. 85, 1900,
    Albany, NY, (CMTS) Past Members
Gilchrist, George M.: (F) Member Temple Lodge, No. 14, 1900,
    Albany, NY
Giles, Henry W.: (F) Member Temple Lodge, No. 14, 1900,
    Albany, NY
Giles, Robert: (NATD) Oct. 23, 1884, (RES) Cohoes, (CMTS) Ireland
Giles, Wm.: (OC) Grocer, (CMTS) Albany 1815 City Directory
Gill, George: (OC) Brewer, (CMTS) Albany 1815 City Directory
Gill, Matthew: (OC) Merchant, (CMTS) Albany 1815 City Directory
Gillan, Michael: (NATD) Oct. 18, 1887, (RES) Cohoes, (CMTS) Ireland
Gillespie, Frank C.: (F) Member Temple Lodge, No. 14, 1900,
    Albany, NY
Gillespie, Robert I.: (OC) Carpenter, (CMTS) Albany 1815 City Directory
Gillespie, William: (F) Member Temple Lodge, No. 14, 1900,
    Albany, NY
Gilling, Luke: (OC) Grocer, (CMTS) Albany 1815 City Directory
Gillis, John: (CMTS) 1790 Federal Census, Watervliet
Gilmartin, James: (NATD) Oct. 27, 1866, (RES) Cohoes, (CMTS) Ireland
Giloon, Patrick: (NATD) Oct. 17, 1860, (RES) Cohoes, (CMTS) Ireland
Gingrich, William H.: (F) Member Temple Lodge, No. 14, 1900,
    Albany, NY
Gladding, Timothy: (OC) Sign Painter, (CMTS) Albany 1815 City
    Directory
Gledhill, J. Edward: (F) Member Temple Lodge, No. 14, 1900,
    Albany, NY
Gledhill, William E.: (F) Member Temple Lodge, No. 14, 1900,
    Albany, NY
Gleichman, Frederick: (CMTS) 1790 Federal Census Rensselaerville
Gleichman, Lawrence: (CMTS) 1790 Federal Census Rensselaerville
Glen, Simon: (RES) 5 W. River, (CMTS) Albany 1815 City Directory

Gleshine, Thos.: (NATD) Mar. 23, 1860, (RES) Cohoes, (CMTS) Ireland
Gloeckner, Louis B.: (F) Member Temple Lodge, No. 14, 1900, Albany, NY
Godfrey, Heber L.: (OC) Barnes & Godfrey, Morning Times, (CMTS) Albany 1859 City Directory
Godfrey, John J.: (OC) Merchant, (RES) 62 State, (CMTS) Albany 1815 City Directory
Godro, Joesph: (OC) Laborer, (CMTS) Albany 1815 City Directory
Godsmark, George: (F) Member Mount Vernon Lodge, No. 3, 1900, Albany, NY, (CMTS) Past Master 1895
Goewey, John A.: (OC) Saddler: (RES) 209 N. Market, (CMTS) Albany 1815 City Directory
Goff, Robert: (CMTS) 1790 Federal Census Rensselaerville
Goffe, John H.: (F) Member Temple Lodge, No. 14, 1900, Albany, NY
Gold, Able: (CMTS) 1790 Federal Census, Watervliet
Goldbergh, John C.: (OC) Professor of Music, (CMTS) Albany 1815 City Directory
Golden, Widow: (RES) Rear 77 Beaver, (CMTS) Albany 1815 City Directory
Goldwait, Jonathan: (OC) Carpenter, (CMTS) Albany 1815 City Directory
Golen, George: (OC) Laborer, (CMTS) Albany 1815 City Directory
Gonyea, John: (OC) Gunsmith, (CMTS) Albany 1815 City Directory
Goodenow, Sterling: (OC) Attorney, (CMTS) Albany 1815 City Directory
Goodfellow, Amos: (CMTS) 1790 Federal Census, Watervliet
Goodfellow, Ichabod: (CMTS) 1790 Federal Census, Watervliet
Goodfellow, Moses: (CMTS) 1790 Federal Census, Watervliet
Goodman, Samuel W.: (F) Member Masters Lodge, No. 5, 1900, Albany, NY
Goodrich, John: (OC) Builder, (CMTS) Albany 1815 City Directory
Goodwin, Scott D'M.: (F) Member Masters Lodge, No. 5, 1900, Albany, NY, (CMTS) Past Master
Goold, James P.: (OC) Coach Maker, (CMTS) Albany 1815 City Directory
Gorden, Patrick: (NATD) Oct. 9, 1866, (RES) Cohoes, (CMTS) Ireland
Gordon, David: (OC) Gunsmith, (CMTS) Albany 1815 City Directory
Gordon, John: (OC) Merchant, (CMTS) Albany 1815 City Directory
Gordon, Thomas: (NATD) Oct. 27, 1866, (RES) Cohoes, (CMTS) Ireland
Gorham, George E.: (F) Member Masters Lodge, No. 5, 1900, Albany, NY
Gorony, Thomas: (NATD) Oct. 21, 1865, (RES) Cohoes, (CMTS) Ireland
Gould, James: (OC) Coach Maker, (CMTS) Albany 1815 City Directory
Gould, Job: (OC) Merchant, (CMTS) Albany 1815 City Directory
Gould, Joseph: (OC) Laborer, (CMTS) Albany 1815 City Directory
Gould, Thomas: (OC) Coachman, (CMTS) Albany 1815 City Directory

Gould, Thomas: (OC) Merchant, (CMTS) Albany 1815 City Directory
Gould, William: (OC) Bookseller, (CMTS) Albany 1815 City Directory
Gourlay, James: (OC) Justice of the Peace, (CMTS) Albany 1815 City Directory
Gouwey, Benjamin: (CMTS) 1790 Federal Census, Watervliet
Gouwey, Solomon: (CMTS) 1790 Federal Census, Watervliet
Gove, Charles L.: (F) Member Temple Lodge, No. 14, 1900, Albany, NY
Gove, Henry C.: (F) Member Temple Lodge, No. 14, 1900, Albany, NY, (CMTS) Life Member
Gowey, John: (CMTS) 1790 Federal Census, Watervliet
Grace, Widow Margaret: (OC) Grocer, (CMTS) Albany 1815 City Directory
Graham, John T. B.: (RES) 225 N. Market, (CMTS) Albany 1815 City Directory
Graham, Joseph B.: (RES) 4 Mark Lane, (CMTS) Albany 1815 City Directory
Graham, T. V. W.: (OC) Judge, (CMTS) Albany 1815 City Directory
Graham, William: (NATD) Oct. 27, 1866, (RES) Cohoes, (CMTS) Ireland
Graham, William H.: (NATD) Oct. 27, 1866, (RES) Cohoes, (CMTS) Ireland
Granger, Lewis: (RES) 22 Hudson, (CMTS) Albany 1815 City Directory
Grant, Alexander: (RES) Accountant, (CMTS) Albany 1815 City Directory
Grant, James: (NATD) Feb. 9, 1874, (RES) Cohoes, (CMTS) Ireland
Grant, Widow: (RES) 281 Washington, (CMTS) Albany 1815 City Directory
Grassfield, Henry: (CMTS) 1790 Federal Census Rensselaerville
Gratenvan, Peter: (CMTS) 1790 Federal Census Rensselaerville
Gratinvan, George: (CMTS) 1790 Federal Census Rensselaerville
Graves, Elisha: (OC) Carpenter, (CMTS) Albany 1815 City Directory
Gray, James: (OC) Mill Wright, (CMTS) Albany 1815 City Directory
Gray, John: (OC) Bakehouse, (CMTS) Albany 1815 City Directory
Gray, John: (OC) Grocer, (CMTS) Albany 1815 City Directory
Gray, Thomas: (OC) Baker, (CMTS) Albany 1815 City Directory
Greb, Henry C.: (F) Member Temple Lodge, No. 14, 1900, Albany, NY
Green, James: (NATD) Oct. 11, 1887, (RES) Cohoes, (CMTS) Ireland
Green, Joseph: (NATD) Aug. 8, 1898, (RES) Cohoes, (CMTS) Ireland
Green, Ralph W.: (F) Member Temple Lodge, No. 14, 1900, Albany, NY
Greene, Jessie: (CMTS) 1790 Federal Census Rensselaerville
Greene, Levy: (CMTS) 1790 Federal Census Rensselaerville
Greene, Rowland: (CMTS) 1790 Federal Census Rensselaerville

Greene, Widow Sarah: (OC) N. Pearl, (CMTS) Albany 1815 City
    Directory
Greene, William H.: (F) Member Mount Vernon Lodge, No. 3, 1900,
    Albany, NY
Greenhalgh, William L.: (F) Member Temple Lodge, No. 14, 1900,
    Albany, NY
Greenlong, James: (NATD) Sep. 25, 1868, (RES) Cohoes, (CMTS)
    Ireland
Greenwood, Peter J. H.: (NATD) Apr. 8, 1887, (RES) Cohoes, (CMTS)
    Ireland
Greenwood, William L: (OC) Public Nortary, (CMTS) Albany 1815 City
    Directory
Greer, James: (OC) Laborer, (CMTS) Albany 1815 City Directory
Gregory, Benjamin: (RES) 17 Division, (CMTS) Albany 1815 City
    Directory
Gregory, David: (OC) Van Schee, (CMTS) Albany 1815 City Directory
Gregory, Matthew: (OC) Public Square, (CMTS) Albany 1815 City
    Directory
Gregory, Silas: (OC) porter & boarding house, (CMTS) Albany 1815 City
    Directory
Grennan, James: (NATD) Mar. 30, 1888, (RES) Cohoes, (CMTS) Ireland
Gresham, Alfred E.: (F) Member Temple Lodge, No. 14, 1900,
    Albany, NY
Grey, Henry A.: (F) Member Temple Lodge, No. 14, 1900,
    Albany, NY
Grey, William W.: (F) Member Temple Lodge, No. 14, 1900,
    Albany, NY
Grier, Andrew: (OC) Cartman, (CMTS) Albany 1815 City Directory
Grier, George: (OC) Cartman, (CMTS) Albany 1815 City Directory
Grier, Samuel: (OC) Shoemaker, (CMTS) Albany 1815 City Directory
Grier, Thomas: (OC) Cartman, (CMTS) Albany 1815 City Directory
Griesman, Frederick V.: (F) Member Temple Lodge, No. 14, 1900,
    Albany, NY
Griffin, Andrew: (CMTS) 1790 Federal Census Rensselaerville
Griffin, Ebenezer: (OC) Blacksmith, (CMTS) Albany 1815 City Directory
Griffin, Ezra: (CMTS) 1790 Federal Census Rensselaerville
Griffin, John: (OC) Shoemaker, (CMTS) Albany 1815 City Directory
Griffin, Joseph: (CMTS) 1790 Federal Census Rensselaerville
Griffin, Richard: (OC) Shoemaker, (CMTS) Albany 1815 City Directory
Griffin, Samuel: (CMTS) 1790 Federal Census Rensselaerville
Griffin, Simon M: (OC) Music instructor, (CMTS) Albany 1815 City
    Directory
Griffins, William: (CMTS) 1790 Federal Census, Watervliet
Griffith, John: (OC) Grocer, (CMTS) Albany 1815 City Directory
Griffith, William H.: (F) Member Masters Lodge, No. 5, 1900,

Albany, NY
Grimley, James: (NATD) Oct. 24, 1877, (RES) Cohoes, (CMTS) Ireland
Grinall, Robert: (CMTS) 1790 Federal Census, Watervliet
Grinham, Patrick: (NATD) Feb. 20, 1879, (RES) Cohoes, (CMTS) Ireland
Grinham, Thomas: (NATD) Feb. 20, 1879, (RES) Cohoes, (CMTS) Ireland
Griswold, A. S.: (OC) Merchant, (CMTS) Albany 1815 City Directory
Griswold, Widow Mary: (OC) Patroon, (CMTS) Albany 1815 City Directory
Groat, Abraham: (CMTS) 1790 Federal Census, Watervliet
Groat, Abraham: (CMTS) 1790 Federal Census, Watervliet
Groat, Aldert: (CMTS) 1790 Federal Census, Watervliet
Groat, Cornelius: (CMTS) 1790 Federal Census, Watervliet
Groat, Derick: (CMTS) 1790 Federal Census, Watervliet
Groat, Jacob: (CMTS) 1790 Federal Census, Watervliet
Groat, Jessie: (CMTS) 1790 Federal Census, Watervliet
Groat, John: (CMTS) 1790 Federal Census, Watervliet
Groat, Peter D.: (CMTS) 1790 Federal Census, Watervliet
Groat, Philip: (CMTS) 1790 Federal Census, Watervliet
Groat, Simon: (CMTS) 1790 Federal Census, Watervliet
Groesbeck, Anthony: (CMTS) 1790 Federal Census, Watervliet
Groesbeck, Gilbert: (CMTS) 1790 Federal Census, Watervliet
Groesbeck, John: (CMTS) 1790 Federal Census, Watervliet
Groesbeck, Peter: (CMTS) 1790 Federal Census, Watervliet
Groesbeec, W. W. (OC) Merchant, (RES) 400 N. Market, (CMTS) Albany 1815 City Directory
Groesbeeck, Abraham: (OC) Merchant, (CMTS) Albany 1815 City Directory
Groesbeeck, C W & Co.: (OC) m. 4 N. Pearl, (CMTS) Albany 1815 City Directory
Groesbeeck, Cornelius W.: (RES) 4 N. Pearl, (CMTS) Albany 1815 City Directory
Groesbeeck, J. I.: (OC) Shoemaker, (CMTS) Albany 1815 City Directory
Groesbeeck, Jacob: (RES) 86 Fox, (CMTS) Albany 1815 City Directory
Groesbeeck, John D.: (OC) Shoemaker, (CMTS) Albany 1815 City Directory
Groesbeeck, Peter R: (RES) 219 N. Market, (CMTS) Albany 1815 City Directory
Groesbeeck, Walter: (OC) Tobacconist, (CMTS) Albany 1815 City Directory
Groesbeeck, Widow Catherine: (RES) 2 N. Pearl, (CMTS) Albany 1815 City Directory
Groesbeeck, William W.: (OC) Merchant, (CMTS) Albany 1815 City Directory

Grogan, Andrew: (NATD) Mar. 25, 1886, (RES) Cohoes, (CMTS) Ireland
Grogan, Dominick: (NATD) Oct. 17, 1874, (RES) Cohoes, (CMTS) Ireland
Grogan, James: (NATD) Mar. 29, 1894, (RES) Cohoes, (CMTS) Ireland
Grogan, John: (NATD) Oct. 26, 1860, (RES) Cohoes, (CMTS) Ireland
Gross, Charles E.: (F) Member Temple Lodge, No. 14, 1900, Albany, NY
Grossfind, Andrew: (CMTS) 1790 Federal Census Rensselaerville
Grounce, Philip: (CMTS) 1790 Federal Census, Watervliet
Guardineer, George H.: (F) Member Temple Lodge, No. 14, 1900, Albany, NY
Guest, Henry: (OC) Leather Dresser, (CMTS) Albany 1815 City Directory
Guest, John I.: (OC) Turner, (CMTS) Albany 1815 City Directory
Guilfoil, Michael: (NATD) Feb. 11, 1874, (RES) Cohoes, (CMTS) Ireland
Guine, James: (NATD) Feb. 26, 1876, (RES) Cohoes, (CMTS) Ireland
Guire, Edward: (NATD) Oct. 26, 1876, (RES) Cohoes, (CMTS) Ireland
Guire, Edward: (NATD) Oct. 26, 1876, (RES) Cohoes, (CMTS) Ireland
Gutherie, Alfred A.: (F) Member Temple Lodge, No. 14, 1900, Albany, NY, (CMTS) Master
Hackett, William S.: (F) Member Masters Lodge, No. 5, 1900, Albany, NY, (CMTS) Master
Hackley, William: (OC) Blacksmith, (CMTS) Albany 1815 City Directory
Hadden, James M.: (NATD) Mar. 27, 1894, (RES) Cohoes, (CMTS) Ireland
Hadden, William: (NATD) Oct. 24, 1891, (RES) Cohoes, (CMTS) Ireland
Hagan, Francis: (F) Member Temple Lodge, No. 14, 1900, Albany, NY
Hagan, William: (OC) Laborer, (CMTS) Albany 1815 City Directory
Hagerdon, John: (CMTS) 1790 Federal Census Rensselaerville
Hagerman, Abraham: (CMTS) 1790 Federal Census, Watervliet
Haggarty, William: (OC) Grocer, (CMTS) Albany 1815 City Directory
Hagy, Jr., John: (F) Member Temple Lodge, No. 14, 1900, Albany, NY
Haight, Horace DeR.: (F) Member Masters Lodge, No. 5, 1900, Albany, NY
Hail, Daniel: (CMTS) 1790 Federal Census Rensselaerville
Hailes, Charles J.: (F) Member Temple Lodge, No. 14, 1900, Albany, NY
Hailes, Theodore C.: (F) Member Temple Lodge, No. 14, 1900, Albany, NY
Haiss, Eugene J.: (F) Member Temple Lodge, No. 14, 1900, Albany, NY
Hale, Daniel: (RES) 70 N. Pearl, (CMTS) Albany 1815 City Directory
Hale, Daniel Jr: (OC) Distiller, (CMTS) Albany 1815 City Directory
Hale, Nathaniel: (CMTS) 1790 Federal Census, Watervliet

Hale, William: (OC) Counsellor, (CMTS) Albany 1815 City Directory
Halenbake, Lawrence: (OC) Carpenter, (CMTS) Albany 1815 City Directory
Hall, Abijah: (OC) Silversmith, (CMTS) Albany 1815 City Directory
Hall, Alonzo: (F) Member Temple Lodge, No. 14, 1900, Albany, NY
Hall, Andrew: (OC) Grocer, (CMTS) Albany 1815 City Directory
Hall, Asahel: (OC) Deputy Wagon Master, (CMTS) Albany 1815 City Directory
Hall, Gadd: (CMTS) 1790 Federal Census Rensselaerville
Hall, Green: (OC) Jeweller, (CMTS) Albany 1815 City Directory
Hall, Joseph: (OC) Gardener, (CMTS) Albany 1815 City Directory
Hall, Rhodolphus: (RES) 68 Washington, (CMTS) Albany 1815 City Directory
Hall, Thomas: (RES) 620 S. Market, (CMTS) Albany 1815 City Directory
Hall, Widow Ann: (RES) 79 N. Pearl, (CMTS) Albany 1815 City Directory
Hall, Widow Margaret: (RES) Boarding House at 31 Hudson, (CMTS) Albany 1815 City Directory
Hallenbake, Jacob: (OC) Laborer, (CMTS) Albany 1815 City Directory
Hallenbeck, Aaron: (CMTS) 1790 Federal Census Rensselaerville
Hallenbeck, Abraham: (CMTS) 1790 Federal Census Rensselaerville
Hallenbeck, Abraham: (CMTS) 1790 Federal Census Rensselaerville
Hallenbeck, Ephraim: (CMTS) 1790 Federal Census Rensselaerville
Hallenbeck, Ephraim: (CMTS) 1790 Federal Census Rensselaerville
Hallenbeck, John: (CMTS) 1790 Federal Census, Watervliet
Hallenbeck, John: (CMTS) 1790 Federal Census Rensselaerville
Hallenbeck, Michael: (CMTS) 1790 Federal Census Rensselaerville
Hallenbeck, Richard: (CMTS) 1790 Federal Census Rensselaerville
Hallett, Jacob: (CMTS) 1790 Federal Census, Watervliet
Hallett, Jacob: (OC) Cartman, (CMTS) Albany 1815 City Directory
Halley, Josephine: (CEN) 6th Ward, Albany, NY, (CMTS) Widow, (A) 28, (OC) Domestic, (BP) NY
Hallivan, John: (NATD) Feb. 23, 1887, (RES) Cohoes, (CMTS) Ireland
Hallock, Silas: (OC) Caulker, (CMTS) Albany 1815 City Directory
Halloman, Patrick: (NATD) Apr. 2, 1891, (RES) Cohoes, (CMTS) Ireland
Halloran, Michael: (NATD) Feb. 26, 1873, (RES) Cohoes, (CMTS) Ireland
Halm, Joseph A.: (F) Member Temple Lodge, No. 14, 1900, Albany, NY
Ham, Fred C.: (F) Member Masters Lodge, No. 5, 1900, Albany, NY
Ham, John: (F) Member Mount Vernon Lodge, No. 3, 1900, Albany, NY
Hamestral, John: (CMTS) 1790 Federal Census, Watervliet

Hamilton, Eliakim: (CMTS) 1790 Federal Census Rensselaerville
Hamilton, Henry N.: (F) Member Temple Lodge, No. 14, 1900,
   Albany, NY
Hamilton, Isaac: (OC) Counsellor, (CMTS) Albany 1815 City Directory
Hamilton, Jane: (CMTS) 1790 Federal Census, Watervliet
Hamilton, John: (OC) Stone Cutter, (CMTS) Albany 1815 City Directory
Hamilton, John A.: (F) Member Temple Lodge, No. 14, 1900,
   Albany, NY
Hammond, Charles D.: (F) Member Temple Lodge, No. 14, 1900,
   Albany, NY
Hamor, Henry: (OC) Slater, (CMTS) Albany 1815 City Directory
Hamton, Martin: (NATD) Feb. 23, 1876, (RES) Cohoes, (CMTS) Ireland
Hanchet, O. C.: (OC) Feather Store, (CMTS) Albany 1815 City
   Directory
Hand, Aaron: (OC) Lumber Merchant, (CMTS) Albany 1815 City
   Directory
Hand, Abraham: (CMTS) 1790 Federal Census Rensselaerville
Hand, Nathan: (OC) Butcher, (CMTS) Albany 1815 City Directory
Hanes, Edward L.: (F) Member Masters Lodge, No. 5, 1900,
   Albany, NY
Haney, Jacob: (OC) Laborer, (CMTS) Albany 1815 City Directory
Hanford, Stephen B.: (RES) 6 Maiden Lane, (CMTS) Albany 1815 City
   Directory
Hankerson, John: (OC) Teamster, (CMTS) Albany 1815 City Directory
Hanlon, Edward: (NATD) Oct. 15, 1868, (RES) Cohoes, (CMTS) Ireland
Hanly, Patrick: (NATD) Oct. 19, 1870, (RES) Cohoes, (CMTS) Ireland
Hanrihan, Thomas: (NATD) Oct. 16, 1872, (RES) Cohoes, (CMTS)
   Ireland
Hansen, Benjamin: (OC) Millener, (CMTS) Albany 1815 City Directory
Hansen, Benjamin: (OC) Shoemaker, (CMTS) Albany 1815 City
   Directory
Hansen, Isaac: (OC) Master in Chancery, (CMTS) Albany 1815 City
   Directory
Hanson, Daniel: (CMTS) 1790 Federal Census, Watervliet
Hanson, Henry: (F) Member Mount Vernon Lodge, No. 3, 1900,
   Albany, NY
Hantay, Thomas: (NATD) Feb. 23, 1875, (RES) Cohoes, (CMTS) Ireland
Happel, William H.: (F) Member Temple Lodge, No. 14, 1900,
   Albany, NY
Harbeck, John: (CMTS) 1790 Federal Census, Watervliet
Harbeck, Samuel: (OC) Taner, (CMTS) Albany 1815 City Directory
Hardick, Daniel: (OC) Laborer, (CMTS) Albany 1815 City Directory
Hardick, W. Clemishire: (F) Member Masters Lodge, No. 5, 1900,
   Albany, NY
Hardiker, Richard: (RES) 108 Beaver, (CMTS) Albany 1815 City

Directory
Hardman, John: (OC) Brass Founder, (CMTS) Albany 1815 City
   Directory
Hare, Daniel: (CMTS) 1790 Federal Census, Watervliet
Hare, Stephen: (CMTS) 1790 Federal Census, Watervliet
Harlow, Hans H.: (F) Member Mount Vernon Lodge, No. 3, 1900,
   Albany, NY
Harp, Michael: (CMTS) 1790 Federal Census Rensselaerville
Harppinger, Frank: (F) Member Mount Vernon Lodge, No. 3, 1900,
   Albany, NY
Harrington, Linn J.: (F) Member Temple Lodge, No. 14, 1900,
   Albany, NY
Harrington, Thomas: (CMTS) 1790 Federal Census Rensselaerville
Harris, Charles B.: (F) Member Temple Lodge, No. 14, 1900,
   Albany, NY
Harris, Frank S.: (F) Member Masters Lodge, No. 5, 1900,
   Albany, NY
Harris, James: (OC) Laborer, (CMTS) Albany 1815 City Directory
Harris, John: (OC) Carpenter, (CMTS) Albany 1815 City
   Directory
Harris, Julius F.: (F) Member Temple Lodge, No. 14, 1900,
   Albany, NY
Harrison, Andrew: (OC) Laborer, (CMTS) Albany 1815 City Directory
Harrow, Peter: (CMTS) 1790 Federal Census Rensselaerville
Hart, Benjamin: (OC) Merchant, (CMTS) Albany 1815 City Directory
Hart, George W.: (F) Member Temple Lodge, No. 14, 1900,
   Albany, NY
Hart, Nehemiah: (CMTS) 1790 Federal Census, Watervliet
Hartness, James: (OC) Chandler, (CMTS) Albany 1815 City Directory
Hartness, John: (OC) Chandler, (CMTS) Albany 1815 City Directory
Hartwick, Christian: (CMTS) 1790 Federal Census Rensselaerville
Hartwick, John: (CMTS) 1790 Federal Census, Watervliet
Harvepson, Robert: (OC) Pedler, (CMTS) Albany 1815 City Directory
Harwood, William: (NATD) Oct. 25, 1876, (RES) Cohoes, (CMTS)
   Ireland
Hasbouck, Peter: (RES) Accountant, (CMTS) Albany 1815 City Directory
Haskell, Clayton K.: (F) Member Masters Lodge, No. 5, 1900,
   Albany, NY
Haskell, Sandford R.: (F) Member Masters Lodge, No. 5, 1900,
   Albany, NY
Haskell, 2d (sic), Clayton K.: (F) Member Masters Lodge, No. 5, 1900,
   Albany, NY
Hastings, Seth: (OC) Merchant, (CMTS) Albany 1815 City Directory
Haswell, Arther: (CMTS) 1790 Federal Census, Watervliet
Haswell, George: (F) Member Temple Lodge, No. 14, 1900,

Albany, NY
Haswell, John: (CMTS) 1790 Federal Census, Watervliet
Haswell, Robert: (CMTS) 1790 Federal Census, Watervliet
Haswell, Willaim H.: (F) Member Temple Lodge, No. 14, 1900,
    Albany, NY
Hatch, Malatiah: (CMTS) 1790 Federal Census Rensselaerville
Hatch, Nathaniel: (CMTS) 1790 Federal Census Rensselaerville
Hatfield, Widow of Edmund: (RES) 1 Chruch, (CMTS) Albany 1815 City
    Directory
Hathorn, David: (OC) Mason, (CMTS) Albany 1815 City Directory
Haveland, William: (CMTS) 1790 Federal Census, Watervliet
Havely, Johannes: (CMTS) 1790 Federal Census, Watervliet
Havens, Morton: (F) Member Mount Vernon Lodge, No. 3, 1900,
    Albany, NY
Hawk, Widow Maria: (RES) Arbor Hill, (CMTS) Albany 1815 City
    Directory
Hawkins, Isaac: (OC) Grocer, (CMTS) Albany 1815 City Directory
Hawley, Adra: (OC) Culler, (CMTS) Albany 1815 City Directory
Hawley, Ebenezer: (CMTS) 1790 Federal Census Rensselaerville
Hawley, Eliphalet: (OC) Merchant, (CMTS) Albany 1815 City Directory
Hawley, Gideon: (OC) Attorney, (CMTS) Albany 1815 City Directory
Hawley, Henry E.: (F) Member Masters Lodge, No. 5, 1900,
    Albany, NY
Hawley, Nathan: (CMTS) 1790 Federal Census Rensselaerville
Hawley, Widow Elizabeth: (RES) 71 Maiden Lane, (CMTS) Albany 1815
    City Directory
Hawn, Orra G.: (F) Member Temple Lodge, No. 14, 1900,
    Albany, NY
Hawsbergen, Daniel: (CMTS) 1790 Federal Census, Watervliet
Hayden, Timothy: (NATD) Oct. 19, 1870, (RES) Cohoes, (CMTS) Ireland
Hayes, Matthew: (NATD) Oct. 23, 1884, (RES) Cohoes, (CMTS) Ireland
Hayes, Michael: (NATD) Oct. 28, 1899, (RES) Cohoes, (CMTS) Ireland
Hayes, Paul N.: (F) Member Masters Lodge, No. 5, 1900,
    Albany, NY
Haynes, George: (CMTS) 1790 Federal Census, Watervliet
Haynes, John: (B) Nov. 14, 1806, (BP) Bethlehem, Albany Co., NY
Haynes, John B.: (CMTS) 1790 Federal Census Rensselaerville
Hanyes, John U.: (B) Feb. 10, 1850, (BP) Cohoes, Albany Co., NY, (D)
    Feb. 23, 1906
Haynes, Stephen: (CMTS) 1790 Federal Census, Watervliet
Hays, Solomon: (OC) Shoemaker, (CMTS) Albany 1815 City
    Directory
Hazen, Widow of General Hazen: (RES) 45 Maden Lane, (CMTS) Albany
    1815 City Directory
Heally, Hugh: (NATD) Mar. 9, 1886, (RES) Cohoes, (CMTS) Ireland

Heamstral, Dirick: (CMTS) 1790 Federal Census, Watervliet
Heamstral, Isaac: (CMTS) 1790 Federal Census, Watervliet
Heamstral, William: (CMTS) 1790 Federal Census, Watervliet
Heamstrial, John: (CMTS) 1790 Federal Census, Watervliet
Hearner, Henry: (CMTS) 1790 Federal Census, Watervliet
Heart, David: (CMTS) 1790 Federal Census, Watervliet
Heath, Henry: (OC) Grocer, (CMTS) Albany 1815 City Directory
Heath, Luther: (OC) Teamster, (CMTS) Albany 1815 City Directory
Heath, Thomas D.: (F) Member Temple Lodge, No. 14, 1900, Albany, NY
Hebberd, Robert W.: (F) Member Masters Lodge, No. 5, 1900, Albany, NY
Hebeysen, Martin: (OC) Grocer, (CMTS) Albany 1815 City Directory
Hedden, Ann: (OC) Millener, (CMTS) Albany 1815 City Directory
Hedlam, William: (F) Member Mount Vernon Lodge, No. 3, 1900, Albany, NY
Heen, Peter: (CMTS) 1790 Federal Census Rensselaerville
Heermance, Orville L.: (F) Member Temple Lodge, No. 14, 1900, Albany, NY
Heermans, John: (OC) Tailor, (CMTS) Albany 1815 City Directory
Heet, Widow Dorothy: (RES) 13 Pine, (CMTS) Albany 1815 City Directory
Heet, Widow Eliza: (OC) Millener, (CMTS) Albany 1815 City Directory
Heineman, Abraham: (F) Member Mount Vernon Lodge, No. 3, 1900, Albany, NY
Helmer, Adam: (OC) Teamster, (CMTS) Albany 1815 City Directory
Hempsted, Isaac: (OC) Sheriff, (CMTS) Albany 1815 City Directory
Hemstral, Direck: (CMTS) 1790 Federal Census, Watervliet
Hemstral, Jacob: (CMTS) 1790 Federal Census, Watervliet
Henderson, James: (NATD) Oct. 17, 1860, (RES) Cohoes, (CMTS) Ireland
Hendrickson, John: (OC) Broker: (RES) 138 State, (CMTS) Albany 1815 City Directory
Henman, Samuel: (OC) Carpenter, (CMTS) Albany 1815 City Directory
Henn, Michael: (OC) Distiller, (CMTS) Albany 1815 City Directory
Henner, Frederick: (CMTS) 1790 Federal Census, Watervliet
Henritte, James: (CMTS) 1790 Federal Census, Watervliet
Henry, Harmanus: (OC) Shoemaker, (CMTS) Albany 1815 City Directory
Henry, James: (CMTS) 1790 Federal Census, Watervliet
Henry, James: (OC) Tailor, (CMTS) Albany 1815 City Directory
Henry, John: (CMTS) 1790 Federal Census, Watervliet
Henry, John V. (OC) Counsellor: (RES) 19 Columbia, (CMTS) Albany 1815 City Directory
Henry, Jonathan: (CMTS) 1790 Federal Census Rensselaerville
Henry, Samuel: (OC) Baker, (CMTS) Albany 1815 City Directory

Henry, Samuel: (OC) Cartman, (CMTS) Albany 1815 City Directory
Henry, Thomas: (CEN) 1880 4th Ward, Albany, NY, (CMTS) Single,
 (A) 62, (BP) Ireland, (OC) Tin SMith
Henry, Widow Ann: (RES) 75 S. Pearl, (CMTS) Albany 1815 City
 Directory
Henry, William: (CMTS) 1790 Federal Census, Watervliet
Henry, William: (CEN) 1880 9th Ward, Albany, NY, (CMTS) Single,
 (A) 48, (BP) Ireland, (OC) Laborer
Henshaw, John V.: (F) Member Temple Lodge, No. 14, 1900,
 Albany, NY
Heplen, James: (NATD) Oct. 24, 1879, (RES) Cohoes, (CMTS) Ireland
Hering, Peter E.: (F) Member Temple Lodge, No. 14, 1900,
 Albany, NY
Herrick, Avery: (F) Member Mount Vernon Lodge, No. 3, 1900,
 Albany, NY
Herrick, Cornelius: *(I) Muscatine, Iowa Journal, May 28, 1927,*
 "Cornelius Herrick, 78, retired farmer, died at his home, 213 West
 Fifth Street, at 9:30 last evening, after an illness of several weeks
 with heart disease and complications. Mr. Herrick was born Nov.
 13, 1848, in Albany, NY, being the son of Stephen and Gertrude
 Breese Herrick. At an early age, he moved to Iowa where he has
 resided since, living in Muscatine County for the past 50 years,
 and in Muscatine for the past seven. He was a member of the
 Methodist Episcopal Church. Mr. Herrick was married to Miss
 Eva Frey of Letts, March 25, 1879. Surviving Mr. Herrick are his
 wife, one daughter, Mrs. Roy Baker, Muscatine, and two sons,
 Charles L. Herrick, Muscatine, and Arthur C. Herrick, Clinton.
 One son, Stephen, died in infancy, and one daughter, Mrs. Andrew
 Cole, died four years ago. Two sisters, Mrs. Sarah Lanning,
 Lyndon, IL, and Mrs. Cornelia Culbertson, Fairfield, IA, also
 survive. Funeral services will be conducted at 2:30 PM Sunday at
 the home of Rev. Victor A. Bloomquist, paster of the Musserville
 Methodist Episcopal church. Burial will be in Greenwood
 Cemetery. The Wittich Funeral Home is in charge of the
 arrangements."
Herrick, Daniel: (CMTS) 1790 Federal Census, Watervliet
Herring, Samuel: (OC) Ferry, (CMTS) Albany 1815 City Directory
Herringgden, Elizabeth: (OC) Orange, (CMTS) Albany 1815 City
 Directory
Herrington, Charles: (OC) Grocer, (CMTS) Albany 1815 City Directory
Herrington, Daniel: (OC) Teamster, (CMTS) Albany 1815 City Directory
Herryman, Gage: (CMTS) 1790 Federal Census Rensselaerville
Herschberger, H. I.: (F) Member Washington Lodge, No. 85, 1900,
 Albany, NY, (CMTS) Past Members
Herttell, Cros: (OC) Sargant at Arms Senate, (CMTS) Albany 1815 City

Directory
Herzog, Jacob H.: (F) Member Masters Lodge, No. 5, 1900, Albany, NY
Hess, Dederick: (CMTS) 1790 Federal Census, Watervliet
Hettinger, William: (F) Member Temple Lodge, No. 14, 1900, Albany, NY
Hewitt, Charles: (OC) Lutheran, (CMTS) Albany 1815 City Directory
Hewitt, Robert: (NATD) Oct. 27, 1876, (RES) Cohoes, (CMTS) Ireland
Hewson, James: (OC) Laborer, (CMTS) Albany 1815 City Directory
Hewson, John: (OC) Mason, (CMTS) Albany 1815 City Directory
Hewson, John: (OC) Silversmith: (RES) 43 Church, (CMTS) Albany 1815 City Directory
Hewson, Thomas: (OC) Brickmaker, (CMTS) Albany 1815 City Directory
Hewson, Widow Mry: (RES) 43 Liberty, (CMTS) Albany 1815 City Directory
Heyer, Mary: (OC) Millener, (CMTS) Albany 1815 City Directory
Hicks, Jacob: (CMTS) 1790 Federal Census Rensselaerville
Hicks, John J.: (F) Member Masters Lodge, No. 5, 1900, Albany, NY
Hicks, Mordecai: (CMTS) 1790 Federal Census, Watervliet
Hicks, Richard: (OC) Laborer, (CMTS) Albany 1815 City Directory
Hicks, Wheeton: (CMTS) 1790 Federal Census, Watervliet
Hicley, Mark: (OC) Laborer, (CMTS) Albany 1815 City Directory
Higby, Edward: (CMTS) 1790 Federal Census Rensselaerville
Higby, Nathaniel: (OC) Grocer, (CMTS) Albany 1815 City Directory
Higgins, J. P.: (OC) Physician, (CMTS) Albany 1815 City Directory
Higham, A.: (OC) Innkeeper: (RES) 569 S. Market, (CMTS) Albany 1815 City Directory
Hill, Cornelia: (RES) 46 Liberty, (CMTS) Albany 1815 City Directory
Hill, Cornelius: (F) Member Temple Lodge, No. 14, 1900, Albany, NY
Hill, Elijah: (CMTS) 1790 Federal Census, Watervliet
Hill, Elijah: (CMTS) 1790 Federal Census, Watervliet
Hill, Erastus: (OC) Hatter, (CMTS) Albany 1815 City Directory
Hill, Erastus C.: (F) Member Temple Lodge, No. 14, 1900, Albany, NY
Hill, George C.: (F) Member Temple Lodge, No. 14, 1900, Albany, NY
Hill, James H.: (F) Member Temple Lodge, No. 14, 1900, Albany, NY
Hill, John: (OC) Merchant, (CMTS) Albany 1815 City Directory
Hill, Robert: (F) Member Temple Lodge, No. 14, 1900, Albany, NY
Hill, Samuel: (OC) Merchant, (CMTS) Albany 1815 City Directory

Hill, Thomas: (CMTS) 1790 Federal Census Rensselaerville
Hill, Thomas: (NATD) Oct. 27, 1876, (RES) Cohoes, (CMTS) Ireland
Hill, Thomas: (OC) leather dresser, (CMTS) Albany 1815 City Directory
Hill, William J. M.: (F) Member Temple Lodge, No. 14, 1900,
    Albany, NY
Hillebrant, Gitty: (CMTS) 1790 Federal Census, Watervliet
Hillebrant, John: (CMTS) 1790 Federal Census, Watervliet
Hillibrant, Jacob: (OC) Teamster, (CMTS) Albany 1815 City Directory
Hilson, Thomas: (OC) Shoemaker, (CMTS) Albany 1815 City Directory
Hilton, Daniel: (NATD) Oct. 18, 1880, (RES) Cohoes, (CMTS) Ireland
Hilton, Jacob W.: (CMTS) 1790 Federal Census, Watervliet
Hilton, James: (OC) Mason, (CMTS) Albany 1815 City Directory
Hilton, James H.: (F) Member Temple Lodge, No. 14, 1900,
    Albany, NY
Hilton, John: (OC) Shoemaker, (CMTS) Albany 1815 City Directory
Hilton, Jonathan: (CMTS) 1790 Federal Census, Watervliet
Hilton, Nicholas: (OC) Carpenter, (CMTS) Albany 1815 City Directory
Hilton, Peter: (OC) Cooper, (CMTS) Albany 1815 City Directory
Hilton, Jr., Peter: (OC) Grocer, (CMTS) Albany 1815 City Directory
Hilton, Phebe: (OC) Morocco Hat and Socks, (CMTS) Albany 1815 City
    Directory
Hilton, Richard: (OC) Cartman, (CMTS) Albany 1815 City Directory
Hilton, Robert: (CMTS) 1790 Federal Census, Watervliet
Hilton, Volkert D.: (OC) Mason, (CMTS) Albany 1815 City Directory
Hilton, Widow: (OC) Nancy, (CMTS) Albany 1815 City Directory
Hilton, William: (OC) Shoemaker, (CMTS) Albany 1815 City Directory
Hinckel, Fredrick: (F) Member Temple Lodge, No. 14, 1900,
    Albany, NY, (CMTS) Life Member
Hinckley, Gershom: (OC) Grocer, (CMTS) Albany 1815 City Directory
Hinckley, John: (OC) Painter, (CMTS) Albany 1815 City Directory
Hinckley, Nathan: (OC) Hatter, (CMTS) Albany 1815 City Directory
Hine, James W.: (F) Member Temple Lodge, No. 14, 1900,
    Albany, NY
Hines, John: (NATD) Oct. 25, 1886, (RES) Cohoes, (CMTS) Ireland
Hinkley, Josiah: (CMTS) 1790 Federal Census, Watervliet
Hinq, Edward P.: (F) Member Temple Lodge, No. 14, 1900,
    Albany, NY, (CMTS) Life Member
Hitchcock, Frank P.: (F) Member Temple Lodge, No. 14, 1900,
    Albany, NY
Hixon, James: (OC) Barber, (CMTS) Albany 1815 City Directory
Hoag, Abraham: (OC) Shoemaker, (CMTS) Albany 1815 City Directory
Hoag, John D.: (F) Member Temple Lodge, No. 14, 1900,
    Albany, NY
Hoag, John S.: (F) Member Mount Vernon Lodge, No. 3, 1900,
    Albany, NY

Hobbs, George W.: (F) Member Masters Lodge, No. 5, 1900, Albany, NY
Hobby, S. Reeve: (RES) 78 N. Pearl, (CMTS) Albany 1815 City Directory
Hobson, John: (OC) Hatter, (CMTS) Albany 1815 City Directory
Hochstrasser, Baltus: (CMTS) 1790 Federal Census Rensselaerville
Hochstrasser, Jacob: (CMTS) 1790 Federal Census Rensselaerville
Hochstrasser, Paul J.: (CMTS) 1790 Federal Census Rensselaerville
Hocknell, John: (OC) Cartman, (CMTS) Albany 1815 City Directory
Hocknell, Richard: (CMTS) 1790 Federal Census, Watervliet
Hocknell, Thomas: (OC) Laborer, (CMTS) Albany 1815 City Directory
Hockstrasser, Paul: (OC) Merchant, (CMTS) Albany 1815 City Directory
Hodge, James: (OC) Stone Cutter, (CMTS) Albany 1815 City Directory
Hodgkins, George R.: (F) Member Temple Lodge, No. 14, 1900, Albany, NY, (CMTS) Past Master 1888
Hodgkins, Stephen C.: (F) Member Temple Lodge, No. 14, 1900, Albany, NY
Hodgson, George R.: (F) Member Temple Lodge, No. 14, 1900, Albany, NY
Hoefferliech, Jacob: (CMTS) 1790 Federal Census Rensselaerville
Hofferlich, Carl: (CMTS) 1790 Federal Census Rensselaerville
Hoffman, George A.: (F) Member Temple Lodge, No. 14, 1900, Albany, NY
Hoffman, Karl R.: (F) Member Masters Lodge, No. 5, 1900, Albany, NY
Hoffman, Paul W.: (F) Member Masters Lodge, No. 5, 1900, Albany, NY
Hoffman, Wenzel: (CMTS) 1790 Federal Census, Watervliet
Hoffman, Widow Patty: (RES) 536 S. Market, (CMTS) Albany 1815 City Directory
Hoffman, William: (F) Member Mount Vernon Lodge, No. 3, 1900, Albany, NY
Hogan, Dennis: (NATD) Oct. 16, 1872, (RES) Cohoes, (CMTS) Ireland
Hogan, George: (CMTS) 1790 Federal Census, Watervliet
Hogan, John: (NATD) Oct. 26, 1876, (RES) Cohoes, (CMTS) Ireland
Hogan, Joseph: (NATD) Oct. 6, 1860, (RES) Cohoes, (CMTS) Ireland
Hogan, Patrick: (NATD) Oct. 17, 1874, (RES) Cohoes, (CMTS) Ireland
Hogle, John: (OC) Innkeeper, (CMTS) Albany 1815 City Directory
Hogner, John: (OC) Ferryman, (CMTS) Albany 1815 City Directory
Hoit, Judson: (F) Member Mount Vernon Lodge, No. 3, 1900, Albany, NY
Hoit, William W.: (F) Member Masters Lodge, No. 5, 1900, Albany, NY
Hoke, Johannes: (CMTS) 1790 Federal Census, Watervliet

Holden, Joseph: (CMTS) 1790 Federal Census, Watervliet
Holkins, Abel D.: (OC) Builder, (CMTS) Albany 1815 City
   Directory
Holland, Almon: (F) Member Masters Lodge, No. 5, 1900,
   Albany, NY
Holland, James: (NATD) Oct. 26, 1887, (RES) Cohoes, (CMTS) Ireland
Hollenbeck, Jacob: (CMTS) 1790 Federal Census, Watervliet
Hollenbeck, Michael: (CMTS) 1790 Federal Census, Watervliet
Holliday, James: (NATD) Feb. 17, 1876, (RES) Cohoes, (CMTS) Ireland
Hollister, Augustin: (OC) Cartman, (CMTS) Albany 1815 City
   Directory
Holloran, Martin: (NATD) Feb. 23, 1876, (RES) Cohoes, (CMTS) Ireland
Holmes, Israel: (OC) Carpenter, (CMTS) Albany 1815 City
   Directory
Holmes, Lewis H.: (F) Member Mount Vernon Lodge, No. 3, 1900,
   Albany, NY
Holmes, Posel: (CMTS) 1790 Federal Census Rensselaerville
Holmes, Samuel: (OC) Cartman, (CMTS) Albany 1815 City
   Directory
Holmes, Jr., James: (CMTS) 1790 Federal Census Rensselaerville
Home, C: (OC) Teacher, (CMTS) Albany 1815 City
   Directory
Hommel, Martin: (CMTS) 1790 Federal Census Rensselaerville
Hood, Salas: (OC) Laborer, (CMTS) Albany 1815 City
   Directory
Hooghkirk, Garret: (OC) Carpenter, (CMTS) Albany 1815 City
   Directory
Hooghkirk, Lucas: (OC) Mason, (CMTS) Albany 1815 City Directory
Hooghkirk, Lucas I.: (OC) Carpenter, (CMTS) Albany 1815 City
   Directory
Hooghkirk, Widow Ann: (RES) 38 Beaver, (CMTS) Albany 1815 City
   Directory
Hooghkirk, Widow Margaret: (RES) 37 Beaver, (CMTS) Albany 1815
   City Directory
Hooker, Philip: (OC) Architect, (CMTS) Albany 1815 City
   Directory
Hoppold, Francis: (CMTS) 1790 Federal Census, Watervliet
Horn, John: (CMTS) 1790 Federal Census, Watervliet
Horn, Peter: (CMTS) 1790 Federal Census, Watervliet
Horr, Marcus M.: (F) Member Temple Lodge, No. 14, 1900,
   Albany, NY
Horsford, Reuben: (CMTS) 1790 Federal Census, Watervliet
Horton, Frederick: (F) Member Temple Lodge, No. 14, 1900,
   Albany, NY
Hosford, David: (OC) Attorney, (CMTS) Albany 1815 City

Directory
Hosford, E.: (OC) Printer and Bookseller, (RES) 100 State, (CMTS) Albany 1815 City Directory
Hoskins, Charles M.: (F) Member Temple Lodge, No. 14, 1900, Albany, NY
Hosmer, Nicholas: (CMTS) 1790 Federal Census, Watervliet
Hotaling, Charles E.: (F) Member Washington Lodge, No. 85, 1900, Albany, NY, (CMTS) Past Members
Hotaling, William R.: (F) Member Mount Vernon Lodge, No. 3, 1900, Albany, NY, (CMTS) Past Master 1882
Hotchkiss, Arthur: (OC) Tailor, (CMTS) Albany 1815 City Directory
Hott, Christopher: (CMTS) 1790 Federal Census Rensselaerville
Houck, Andress: (CMTS) 1790 Federal Census, Watervliet
Houck, George: (CMTS) 1790 Federal Census, Watervliet
Houck, Lodowick: (CMTS) 1790 Federal Census, Watervliet
Houck, Nicholas: (CMTS) 1790 Federal Census, Watervliet
Houghenpack, Peter: (CMTS) 1790 Federal Census, Watervliet
Houghkerk, Silas H.: (F) Member Temple Lodge, No. 14, 1900, Albany, NY
Houghtalen, Abraham: (CMTS) 1790 Federal Census, Watervliet
Houghtalen, David: (CMTS) 1790 Federal Census, Watervliet
Houghtalen, Dirick: (CMTS) 1790 Federal Census, Watervliet
Houghtalen, Garret: (CMTS) 1790 Federal Census, Watervliet
Houghtalen, John H.: (CMTS) 1790 Federal Census, Watervliet
Houghtalen, John M: (CMTS) 1790 Federal Census, Watervliet
Houghtalen, Storm: (CMTS) 1790 Federal Census, Watervliet
Houghtalen, Teunis M: (CMTS) 1790 Federal Census, Watervliet
Houghtalen, William: (CMTS) 1790 Federal Census, Watervliet
Houghton, George H.: (F) Member Mount Vernon Lodge, No. 3, 1900, Albany, NY
Houk, Isaac C: (CMTS) 1790 Federal Census, Watervliet
Houk, Jacob: (CMTS) 1790 Federal Census, Watervliet
Houk, John: (CMTS) 1790 Federal Census, Watervliet
Houk, Peter: (CMTS) 1790 Federal Census, Watervliet
Houk, Ruluff: (CMTS) 1790 Federal Census, Watervliet
Houk, Jr., John: (CMTS) 1790 Federal Census, Watervliet
Hourigan, William F.: (F) Member Temple Lodge, No. 14, 1900, Albany, NY
House, Joseph S.: (F) Member Masters Lodge, No. 5, 1900, Albany, NY
Hovey, Phineas: (RES) 34 Fox, (CMTS) Albany 1815 City Directory
How, Benjamin: (CMTS) 1790 Federal Census, Watervliet
How, Samuel: (CMTS) 1790 Federal Census Rensselaerville
How, Solomon: (CMTS) 1790 Federal Census, Watervliet
How, Thomas: (CMTS) 1790 Federal Census, Watervliet

Howard, Ephrain: (OC) Blacksmith, (CMTS) Albany 1815 City Directory
Howard, Noah: (OC) Nailer, (CMTS) Albany 1815 City Directory
Howard, Peter: (OC) Carpenter, (CMTS) Albany 1815 City Directory
Howe, Estes: (OC) Merchant, (CMTS) Albany 1815 City Directory
Howell, J.: (OC) Trumak & Papsta, (CMTS) Albany 1815 City
   Directory
Howell, John: (OC) Paper Stainer, (CMTS) Albany 1815 City Directory
Howell, Maltby: (OC) Cabinetmaker, (CMTS) Albany 1815 City
   Directory
Howell, Richard: (OC) Flour Store, (CMTS) Albany 1815 City Directory
Howell, William: (OC) Grocery and Flour Store, (CMTS) Albany 1815
   City Directory
Hoxie, Charles A.: (F) Member Temple Lodge, No. 14, 1900,
   Albany, NY
Hoy, Richard: (OC) Shoemaker, (CMTS) Albany 1815 City Directory
Hoyt, Goold: (RES) 167 and 339 N. Market, (CMTS) Albany 1815 City
   Directory
Hubbell, Amos: (RES) Boarding House at 25 S. Pearl, (CMTS) Albany
   1815 City Directory
Hudson, Moses: (CMTS) 1790 Federal Census, Watervliet
Hudson, William: (OC) Butcher, (CMTS) Albany 1815 City Directory
Hughes, Daniel W.: (OC) Constable, (CMTS) Albany 1815 City Directory
Hughes, Patrick: (NATD) Oct. 25, 1864, (RES) Cohoes, (CMTS) Ireland
Hulbut, Widow Ann: (RES) Boarding House at 43 Union, (CMTS)
   Albany 1815 City Directory
Hull, Stephen: (CMTS) 1790 Federal Census Rensselaerville
Hummel, Henry: (OC) Coachman, (CMTS) Albany 1815 City Directory
Humphrey, Chauncey: (RES) 59 State cont., (CMTS) Albany 1815 City
   Directory
Humphrey, George: (OC) Merchant, (CMTS) Albany 1815 City Directory
Humphrey, Grien: (OC) Currier, (CMTS) Albany 1815 City Directory
Humphrey, Hugh: (OC) Carpenter, (CMTS) Albany 1815 City Directory
Humphrey, John: (OC) Innkeeper, (CMTS) Albany 1815 City Directory
Humphrey, Jr., John: (OC) Grocer, (CMTS) Albany 1815 City Directory
Humphrey, William: (OC) Merchant, (RES) 389 S. Market, (CMTS)
   Albany 1815 City Directory
Humphries, William: (OC) Shoe Store, (CMTS) Albany 1815 City
   Directory
Hun, Derick: (OC) Carpenter, (CMTS) Albany 1815 City Directory
Hun, Richard T: (OC) Shoemaker, (CMTS) Albany 1815 City Directory
Hun, Widow Sarah: (RES) 243 N. Market, (CMTS) Albany 1815 City
   Directory
Hunderman, Hendrick: (CMTS) 1790 Federal Census, Watervliet
Hundicker, Samuel: (CMTS) 1790 Federal Census, Watervliet
Hungeford, Elisha: (CMTS) 1790 Federal Census, Watervliet

Hunt, Abijah: (OC) Ordinary, (CMTS) Albany 1815 City Directory
Hunt, William I.: (OC) Jeweller, (CMTS) Albany 1815 City Directory
Hunter, John: (CMTS) 1790 Federal Census, Watervliet
Hunter, Widow Isabella: (RES) 88 Beaver, (CMTS) Albany 1815 City Directory
Hunting, Edwin F.: (F) Member Mount Vernon Lodge, No. 3, 1900, Albany, NY
Huntley, Ava: (F) Member Temple Lodge, No. 14, 1900, Albany, NY
Hurd, Zadock: (CMTS) 1790 Federal Census Rensselaerville
Hurlburt, Asa: (RES) Boarding House at 43 Union, (CMTS) Albany 1815 City Directory
Hurst, Harvey: (OC) Umbrella Factory, (CMTS) Albany 1815 City Directory
Huss, Albert: (CMTS) 1790 Federal Census Rensselaerville
Husted, Alfred B.: (F) Member Temple Lodge, No. 14, 1900, Albany, NY
Husted, Israel: (OC) Merchant, (CMTS) Albany 1815 City Directory
Husted, Lewis: (OC) Merchant, (CMTS) Albany 1815 City Directory
Hutchins, Amos: (OC) Carpenter, (CMTS) Albany 1815 City Directory
Hutchins, Daniel: (OC) Mason, (CMTS) Albany 1815 City Directory
Hutchins, Jacob: (OC) Carpenter, (CMTS) Albany 1815 City Directory
Hutchins, Joshua: (CMTS) 1790 Federal Census Rensselaerville
Hutton, G.: (OC) Merchant, (CMTS) Albany 1815 City Directory
Hutton, I.: (OC) Merchant, (CMTS) Albany 1815 City Directory
Hutton, I. G.: (OC) Pocketbook and Purse factory, (CMTS) Albany 1815 City Directory
Hutton, Patrick: (OC) Nailer, (CMTS) Albany 1815 City Directory
Huxley, James: (OC) Cartman, (CMTS) Albany 1815 City Directory
Hyette, Menegh: (CMTS) 1790 Federal Census, Watervliet
Hyslop, Robert: (RES) 224 S. Mark. & 37 Montgomery, (CMTS) Albany 1815 City Directory
Iggatt, Edward: (OC) Grocer, (CMTS) Albany 1815 City Directory
Illch, William: (F) Member Mount Vernon Lodge, No. 3, 1900, Albany, NY
Ingenthron, Frank: (F) Member Temple Lodge, No. 14, 1900, Albany, NY
Inglis, Adam: (CMTS) 1790 Federal Census Rensselaerville
Ingraham, James: (OC) Merchant, (CMTS) Albany 1815 City Directory
Ingraham, Jarvis S.: (F) Member Temple Lodge, No. 14, 1900, Albany, NY
Ireland, Arthur J.: (F) Member Temple Lodge, No. 14, 1900, Albany, NY
Ireland, Edwin D.: (F) Member Temple Lodge, No. 14, 1900, Albany, NY

Ireland, Harry D.: (F) Member Temple Lodge, No. 14, 1900,
    Albany, NY
Ireland, Julis D.: (F) Member Temple Lodge, No. 14, 1900,
    Albany, NY, (CMTS) Life Member
Irwin, John: (CMTS) 1790 Federal Census, Watervliet
Ives, Joseph: (RES) 53 Eagle, (CMTS) Albany 1815 City Directory
Ives, Joseph: (OC) Merchant, (CMTS) Albany 1815 City Directory
Ives, Samuel: (OC) Innkeeper, (CMTS) Albany 1815 City Directory
Iveson, William: (CMTS) 1790 Federal Census, Watervliet
Jackson, Abraham: (OC) Bassett, (CMTS) Albany 1815 City Directory
Jackson, Ebenezer: (CMTS) 1790 Federal Census Rensselaerville
Jackson, Jack: (OC) Waterman, (CMTS) Albany 1815 City Directory
Jackson, James: (OC) Shoe Black, (CMTS) Albany 1815 City Directory
Jackson, Jeremiah: (CMTS) 1790 Federal Census Rensselaerville
Jackson, John: (CMTS) 1790 Federal Census, Watervliet
Jackson, John: (OC) Laborer, (CMTS) Albany 1815 City Directory
Jackson, Lewis: (OC) Waterman, (CMTS) Albany 1815 City Directory
Jackson, Widow Dinah: (RES) 31 Maiden Lane, (CMTS) Albany 1815
    City Directory
Jacobs, Francis: (OC) Sweep Master, (CMTS) Albany 1815 City
    Directory
Jacobs, Jacob: (CMTS) 1790 Federal Census, Watervliet
Jacobs, Myer C.: (F) Member Washington Lodge, No. 85, 1900,
    Albany, NY, (CMTS) Master
Jacobs, Wilson: (CMTS) 1790 Federal Census, Watervliet
James, Daniel: (OC) Physician, (CMTS) Albany 1815 City Directory
James, H.: (OC) Druggist, (CMTS) Albany 1815 City Directory
James, Thomas: (CMTS) 1790 Federal Census, Watervliet
James, William: (OC) Merchant, (CMTS) Albany 1815 City Directory
Janes, Franklin H.: (F) Member Temple Lodge, No. 14, 1900,
    Albany, NY
Janes, J. Edward: (F) Member Temple Lodge, No. 14, 1900,
    Albany, NY
Janes, William G.: (F) Member Temple Lodge, No. 14, 1900,
    Albany, NY, (CMTS) Past Master 1881
Jeannin, Lewis J.: (F) Member Temple Lodge, No. 14, 1900,
    Albany, NY
Jenkins, Elisha: (OC) Quarter Master General, (CMTS) Albany 1815 City
    Directory
Jenkins, G. A.: (OC) Millener, (CMTS) Albany 1815 City Directory
Jenkins, H.: (OC) Watchmaker, (CMTS) Albany 1815 City Directory
Jenkins, Harman: (CMTS) Albany 1815 City Directory
Jenkins, Ira: (OC) Watchmaker, (CMTS) Albany 1815 City Directory
Jenkins, J.: (OC) Watchmaker, (CMTS) Albany 1815 City Directory
Jenkins, Jacob: (OC) Hatter, (CMTS) Albany 1815 City Directory

Jenkins, James: (OC) Grocer, (CMTS) Albany 1815 City Directory
Jenkins, Lemuel: (OC) Attorney, (CMTS) Albany 1815 City Directory
Jenkins, Samuel: (CMTS) 1790 Federal Census Rensselaerville
Jenks, Nathan: (OC) Grocer, (CMTS) Albany 1815 City Directory
Jenne, Ira G.: (OC) Grocer, (CMTS) Albany 1815 City Directory
Jennings, Ebenezer: (CMTS) 1790 Federal Census Rensselaerville
Jennings, James: (NATD) Oct. 23, 1886, (RES) Cohoes, (CMTS) Ireland
Jephson, William H.: (OC) Merchant, (CMTS) Albany 1815 City Directory
Jeraleway, Nicholas: (CMTS) 1790 Federal Census, Watervliet
Jeraloman, Jr., Nicholas: (OC) Mason, (CMTS) Albany 1815 City Directory
Jermain, Sylvanus P.: (OC) Merchant, (CMTS) Albany 1815 City Directory
Jessup, Isaac: (OC) Merchant, (CMTS) Albany 1815 City Directory
Jewell, Jeremiah P.: (OC) Blacksmith, (CMTS) Albany 1815 City Directory
Jewell, Volkert D.: (OC) Blacksmith, (CMTS) Albany 1815 City Directory
Jewett, George G.: (OC) Merchant, (CMTS) Albany 1815 City Directory
Jimpson, James: (RES) 39 Division, (CMTS) Albany 1815 City Directory
Jlodge, Jr., Barington: (F) Member Temple Lodge, No. 14, 1900, Albany, NY, (CMTS) Life Member
Johnson, Bristol: (OC) Waterman, (CMTS) Albany 1815 City Directory
Johnson, Cleb: (OC) Laborer, (CMTS) Albany 1815 City Directory
Johnson, Eugene C.: (F) Member Masters Lodge, No. 5, 1900, Albany, NY
Johnson, James: (OC) Caulker, (CMTS) Albany 1815 City Directory
Johnson, Jermiah: (OC) Harness Maker, (CMTS) Albany 1815 City Directory
Johnson, John: (OC) Butcher, (CMTS) Albany 1815 City Directory
Johnson, John: (NATD) Feb. 23, 1878, (RES) Cohoes, (CMTS) Ireland
Johnson, John: (OC) Grocer, (CMTS) Albany 1815 City Directory
Johnson, John: (OC) Laborer, (CMTS) Albany 1815 City Directory
Johnson, John: (OC) Waterman, (CMTS) Albany 1815 City Directory
Johnson, John C.: (OC) Shoemaker, (CMTS) Albany 1815 City Directory
Johnson, John M.: (F) Member Temple Lodge, No. 14, 1900, Albany, NY
Johnson, John T.: (F) Member Temple Lodge, No. 14, 1900, Albany, NY
Johnson, Lewis: (OC) Tailor, (CMTS) Albany 1815 City Directory
Johnson, Mary: (CMTS) 1790 Federal Census, Watervliet
Johnson, Maycock W.: (OC) Silversmith, (CMTS) Albany 1815 City Directory
Johnson, Nathan P.: (RES) 17 Washington, (CMTS) Albany 1815 City

Johnson, Stephen W.: (RES) Boarding House at 3 S. Pearl, (CMTS) Albany 1815 City Directory
Johnson, Thomas: (OC) Cooper, (CMTS) Albany 1815 City Directory
Johnson, Widow Laney: (OC) Lumber, (CMTS) Albany 1815 City Directory
Johnson, Widow Lucretia: (RES) Boarding House at 49 Green, (CMTS) Albany 1815 City Directory
Johnson, William: (F) Member Temple Lodge, No. 14, 1900, Albany, NY
Johnson, William: (OC) Grocer, (CMTS) Albany 1815 City Directory
Johnston, Evert: (CMTS) 1790 Federal Census, Watervliet
Johnston, James: (CMTS) 1790 Federal Census, Watervliet
Johnston, James: (CMTS) 1790 Federal Census Rensselaerville
Johnston, John: (CMTS) 1790 Federal Census, Watervliet
Johnston, Joseph: (CMTS) 1790 Federal Census Rensselaerville
Johnston, Reubin: (CMTS) 1790 Federal Census Rensselaerville
Johnston, Russell M.: (F) Member Masters Lodge, No. 5, 1900, Albany, NY
Johnston, William: (CMTS) 1790 Federal Census, Watervliet
Jolly, Hugh: (CMTS) 1790 Federal Census, Watervliet
Jones, Amos: (CMTS) 1790 Federal Census Rensselaerville
Jones, Amos: (OC) Grocer, (CMTS) Albany 1815 City Directory
Jones, Benjamin: (OC) Carpenter, (CMTS) Albany 1815 City Directory
Jones, Casper: (RES) 17 Quay, (CMTS) Albany 1815 City Directory
Jones, Elisha: (OC) Carpenter, (CMTS) Albany 1815 City Directory
Jones, Eliza: (CEN) 1880 4th Ward, Albany, NY, (CMTS) Widow, (A) 52, (OC) Dressmaking, (BP) NY, Listed with John Jones, 34, son, Laborer, Robert Jones, 32, Carpenter, son, Edward Jones, 26, Tin Smith, son
Jones, Elizabeth: (CEN) 1880 6th Ward, Albany, NY, (CMTS) Widow, (A) 57, (BP) MA, (OC) Matron
Jones, Gillet: (CMTS) 1790 Federal Census Rensselaerville
Jones, Henry: (CMTS) 1790 Federal Census Rensselaerville
Jones, Henry T: (OC) Counsellor, (CMTS) Albany 1815 City Directory
Jones, James: (OC) Merchant, (CMTS) Albany 1815 City Directory
Jones, Jenny: (CEN) 1880 4th Ward, Albany, NY, (CMTS) Single, (A) 19, (BP) NY, (OC) Dressmaker
Jones, Jeremaih: (OC) Carpenter, (CMTS) Albany 1815 City Directory
Jones, Johannes: (CMTS) 1790 Federal Census Rensselaerville
Jones, John: (CEN) 1880 4th Ward, Albany, NY, (CMTS) Married, (A) 32, (OC) Lumber Merchant, (B) NY, Listed with Mercy, 29, wife, Isibel E., 6, daughter, William T., 3, son
Jones, John: (CMTS) 1790 Federal Census, Watervliet
Jones, John: (OC) Carpenter, (CMTS) Albany 1815 City Directory

Jones, John P.: (OC) Merchant, (CMTS) Albany 1815 City Directory
Jones, Louisa: (CEN) 1880 6rh Ward, Albany, NY, (CMTS) Single, Black, (A) 29, (BP) NY, (OC) Laborer, Listed with Cora, 10, MA, daughter
Jones, Luther: (OC) Drummaker, (CMTS) Albany 1815 City Directory
Jones, Marshal: (RES) 23 Hamilton, (CMTS) Albany 1815 City Directory
Jones, Peter: (OC) Morocco Dresser, (CMTS) Albany 1815 City Directory
Jones, Robert: (CEN) 1880 4th Ward, Albany, NY, (CMTS) Married, (A) 32, (BP) NY,)OC) Huckster, Listed with Ellen, 22, wife
Jones, Roger: (CMTS) 1790 Federal Census Rensselaerville
Jones, Seth: (OC) Laborer, (CMTS) Albany 1815 City Directory
Jones, Thomas: (OC) Carpenter, (CMTS) Albany 1815 City Directory
Jones, Thomas: (OC) Grocer, (CMTS) Albany 1815 City Directory
Joralemon, John: (OC) Bailey & Joralemon, Stoves, (CMTS) Albany 1859 City Directory
Jordan, Martin: (NATD) Oct. 25, 1879, (RES) Cohoes, (CMTS) Ireland
Josling, Henry: (CMTS) 1790 Federal Census, Watervliet
Joslyn, Jesse: (OC) Innkeeper, (CMTS) Albany 1815 City Directory
Joyce, George: (OC) Cartman, (CMTS) Albany 1815 City Directory
Joyce, John: (OC) Cartman, (CMTS) Albany 1815 City Directory
Joyce, Jonathan: (CMTS) 1790 Federal Census Rensselaerville
Joyce, Patrick: (NATD) Mar. 30, 1885, (RES) Cohoes, (CMTS) Ireland
Joyce, Patrick: (NATD) Oct. 19, 1887, (RES) Cohoes, (CMTS) Ireland
Judge, Hugh: (NATD) Oct. 26, 1887, (RES) Cohoes, (CMTS) Ireland
Judson, Albert L.: (F) Member Masters Lodge, No. 5, 1900, Albany, NY
Judson, Nathaniel: (OC) Innkeeper, (CMTS) Albany 1815 City Directory
Kaack, Henry: (F) Member Temple Lodge, No. 14, 1900, Albany, NY
Kaiser, John: (F) Member Temple Lodge, No. 14, 1900, Albany, NY
Kaley, John R.: (F) Member Masters Lodge, No. 5, 1900, Albany, NY
Kane, Archibald: (OC) Merchant, (CMTS) Albany 1815 City Directory
Kane, Earnest: (CMTS) 1790 Federal Census, Watervliet
Kane, George: (OC) Ordinary, (CMTS) Albany 1815 City Directory
Kane, James: (OC) Merchant, (CMTS) Albany 1815 City Directory
Kane, Martin: (NATD) Oct. 24, 1874, (RES) Cohoes, (CMTS) Ireland
Kane, Michael: (OC) Laborer, (CMTS) Albany 1815 City Directory
Kane, Patrick: (NATD) Oct. 15, 1860, (RES) Cohoes, (CMTS) Ireland
Kane, William: (CMTS) 1790 Federal Census, Watervliet
Kane, William: (OC) Carpenter, (CMTS) Albany 1815 City Directory
Kanzelmyer, J. Chas.: (F) Member Mount Vernon Lodge, No. 3, 1900, Albany, NY
Kaufman, Levi H.: (F) Member Mount Vernon Lodge, No. 3, 1900,

Albany, NY, (CMTS) Past Master 1878
Kavanaugh, William: (F) Member Mount Vernon Lodge, No. 3, 1900, Albany, NY
Kearney, Cornelius: (NATD) Mar. 1, 1875, (RES) Cohoes, (CMTS) Ireland
Kearney, James: (NATD) Jan. 24, 1876, (RES) Cohoes, (CMTS) Ireland
Kearney, John: (NATD) Mar. 29, 1892, (RES) Cohoes, (CMTS) Ireland
Kearney, John: (OC) Porter House, (CMTS) Albany 1815 City Directory
Kearney, Owen: (NATD) Jan. 28, 1876, (RES) Cohoes, (CMTS) Ireland
Kearney, Widow·Mary: (OC) Lutheran, (CMTS) Albany 1815 City Directory
Kearny, William: (OC) Lunber, (CMTS) Albany 1815 City Directory
Keays, Edward: (F) Member Temple Lodge, No. 14, 1900, Albany, NY
Keefe, Daniel: (NATD) Oct. 17, 1860, (RES) Cohoes, (CMTS) Ireland
Keefe, Edward: (NATD) Oct. 27, 1866, (RES) Cohoes, (CMTS) Ireland
Keefe, Margaret: (OC) Millener, (CMTS) Albany 1815 City Directory
Keefe, Thomas: (NATD) Oct. 22, 1860, (RES) Cohoes, (CMTS) Ireland
Keefer, David H.: (F) Member Temple Lodge, No. 14, 1900, Albany, NY
Keegan, Timothy: (NATD) Oct. 23, 1868, (RES) Cohoes, (CMTS) Ireland
Keeler, Frederick H.: (F) Member Temple Lodge, No. 14, 1900, Albany, NY
Keeler, Isaac: (RES) 18 Hamilton, (CMTS) Albany 1815 City Directory
Keeler, Jacob: (OC) Waterman 528 N. Market, (CMTS) Albany 1815 City Directory
Keeler, James: (OC) Merchant, (CMTS) Albany 1815 City Directory
Keeler, Jasper S.: (OC) Merchant, (CMTS) Albany 1815 City Directory
Keeler, John: (F) Member Temple Lodge, No. 14, 1900, Albany, NY
Keenan, James: (NATD) Oct. 25, 1862, (RES) Cohoes, (CMTS) Ireland
Keenholts, James C.: (F) Member Temple Lodge, No. 14, 1900, Albany, NY
Keenholts, Walter S.: (F) Member Temple Lodge, No. 14, 1900, Albany, NY
Keens, Joseph W.: (F) Member Mount Vernon Lodge, No. 3, 1900, Albany, NY
Keer, Charles: (OC) Carpenter, (CMTS) Albany 1815 City Directory
Kelihan, Daniel: (NATD) Oct. 22, 1864, (RES) Cohoes, (CMTS) Ireland
Keller, George A.: (F) Member Masters Lodge, No. 5, 1900, Albany, NY
Kelley, Bernard: (NATD) Oct. 24, 1874, (RES) Cohoes, (CMTS) Ireland
Kelly, Daniel: (NATD) Oct. 16, 1872, (RES) Cohoes, (CMTS) Ireland
Kelly, James: (NATD) Mar. 21, 1894, (RES) Cohoes, (CMTS) Ireland
Kelly, James: (NATD) Oct. 26, 1887, (RES) Cohoes, (CMTS) Ireland

Kelly, Michael H.: (NATD) Oct. 25, 1879, (RES) Cohoes, (CMTS) Ireland
Kelly, Robert: (NATD) Oct.' 24, 1882, (RES) Cohoes, (CMTS) Ireland
Kelly, Stephen: (CMTS) 1790 Federal Census Rensselaerville
Kelly, Thomas: (NATD) Oct. 20, 1868, (RES) Cohoes, (CMTS) Ireland
Kelly, William: (NATD) Mar. 29, 1892, (RES) Cohoes, (CMTS) Ireland
Kelly, William: (NATD) Oct. 21, 1874, (RES) Cohoes, (CMTS) Ireland
Kelsey, Gideon: (CMTS) 1790 Federal Census Rensselaerville
Kelsey, Israel: (CMTS) 1790 Federal Census, Watervliet
Kelsey, Jonas: (CMTS) 1790 Federal Census Rensselaerville
Kemmer, Hermanus: (CMTS) 1790 Federal Census, Watervliet
Kemp, James: (OC) Waiter on a Steam Boat, (CMTS) Albany 1815 City Directory
Kemp, Joseph: (OC) Flour Merchant, (CMTS) Albany 1815 City Directory
Kendal, Enoch: (OC) Hair Dresser, (CMTS) Albany 1815 City Directory
Kendrick, Fred M. H.: (F) Member Masters Lodge, No. 5, 1900, Albany, NY
Kenerkern, Christian: (CMTS) 1790 Federal Census Rensselaerville
Keniskern, Henry: (CMTS) 1790 Federal Census Rensselaerville
Kennear, George: (OC) Blacksmith, (CMTS) Albany 1815 City Directory
Kennear, Robert: (CMTS) 1790 Federal Census, Watervliet
Kenneary, Martin: (NATD) Aug. 8, 1898, (RES) Cohoes, (CMTS) Ireland
Kennedy, Daniel: (NATD) Feb. 20, 1880, (RES) Cohoes, (CMTS) Ireland
Kennedy, Edward: (NATD) Mar. 29, 1893, (RES) Cohoes, (CMTS) Ireland
Kennedy, Frank I.: (F) Member Temple Lodge, No. 14, 1900, Albany, NY
Kennedy, James: (RES) 83 Beaver, (CMTS) Albany 1815 City Directory
Kennedy, James: (OC) Mason, (CMTS) Albany 1815 City Directory
Kennedy, John: (NATD) Feb. 20, 1879, (RES) Cohoes, (CMTS) Ireland
Kennedy, John: (NATD) Oct. 15, 1872, (RES) Cohoes, (CMTS) Ireland
Kent, Benjamin: (OC) Laborer, (CMTS) Albany 1815 City Directory
Kent, James: (OC) Chancellor, (CMTS) Albany 1815 City Directory
Kenyon, Moses: (OC) Ship Builder, (CMTS) Albany 1815 City Directory
Kerker, Conradt: (CMTS) 1790 Federal Census, Watervliet
Kerker, David: (CMTS) 1790 Federal Census, Watervliet
Kerker, Henry: (CMTS) 1790 Federal Census, Watervliet
Kerney, Widow Ann: (RES) 52 Chapel, (CMTS) Albany 1815 City Directory
Kerr, Hugh: (OC) Merchant, (CMTS) Albany 1815 City Directory
Ketcham, Joseph: (OC) Brewer, (CMTS) Albany 1815 City Directory
Ketchum, Ephraim: (CMTS) 1790 Federal Census Rensselaerville
Keyser, Edward: (F) Member Temple Lodge, No. 14, 1900, Albany, NY

Kidd, Thomas: (OC) Constable, (CMTS) Albany 1815 City Directory
Kidney, John: (OC) Blacksmith, (CMTS) Albany 1815 City Directory
Kidney, Jonathan: (OC) Blacksmith, (CMTS) Albany 1815 City Directory
Kiernan, Charles B.: (F) Member Temple Lodge, No. 14, 1900,
    Albany, NY
Kilbourn, George: (OC) Music Instructor, (CMTS) Albany 1815 City
    Directory
Kilbourne, James B.: (F) Member Mount Vernon Lodge, No. 3, 1900,
    Albany, NY
Killam, Jr., Eliphalet: (RES) 51 Washington, (CMTS) Albany 1815 City
    Directory
Killey, Philip: (OC) Laborer, (CMTS) Albany 1815 City Directory
Killy, John: (OC) Laborer, (CMTS) Albany 1815 City Directory
Kimme, Jacob: (CMTS) 1790 Federal Census, Watervliet
Kimmey, Edson: (F) Member Masters Lodge, No. 5, 1900,
    Albany, NY
King, James: (OC) Attorney, (CMTS) Albany 1815 City Directory
King, Reuben: (CMTS) 1790 Federal Census Rensselaerville
King, William S.: (OC) Trunkmaker, (CMTS) Albany 1815
    City Directory
Kiniskern, Martinus: (CMTS) 1790 Federal Census Rensselaerville
Kinnicut, R. S.: (OC) Accountant, (CMTS) Albany 1815 City Directory
Kinnicut, Robert S.: (OC) Auctineer, (CMTS) Albany 1815 City Directory
Kinnier, Widow Susan: (RES) Schecectady Turnpike, (CMTS) Albany
    1815 City Directory
Kirk, Henry: (OC) Coppersmith, (CMTS) Albany 1815 City Directory
Kirk, John: (RES) 37 Columbia, (CMTS) Albany 1815 City Directory
Kirk, William: (OC) Gilder, (CMTS) Albany 1815 City Directory
Kirkland, Widow Margaret: (RES) 108 Beaver, (CMTS) Albany 1815
    City Directory
Kirkner, Nicholas: (CMTS) 1790 Federal Census, Watervliet
Kittle, John: (OC) Teamster, (CMTS) Albany 1815 City Directory
Kittle, Nicholas D.: (OC) Cartman, (CMTS) Albany 1815 City Directory
Kittle, Sybrant: (OC) Grocer, (CMTS) Albany 1815 City Directory
Klinch, George: (OC) Cabinet Maker, (CMTS) Albany 1815 City
    Directory
Klinck, John G.: (OC) Printer, (CMTS) Albany 1815 City Directory
Kline, George: (OC) Tanner, (CMTS) Albany 1815 City Directory
Kline, Nicholas: (CMTS) 1790 Federal Census, Watervliet
Knap, Hubbee: (OC) Merchant, (CMTS) Albany 1815 City Directory
Knap, Josiah: (CMTS) 1790 Federal Census, Watervliet
Knapp, Ephraim D.: (CMTS) 1790 Federal Census Rensselaerville
Knapp, George B.: (F) Member Temple Lodge, No. 14, 1900,
    Albany, NY
Knapp, Ira G.: (F) Member Temple Lodge, No. 14, 1900,

Albany, NY
Knapp, Moses: (CMTS) 1790 Federal Census Rensselaerville
Knauff, John G.: (OC) Merchant, (CMTS) Albany 1815 City Directory
Knight, Charles F.: (F) Member Temple Lodge, No. 14, 1900, Albany, NY
Kniver, David: (CMTS) 1790 Federal Census, Watervliet
Kniver, Henry: (CMTS) 1790 Federal Census Rensselaerville
Knolton, George: (CMTS) 1790 Federal Census Rensselaerville
Knower, Benjamin: (OC) Hatter, (CMTS) Albany 1815 City Directory
Knower, Daniel: (RES) 19 Green, (CMTS) Albany 1815 City Directory
Knower, George: (OC) Merchant, (CMTS) Albany 1815 City Directory
Knower, Samuel: (OC) Inspector of Ashes, (CMTS) Albany 1815 City Directory
Knowles, George E.: (F) Member Temple Lodge, No. 14, 1900, Albany, NY
Knowlson, Richard: (RES) 38 Lydius, (CMTS) Albany 1815 City Directory
Knowlson, Thomas: (OC) Grocer, (CMTS) Albany 1815 City Directory
Knox, George: (OC) Grocer, (CMTS) Albany 1815 City Directory
Knox, Samuel J.: (F) Member Temple Lodge, No. 14, 1900, Albany, NY
Koch, Andress: (CMTS) 1790 Federal Census Rensselaerville
Komsales, John: (CMTS) 1790 Federal Census, Watervliet
Kosboth, Cutlip: (CMTS) 1790 Federal Census Rensselaerville
Kramrath, Alexander: (F) Member Temple Lodge, No. 14, 1900, Albany, NY
Kramrath, Henry M.: (F) Member Temple Lodge, No. 14, 1900, Albany, NY
Kratz, Conrad: (F) Member Temple Lodge, No. 14, 1900, Albany, NY
Kregier, Bastian: (CMTS) 1790 Federal Census, Watervliet
Kregier, Hester: (CMTS) 1790 Federal Census, Watervliet
Kregier, Martinus: (CMTS) 1790 Federal Census, Watervliet
Kullman, Augustus: (F) Member Temple Lodge, No. 14, 1900, Albany, NY
Kullman, Theodore C.: (F) Member Temple Lodge, No. 14, 1900, Albany, NY
Kumsales, Petrus: (CMTS) 1790 Federal Census, Watervliet
Kunholtz, Christopher: (CMTS) 1790 Federal Census Rensselaerville
Kunkel, Martin: (F) Member Temple Lodge, No. 14, 1900, Albany, NY
La Grange, Conrad: (OC) Blacksmith, (CMTS) Albany 1815 City Directory
La Grange, G. (OC) Merchant, (CMTS) Albany 1815 City Directory
La Grange, James: (RES) 240 Washington, (CMTS) Albany 1815 City

La Grange, James: (RES) 68 Hudson, (CMTS) Albany 1815 City Directory
Ladd, James: (OC) Innkeeper, (CMTS) Albany 1815 City Directory
Ladew, Stephen: (OC) Grocer, (CMTS) Albany 1815 City Directory
Ladew, Tusant: (OC) Mason, (CMTS) Albany 1815 City Directory
Lamb, Anthony: (RES) 66 Hudson, (CMTS) Albany 1815 City Directory
Lamb, Charles W.: (F) Member Temple Lodge, No. 14, 1900, Albany, NY
Lamberse, Nicholas: (CMTS) 1790 Federal Census, Watervliet
Lamoureux, Andrew: (OC) Teamster, (CMTS) Albany 1815 City Directory
Lamoureux, Joseph: (OC) Merchant, (CMTS) Albany 1815 City Directory
Lamoureux, Timothy: (OC) Carpenter, (CMTS) Albany 1815 City Directory
Lamourex, Reuben: (OC) Teamster, (CMTS) Albany 1815 City Directory
Lamp, Michael: (F) Member Temple Lodge, No. 14, 1900, Albany, NY
Lanagan, Elmer D.: (F) Member Temple Lodge, No. 14, 1900, Albany, NY
Lanaway, Isaac: (CMTS) 1790 Federal Census Rensselaerville
Landers, Ebenezer: (CMTS) 1790 Federal Census Rensselaerville
Lane, Charles B.: (F) Member Masters Lodge, No. 5, 1900, Albany, NY
Lane, Joseph J: (CMTS) 1790 Federal Census, Watervliet
Lane, Nathaniel: (CMTS) 1790 Federal Census, Watervliet
Lanehart, Michael: (CMTS) 1790 Federal Census, Watervliet
Laney, Dennis: (OC) Mason, (CMTS) Albany 1815 City Directory
Lang, Charles M.: (F) Member Temple Lodge, No. 14, 1900, Albany, NY
Lansing, A. T. E.: (OC) Merchant, (CMTS) Albany 1815 City Directory
Lansing, Abraham H.: (CMTS) 1790 Federal Census, Watervliet
Lansing, Abram F.: (OC) Shoemaker, (CMTS) Albany 1815 City Directory
Lansing, Charles E.: (F) Member Temple Lodge, No. 14, 1900, Albany, NY
Lansing, Christopher: (CMTS) 1790 Federal Census, Watervliet
Lansing, Garret: (CMTS) 1790 Federal Census, Watervliet
Lansing, Garret A: (RES) 34 Church, (CMTS) Albany 1815 City Directory
Lansing, Garret Y.: (OC) Counsellor, (CMTS) Albany 1815 City Directory
Lansing, Henry: (OC) Wheelwright 59 N. Market, (CMTS) Albany 1815 City Directory
Lansing, Henry J.: (CMTS) 1790 Federal Census, Watervliet

Lansing, Henry R.: (OC) Merchant, (CMTS) Albany 1815 City Directory
Lansing, Isaac: (CMTS) 1790 Federal Census, Watervliet
Lansing, Jacob: (CMTS) 1790 Federal Census, Watervliet
Lansing, Jacob: (RES) 216 N. Market, (CMTS) Albany 1815 City Directory
Lansing, Jacob: (OC) Mason, (CMTS) Albany 1815 City Directory
Lansing, Jacob F.: (CMTS) 1790 Federal Census, Watervliet
Lansing, Jacob H.: (CMTS) 1790 Federal Census, Watervliet
Lansing, Jacob J.: (CMTS) 1790 Federal Census, Watervliet
Lansing, Jacob J.: (RES) 85 N. Market, (CMTS) Albany 1815 City Directory
Lansing, Jr., Jacob: (OC) Wheelwright, (CMTS) Albany 1815 City Directory
Lansing, James: (OC) Merchant, (CMTS) Albany 1815 City Directory
Lansing, John: (CMTS) 1790 Federal Census, Watervliet
Lansing, John A.: (OC) Baker, (CMTS) Albany 1815 City Directory
Lansing, Jr., John: (OC) Late Chancellor, (CMTS) Albany 1815 City Directory
Lansing, John V. A.: (CMTS) 1790 Federal Census, Watervliet
Lansing, Rutger: (CMTS) 1790 Federal Census, Watervliet
Lansing, Sanders: (OC) Register in Chancery, (CMTS) Albany 1815 City Directory
Lansing, Widow Ann: (RES) 216 N. Market, (CMTS) Albany 1815 City Directory
Lansing, Widow of Myndert: (RES) 617 S. Market, (CMTS) Albany 1815 City Directory
Lansing, Jr., Jacob J.: (CMTS) 1790 Federal Census, Watervliet
Lansing, Sr., Jacob J.: (CMTS) 1790 Federal Census, Watervliet
Lansingh, Jeremiah: (RES) 80 N. Pearl, (CMTS) Albany 1815 City Directory
Lansinh, Abraham A: (RES) 652 S. Market, (CMTS) Albany 1815 City Directory
Laraway, Frank J.: (F) Member Temple Lodge, No. 14, 1900, Albany, NY
Larcher, Joseph W.: (OC) Tailor, (CMTS) Albany 1815 City Directory
Larraway, Isaac: (CMTS) 1790 Federal Census, Watervliet
Larraway, Jacob: (CMTS) 1790 Federal Census, Watervliet
Larraway, John W.: (F) Member Temple Lodge, No. 14, 1900, Albany, NY, (CMTS) Life Member
Larraway, Jonas: (CMTS) 1790 Federal Census, Watervliet
Larraway, Nicholas: (CMTS) 1790 Federal Census, Watervliet
Larraway, William: (CMTS) 1790 Federal Census, Watervliet
Larvey, James: (OC) Mason, (CMTS) Albany 1815 City Directory
Larwood, Thomas W.: (F) Member Masters Lodge, No. 5, 1900, Albany, NY

Lassing, John: (OC) Blacksmith, (CMTS) Albany 1815 City Directory
Latham, George E.: (F) Member Temple Lodge, No. 14, 1900,
    Albany, NY
Lathrop, Augustus H.: (F) Member Temple Lodge, No. 14, 1900,
    Albany, NY
Lathrop, Dyer: (OC) Merchant, (CMTS) Albany 1815 City Directory
Lathrop, Gorden: (OC) Laborer, (CMTS) Albany 1815 City Directory
Lathrop, Oliver: (OC) Physician, (CMTS) Albany 1815 City Directory
Latta, William: (CMTS) 1790 Federal Census, Watervliet
Lattimer, Benjamin: (RES) 9 Plain, (CMTS) Albany 1815 City Directory
Lavally, Cook: (CMTS) 1790 Federal Census, Watervliet
Lavally, John: (CMTS) 1790 Federal Census, Watervliet
Lawlew, William: (OC) Gilder, (CMTS) Albany 1815 City Directory
Lawrence, Charles E.: (F) Member Temple Lodge, No. 14, 1900,
    Albany, NY
Lawrence, Fred J.: (F) Member Temple Lodge, No. 14, 1900,
    Albany, NY
Lawrence, Thomas: (RES) 174 Washington, (CMTS) Albany 1815 City
    Directory
Lawson, Andrew P.: (CMTS) 1790 Federal Census Rensselaerville
Lawson, Henry: (CMTS) 1790 Federal Census Rensselaerville
Lawson, Joseph A.: (F) Member Masters Lodge, No. 5, 1900,
    Albany, NY, (CMTS) Past Master
Lawson, Lawrence: (CMTS) 1790 Federal Census, Watervliet
Lawtenslager, Albert: (F) Member Masters Lodge, No. 5, 1900,
    Albany, NY
Lawtenslager, Joseph J.: (F) Member Masters Lodge, No. 5, 1900,
    Albany, NY
Lawther, Robert: (OC) Carpenter, (CMTS) Albany 1815 City Directory
Lawton, George: (F) Member Mount Vernon Lodge, No. 3, 1900,
    Albany, NY
Lawton, George: (F) Member Temple Lodge, No. 14, 1900,
    Albany, NY
Lawyer, Abraham L.: (F) Member Mount Vernon Lodge, No. 3, 1900,
    Albany, NY
Lawyer, Abram S.: (F) Member Washington Lodge, No. 85, 1900,
    Albany, NY, (CMTS) Past Members
Lawyer, Christopher: (CMTS) 1790 Federal Census, Watervliet
Lawyer, George: (F) Member Temple Lodge, No. 14, 1900,
    Albany, NY
Lay, Amos: (OC) Surveyor, (CMTS) Albany 1815 City Directory
Le Boeuf, Randall J.: (F) Member Masters Lodge, No. 5, 1900,
    Albany, NY
Le Brun, Louis: (F) Member Masters Lodge, No. 5, 1900,
    Albany, NY

Le Fevre, Claude B.: (F) Member Masters Lodge, No. 5, 1900, Albany, NY
Le Que, Enos: (OC) Laborer, (CMTS) Albany 1815 City Directory
Le Rue, John: (OC) Confectioner, (CMTS) Albany 1815 City Directory
Le Ruso, Angelow: (CMTS) 1915, Census, District No. 3 Ward No. 13
Le Ruso, Max: (CMTS) 1915, Census, District No. 3 Ward No. 13
Le Ruso, Rose: (CMTS) 1915, Census, District No. 3 Ward No. 13
Leach, Hosea K.: (F) Member Temple Lodge, No. 14, 1900, Albany, NY
Leach, William: (OC) Weaver, (CMTS) Albany 1815 City Directory
Leak, Henry: (CMTS) 1790 Federal Census, Watervliet
Leake, John: (RES) 49 Green Leake, (CMTS) Albany 1815 City Directory
Leanhart, Johannes: (CMTS) 1790 Federal Census Rensselaerville
Leanord, Widow Maria: (RES) 199 N. Market, (CMTS) Albany 1815 City Directory
Lee, Charles: (RES) 45 Lydius, (CMTS) Albany 1815 City Directory
Lee, Joseph: (CMTS) 1790 Federal Census Rensselaerville
Lee, Philomon: (CMTS) 1790 Federal Census Rensselaerville
Lee, Uriah: (CMTS) 1790 Federal Census, Watervliet
Lefevre, Arthur N.: (F) Member Temple Lodge, No. 14, 1900, Albany, NY
Lefevre, Sherwood: (F) Member Temple Lodge, No. 14, 1900, Albany, NY
Leffingwell, Christopher: (OC) Merchant, (CMTS) Albany 1815 City Directory
Legrange, Christian: (CMTS) 1790 Federal Census, Watervliet
Legrange, Christian J: (CMTS) 1790 Federal Census, Watervliet
Legrange, Conradt: (CMTS) 1790 Federal Census, Watervliet
Legrange, Isaac: (CMTS) 1790 Federal Census, Watervliet
Legrange, Jacob: (CMTS) 1790 Federal Census, Watervliet
Legrange, John: (CMTS) 1790 Federal Census, Watervliet
Legrange, John J.: (CMTS) 1790 Federal Census, Watervliet
Legrange, Omie: (CMTS) 1790 Federal Census, Watervliet
Legrange, Omie S.: (CMTS) 1790 Federal Census, Watervliet
Legrange, Peter: (CMTS) 1790 Federal Census, Watervliet
Legrange, Jr., Jacob: (CMTS) 1790 Federal Census, Watervliet
Leit, Helen E.: (CEN) 1880 6th Ward, Albany, NY, (CMTS) Single, (A) 44, (BP) Ireland, (OC) Laundress
Leland, Charles E.: (F) Member Masters Lodge, No. 5, 1900, Albany, NY
Lemet, Louis: (OC) Gold Beater, (CMTS) Albany 1815 City Directory
Lenington, Thomas: (OC) Col. U.S., (CMTS) Albany 1815 City Directory
Lent, David: (OC) Whip Maker, (CMTS) Albany 1815 City Directory
Leonard, Gardner C.: (F) Member Masters Lodge, No. 5, 1900, Albany, NY

Leonard, Jesse Hoyt: (F) Member Temple Lodge, No. 14, 1900,
Albany, NY
Leonard, John: (CMTS) 1790 Federal Census, Watervliet
Leonard, Philip: (OC) Grocer, (CMTS) Albany 1815 City Directory
Leslie, Harry W.: (F) Member Temple Lodge, No. 14, 1900,
Albany, NY
Lester, Mordecia: (OC), (CMTS) Albany 1815 City Directory
Leverson, Peter: (CMTS) 1790 Federal Census, Watervliet
Levings, Amos W.: (F) Member Temple Lodge, No. 14, 1900,
Albany, NY
Levy, Michael: (CMTS) 1790 Federal Census, Watervliet
Lewi, Isadore: (F) Member Mount Vernon Lodge, No. 3, 1900,
Albany, NY
Lewis, Benedict: (OC) Shoemaker, (CMTS) Albany 1815 City Directory
Lewis, Clear: (CMTS) 1790 Federal Census Rensselaerville
Lewis, David D.: (OC) Carpenter, (CMTS) Albany 1815 City Directory
Lewis, Garret: (OC) Shoemaker, (CMTS) Albany 1815 City Directory
Lewis, Henry: (CMTS) 1790 Federal Census Rensselaerville
Lewis, James: (OC) Harness Maker, (CMTS) Albany 1815 City Directory
Lewis, Leonard: (RES) 45 Union, (CMTS) Albany 1815 City Directory
Lewis, Lewis: (OC) Carpenter, (CMTS) Albany 1815 City Directory
Lewis, Nancy: (RES) 11 Fox, (CMTS) Albany 1815 City Directory
Lewis, Nathan: (CMTS) 1790 Federal Census, Watervliet
Lewis, Russel: (OC) Cooper, (CMTS) Albany 1815 City Directory
Lewis, Stewart: (RES) 8 S. Pearl, (CMTS) Albany 1815 City Directory
Lewis, William A.: (F) Member Temple Lodge, No. 14, 1900,
Albany, NY
Lexon, Class: (CMTS) 1790 Federal Census, Watervliet
Lieb, Johannes: (CMTS) 1790 Federal Census Rensselaerville
Lighhall, Nicholas: (OC) Blacksmith, (CMTS) Albany 1815 City
Directory
Lightbody, Andrew: (OC) Clerk, (CMTS) Albany 1815 City Directory
Lightbody, James: (RES) Schecectady Turnpike, (CMTS) Albany 1815
City Directory
Linacre, James: (OC) Cabinet Maker, (CMTS) Albany 1815 City
Directory
Linacre, Thomas: (OC) Cabinet Maker, (CMTS) Albany 1815 City
Directory
Lincoln, Joseph: (CMTS) 1790 Federal Census Rensselaerville
Lincoln, William: (F) Member Mount Vernon Lodge, No. 3, 1900,
Albany, NY
Linder, Nicholas C.: (F) Member Temple Lodge, No. 14, 1900,
Albany, NY
Lindsay, J. Hally: (F) Member Temple Lodge, No. 14, 1900,
Albany, NY

Ling, Daniel Joseph: (CMTS) 1790 Federal Census Rensselaerville
Lisbrow, Nathan: (RES) 34 Fox, (CMTS) Albany 1815 City Directory
Lister, Benjamin: (CMTS) 1790 Federal Census, Watervliet
Liswell, John: (CMTS) 1790 Federal Census, Watervliet
Liswell, John: (RES) 152 N. Market, (CMTS) Albany 1815 City Directory
Liswell, Widow Ann: (RES) 150 N. Market, (CMTS) Albany 1815 City Directory
Little, Stephen: (OC) Laborer, (CMTS) Albany 1815 City Directory
Littlefield, Henry C.: (F) Member Masters Lodge, No. 5, 1900, Albany, NY
Livingston, Johannes: (CMTS) 1790 Federal Census, Watervliet
Livingston, Moncrief: (CMTS) 1790 Federal Census, Watervliet
Livingston, Peter: (CMTS) 1790 Federal Census, Watervliet
Livingston, Robert: (CMTS) 1790 Federal Census Rensselaerville
Livingston, William: (CMTS) 1790 Federal Census, Watervliet
Lloyd, James: (OC) Merchant, (CMTS) Albany 1815 City Directory
Lloyd, William: (OC) Stage Driver, (CMTS) Albany 1815 City Directory
Lloyd, William L.: (F) Member Mount Vernon Lodge, No. 3, 1900, Albany, NY, (CMTS) Life Member
Loadman, Samuel: (CMTS) 1790 Federal Census, Watervliet
Lobdell, Isaac: (CMTS) 1790 Federal Census Rensselaerville
Lobdell, Stephen: (RES) 52 Church, (CMTS) Albany 1815 City Directory
Lochner, G. Emory: (F) Member Masters Lodge, No. 5, 1900, Albany, NY
Lochner, Jacob L.: (F) Member Mount Vernon Lodge, No. 3, 1900, Albany, NY
Lock, Charles O.: (F) Member Temple Lodge, No. 14, 1900, Albany, NY
Lock, James B.: (F) Member Mount Vernon Lodge, No. 3, 1900, Albany, NY
Lockery, Widow: (OC) Washing House, (CMTS) Albany 1815 City Directory
Lockrow, Charles: (OC) Shoemaker, (CMTS) Albany 1815 City Directory
Lockwood, Horace: (RES) 50 Lydius, (CMTS) Albany 1815 City Directory
Lockwood, Jared: (OC) Merchant, (CMTS) Albany 1815 City Directory
Lockwood, Millington: (OC) Tailor, (CMTS) Albany 1815 City Directory
Lockwood, Samuel S.: (RES) 21 Steuben, (CMTS) Albany 1815 City Directory
Lockwood, Solomon: (CMTS) 1790 Federal Census, Watervliet
Locy, Alexander: (OC) Shoemaker, (CMTS) Albany 1815 City Directory
Logan, Geoge: (F) Member Mount Vernon Lodge, No. 3, 1900, Albany, NY
Lomax, John: (F) Member Mount Vernon Lodge, No. 3, 1900, Albany, NY, (CMTS) Past Master 1870

Lomis, George J.: (OC) Bookbinder, (CMTS) Albany 1815 City Directory
Lommerce, Aaron: (CMTS) 1790 Federal Census, Watervliet
Long, Adam: (CMTS) 1790 Federal Census, Watervliet
Long, Leroy Y.: (F) Member Temple Lodge, No. 14, 1900,
    Albany, NY
Long, Moses: (OC) Printer, (CMTS) Albany 1815 City Directory
Longsdon, William: (OC) Laborer, (CMTS) Albany 1815 City Directory
Loom, Samuel: (OC) Sawyer, (CMTS) Albany 1815 City Directory
Loomis, George: (OC) Teacher, (CMTS) Albany 1815 City Directory
Loomis, Harvry: (OC) Saddler, (CMTS) Albany 1815 City Directory
Loran, Frank: (F) Member Temple Lodge, No. 14, 1900,
    Albany, NY
Lord, Eliphilet: (CMTS) 1790 Federal Census Rensselaerville
Lord, Nehemiah: (CMTS) 1790 Federal Census Rensselaerville
Lothridge, William E.: (F) Member Temple Lodge, No. 14, 1900,
    Albany, NY
Lottridge, Abraham: (OC) Tobacconist, (CMTS) Albany 1815 City
    Directory
Lottridge, Robert: (OC) Teamster, (CMTS) Albany 1815 City Directory
Loucks, Henry: (OC) Counsellor, (CMTS) Albany 1815 City Directory
Louden, John: (OC) Carpenter, (CMTS) Albany 1815 City Directory
Loughlan, Jorn: (OC) Brass Founder, (CMTS) Albany 1815 City
    Directory
Loughran, Francis: (OC) Grocer, (CMTS) Albany 1815 City Directory
Lovely, Libbey: (CEN) 1880 6th Ward, Albany, NY, (CMTS) Single, (A)
    18, (BP) NY, (OC) Dressmaker
Lovet, John: (OC) Representative to Congress, (CMTS) Albany 1815 City
    Directory
Low, Francis: (OC) Furnaceman, (CMTS) Albany 1815 City Directory
Low, James: (OC) Physician, (CMTS) Albany 1815 City Directory
Low, John: (OC) Shoemaker, (CMTS) Albany 1815 City Directory
Low, Thomas: (CMTS) 1790 Federal Census, Watervliet
Lownsberry, Nathan: (CMTS) 1790 Federal Census Rensselaerville
Lownsberry, Silvanus: (CMTS) 1790 Federal Census Rensselaerville
Lowry, James: (CMTS) 1790 Federal Census, Watervliet
Lowry, Robert: (OC) Grocer, (CMTS) Albany 1815 City Directory
Lucas, Isaac: (OC) Builder, (CMTS) Albany 1815 City Directory
Luce, Israel: (CMTS) 1790 Federal Census Rensselaerville
Luce, Vinal: (OC) Druggist, (CMTS) Albany 1815 City Directory
Luck, Edward: (RES) 111 N. Market St., (CMTS) Albany 1815 City
    Directory
Luck, William H.: (F) Member Mount Vernon Lodge, No. 3, 1900,
    Albany, NY
Lucky, James: (CMTS) 1790 Federal Census Rensselaerville
Lucky, William: (CMTS) 1790 Federal Census Rensselaerville

Lucy, James: (F) Member Temple Lodge, No. 14, 1900, Albany, NY
Luddington, Charles H.: (F) Member Masters Lodge, No. 5, 1900, Albany, NY
Luddington, James S.: (F) Member Temple Lodge, No. 14, 1900, Albany, NY
Ludlow, Joseph: (OC) Tailor, (CMTS) Albany 1815 City Directory
Ludlum, Richard T.: (F) Member Temple Lodge, No. 14, 1900, Albany, NY
Luke, Conradt: (CMTS) 1790 Federal Census, Watervliet
Luke, Jacob: (CMTS) 1790 Federal Census, Watervliet
Lumaree, James: (OC) Ship Carpenter, (CMTS) Albany 1815 City Directory
Lumbert, Ezra: (OC) Laborer, (CMTS) Albany 1815 City Directory
Lumley, John: (OC) Cartman, (CMTS) Albany 1815 City Directory
Lummeree, Daniel: (CMTS) 1790 Federal Census, Watervliet
Lummis, Lorey: (CMTS) 1790 Federal Census Rensselaerville
Lumsden, David: (OC) Grocer, (CMTS) Albany 1815 City Directory
Lush, John: (RES) 320 N. Market, (CMTS) Albany 1815 City Directory
Lush, Richard: (CMTS) Albany 1815 City Directory
Lush, Samuel S.: (OC) Counsellor, (CMTS) Albany 1815 City Directory
Lush, Stephen: (OC) Counsellor, (CMTS) Albany 1815 City Directory
Luther, Jermiah: (RES) Arbor hill, (CMTS) Albany 1815 City Directory
Luther, John: (CMTS) 1790 Federal Census, Watervliet
Luther, John: (RES) Arbor hill, (CMTS) Albany 1815 City Directory
Luther, Robert: (OC) Carpenter, (CMTS) Albany 1815 City Directory
Lutridge, Hannah: (CMTS) 1790 Federal Census, Watervliet
Luyster, Garret: (RES) Boarding House at 12 Van Tromp, (CMTS) Albany 1815 City Directory
Lyduis, Baltus: (RES) 104 N. Pearl, (CMTS) Albany 1815 City Directory
Lyker, Hendrick: (CMTS) 1790 Federal Census, Watervliet
Lyman, Charles R.: (OC) Artcher & Lyman, Flour, (CMTS) Albany 1859 City Directory
Lynch, Widow Margaret: (RES) Boarding House at 42 Chapel, (CMTS) Albany 1815 City Directory
Lynn, William: (OC) Grocer, (CMTS) Albany 1815 City Directory
Lyon, Aaron: (OC) Grocer, (CMTS) Albany 1815 City Directory
Lyon, John: (OC) Shoemaker, (CMTS) Albany 1815 City Directory
Lyons, David: (OC) Laborer, (CMTS) Albany 1815 City Directory
Lyons, Edward: (F) Member Mount Vernon Lodge, No. 3, 1900, Albany, NY
Lyons, Luke: (OC) Teacher, (CMTS) Albany 1815 City Directory
Lyons, Widow: (OC) Margaret, (CMTS) Albany 1815 City Directory
Mabbett, James: (OC) Merchant, (CMTS) Albany 1815 City Directory
MacAuly, John: (OC) Artist, (CMTS) Albany 1815 City Directory

MacDonald, George H.: (F) Member Temple Lodge, No. 14, 1900, Albany, NY
MacDonald, Pirie (sic): (F) Member Temple Lodge, No. 14, 1900, Albany, NY
MacFadgen, J. L.: (F) Member Temple Lodge, No. 14, 1900, Albany, NY
MacHarg, Martin: (F) Member Masters Lodge, No. 5, 1900, Albany, NY
Machet, James: (OC) Laborer, (CMTS) Albany 1815 City Directory
Mackey, Alexander: (CMTS) 1790 Federal Census Rensselaerville
Mackey, James: (OC) Carpenter, (CMTS) Albany 1815 City Directory
Mackey, Samuel J.: (F) Member Temple Lodge, No. 14, 1900, Albany, NY
Magoffin, John: (RES) 35 State, (CMTS) Albany 1815 City Directory
Maher, James: (RES) 21 Hamilton, (CMTS) Albany 1815 City Directory
Maher, John: (RES) 55 Hudson, (CMTS) Albany 1815 City Directory
Mahler, Jacob P.: (F) Member Temple Lodge, No. 14, 1900, Albany, NY
Malcom, Charles: (RES) 6 Fox, (CMTS) Albany 1815 City Directory
Malcomb, Anrew: (OC) Laborer, (CMTS) Albany 1815 City Directory
Mallary, David: (OC) Merchant, (CMTS) Albany 1815 City Directory
Mallery, Sheldon: (OC) Merchant, (CMTS) Albany 1815 City Directory
Mallet, Francis: (OC) Teacher of Music, (CMTS) Albany 1815 City Directory
Mancius, G. W.: (RES) 22 Montgomery St., (CMTS) Albany 1815 City Directory
Mandell, Ephraim: (OC) Attorney, (CMTS) Albany 1815 City Directory
Mandeville, Mathew: (OC) Crier, (CMTS) Albany 1815 City Directory
Mandeville, Robert P.: (F) Member Mount Vernon Lodge, No. 3, 1900, Albany, NY
Manicus, John: (RES) 316 N. Market, (CMTS) Albany 1815 City Directory
Mann, John: (CMTS) 1790 Federal Census, Watervliet
Mann, Joseph: (CMTS) 1790 Federal Census, Watervliet
Mann, Samuel: (CMTS) 1790 Federal Census Rensselaerville
Manning, Catharine: (OC) Millener, (CMTS) Albany 1815 City Directory
Manning, James H.: (F) Member Temple Lodge, No. 14, 1900, Albany, NY
Manning, Samuel W.: (F) Member Masters Lodge, No. 5, 1900, Albany, NY
Manning, William: (CMTS) 1790 Federal Census, Watervliet
Manning, William S.: (F) Member Masters Lodge, No. 5, 1900, Albany, NY
Mans, Jacob: (CMTS) 1790 Federal Census, Watervliet
Marcelis, Widow Alida: (RES) 48 Chapel, (CMTS) Albany 1815 City

Directory
March, Francis: (OC) Skipper, (CMTS) Albany 1815 City Directory
Marchell, Charles: (F) Member Masters Lodge, No. 5, 1900,
  Albany, NY
Mark, Isaac: (CMTS) 1790 Federal Census, Watervliet
Marseilus, John: (CMTS) 1790 Federal Census, Watervliet
Marsh, Enos: (CMTS) 1790 Federal Census Rensselaerville
Marsh, John B.: (F) Member Masters Lodge, No. 5, 1900,
  Albany, NY
Marsh, Joshua: (OC) Tailor, (CMTS) Albany 1815 City Directory
Marsh, Widow Hannah: (RES) 116 Fox, (CMTS) Albany 1815 City
  Directory
Marshal, Francis: (CMTS) 1790 Federal Census, Watervliet
Marshal, William: (OC) Shoemaker, (CMTS) Albany 1815 City Directory
Marshall, Benj.: (OC) Soda Water, (CMTS) Albany 1815 City Directory
Marshall, Robert: (CMTS) 1790 Federal Census Rensselaerville
Marshall, William: (CMTS) 1790 Federal Census Rensselaerville
Marston, Ephraim: (OC) Grocer, (CMTS) Albany 1815 City Directory
Martin, Abraham: (OC) Hatter, (CMTS) Albany 1815 City Directory
Martin, James: (OC) Bricklayer, (CMTS) Albany 1815 City Directory
Martin, James B.: (F) Member Mount Vernon Lodge, No. 3, 1900,
  Albany, NY
Martin, John: (CMTS) 1790 Federal Census, Watervliet
Martin, Medad: (OC) Carpenter, (CMTS) Albany 1815 City Directory
Martin, Samuel: (CMTS) 1790 Federal Census Rensselaerville
Martin, Widow Mary: (RES) 24 Union, (CMTS) Albany 1815 City
  Directory
Martin, William: (CMTS) 1790 Federal Census, Watervliet
Martin, William: (OC) Coach Maker, (CMTS) Albany 1815 City
  Directory
Martin, William L.: (F) Member Masters Lodge, No. 5, 1900,
  Albany, NY
Martin , Dadin: (OC) Carpenter, (CMTS) Albany 1815 City Directory
Marvin, John: (OC) Merchant, (CMTS) Albany 1815 City Directory
Marvin, Richard: (OC) Merchant, (CMTS) Albany 1815 City Directory
Marvin, Uriah: (OC) Merchant, (CMTS) Albany 1815 City Directory
Marvin, William: (OC) Merchant, (CMTS) Albany 1815 City Directory
Marvin, Wm.: (OC) Merchant, (CMTS) Albany 1815 City Directory
Marvin, Jr., Selden E.: (F) Member Masters Lodge, No. 5, 1900,
  Albany, NY
Marwill, Harris: (F) Member Temple Lodge, No. 14, 1900,
  Albany, NY
Mascraft, John: (OC) Wheelwright: (RES) 65 N. Market, (CMTS) Albany
  1815 City Directory
Mascraft, Wm.: (OC) Wheelright, (CMTS) Albany 1815 City Directory

Mason, Frank J.: (F) Member Temple Lodge, No. 14, 1900, Albany, NY
Mason, James: (CMTS) 1790 Federal Census, Watervliet
Masten, Edson W.: (F) Member Temple Lodge, No. 14, 1900, Albany, NY
Matcalf, Levi: (OC) Grocer, (CMTS) Albany 1815 City Directory
Matchcraft, John: (CMTS) 1790 Federal Census, Watervliet
Mather, Elias: (OC) Merchant, (CMTS) Albany 1815 City Directory
Matthews, Caleb: (OC) Laborer, (CMTS) Albany 1815 City Directory
Maurice, Thomas: (OC) Grocer, (CMTS) Albany 1815 City Directory
Maurice, Widow: (RES) 557 S. Market, (CMTS) Albany 1815 City Directory
Maxwell, James: (OC) Porterhouse, (CMTS) Albany 1815 City Directory
May, Anthony: (OC) Carpenter, (CMTS) Albany 1815 City Directory
Mayell, Ten Broeck: (F) Member Temple Lodge, No. 14, 1900, Albany, NY
Mayhew, Thomas: (OC) Grocer, (CMTS) Albany 1815 City Directory
Mc Hench, Peter: (OC) Carpenter, (CMTS) Albany 1815 City Directory
McAlvey, Daniel: (OC) Baker, (CMTS) Albany 1815 City Directory
McAvenue, Owen F.: (F) Member Temple Lodge, No. 14, 1900, Albany, NY
McCabe, Widow Hannah: (OC) Grocer, (CMTS) Albany 1815 City Directory
McCall, Henry S.: (F) Member Masters Lodge, No. 5, 1900, Albany, NY
McCalligan, Patrick: (CMTS) 1790 Federal Census, Watervliet
McCalvin, Daniel: (CMTS) 1790 Federal Census, Watervliet
McCammon, Enoch: (RES) 94 Hawl, (CMTS) Albany 1815 City Directory
McCarty, Alexander: (OC) Teamster, (CMTS) Albany 1815 City Directory
McCarty, David: (CMTS) 1790 Federal Census, Watervliet
McCarty, Jeremiah: (OC) Tailor, (CMTS) Albany 1815 City Directory
McCaughan, James B.: (F) Member Mount Vernon Lodge, No. 3, 1900, Albany, NY
McCauley, Robert J.: (F) Member Temple Lodge, No. 14, 1900, Albany, NY
McChesney, Joseph: (CMTS) 1790 Federal Census, Watervliet
McChestney, John: (OC) Carpenter, (CMTS) Albany 1815 City Directory
McClallen, Hugh: (OC) Gunsmith, (CMTS) Albany 1815 City Directory
McClallen, Robert: (RES) Boarding House at 32 Dock, (CMTS) Albany 1815 City Directory
McClellan, George W.: (F) Member Temple Lodge, No. 14, 1900, Albany, NY
McClinton, Ralph: (OC) Cartman, (CMTS) Albany 1815 City Directory

McClum, John: (OC) Laborer, (CMTS) Albany 1815 City Directory
McClure, James H.: (F) Member Masters Lodge, No. 5, 1900,
    Albany, NY
McCollister, Chester: (OC) Cartman, (CMTS) Albany 1815 City Directory
McCollister, William: (CMTS) 1790 Federal Census Rensselaerville
McCollough, William: (CMTS) 1790 Federal Census, Watervliet
McCollum, John: (OC) Grocer, (CMTS) Albany 1815 City Directory
McCollum, Randel: (OC) Grocer, (CMTS) Albany 1815 City Directory
McConly, John: (CMTS) 1790 Federal Census, Watervliet
McConnoly, Mrs. (OC) Millenier: (RES) 70 State, (CMTS) Albany 1815
    City Directory
McCoughtry, Jr., John: (CMTS) 1790 Federal Census, Watervliet
McCoughtry, Sr., John: (CMTS) 1790 Federal Census, Watervliet
McCoy, Widow: (RES) 17 S. Market, (CMTS) Albany 1815 City
    Directory
McCracket, Ellinor: (OC) Millener, (CMTS) Albany 1815 City Directory
McCreery, William: (OC) Stone Cutter, (CMTS) Albany 1815 City
    Directory
McCue, John: (OC) Cartman, (CMTS) Albany 1815 City Directory
McCullock, Hathorn: (OC) Brewer, (CMTS) Albany 1815 City Directory
McCullough, William: (CMTS) 1790 Federal Census Rensselaerville
McCumber, George A.: (F) Member Temple Lodge, No. 14, 1900,
    Albany, NY
McDole, Charles: (RES) 52 Liberty, (CMTS) Albany 1815 City Directory
McDole, George: (CMTS) 1790 Federal Census, Watervliet
McDole, Wiliam: (OC) Laborer, (CMTS) Albany 1815 City Directory
McDonald, Alton P.: (F) Member Temple Lodge, No. 14, 1900,
    Albany, NY
McDonald, Angus: (OC) Capt. O Chief, (CMTS) Albany 1815 City
    Directory
McDonald, D.: (OC) Hair Dresser, (CMTS) Albany 1815 City Directory
McDonald, Donald: (F) Member Masters Lodge, No. 5, 1900,
    Albany, NY
McDonald, Donald: (RES) 171 S. Pearl, (CMTS) Albany 1815 City
    Directory
McDonald, John: (CMTS) 1790 Federal Census, Watervliet
McDonald, John: (OC) Past Unit President, (CMTS) Albany 1815 City
    Directory
McDonald, William: (F) Member Temple Lodge, No. 14, 1900,
    Albany, NY
McDougall, William: (RES) 265 N. Market, (CMTS) Albany 1815 City
    Directory
McDowell, Robert P.: (F) Member Mount Vernon Lodge, No. 3, 1900,
    Albany, NY
McDowle, John: (RES) 52 Liberty, (CMTS) Albany 1815 City Directory

McElroy, James: (OC) Mason, (CMTS) Albany 1815 City Directory
McElroy, Samuel: (OC) Merchant, (CMTS) Albany 1815 City Directory
McEwan, Alex. M.: (F) Member Temple Lodge, No. 14, 1900,
    Albany, NY
McEwan, James B.: (F) Member Temple Lodge, No. 14, 1900,
    Albany, NY, (CMTS) Past Master 1892
McEwan, John P.: (F) Member Temple Lodge, No. 14, 1900,
    Albany, NY
McEwan, John S.: (F) Member Temple Lodge, No. 14, 1900,
    Albany, NY
McEwan, Walter: (F) Member Temple Lodge, No. 14, 1900,
    Albany, NY, (CMTS) Life Member
McEwan, Walter S.: (F) Member Temple Lodge, No. 14, 1900,
    Albany, NY
McEwan, William: (F) Member Temple Lodge, No. 14, 1900,
    Albany, NY, (CMTS) Life Member
McEwan, Jr., John S.: (F) Member Temple Lodge, No. 14, 1900,
    Albany, NY
McGee, James: (CMTS) 1790 Federal Census, Watervliet
McGee, John: (CMTS) 1790 Federal Census, Watervliet
McGill, William: (CMTS) 1790 Federal Census, Watervliet
McGillivray, Wm.: (RES) Accountant, (CMTS) Albany 1815 City
    Directory
McGlasban, Daniel: (OC) Grocer, (CMTS) Albany 1815 City Directory
McGlasban, Mrs: (RES) 51 Beaver, (CMTS) Albany 1815 City Directory
McGourky, Edward: (OC) Grocer, (CMTS) Albany 1815 City Directory
McGourky, John: (OC) Chocolate Maker, (CMTS) Albany 1815 City
    Directory
McGourky, Sally: (RES) 59 Orange, (CMTS) Albany 1815 City Directory
McGrath, Thomas: (OC) Cooper, (CMTS) Albany 1815 City Directory
McGrigger, Malcom: (CMTS) 1790 Federal Census, Watervliet
McGuyre, John: (OC) Morocco Dresser, (CMTS) Albany 1815 City
    Directory
McHaffle, Robert: (F) Member Temple Lodge, No. 14, 1900,
    Albany, NY
McHarg, Widow Grissel: (RES) 429 S. Market, (CMTS) Albany 1815
    City Directory
McHarg, Widow Janet: (OC) Grocer, (CMTS) Albany 1815 City
    Directory
McHarg, William: (OC) Merchant, (CMTS) Albany 1815 City Directory
McIntosh, Abigail: (CMTS) 1790 Federal Census, Watervliet
McIntosh, Alexander: (CMTS) 1790 Federal Census, Watervliet
McIntosh, John: (CMTS) 1790 Federal Census, Watervliet
McIntosh, Matthias: (CMTS) 1790 Federal Census Rensselaerville
McIntosh, Peter: (OC) Merchant, (CMTS) Albany 1815 City Directory

McIntosh, Robert: (OC) Carpenter, (CMTS) Albany 1815 City Directory
McIntosh, William: (OC) Sawyer, (CMTS) Albany 1815 City Directory
McIntyre, Archibald: (F) Member Temple Lodge, No. 14, 1900, Albany, NY
McIntyre, Charles A.: (F) Member Temple Lodge, No. 14, 1900, Albany, NY
McIntyre, Peter C.: (F) Member Temple Lodge, No. 14, 1900, Albany, NY
McIntyre, Thomas: (OC) Chair Maker, (CMTS) Albany 1815 City Directory
McKargh, Peter: (CMTS) 1790 Federal Census, Watervliet
McKay, Alexander: (OC) Constable, (CMTS) Albany 1815 City Directory
McKercher, Duncan: (OC) Grocer, (CMTS) Albany 1815 City Directory
McKilvey, John: (OC) Baker, (CMTS) Albany 1815 City Directory
McKin, James: (CMTS) 1790 Federal Census, Watervliet
McKinsey, James: (CMTS) 1790 Federal Census, Watervliet
McKnight, Wm. G.: (F) Member Temple Lodge, No. 14, 1900, Albany, NY, (CMTS) Past Master 1872
McKnower, Thomas: (OC) Flour Store, (CMTS) Albany 1815 City Directory
McKonney, Robert: (CMTS) 1790 Federal Census, Watervliet
McKoy, John: (CMTS) 1790 Federal Census, Watervliet
McLachlan, D.: (OC) Flour Store, (CMTS) Albany 1815 City Directory
McLachlan, John: (OC) Flour Store, (CMTS) Albany 1815 City Directory
McLean, F. St. George: (F) Member Masters Lodge, No. 5, 1900, Albany, NY
McLean, Hugh B.: (F) Member Masters Lodge, No. 5, 1900, Albany, NY
McLeod, Alexander: (OC) Shoemaker, (CMTS) Albany 1815 City Directory
McLeod, Alexander: (OC) Shoemaker, (CMTS) Albany 1815 City Directory
McMichael, Hester: (RES) 1 Chapel, (CMTS) Albany 1815 City Directory
McMickin, John: (RES) Boarding House at 84 N. Pearl, (CMTS) Albany 1815 City Directory
McMillan, John: (OC) Flour Merchant, (CMTS) Albany 1815 City Directory
McMontry, John: (CMTS) 1790 Federal Census Rensselaerville
McMullen, Andrew: (OC) Merchant, (CMTS) Albany 1815 City Directory
McMullen, James: (CMTS) 1790 Federal Census, Watervliet
McMullen, James: (OC) Grocer, (CMTS) Albany 1815 City Directory
McMullen, John: (CMTS) 1790 Federal Census, Watervliet
McMullen, Lawrence: (OC) Laborer, (CMTS) Albany 1815 City Directory
McMullen, Peter: (CMTS) 1790 Federal Census, Watervliet

McMullen, William: (OC) Mason, (CMTS) Albany 1815 City Directory
McMurray, James: (OC) Bricklayer, (CMTS) Albany 1815 City Directory
McNab, Archibald: (OC) Grocer, (CMTS) Albany 1815 City Directory
McNally, Robert: (OC) Grocer, (CMTS) Albany 1815 City Directory
McNelly, John: (OC) Laborer, (CMTS) Albany 1815 City Directory
McNevin, Duncan: (OC) Laborer, (CMTS) Albany 1815 City Directory
McNiven, Thomas: (OC) Stone Cutter, (CMTS) Albany 1815 City Directory
McPherson, George: (OC) Merchant, (CMTS) Albany 1815 City Directory
McPherson, John: (RES) 27 Chapel, (CMTS) Albany 1815 City Directory
McPherson, Widow Janet: (RES) 51 Beaver, (CMTS) Albany 1815 City Directory
McPherson, William: (OC) Grocer, (CMTS) Albany 1815 City Directory
McQuade, Paul: (OC) Pastor of St. Mary's church, (CMTS) Albany 1815 City Directory
McTavish, Alexander: (RES) 38 N. Pearl, (CMTS) Albany 1815 City Directory
McWilliams, Janes: (CMTS) 1790 Federal Census Rensselaerville
Meacham, H.: (OC) Musical Instrument Maker, (CMTS) Albany 1815 City Directory
Meacham, J.: (OC) Musical Instrument Makers, (CMTS) Albany 1815 City Directory
Meacham, John: (OC) Lodge, (CMTS) Albany 1815 City Directory
Meacham, L.:D.: (RES) 19 N. Pearl, (CMTS) Albany 1815 City Directory
Meachum, David: (CMTS) 1790 Federal Census, Watervliet
Mead, Charles W.: (F) Member Temple Lodge, No. 14, 1900, Albany, NY, (CMTS) Past Master 1886
Mead, Charles W.: (F) Member Temple Lodge, No. 14, 1900, Albany, NY, (CMTS) Life Member
Mead, Eugene: (F) Member Temple Lodge, No. 14, 1900, Albany, NY
Mead, Jeremiah: (CMTS) 1790 Federal Census, Watervliet
Mead, Selick: (OC) Shoemaker, (CMTS) Albany 1815 City Directory
Meadon, John: (OC) Rope Maker, (CMTS) Albany 1815 City Directory
Meadon, William: (OC) Grocer, (CMTS) Albany 1815 City Directory
Meads, Jno: (OC) Cabinet Maker, (CMTS) Albany 1815 City Directory
Mealy, William: (OC) Innkeeper, (CMTS) Albany 1815 City Directory
Megree, Andrew: (RES) 108 Beaver, (CMTS) Albany 1815 City Directory
Meigs, John: (OC) Constable, (CMTS) Albany 1815 City Directory
Meigs, Richard M: (OC) Druggist, (CMTS) Albany 1815 City Directory
Melich, David: (RES) 175 S. Pearl, (CMTS) Albany 1815 City Directory
Melick, James H.: (F) Member Temple Lodge, No. 14, 1900, Albany, NY

Melville, Allen: (RES) 316 N. Market, (CMTS) Albany 1815 City Directory
Melville, Andrew: (OC) Paver, (CMTS) Albany 1815 City Directory
Memyer, Henry: (CMTS) 1790 Federal Census Rensselaerville
Merchant, Heratio: (OC) Justice of the Peace, (CMTS) Albany 1815 City Directory
Merchant, George: (OC) County Clerk, (CMTS) Albany 1815 City Directory
Merchant, S.: (RES) 12 Washington, (CMTS) Albany 1815 City Directory
Merchant, Samuel L: (RES) 59 Washington, (CMTS) Albany 1815 City Directory
Merchant, Stephen: (OC) Merchant, (CMTS) Albany 1815 City Directory
Merkle, John: (CMTS) 1790 Federal Census, Watervliet
Merkle, Matthew: (CMTS) 1790 Federal Census, Watervliet
Merridy, Hillida: (CMTS) 1790 Federal Census, Watervliet
Merrihew, Rufus: (F) Member Mount Vernon Lodge, No. 3, 1900, Albany, NY
Merrill, Cyrus S.: (F) Member Masters Lodge, No. 5, 1900, Albany, NY
Merrit, Ebenezer: (RES) 57 N. Pearl, (CMTS) Albany 1815 City Directory
Merritt, Charles: (CMTS) 1790 Federal Census Rensselaerville
Merryfield, Mary: (OC) Grocer, (CMTS) Albany 1815 City Directory
Merryfield, Richard: (OC) Shoemaker, (CMTS) Albany 1815 City Directory
Merryfield, Richard: (MD) Nov. 3, 1810, (Spouse) Sally Van Hoesen, (PMD) First Dutch Reformed Church, Albany, NY
Merseilus, Andrew: (CMTS) 1790 Federal Census, Watervliet
Merseilus, Garrit: (CMTS) 1790 Federal Census, Watervliet
Mesick, Charles E.: (F) Member Mount Vernon Lodge, No. 3, 1900, Albany, NY
Metcalf, Edward B.: (F) Member Temple Lodge, No. 14, 1900, Albany, NY
Meyer, John: (F) Member Mount Vernon Lodge, No. 3, 1900, Albany, NY
Meyer, Oscar A.: (F) Member Temple Lodge, No. 14, 1900, Albany, NY
Michael, Anthony M.: (F) Member Mount Vernon Lodge, No. 3, 1900, Albany, NY
Michaelis, Gustavus: (F) Member Masters Lodge, No. 5, 1900, Albany, NY
Mickel, Augustus: (F) Member Temple Lodge, No. 14, 1900, Albany, NY
Miel, Charles: (CMTS) 1790 Federal Census Rensselaerville
Miligan, James: (OC) Grocer, (CMTS) Albany 1815 City Directory
Miller, Albert T.: (F) Member Temple Lodge, No. 14, 1900,

Albany, NY
Miller, Christian: (OC) Merchant, (CMTS) Albany 1815 City Directory
Miller, Christian: (MD) Jun. 25, 1791, (Spouse) Martie Van Schiac, (PM) Reformed Dutch Church, Albany, NY
Miller, Conradt: (CMTS) 1790 Federal Census Rensselaerville
Miller, Ernest L.: (F) Member Masters Lodge, No. 5, 1900, Albany, NY
Miller, Frederick: (CMTS) 1790 Federal Census, Watervliet
Miller, Frederick, (D) Oct. 24, 1881, (PD) Watervliet, (PRTS) Nicholas Miller and Elizabeth Dampf
Miller, Harry S.: (F) Member Masters Lodge, No. 5, 1900, Albany, NY
Miller, Hendrick: (CMTS) 1790 Federal Census Rensselaerville
Miller, Jacob: (CMTS) 1790 Federal Census, Watervliet
Miller, Jacob: (CMTS) 1790 Federal Census Rensselaerville
Miller, Jacob P.: (OC) Cooper, (CMTS) Albany 1815 City Directory
Miller, Jno.: (OC) Tin Plate Worker, (CMTS) Albany 1815 City Directory
Miller, John: (RES) 5 W. bank of river, (CMTS) Albany 1815 City Directory
Miller, John H.: (F) Member Temple Lodge, No. 14, 1900, Albany, NY
Miller, Lyman E.: (F) Member Mount Vernon Lodge, No. 3, 1900, Albany, NY
Miller, Nathaniel: (RES) 40 Fox, (CMTS) Albany 1815 City Directory
Miller, Pelegg R: (OC) Printer, (CMTS) Albany 1815 City Directory
Miller, Philip: (OC) Mason, (CMTS) Albany 1815 City Directory
Miller, Philips: (RES) 28 Orange, (CMTS) Albany 1815 City Directory
Miller, Samuel: (CMTS) 1790 Federal Census, Watervliet
Miller, Wiliam: (OC) Laborer, (CMTS) Albany 1815 City Directory
Miller, William C.: (F) Member Masters Lodge, No. 5, 1900, Albany, NY
Milliman, Frank: (F) Member Temple Lodge, No. 14, 1900, Albany, NY
Mills, Charles H.: (F) Member Temple Lodge, No. 14, 1900, Albany, NY
Mills, Rufus: (RES) Boarding House at 61 Washington, (CMTS) Albany 1815 City Directory
Mills, Samuel: (CMTS) 1790 Federal Census, Watervliet
Milton, George: (OC) Mason, (CMTS) Albany 1815 City Directory
Milton, Henry: (OC) Laborer, (CMTS) Albany 1815 City Directory
Milton, William: (CMTS) 1790 Federal Census, Watervliet
Milven, Andrew: (OC) Laborer, (CMTS) Albany 1815 City Directory
Minckler, Isaiah: (CMTS) 1790 Federal Census, Watervliet
Minderse, Barent: (CMTS) 1790 Federal Census, Watervliet
Mindersee, Frederick: (CMTS) 1790 Federal Census, Watervliet

Mindersen, Nicholas V.: (CMTS) 1790 Federal Census Rensselaerville
Mingo, Peter: (OC) Waterman, (CMTS) Albany 1815 City Directory
Minor, Epariam: (RES) 11 Hamilton, (CMTS) Albany 1815 City Directory
Minor, Noyes: (OC), (CMTS) Albany 1815 City Directory
Minthine, John: (OC) Skinner, (CMTS) Albany 1815 City Directory
Mitchell, James: (RES) Boarding House at 60 Hudson, (CMTS) Albany 1815 City Directory
Mix, Frederick L.: (F) Member Temple Lodge, No. 14, 1900, Albany, NY, (CMTS) Life Member
Moak, Jon M.: (F) Member Temple Lodge, No. 14, 1900, Albany, NY
Moakley, Peter: (OC) Sail Maker, (CMTS) Albany 1815 City Directory
Moke, Christian: (CMTS) 1790 Federal Census, Watervliet
Moke, Francis: (CMTS) 1790 Federal Census, Watervliet
Moke, Henry: (CMTS) 1790 Federal Census, Watervliet
Moke, Jacob: (CMTS) 1790 Federal Census, Watervliet
Moke, John: (CMTS) 1790 Federal Census, Watervliet
Moll, Jacobus: (CMTS) 1790 Federal Census, Watervliet
Monchus, Thomas: (CMTS) 1790 Federal Census, Watervliet
Monk, Christopher: (CMTS) 1790 Federal Census, Watervliet
Monk, Christopher: (OC) Cartman, (CMTS) Albany 1815 City Directory
Monk, William: (CMTS) 1790 Federal Census, Watervliet
Monsion, Lewis: (OC) Confectioner, (CMTS) Albany 1815 City Directory
Montague, William: (OC) Blacksmith, (CMTS) Albany 1815 City Directory
Monteith, George: (OC) Skipper, (CMTS) Albany 1815 City Directory
Moody, Adonijah: (OC) Innkeeper, (CMTS) Albany 1815 City Directory
Moore, James: (OC) Cartman, (CMTS) Albany 1815 City Directory
Moore, James: (OC) Innkeeper, (CMTS) Albany 1815 City Directory
Moore, James N.: (F) Member Masters Lodge, No. 5, 1900, Albany, NY
Moore, John: (OC) Cartman, (CMTS) Albany 1815 City Directory
Moore, Richard: (OC) Grocer, (CMTS) Albany 1815 City Directory
Moore, Thomas: (OC) Slater, (CMTS) Albany 1815 City Directory
Moore, Timothy: (CMTS) 1790 Federal Census Rensselaerville
Moore, William: (OC) Mason, (CMTS) Albany 1815 City Directory
Moorehead, John: (F) Member Temple Lodge, No. 14, 1900, Albany, NY
Morange, J. W.: (F) Member Masters Lodge, No. 5, 1900, Albany, NY
Morange, Lewis: (OC) Upholsterer, (CMTS) Albany 1815 City Directory
Morange, Peter M.: (OC) Pianoware Room, (CMTS) Albany 1859 City Directory
Moredock, Elisha: (CMTS) 1790 Federal Census Rensselaerville

Morgan, Charles A.: (F) Member Masters Lodge, No. 5, 1900,
   Albany, NY
Morgan, Francis: (RES) 13 Maiden Lane, (CMTS) Albany 1815 City
   Directory
Morgan, James: (CMTS) 1790 Federal Census Rensselaerville
Morgan, Jeremiah: (RES) 41 Hudson, (CMTS) Albany 1815 City
   Directory
Morgan, Thomas: (OC) Employer of laborers, (CMTS) Albany 1815 City
   Directory
Morgan, W. S.: (F) Member Mount Vernon Lodge, No. 3, 1900,
   Albany, NY
Morre, Ira: (OC) Laborer, (CMTS) Albany 1815 City Directory
Morrel, Widow Cornelia: (RES) 21 Chapel, (CMTS) Albany 1815 City
   Directory
Morrell, Jonathan: (OC) Cooper, (CMTS) Albany 1815 City Directory
Morrell, Samuel: (CMTS) 1790 Federal Census, Watervliet
Morrill, John R.: (F) Member Temple Lodge, No. 14, 1900,
   Albany, NY
Morris, Isaiah: (CMTS) 1790 Federal Census Rensselaerville
Morris, Joseph: (OC) Tobaconist, (CMTS) Albany 1815 City Directory
Morris, Richard: (OC) Laborer, (CMTS) Albany 1815 City Directory
Morris, Widow Rachael: (RES) 31 Sand, (CMTS) Albany 1815 City
   Directory
Morrison, Connel: (OC) Laborer, (CMTS) Albany 1815 City Directory
Morrow, Jacob: (OC) Shoemaker, (CMTS) Albany 1815 City Directory
Morrow, Robert: (OC) Grocer, (CMTS) Albany 1815 City Directory
Morse, Ebenezer: (OC) Grocer, (CMTS) Albany 1815 City Directory
Morse, Noah: (OC) Painter, (CMTS) Albany 1815 City Directory
Moseley, Frank E.: (F) Member Temple Lodge, No. 14, 1900,
   Albany, NY
Mosier, Stephen: (CMTS) 1790 Federal Census, Watervliet
Mosser, Ebenezer: (RES) 45 Church, (CMTS) Albany 1815 City
   Directory
Moston, George T.: (F) Member Temple Lodge, No. 14, 1900,
   Albany, NY
Mott, Athanias: (OC) Shoemaker, (CMTS) Albany 1815 City Directory
Mott, James: (OC) Carpenter, (CMTS) Albany 1815 City Directory
Moulton, Josiah: (RES) Boarding House at 4 Maiden Lane, (CMTS)
   Albany 1815 City Directory
Mounsey, Thomas: (OC) Tanner, (CMTS) Albany 1815 City Directory
Mowers, Philip: (OC) Laborer, (CMTS) Albany 1815 City Directory
Mudge, Aaron: (CMTS) 1790 Federal Census Rensselaerville
Mudge, Daniel: (CMTS) 1790 Federal Census Rensselaerville
Mudge, David: (CMTS) 1790 Federal Census Rensselaerville
Mudge, Joseph: (CMTS) 1790 Federal Census Rensselaerville

Muer, Jr., Peter: (CMTS) 1790 Federal Census, Watervliet
Muer, William: (CMTS) 1790 Federal Census, Watervliet
Muer, Jr., William: (CMTS) 1790 Federal Census, Watervliet
Mull, Abram M.: (F) Member Washington Lodge, No. 85, 1900, Albany, NY, (CMTS) Past Members
Mull, Leonard M.: (F) Member Washington Lodge, No. 85, 1900, Albany, NY, (CMTS) Past Members
Muller, Nicholas: (B) Nov. 23, 1768, (DP) Watervliet, (Spouse) Elizabeth Dampf, (MD) Feb. 28, 1796.
Multon, William: (CMTS) 1790 Federal Census, Watervliet
Mulwan, Thomas: (CMTS) 1790 Federal Census, Watervliet
Munger, Curtis: (OC) Innkeeper, (CMTS) Albany 1815 City Directory
Munson, George S.: (F) Member Masters Lodge, No. 5, 1900, Albany, NY
Munson, Samuel L.: (F) Member Masters Lodge, No. 5, 1900, Albany, NY
Murdoch, Ebenezer: (OC) Grocer, (CMTS) Albany 1815 City Directory
Murdock, Ariel: (CMTS) 1790 Federal Census Rensselaerville
Murdock, Ariel: (MD) Jan. 8, 1783, (PMD) Lebanon, New London, CT, (PD) Rensselaerville, Albany, NY, (Spouse) Eunice Murdock (GPRTS) Amas Murdock and Sybil Flint, (BPTS) William Murdock and Mary Pierce
Murdock, Clarissa: (B) Sep. 17, 1801, (BP) Rensselaerville, Albany, (PRTS) Ariel and Eunice Murdock
Murdock, Eliphalet: (B) Nov. 28, 1796, (BP) Rensselaerville, Albany, (PRTS) Ariel and Eunice Murdock
Murdock, Gurdon S.: (B) Aug. 4, 1799, (BP) Rensselaerville, Albany, (PRTS) Ariel and Eunice Murdock
Murdock, Irvine: (B) Mar. 1, 1797, (BP) Rensselaerville, Albany, (PRTS) Ariel and Eunice Murdock
Murdock, Newell Flint: (B) Jul. 24, 1792, (BP) Rensselaerville, Albany, (PRTS) Ariel and Eunice Murdock
Murdock, Polly: (B) Jul. 17, 1790, (BP) Rensselaerville, Albany, (PRTS) Ariel and Eunice Murdock
Murdock, Sally: (B) Aug. 7, 1768, (BP) Rensselaerville, Albany, (PRTS) Ariel and Eunice Murdock
Murdock, Zera: (OC) Grocer, (CMTS) Albany 1815 City Directory
Murphy, James B.: (F) Member Mount Vernon Lodge, No. 3, 1900, Albany, NY
Murphy, Martin: (RES) 7 Capital, (CMTS) Albany 1815 City Directory
Murphy, Patrick: (CMTS) 1790 Federal Census, Watervliet
Murphy, Thomas S.: (F) Member Temple Lodge, No. 14, 1900, Albany, NY
Murray, James: (OC) Cartman, (CMTS) Albany 1815 City Directory
Murray, John: (CMTS) 1790 Federal Census, Watervliet

Murray, John: (OC) Grocer, (CMTS) Albany 1815 City Directory
Murray, Mrs: (OC) Teacher, (CMTS) Albany 1815 City Directory
Murray, William: (OC) Grocer, (CMTS) Albany 1815 City Directory
Murray, William: (OC) Mason, (CMTS) Albany 1815 City Directory
Mutari, Rosario: (F) Member Mount Vernon Lodge, No. 3, 1900,
 Albany, NY
Mutter, Philip: (CMTS) 1790 Federal Census, Watervliet
Muudock, Ebenezer: (OC) Grocer, (CMTS) Albany 1815 City Directory
Myers, Andrew: (CMTS) 1790 Federal Census, Watervliet
Myers, Christiana: (RES) 39 Fox, (CMTS) Albany 1815 City Directory
Myers, Ephraim: (CMTS) 1790 Federal Census, Watervliet
Myers, John: (OC) Teamster, (CMTS) Albany 1815 City Directory
Myers, Philip: (CMTS) 1790 Federal Census, Watervliet
Myers, Philip: (CMTS) 1790 Federal Census Rensselaerville
Myers, Stephen: (OC) Ferryman, (CMTS) Albany 1815 City Directory
Myers, Jr., John: (F) Member Mount Vernon Lodge, No. 3, 1900,
 Albany, NY
Mynderse, William: (OC) Mason, (CMTS) Albany 1815 City Directory
Naegeley, Jr., John: (F) Member Mount Vernon Lodge, No. 3, 1900,
 Albany, NY
Naler, Widow Dorothy: (RES) 40 Chapel, (CMTS) Albany 1815 City
 Directory
Needham, George J.: (F) Member Temple Lodge, No. 14, 1900,
 Albany, NY
Nehemiah, Charles H.: (OC) Culler, (CMTS) Albany 1815 City Directory
Nehemiah, John C: (OC) Glover, (CMTS) Albany 1815 City Directory
Neill, William: (OC) Pastor of Presbyterian Church, (CMTS) Albany 1815
 City Directory
Neilliger, John: (OC) Mason, (CMTS) Albany 1815 City Directory
Nelliger, Joheph: (OC) Cartman, (CMTS) Albany 1815 City Directory
Nellis, William J.: (F) Member Masters Lodge, No. 5, 1900,
 Albany, NY
Neson, Henry S.: (F) Member Temple Lodge, No. 14, 1900,
 Albany, NY
Nestler, George: (CMTS) 1790 Federal Census, Watervliet
Nestley, Christian: (CMTS) 1790 Federal Census, Watervliet
Neudorf, Jr., Frederick: (F) Member Masters Lodge, No. 5, 1900,
 Albany, NY
Nevin, Alexander: (OC) Patroon, (CMTS) Albany 1815 City Directory
Newcomb, Grant: (F) Member Washington Lodge, No. 85, 1900,
 Albany, NY, (CMTS) Past Members
Newell, John: (F) Member Temple Lodge, No. 14, 1900,
 Albany, NY
Newell, William: (OC) Constable, (CMTS) Albany 1815 City Directory
Newell, Ziba: (OC) Shoemaker, (CMTS) Albany 1815 City Directory

Newland, David: (OC) ner, (CMTS) Albany 1815 City Directory
Newman, Charles: (F) Member Masters Lodge, No. 5, 1900, Albany, NY
Newman, Frederick W.: (F) Member Temple Lodge, No. 14, 1900, Albany, NY
Newman, Henry: (OC) Leather Dresser, (CMTS) Albany 1815 City Directory
Newman, Lewis: (OC) Mason, (CMTS) Albany 1815 City Directory
Newton, Aaron L.: (F) Member Temple Lodge, No. 14, 1900, Albany, NY
Newton, Henry A.: (F) Member Temple Lodge, No. 14, 1900, Albany, NY
Newton, Thomas C.: (F) Member Temple Lodge, No. 14, 1900, Albany, NY
Newton, D. (OC) Grocer, (CMTS) Albany 1815 City Directory
Newton, W. (OC) Grocer, (CMTS) Albany 1815 City Directory
Newton, Walter M.: (F) Member Masters Lodge, No. 5, 1900, Albany, NY
Newton, Widow Ellis: (RES) 32 Union, (CMTS) Albany 1815 City Directory
Nicholls, Samuel: (CMTS) 1790 Federal Census Rensselaerville
Nichols, Francis: (CMTS) 1790 Federal Census, Watervliet
Nichols, John: (CMTS) 1790 Federal Census Rensselaerville
Nielson, Bloomy: (CMTS) 1790 Federal Census, Watervliet
Niles, Nathaniel: (RES) 275 Washington, (CMTS) Albany 1815 City Directory
Nimo, Charles: (OC) Baker, (CMTS) Albany 1815 City Directory
Noble, Edward B.: (F) Member Temple Lodge, No. 14, 1900, Albany, NY
Noble, Francis: (OC) Mason, (CMTS) Albany 1815 City Directory
Noble, Hezekiah: (CMTS) 1790 Federal Census, Watervliet
Noble, James E.: (F) Member Temple Lodge, No. 14, 1900, Albany, NY
Norris, Jacob: (OC) Turner, (CMTS) Albany 1815 City Directory
Norris, John: (OC) Shoemaker, (CMTS) Albany 1815 City Directory
Norris, Samuel: (CMTS) 1790 Federal Census, Watervliet
Northrop, Millington E.: (F) Member Temple Lodge, No. 14, 1900, Albany, NY
Norton, Charles: (CMTS) 1790 Federal Census Rensselaerville
Norton, Samuel: (OC) Mason, (CMTS) Albany 1815 City Directory
Norton, Thomas: (RES) Mansion of late Gen. Schuyler, (CMTS) Albany 1815 City Directory
Nortrip, Cornel: (CMTS) 1790 Federal Census, Watervliet
Noye, James: (CMTS) 1790 Federal Census, Watervliet
Noyes, Aaron: (OC) Shoemaker, (CMTS) Albany 1815 City Directory

Nugent, John: (OC) Young Ladies' Seminary, (CMTS) Albany 1815 City Directory
Nutt, James: (OC) Blacksmith, (CMTS) Albany 1815 City Directory
Nye, Ichabod: (OC) Butcher, (CMTS) Albany 1815 City Directory
Oake, Abraham: (OC) Surveyor, (CMTS) Albany 1815 City Directory
Oake, Jacob: (OC) Shoemaker, (CMTS) Albany 1815 City Directory
Oakley, Benjamin: (OC) Shoemaker, (CMTS) Albany 1815 City Directory
Oaks, Charles J.: (F) Member Masters Lodge, No. 5, 1900, Albany, NY
Oaky, John: (OC) Shoemaker, (CMTS) Albany 1815 City Directory
O'Brien, Lewis: (OC) Laborer, (CMTS) Albany 1815 City Directory
O'Brien, Lodowick: (CMTS) 1790 Federal Census, Watervliet
O'Conner, Bernard: (OC) Grocer, (CMTS) Albany 1815 City Directory
O'Conner, Thomas: (OC) Cartman, (CMTS) Albany 1815 City Directory
O'Donnald, Terrence: (CMTS) 1790 Federal Census, Watervliet
Ogden, John: (OC) Shoemaker, (CMTS) Albany 1815 City Directory
Ogden, Nathaniel: (CMTS) 1790 Federal Census, Watervliet
Ogden, Widow Phebe: (OC), (CMTS) Albany 1815 City Directory
Ogsburry, David: (CMTS) 1790 Federal Census, Watervliet
Olds, George D.: (F) Member Masters Lodge, No. 5, 1900, Albany, NY
Oliver, Arie: (CMTS) 1790 Federal Census, Watervliet
Oliver, Benjamin: (OC) Stone Cutter, (CMTS) Albany 1815 City Directory
Oliver, George E.: (F) Member Mount Vernon Lodge, No. 3, 1900, Albany, NY
Oliver, Jacobus: (CMTS) 1790 Federal Census, Watervliet
Oliver, John: (CMTS) 1790 Federal Census, Watervliet
Oliver, John: (CMTS) 1790 Federal Census, Watervliet
Oliver, Robert: (OC) Stone Cutter, (CMTS) Albany 1815 City Directory
Oliver, Jr., John: (CMTS) 1790 Federal Census, Watervliet
Olmstead, Jr., Daniel: (OC) Merchant, (CMTS) Albany 1815 City Directory
Olmstead, David: (OC) City Superintendent, (CMTS) Albany 1815 City Directory
Olmsted, Betsy: (RES) rear of 181 S. Pearl, (CMTS) Albany 1815 City Directory
Olney, Christopher: (OC) Wheelwright, (CMTS) Albany 1815 City Directory
Onderkirk, Abraham: (CMTS) 1790 Federal Census, Watervliet
Onderkirk, Andrew: (CMTS) 1790 Federal Census, Watervliet
Onderkirk, Cornelius: (CMTS) 1790 Federal Census, Watervliet
Onderkirk, Jacob: (CMTS) 1790 Federal Census, Watervliet
Onderkirk, John: (CMTS) 1790 Federal Census, Watervliet
Onderkirk, John: (CMTS) 1790 Federal Census, Watervliet

Onderkirk, Magdaline: (CMTS) 1790 Federal Census, Watervliet
Onderkirk, Mendirt: (CMTS) 1790 Federal Census, Watervliet
Onderkirk, Peter P.: (CMTS) 1790 Federal Census, Watervliet
Onderkirk, Petrus: (CMTS) 1790 Federal Census, Watervliet
Onger, Frederick: (CMTS) 1790 Federal Census, Watervliet
Oothout, Evert: (CMTS) 1790 Federal Census, Watervliet
Oothout, Hendrick: (CMTS) 1790 Federal Census, Watervliet
Oothout, Henry A.: (RES) 247 N. Market, (CMTS) Albany 1815 City
    Directory
Oothout, Volkert: (CMTS) 1790 Federal Census, Watervliet
Opie, Richard: (F) Member Mount Vernon Lodge, No. 3, 1900,
    Albany, NY
Oppenheim, Wm. L.: (F) Member Mount Vernon Lodge, No. 3, 1900,
    Albany, NY
Orcut, John: (OC) Grocer, (CMTS) Albany 1815 City Directory
O'Rielly, Patrick: (RES) 113 Fox, (CMTS) Albany 1815 City Directory
Orlop, Frederick: (CMTS) 1790 Federal Census, Watervliet
Orlop, Hendrick: (CMTS) 1790 Federal Census, Watervliet
Orlop, William: (CMTS) 1790 Federal Census, Watervliet
Ornhout, Christian: (CMTS) 1790 Federal Census, Watervliet
Ornhout, John: (CMTS) 1790 Federal Census, Watervliet
Oroke, Manly: (OC) Tailor, (CMTS) Albany 1815 City Directory
Osterhout, Hendrick: (CMTS) 1790 Federal Census, Watervliet
Osterhout, John: (CMTS) 1790 Federal Census, Watervliet
Ostrander, Benjamin: (OC) Cabinet Maker, (CMTS) Albany 1815 City
    Directory
Ostrander, Hendrick: (CMTS) 1790 Federal Census, Watervliet
Ostrander, John: (CMTS) 1790 Federal Census, Watervliet
Ostrander, John I.: (OC) Exam in Chancery, (CMTS) Albany 1815 City
    Directory
Ostrom, Dinah: (CMTS) 1790 Federal Census, Watervliet
Ostrom, Henry: (CMTS) 1790 Federal Census, Watervliet
Otefield, Henry: (OC) Ferryman, (CMTS) Albany 1815 City Directory
Ousterhout, Wilhelmus: (CMTS) 1790 Federal Census, Watervliet
Owens, Abraham L.: (F) Member Temple Lodge, No. 14, 1900,
    Albany, NY
Owens, John: (CMTS) 1790 Federal Census Rensselaerville
Owens, Owen: (OC) Baker, (CMTS) Albany 1815 City Directory
Ox, Melchor: (CMTS) 1790 Federal Census Rensselaerville
Ozbart, Joseph: (CMTS) 1790 Federal Census, Watervliet
Pabst, William: (F) Member Mount Vernon Lodge, No. 3, 1900,
    Albany, NY
Pacinger, Andrew: (CMTS) 1790 Federal Census, Watervliet
Packard, Benjamin D.: (OC) Bookseller, (CMTS) Albany 1815 City
    Directory

Packard, Isaac: (OC) Carpenter, (CMTS) Albany 1815 City Directory
Packard, Isaac: (MD) Mar. 25, 1810, (Spouse) Lucinda Hale, (PMD)
    First Lutheran Church, Albany, NY
Packard, Isaac: (B) Jun. 11, 1817, (BP) Albany, (D) Jan. 16, 1818, (DP)
    Albany, (PRTS) Isaac Packard and Lucinda Hale
Packard, S. H.: (OC) Painter: (RES) 473 S. Market, (CMTS) Albany 1815
    City Directory
Paddock, Edward: (F) Member Temple Lodge, No. 14, 1900,
    Albany, NY
Paddock, William G.: (F) Member Masters Lodge, No. 5, 1900,
    Albany, NY
Page, Frederick G.: (F) Member Temple Lodge, No. 14, 1900,
    Albany, NY
Page, Levi: (OC) Carpenter, (CMTS) Albany 1815 City Directory
Page, Nicholas: (OC) Skipper, (CMTS) Albany 1815 City Directory
Paige, Joseph Yates: (F) Member Masters Lodge, No. 5, 1900,
    Albany, NY
Paige, Levi: (B) Sep. 16, 1906, (PB) Pine Bush, Albany, NY,
Palmer, Allen S.: (OC) Shoemaker, (CMTS) Albany 1815 City Directory
Palmer, Daniel: (OC) Carpenter, (CMTS) Albany 1815 City Directory
Palmer, Darias: (CMTS) 1790 Federal Census, Watervliet
Palmer, Edwin: (F) Member Temple Lodge, No. 14, 1900,
    Albany, NY
Palmer, Frank R.: (F) Member Masters Lodge, No. 5, 1900,
    Albany, NY
Palmer, Gamaliel: (CMTS) 1790 Federal Census Rensselaerville
Palmer, John: (F) Member Washington Lodge, No. 85, 1900,
    Albany, NY, (CMTS) Past Members
Palmer, John: (CMTS) 1790 Federal Census Rensselaerville
Palmer, John: (MD) Aug. 28, 1776, (Spouse) Mary, (PMD) Albany
Palmer, Joseph: (OC) Innkeeper, (CMTS) Albany 1815 City Directory
Palmer, Louis G.: (F) Member Temple Lodge, No. 14, 1900,
    Albany, NY
Palmeter, Henry: (CMTS) 1790 Federal Census, Watervliet
Palmeter, John: (CMTS) 1790 Federal Census, Watervliet
Palmeter, Peter: (CMTS) 1790 Federal Census, Watervliet
Pangburn, Edmund: (CMTS) 1790 Federal Census, Watervliet
Pangburn, William: (CMTS) 1790 Federal Census, Watervliet
Pangburn, William C.: (F) Member Temple Lodge, No. 14, 1900,
    Albany, NY
Parker, Elizabeth: (OC) Widow of Thomas, (CMTS) Albany 1815 City
    Directory
Parker, Lewis R.: (F) Member Masters Lodge, No. 5, 1900,
    Albany, NY
Parker, Jr., Amasa J.: (F) Member Masters Lodge, No. 5, 1900,

Albany, NY
Parkerson, John: (OC) Teamster, (CMTS) Albany 1815 City Directory
Parkinson, Eliza: (OC) Millener, (CMTS) Albany 1815 City Directory
Parks, David: (OC) Carpenter, (CMTS) Albany 1815 City Directory
Parson, Joseph: (CMTS) 1790 Federal Census, Watervliet
Parsons, Henry C.: (F) Member Temple Lodge, No. 14, 1900, Albany, NY
Parsons, Samuel: (RES) 591 S. Market, (CMTS) Albany 1815 City Directory
Parsons, Jr., John D.: (F) Member Masters Lodge, No. 5, 1900, Albany, NY
Partington, John: (CMTS) 1790 Federal Census, Watervliet
Partridge, John: (OC) Shoemaker, (CMTS) Albany 1815 City Directory
Passage, George M.: (F) Member Mount Vernon Lodge, No. 3, 1900, Albany, NY
Patrick, Benjamin: (OC) Cartman, (CMTS) Albany 1815 City Directory
Patrick, Ebenezer: (OC) Innkeeper, (CMTS) Albany 1815 City Directory
Patrick, John: (OC) Carpenter, (CMTS) Albany 1815 City Directory
Patridge, Wharton: (OC) Shoemaker, (CMTS) Albany 1815 City Directory
Patterson, John: (F) Member Temple Lodge, No. 14, 1900, Albany, NY
Patterson, John: (CMTS) 1790 Federal Census, Watervliet
Patterson, Sunderland: (CMTS) 1790 Federal Census Rensselaerville
Patterson, William: (CMTS) 1790 Federal Census, Watervliet
Patterson, Williamson: (OC) Grocer, (CMTS) Albany 1815 City Directory
Paul, James: (OC) Stone Cutter, (CMTS) Albany 1815 City Directory
Payn, C. S.: (OC) Watch Maker, (CMTS) Albany 1815 City Directory
Payn, Hiram: (OC) Watch Maker, (CMTS) Albany 1815 City Directory
Payn, Samuel: (OC) Innkeeper, (CMTS) Albany 1815 City Directory
Pearce, Barton: (OC) Printer, (CMTS) Albany 1815 City Directory
Pearce, Caleb: (CMTS) 1790 Federal Census Rensselaerville
Pearce, John: (CMTS) 1790 Federal Census, Watervliet
Pearce, John: (CMTS) 1790 Federal Census Rensselaerville
Pearce, Levy: (CMTS) 1790 Federal Census Rensselaerville
Pearce, Rykirt: (CMTS) 1790 Federal Census, Watervliet
Pearce, Thomas: (CMTS) 1790 Federal Census Rensselaerville
Peare, Levy: (CMTS) 1790 Federal Census Rensselaerville
Pearee, Sylvister: (CMTS) 1790 Federal Census Rensselaerville
Pearl, John J.: (F) Member Temple Lodge, No. 14, 1900, Albany, NY
Pearson, Pool: (OC) Tailor, (CMTS) Albany 1815 City Directory
Pearson, Timothy: (OC) Currier, (CMTS) Albany 1815 City Directory
Peck, Edward A.: (F) Member Mount Vernon Lodge, No. 3, 1900, Albany, NY

Peck, James H.: (F) Member Mount Vernon Lodge, No. 3, 1900, Albany, NY
Peckham, Audley C: (OC) Merchant, (CMTS) Albany 1815 City Directory
Peebles, Harry: (OC) Laborer, (CMTS) Albany 1815 City Directory
Pemberton, Ebenezer: (OC) Paper Stainer, (CMTS) Albany 1815 City Directory
Pemberton, Thos. L: (OC) Millener, (CMTS) Albany 1815 City Directory
Pendergrass, John: (OC) Laborer, (CMTS) Albany 1815 City Directory
Pennery, Thomas: (OC) Carman, (CMTS) Albany 1815 City Directory
Pennery, Thomas: (OC) Teamster, (CMTS) Albany 1815 City Directory
Penny, Samuel T: (OC) Merchant, (CMTS) Albany 1815 City Directory
Peper, Calvin: (OC) Attorney, (CMTS) Albany 1815 City Directory
Pepper, William: (CMTS) 1790 Federal Census, Watervliet
Pepper, William: (OC) Laborer, (CMTS) Albany 1815 City Directory
Percy, William E.: (F) Member Temple Lodge, No. 14, 1900, Albany, NY
Perry, John: (OC) Butcher, (CMTS) Albany 1815 City Directory
Perry, Obediah: (CMTS) 1790 Federal Census, Watervliet
Perry, Thornton K.: (F) Member Temple Lodge, No. 14, 1900, Albany, NY
Person, Abraham: (CMTS) 1790 Federal Census Rensselaerville
Peterson, William J.: (F) Member Temple Lodge, No. 14, 1900, Albany, NY
Pettinger, Mary: (RES) 71 Maiden Lane, (CMTS) Albany 1815 City Directory
Pettit, Ira: (OC) Merchant, (CMTS) Albany 1815 City Directory
Pew, Widow Margaret: (RES) Rear of 8 Lutheran, (CMTS) Albany 1815 City Directory
Phelps, Joshua: (CMTS) 1790 Federal Census, Watervliet
Phelps, Philip: (OC) Clerk in quarter master department, (CMTS) Albany 1815 City Directory
Phelt, Asahel: (OC) Teamster, (CMTS) Albany 1815 City Directory
Philips, Philip: (OC) Mason, (CMTS) Albany 1815 City Directory
Phillips, James: (CMTS) 1790 Federal Census, Watervliet
Phillips, John S.: (CMTS) 1790 Federal Census, Watervliet
Phillips, Joseph: (CMTS) 1790 Federal Census, Watervliet
Philps, Asa: (CMTS) 1790 Federal Census Rensselaerville
Philps, Belah: (CMTS) 1790 Federal Census Rensselaerville
Pierce, Christian: (CMTS) 1790 Federal Census, Watervliet
Pierce, John: (OC) Cartman, (CMTS) Albany 1815 City Directory
Pierce, Lemuel: (RES) 13 Maiden Lane, (CMTS) Albany 1815 City Directory
Pierson, Caleb: (OC) Innkeeper, (CMTS) Albany 1815 City Directory
Pike, Samuel: (CMTS) 1790 Federal Census, Watervliet

Pine, J. G.: (RES) Boarding House at 68 N. Pearl, (CMTS) Albany 1815 City Directory
Pinkerton, James: (CMTS) 1790 Federal Census, Watervliet
Pinne, Joseph G.: (OC) Teacher, (CMTS) Albany 1815 City Directory
Pinney, Joel: (RES) 166 Washington, (CMTS) Albany 1815 City Directory
Pitkin, William: (OC) Druggist, (CMTS) Albany 1815 City Directory
Pladwell, John: (F) Member Temple Lodge, No. 14, 1900, Albany, NY
Plamer, E. W.: (OC) Druggist, (CMTS) Albany 1815 City Directory
Plank, Peter: (CMTS) 1790 Federal Census Rensselaerville
Plantai, Anthony: (OC) Blacksmith, (CMTS) Albany 1815 City Directory
Plato, Alexander: (CMTS) 1790 Federal Census, Watervliet
Platt, Andrew: (F) Member Mount Vernon Lodge, No. 3, 1900, Albany, NY
Platt, Charles Z.: (OC) State Treasurer, (CMTS) Albany 1815 City Directory
Platt, Elnathan: (OC) Merchant, (CMTS) Albany 1815 City Directory
Platt, Israel: (OC) Merchant, (CMTS) Albany 1815 City Directory
Platt, James: (OC) Judge, (CMTS) Albany 1815 City Directory
Pointer, Charles P.: (OC) Distiller, (CMTS) Albany 1815 City Directory
Poltscroft, Peter: (OC), (CMTS) Albany 1815 City Directory
Pool, William: (CMTS) 1790 Federal Census, Watervliet
Poole, Edward A.: (F) Member Temple Lodge, No. 14, 1900, Albany, NY
Porter, Ira: (OC) Tailor, (CMTS) Albany 1815 City Directory
Possoon, Peter: (CMTS) 1790 Federal Census Rensselaerville
Post, Benjamin: (CMTS) 1790 Federal Census, Watervliet
Post, Henry: (CMTS) 1790 Federal Census Rensselaerville
Post, Jacob: (CMTS) 1790 Federal Census Rensselaerville
Post, Richard: (CMTS) 1790 Federal Census, Watervliet
Post, Jr., Jacob: (CMTS) 1790 Federal Census Rensselaerville
Potter, Eugene L.: (F) Member Masters Lodge, No. 5, 1900, Albany, NY
Potter, William C.: (F) Member Temple Lodge, No. 14, 1900, Albany, NY
Potts, Widow of Jesse: (RES) Boarding House at 44 Quay, (CMTS) Albany 1815 City Directory
Potwine, John S.: (OC) Merchant, (CMTS) Albany 1815 City Directory
Povert, Daniel: (CMTS) 1790 Federal Census, Watervliet
Powers, Daniel: (OC) Ffruiterer, (CMTS) Albany 1815 City Directory
Powers, John: (OC) Coachman, (CMTS) Albany 1815 City Directory
Pratt, Jr., Moses: (OC) Printer, (CMTS) Albany 1815 City Directory
Pratt, Peabody: (CMTS) 1790 Federal Census Rensselaerville
Pratt, Ralph: (OC) Merchant, (CMTS) Albany 1815 City Directory

Pratt, Widow Chloe: (RES) 45 Columbia, (CMTS) Albany 1815 City
   Directory
Prereau, Elizabeth: (RES) 53 Fox, (CMTS) Albany 1815 City Directory
Presseau, Daniel: (OC) Laborer, (CMTS) Albany 1815 City Directory
Prest, George M.: (F) Member Temple Lodge, No. 14, 1900,
   Albany, NY
Prest, John B.: (F) Member Temple Lodge, No. 14, 1900,
   Albany, NY
Preston, Eliphilet: (CMTS) 1790 Federal Census Rensselaerville
Preston, John: (CMTS) 1790 Federal Census Rensselaerville
Price, Daniel: (OC) Carpenter, (CMTS) Albany 1815 City Directory
Price, Isaac: (CMTS) 1790 Federal Census, Watervliet
Price, Lamuel: (OC) Shoemaker, (CMTS) Albany 1815 City Directory
Price, Seth: (CMTS) 1790 Federal Census, Watervliet
Price, Widow Mary: (RES) 69 S. Pearl, (CMTS) Albany 1815 City
   Directory
Pritchard, William: (OC) Stonecutter, (CMTS) Albany 1815 City
   Directory
Proby, Edward: (OC) Sail Maker, (CMTS) Albany 1815 City Directory
Proctor, Albert H.: (F) Member Temple Lodge, No. 14, 1900,
   Albany, NY, (CMTS) Life Member
Pruyn, Casparus: (OC) Blacksmith, (CMTS) Albany 1815 City Directory
Pruyn, David: (OC) Shoemaker, (CMTS) Albany 1815 City Directory
Pruyn, Issac: (OC) Laborer, (CMTS) Albany 1815 City Directory
Pruyn, Jacob S.: (OC) Skipper, (CMTS) Albany 1815 City Directory
Pruyn, John: (OC) Merchant, (CMTS) Albany 1815 City Directory
Pruyn, John S.: (RES) 203 N. Market, (CMTS) Albany 1815 City
   Directory
Pruyn, Mass: (RES) 59 Van Schaick, (CMTS) Albany 1815 City Directory
Pugsley, Abraham B.: (RES) 551 S. Market, (CMTS) Albany 1815 City
   Directory
Pumpelly, John H.: (F) Member Masters Lodge, No. 5, 1900,
   Albany, NY
Putnam, David: (OC) Butcher, (CMTS) Albany 1815 City Directory
Putnam, Elisha: (OC) Builder, (CMTS) Albany 1815 City Directory
Putnam, John: (CMTS) 1790 Federal Census, Watervliet
Putnam, Rufus: (OC) Silversmith, (CMTS) Albany 1815 City Directory
Putnam, Salter: (CMTS) 1790 Federal Census Rensselaerville
Pyrke, Henry W.: (F) Member Temple Lodge, No. 14, 1900,
   Albany, NY
Quackenboss, Isaac A: (OC) Attorney, (CMTS) Albany 1815 City
   Directory
Quackenbush, Abraham: (OC) Cooper, (CMTS) Albany 1815 City
   Directory
Quackenbush, Benjamin: (OC) Blacksmith, (CMTS) Albany 1815 City

Directory
Quackenbush, John: (OC) Lumber Merchant, (CMTS) Albany 1815 City Directory
Quackenbush, Nicholas: (OC) Attorney, (CMTS) Albany 1815 City Directory
Quackenbush, Walter: (RES) 240 N. Market, (CMTS) Albany 1815 City Directory
Quackenbush, Widow: (RES) Rear 51 Beaver St., (CMTS) Albany 1815 City Directory
Quackenbuss, Adrian: (CMTS) 1790 Federal Census, Watervliet
Quackenbuss, Frederick: (CMTS) 1790 Federal Census, Watervliet
Quackenbuss, Henry: (CMTS) 1790 Federal Census, Watervliet
Quackenbuss, Isaac: (CMTS) 1790 Federal Census, Watervliet
Quackenbuss, John: (CMTS) 1790 Federal Census, Watervliet
Quackenbuss, John: (CMTS) 1790 Federal Census, Watervliet
Quackenbuss, Nicholas: (CMTS) 1790 Federal Census, Watervliet
Quant, Frederick: (CMTS) 1790 Federal Census, Watervliet
Quant, Frederick: (CMTS) 1790 Federal Census, Watervliet
Quant, Jr., Frederick: (CMTS) 1790 Federal Census, Watervliet
Quay, William A.: (F) Member Temple Lodge, No. 14, 1900, Albany, NY
Quayle, Oliver A.: (F) Member Temple Lodge, No. 14, 1900, Albany, NY
Quick, Geraous: (OC) Nailer, (CMTS) Albany 1815 City Directory
Quiclin, John: (OC) Gardener, (CMTS) Albany 1815 City Directory
Quigley, Philip: (OC) Laborer, (CMTS) Albany 1815 City Directory
Quinby, John H.: (F) Member Masters Lodge, No. 5, 1900, Albany, NY, (CMTS) Past Master
Racter, John: (OC) Laborer, (CMTS) Albany 1815 City Directory
Radcliff, Catalyna: (B) Nov. 1, 1730, (PB) Albany, Albany Co., NY, (PRTS) Johannes Radcliff and Celia Yates
Radcliff, James: (OC) Grocer, (CMTS) Albany 1815 City Directory
Radcliff, James: (OC) Laborer, (CMTS) Albany 1815 City Directory
Radcliff, Nicholas: (RES) 6 Union, (CMTS) Albany 1815 City Directory
Radcliff, Widow of Philip: (RES) 68 Beaver, (CMTS) Albany 1815 City Directory
Radcliff, William: (OC) Tailor, (CMTS) Albany 1815 City Directory
Radcliff, Catherina: (B) May 21, 1790, (PB) Albany, Albany Co., NY, (PRTS) Jacobus Radcliffe and Maria Ottman
Radcliffe, Catharina: (B) Oct. 25, 1775, (PB) Albany, Albany Co., NY, (PRTS) Johannes Radcliffe and Margarita Passage
Radcliffe, James W.: (B) Mar. 30, 1810, (PB) Jerusalem, Albany, NY, (PRTS) William Radcliffe and Elizabeth Pangborn
Radcliffe, Jacobus: (B) Sep. 12, 1703, (PB) Albany, Abany Co., NY, (PRTS) Jan Radcliffe and Rachel Van Valkenburgh

Radcliffe, Philip: (B) Oct. 26, 1735, (PB) Albany, Abany Co., NY, (PRTS) Jacobus Radcliffe and Catharine Bovie

Radcliffe, Phillip: (B) Sep. 23, 1804, (PB) Jerusalem, Albany Co., NY, (PRTS) Rykert Radcliffe and Elizabeth Schut

Radcliffe, Philip: (MD) Feb. 23, 1786, (Spouse) Naomi Hall, (PMD) Albany

Radley, Catherine: (CMTS) 1790 Federal Census, Watervliet

Radley, Richard: (CMTS) 1790 Federal Census, Watervliet

Ramsay, Frederick: (CMTS) 1790 Federal Census, Watervliet

Ramsay, George: (CMTS) 1790 Federal Census, Watervliet

Ramsay, Samuel: (CMTS) 1790 Federal Census, Watervliet

Randal, John: (OC) Brass Founder, (CMTS) Albany 1815 City Directory

Randal, Miss: (RES) Lumber street, (CMTS) Albany 1815 City Directory

Randall, Thomas J.: (F) Member Mount Vernon Lodge, No. 3, 1900, Albany, NY

Randdolph, Jackson F.: (OC) Cartman, (CMTS) Albany 1815 City Directory

Randell, John: (CMTS) 1790 Federal Census, Watervliet

Ransier, John: (CMTS) 1790 Federal Census Rensselaerville

Rasey, Ammon: (OC) Innkeeper, (CMTS) Albany 1815 City Directory

Rathbone, Charles D.: (F) Member Masters Lodge, No. 5, 1900, Albany, NY

Rathbone, Clarence: (F) Member Masters Lodge, No. 5, 1900, Albany, NY, (CMTS) Past Master

Rathbone, J. L.: (RES) 2 Hudson, (CMTS) Albany 1815 City Directory

Rathbone, John F.: (F) Member Masters Lodge, No. 5, 1900, Albany, NY

Rathbone, S.: (RES) 2 Hudson, (CMTS) Albany 1815 City Directory

Rathbone, Valentine: (OC) Merchant, (CMTS) Albany 1815 City Directory

Rathbone, William F.: (F) Member Masters Lodge, No. 5, 1900, Albany, NY

Rathbone, Jr., C. D.: (F) Member Masters Lodge, No. 5, 1900, Albany, NY

Rawls, Widow Hannah: (RES) Rear of 181 S. Pearl, (CMTS) Albany 1815 City Directory

Raynsford, George W.: (F) Member Temple Lodge, No. 14, 1900, Albany, NY

Read, Daniel P.: (F) Member Temple Lodge, No. 14, 1900, Albany, NY

Read, Harmon P.: (F) Member Masters Lodge, No. 5, 1900, Albany, NY

Read, J. Meredith: (F) Member Masters Lodge, No. 5, 1900, Albany, NY

Rebhun, Charles A.: (F) Member Temple Lodge, No. 14, 1900,

Albany, NY
Rechenberg, John H.: (F) Member Temple Lodge, No. 14, 1900,
   Albany, NY
Reckhow, John: (RES) Albany Oyster & Porter, (CMTS) Albany 1815
   City Directory
Reddington, Daniel: (CMTS) 1790 Federal Census Rensselaerville
Redhun, Daniel C.: (F) Member Temple Lodge, No. 14, 1900,
   Albany, NY
Redliker, Peter: (CMTS) 1790 Federal Census, Watervliet
Redway, George H.: (F) Member Masters Lodge, No. 5, 1900,
   Albany, NY
Reed, George: (CMTS) 1790 Federal Census, Watervliet
Reed, Joseph P.: (F) Member Temple Lodge, No. 14, 1900,
   Albany, NY
Rees, George: (CMTS) 1790 Federal Census, Watervliet
Rees, Philip: (CMTS) 1790 Federal Census, Watervliet
Rees, Zachariah: (OC) Carpenter, (CMTS) Albany 1815 City Directory
Reid, George: (OC) Shoemaker, (CMTS) Albany 1815 City Directory
Reid, John: (OC) Merchant, (CMTS) Albany 1815 City Directory
Reid, John: (OC) Stonecutter, (CMTS) Albany 1815 City Directory
Reid, William: (OC) Teamster, (CMTS) Albany 1815 City Directory
Reiffenburgh, Peter: (CMTS) 1790 Federal Census Rensselaerville
Rekinburgh, John: (CMTS) 1790 Federal Census, Watervliet
Relleyea, Jacob: (CMTS) 1790 Federal Census, Watervliet
Rellyea, David: (CMTS) 1790 Federal Census, Watervliet
Rellyea, Simon: (CMTS) 1790 Federal Census, Watervliet
Rellyea, Jr., David: (CMTS) 1790 Federal Census, Watervliet
Rellyie, Peter: (CMTS) 1790 Federal Census, Watervliet
Relyea, Lewis L.: (F) Member Mount Vernon Lodge, No. 3, 1900,
   Albany, NY
Repenburgh, Adam: (CMTS) 1790 Federal Census, Watervliet
Repenburgh, Daniel: (CMTS) 1790 Federal Census, Watervliet
Requa, James: (OC) Merchant, (CMTS) Albany 1815 City Directory
Resegrans, Frederick: (CMTS) 1790 Federal Census Rensselaerville
Resseguie, James E.: (F) Member Temple Lodge, No. 14, 1900,
   Albany, NY
Revie, Joseph: (OC) Laborer, (CMTS) Albany 1815 City Directory
Reymond, Gamaliel: (CMTS) 1790 Federal Census Rensselaerville
Reynders, John C.: (F) Member Temple Lodge, No. 14, 1900,
   Albany, NY
Reynolds, Edward: (OC) Cartman, (CMTS) Albany 1815 City Directory
Reynolds, John: (OC) Cartman, (CMTS) Albany 1815 City Directory
Reynolds, John H.: (F) Member Masters Lodge, No. 5, 1900,
   Albany, NY
Reynolds, William A.: (F) Member Mount Vernon Lodge, No. 3, 1900,

Rhino, Rebecca: (OC) Merchant, (CMTS) Albany 1815 City Directory
Rian, John: (OC) Grocer, (CMTS) Albany 1815 City Directory
Rice, Charles: (OC) Carpenter, (CMTS) Albany 1815 City Directory
Rice, Frederick H.: (F) Member Temple Lodge, No. 14, 1900,
    Albany, NY
Rice, James D.: (F) Member Temple Lodge, No. 14, 1900,
    Albany, NY
Rice, Joesph T: (OC) Watchmaker, (CMTS) Albany 1815 City Directory
Rice, Nahum: (OC) Merchant, (CMTS) Albany 1815 City Directory
Rice, Samuel: (CMTS) 1790 Federal Census Rensselaerville
Rice, Ward: (OC) Carpenter, (CMTS) Albany 1815 City Directory
Rice, Woodis: (OC) Merchant, (CMTS) Albany 1815 City Directory
Richards, Joseph: (OC) Butcher, (CMTS) Albany 1815 City Directory
Richards, Walter Scott: (F) Member Temple Lodge, No. 14, 1900,
    Albany, NY
Richards, Widow Ann: (RES) 51 Columbis, (CMTS) Albany 1815 City
    Directory
Richardson, Frank: (F) Member Temple Lodge, No. 14, 1900,
    Albany, NY
Richter, Michael: (CMTS) 1790 Federal Census Rensselaerville
Rickerson, Abednego: (CMTS) 1790 Federal Census, Watervliet
Rickert, George C.: (F) Member Temple Lodge, No. 14, 1900,
    Albany, NY
Rickey, Jeremiah: (OC) Laborer, (CMTS) Albany 1815 City Directory
Riddeker, Peter: (OC) Laborer, (CMTS) Albany 1815 City Directory
Riddy, Ella: (RES) 35 Eagle, (CMTS) Albany 1815 City Directory
Rider, Stephen J: (OC) Carpenter, (CMTS) Albany 1815 City Directory
Ridgeway, Thomas: (OC) Shoemaker, (CMTS) Albany 1815 City
    Directory
Rieb, George: (CMTS) 1790 Federal Census, Watervliet
Rieck, Ernest W.: (F) Member Mount Vernon Lodge, No. 3, 1900,
    Albany, NY
Riemer, Adam: (CMTS) 1790 Federal Census Rensselaerville
Riley, Ashur: (OC) Builder, (CMTS) Albany 1815 City Directory
Riley, Widow: (RES) 49 Chapel, (CMTS) Albany 1815 City Directory
Rillman, George: (CMTS) 1790 Federal Census, Watervliet
Rinehart, George: (CMTS) 1790 Federal Census Rensselaerville
Rinehart, John: (CMTS) 1790 Federal Census Rensselaerville
Rink, Niccholas: (F) Member Temple Lodge, No. 14, 1900,
    Albany, NY
Rivenburgh, Clarence H.: (F) Member Temple Lodge, No. 14, 1900,
    Albany, NY
Rivenburgh, James: (F) Member Temple Lodge, No. 14, 1900,
    Albany, NY

Rivington, James: (RES) 671 S. Market, (CMTS) Albany 1815 City
    Directory
Robbbins, Joseph: (OC) Blacksmith, (CMTS) Albany 1815 City Directory
Robbins, James B.: (OC) Printer, (CMTS) Albany 1815 City Directory
Robe, Lawrence: (CMTS) 1915, Census, District No. 1 Ward No. 6
Robe, Richard: (CMTS) 1915, Census, District No. 2 Ward No. 6
Roberts, Israel: (OC) Teacher, (CMTS) Albany 1815 City Directory
Robertson, James: (OC) Stonecutter, (CMTS) Albany 1815 City Directory
Robins, Abinel: (CMTS) 1790 Federal Census, Watervliet
Robins, Henry: (CMTS) 1790 Federal Census, Watervliet
Robins, Thomas: (CMTS) 1790 Federal Census, Watervliet
Robins, William: (CMTS) 1790 Federal Census, Watervliet
Robinson, Andrew: (CMTS) 1790 Federal Census, Watervliet
Robinson, Daniel S.: (OC) Mason, (CMTS) Albany 1815 City Directory
Robinson, Duncan: (OC) Flour Store, (CMTS) Albany 1815 City
    Directory
Robinson, Francis: (OC) Cartman, (CMTS) Albany 1815 City Directory
Robinson, George W.: (F) Member Temple Lodge, No. 14, 1900,
    Albany, NY, (CMTS) Life Member
Robinson, James: (OC) Coach Maker, (CMTS) Albany 1815 City
    Directory
Robinson, James E.: (F) Member Mount Vernon Lodge, No. 3, 1900,
    Albany, NY
Robinson, Johnathan: (OC) Morocco Dresser, (CMTS) Albany 1815 City
    Directory
Robinson, Margaret: (OC) Millener, (CMTS) Albany 1815 City Directory
Robinson, R. G.: (F) Member Mount Vernon Lodge, No. 3, 1900,
    Albany, NY
Robinson, Robert: (CMTS) 1790 Federal Census, Watervliet
Robison, John: (RES) 34 Dock, (CMTS) Albany 1815 City Directory
Robson, Peter R.: (F) Member Temple Lodge, No. 14, 1900,
    Albany, NY
Rock, Samuel: (CMTS) 1790 Federal Census Rensselaerville
Rocket, Doug: (OC) Ferryman, (CMTS) Albany 1815 City Directory
Rockistile, Daniel: (CMTS) 1790 Federal Census, Watervliet
Rockwell, Lewis H.: (F) Member Temple Lodge, No. 14, 1900,
    Albany, NY
Rodgers, Jedediah: (OC) Merchant, (CMTS) Albany 1815 City Directory
Rodgers, Lemuel L.: (F) Member Mount Vernon Lodge, No. 3, 1900,
    Albany, NY
Rodgers, Widow Elizabeth: (RES) 30 N. Pearl, (CMTS) Albany 1815 City
    Directory
Rodgers, William: (OC) Blacksmith, (CMTS) Albany 1815 City Directory
Rodman, Daniel: (OC) Attorney, (CMTS) Albany 1815 City Directory
Roff, Christopher: (CMTS) 1790 Federal Census, Watervliet

Roff, Frederick: (CMTS) 1790 Federal Census, Watervliet
Roff, John: (OC) Grocer, (CMTS) Albany 1815 City Directory
Rogers, Halsey: (OC) Merchant, (CMTS) Albany 1815 City Directory
Rogers, Nathaniel: (CMTS) 1790 Federal Census Rensselaerville
Roggen, Peter: (RES) 83 State, (CMTS) Albany 1815 City Directory
Rollins, Andrew M.: (F) Member Temple Lodge, No. 14, 1900, Albany, NY
Rollo, Daniel: (CMTS) 1790 Federal Census Rensselaerville
Rom, Catharine: (RES) 31 Columbia, (CMTS) Albany 1815 City Directory
Roman, Peter: (CMTS) 1790 Federal Census, Watervliet
Rooker, William H. A.: (F) Member Temple Lodge, No. 14, 1900, Albany, NY
Roorbach, Arthur: (OC) Capt, (CMTS) Albany 1815 City Directory
Root, Dr. A. T.: (CMTS) 1915, Census, District No. 3 Ward No. 14
Root, Andrew: (CMTS) 1915, Census, District No. 1 Ward No. 10
Root, Andrew J.: (F) Member Masters Lodge, No. 5, 1900, Albany, NY
Root, Arthur G.: (F) Member Masters Lodge, No. 5, 1900, Albany, NY
Root, Arthur Jr.: (CMTS) 1915, Census, District No. 3 Ward No. 18
Root, Arthur M.: (CMTS) 1915, Census, District No. 3 Ward No. 18
Root, Charlet S.: (CMTS) 1915, Census, District No. 7 Ward No. 16
Root, Claire E.: (CMTS) 1915, Census, District No. 7 Ward No. 16
Root, Edith H.: (CMTS) 1915, Census, District No. 5 Ward No. 6
Root, Francis: (CMTS) 1915, Census, District No. 3 Ward No. 18
Root, Frank: (CMTS) 1915, Census, District No. 7 Ward No. 19
Root, Fred W.: (CMTS) 1915, Census, District No. 5 Ward No. 6
Root, Grace: (CMTS) 1915, Census, District No. 7 Ward No. 19
Root, John W.: (CMTS) 1915, Census, District No. 7 Ward No. 16
Root, Laura: (CMTS) 1915, Census, District No. 6 Ward No. 19
Root, Lyman: (OC) Merchant, (CMTS) Albany 1815 City Directory
Root, Marguerite G.: (CMTS) 1915, Census, District No. 5 Ward No. 6
Root, Marlon: (CMTS) 1915, Census, District No. 4 Ward No. 16
Root, Martha E.: (CMTS) 1915, Census, District No. 7 Ward No. 16
Root, Maude D.: (CMTS) 1915, Census, District No. 3 Ward No. 18
Root, May: (CMTS) 1915, Census, District No. 7 Ward No. 19
Root, Nellie A.: (CMTS) 1915, Census, District No. 5 Ward No. 6
Root, R H.: (OC) Merchant, (CMTS) Albany 1815 City Directory
Root, Richard: (RES) Boarding House at 10 Hudson, (CMTS) Albany 1815 City Directory
Root, Theo S.: (CMTS) 1915, Census, District No. 4 Ward No. 16
Root, Theo Z.: (CMTS) 1915, Census, District No. 4 Ward No. 16
Root, William: (CMTS) 1915, Census, District No. 5 Ward No. 6
Rose, James: (CMTS) 1790 Federal Census, Watervliet

Rose, Samuel: (CMTS) 1790 Federal Census Rensselaerville
Roseboom, Widow Hester: (RES) 59 Hudson, (CMTS) Albany 1815 City
  Directory
Rosekrans, Henry: (OC) Laborer, (CMTS) Albany 1815 City Directory
Rosenbarack, John: (CMTS) 1790 Federal Census, Watervliet
Rosendale, Simon W.: (F) Member Washington Lodge, No. 85, 1900,
  Albany, NY, (CMTS) Past Members
Roser, Richard: (OC) Mason, (CMTS) Albany 1815 City Directory
Ross, Charles H.: (F) Member Temple Lodge, No. 14, 1900,
  Albany, NY
Rossman, Jacob J.: (CMTS) 1790 Federal Census Rensselaerville
Rotnen, John: (CMTS) 1790 Federal Census, Watervliet
Round, Charles: (CMTS) 1790 Federal Census Rensselaerville
Roush, Thomas: (CMTS) 1790 Federal Census, Watervliet
Rousseau, Francis: (CMTS) 1790 Federal Census, Watervliet
Row, Johannes: (CMTS) 1790 Federal Census Rensselaerville
Row, Joseph: (CMTS) 1790 Federal Census Rensselaerville
Row, Rachel: (CMTS) 1790 Federal Census, Watervliet
Row, Wilhelmus: (CMTS) 1790 Federal Census, Watervliet
Row, Wilhelmus: (CMTS) 1790 Federal Census, Watervliet
Rowe, Nicholas: (OC) Umbrella Maker, (CMTS) Albany 1815 City
  Directory
Rowel, Simeon: (OC) Carpenter, (CMTS) Albany 1815 City Directory
Rowson, William: (RES) 4 Lutheran, (CMTS) Albany 1815 City
  Directory
Ruby, Christopher: (OC) Grocer, (CMTS) Albany 1815 City Directory
Ruby, Robert: (OC) Cooper, (CMTS) Albany 1815 City Directory
Rudes, Jason: (RES) 43 Van Schaick, (CMTS) Albany 1815 City
  Directory
Ruggles, V.P.: (OC) Averill & Ruggles, Flour and Grain, (CMTS) Albany
  1859 City Directory
Rugs, John: (OC) Rope Maker, (CMTS) Albany 1815 City Directory
Ruland, Benjamin: (CMTS) 1790 Federal Census Rensselaerville
Runkie, John: (CMTS) 1790 Federal Census, Watervliet
Runkle, Jr., John: (CMTS) 1790 Federal Census, Watervliet
Runnelis, Andrew: (CMTS) 1790 Federal Census Rensselaerville
Runnells, Abraham: (CMTS) 1790 Federal Census, Watervliet
Runnels, Jacob: (CMTS) 1790 Federal Census Rensselaerville
Ruso, Ada: (CMTS) 1915, Census, District No. 1 Ward No. 8
Ruso, Angleo: (CMTS) 1915, Census, District No. 2 Ward No. 12
Ruso, Anna: (CMTS) 1915, Census, District No. 2 Ward No. 12
Ruso, Antonio: (CMTS) 1915, Census, District No. 3 Ward No. 4
Ruso, Bernard: (CMTS) 1915, Census, District No. 3 Ward No. 4
Ruso, Charles E.: (CMTS) 1915, Census, District No. 1 Ward No. 8
Ruso, Conrad: (F) Member Temple Lodge, No. 14, 1900,

Albany, NY
Ruso, Cosimo: (CMTS) 1915, Census, District No. 3 Ward No. 4
Ruso, Elizabeth A.: (CMTS) 1915, Census, District No. 4 Ward No. 14
Ruso, Floyd H.: (CMTS) 1915, Census, District No. 1 Ward No. 8
Ruso, George: (CMTS) 1915, Census, District No. 2 Ward No. 17
Ruso, George W.: (CMTS) 1915, Census, District No. 4 Ward No. 14
Ruso, Jacob: (CMTS) 1915, Census, District No. 1 Ward No. 8
Ruso, James M.: (F) Member Temple Lodge, No. 14, 1900,
    Albany, NY, (CMTS) Life Member
Ruso, Joseph: (CMTS) 1915, Census, District No. 2 Ward No. 7
Ruso, Lena: (CMTS) 1915, Census, District No. 2 Ward No. 12
Ruso, Leo: (CMTS) 1915, Census, District No. 2 Ward No. 12
Ruso, Leonora: (CMTS) 1915, Census, District No. 2 Ward No. 17
Ruso, Louis: (CMTS) 1915, Census, District No. 2 Ward No. 12
Ruso, Lucy: (CMTS) 1915, Census, District No. 2 Ward No. 12
Ruso, Mary: (CMTS) 1915, Census, District No. 3 Ward No. 4
Ruso, Molly: (CMTS) 1915, Census, District No. 2 Ward No. 12
Ruso, Samuel: (CMTS) 1915, Census, District No. 2 Ward No. 12
Ruso, Sebastian: (CMTS) 1915, Census, District No. 2 Ward No. 12
Ruso, William: (CMTS) 1915, Census, District No. 2 Ward No. 12
Russ, Adam: (OC) Cartman, (CMTS) Albany 1815 City Directory
Russ, Alanson B.: (F) Member Temple Lodge, No. 14, 1900,
    Albany, NY
Russ, Jr., Jonathan: (CMTS) 1790 Federal Census, Watervliet
Russell, David: (OC) Mason, (CMTS) Albany 1815 City Directory
Russell, Eli: (OC) Brickmaker, (CMTS) Albany 1815 City Directory
Russell, Elihu: (OC) Painter, (CMTS) Albany 1815 City Directory
Russell, J.: (OC) Painter, (CMTS) Albany 1815 City Directory
Russell, Joseph: (OC) Grocer, (CMTS) Albany 1815 City Directory
Russell, Joseph: (OC) Painter, (CMTS) Albany 1815 City Directory
Russell, Robert B.: (F) Member Mount Vernon Lodge, No. 3, 1900,
    Albany, NY
Russell, T.: (OC) Painters, (CMTS) Albany 1815 City Directory
Russell, Thomas: (OC) Painter, (CMTS) Albany 1815 City Directory
Rust, Nathan: (CMTS) 1790 Federal Census, Watervliet
Ryer, James: (OC) Blacksmith, (CMTS) Albany 1815 City Directory
Sackrider, D. W.: (OC) Merchant, (CMTS) Albany 1815 City Directory
Safford, Elias: (OC) plane maker, (CMTS) Albany 1815 City Directory
Sage, Benjamin: (CMTS) 1790 Federal Census Rensselaerville
Sager, John: (CMTS) 1790 Federal Census, Watervliet
Sager, Peter: (CMTS) 1790 Federal Census, Watervliet
Salisburry, Joseph: (CMTS) 1790 Federal Census, Watervliet
Salisbury, Henry: (OC) Culler, (CMTS) Albany 1815 City Directory
Salisbury, Tobias: (OC) Ferryman, (CMTS) Albany 1815 City Directory
Sanaders, Francis N.: (F) Member Temple Lodge, No. 14, 1900,

Albany, NY
Sanders, Barent: (RES) 54 S. Pearl, (CMTS) Albany 1815 City Directory
Sanders, Eugene: (F) Member Temple Lodge, No. 14, 1900,
Albany, NY
Sanders, William N. S.: (F) Member Masters Lodge, No. 5, 1900,
Albany, NY
Sanderson, George: (F) Member Temple Lodge, No. 14, 1900,
Albany, NY
Sandford, Cornelius: (CMTS) 1790 Federal Census, Watervliet
Sands, Widow Elizabeth: (RES) 31 Union, (CMTS) Albany 1815 City Directory
Sanford, Ashbel N.: (OC) Grocer, (CMTS) Albany 1815 City Directory
Sanford, Staats: (CMTS) 1790 Federal Census, Watervliet
Sanford, Stephen: (OC) Merchant, (CMTS) Albany 1815 City Directory
Sann, Charles: (F) Member Temple Lodge, No. 14, 1900,
Albany, NY
Sann, Fredrick: (F) Member Temple Lodge, No. 14, 1900,
Albany, NY
Sanson, Adam: (CMTS) 1790 Federal Census Rensselaerville
Saop, Conradt: (CMTS) 1790 Federal Census, Watervliet
Satterlee, Edward: (OC) Retail Merchant, (CMTS) Albany 1815 City Directory
Sautter, Jr., Louis: (F) Member Mount Vernon Lodge, No. 3, 1900,
Albany, NY
Sayles, Alexander: (CMTS) 1915, Census, District No. 8 Ward No. 1
Sayles, Anna: (CMTS) 1915, Census, District No. 8 Ward No. 1
Sayles, Anna Hanna: (CMTS) 1915, Census, District No. 7 Ward No. 16
Sayles, Anna K.: (CMTS) 1915, Census, District No. 3 Ward No. 14
Sayles, Bessie: (CMTS) 1915, Census, District No. 7 Ward No. 16
Sayles, Caroline B.: (CMTS) 1915, Census, District No. 3 Ward No. 14
Sayles, Edw C.: (CMTS) 1915, Census, District No. 8 Ward No. 19
Sayles, Edward: (CMTS) 1915, Census, District No. 7 Ward No. 16
Sayles, Ellen: (CMTS) 1915, Census, District No. 7 Ward No. 16
Sayles, Frances: (CMTS) 1915, Census, District No. 8 Ward No. 1
Sayles, George: (CMTS) 1915, Census, District No. 7 Ward No. 16
Sayles, Harry: (CMTS) 1915, Census, District No. 7 Ward No. 16
Sayles, James H.: (CMTS) 1915, Census, District No. 8 Ward No. 1
Sayles, James M.: (F) Member Temple Lodge, No. 14, 1900,
Albany, NY, (CMTS) Past Maser 1869
Sayles, Marion: (CMTS) 1915, Census, District No. 3 Ward No. 19
Sayles, Mary A.: (CMTS) 1915, Census, District No. 3 Ward No. 14
Sayles, Miss Lottie A.: (CMTS) 1915, Census, District No. 2 Ward No. 8
Sayles, Thomas: (CMTS) 1915, Census, District No. 3 Ward No. 19
Sayles, Wm.: (CMTS) 1915, Census, District No. 7 Ward No. 16
Schaelffer, Fredrick: (OC) Morocco Dresser, (CMTS) Albany 1815 City

Schafer, Henry: (F) Member Mount Vernon Lodge, No. 3, 1900, Albany, NY
Schaler, William: (F) Member Mount Vernon Lodge, No. 3, 1900, Albany, NY
Schanck, Paul: (CMTS) 1790 Federal Census, Watervliet
Schell, John: (OC) Carpenter, (CMTS) Albany 1815 City Directory
Scherer, Robert G.: (F) Member Temple Lodge, No. 14, 1900, Albany, NY
Schermerhorn, Cornelius: (CMTS) 1790 Federal Census Rensselaerville
Schermerhorn, Cornelius: (B) Mar. 1, 1778, (PM) Albany, Albany Co., NY, (PRTS) Johannes Winnie Schermerhorn and Cathelgetje Van Valkenberg
Schermerhorn, Cornelius: (OC) Innkeeper, (CMTS) Albany 1815 City Directory
Schermerhorn, Henry: (CMTS) 1790 Federal Census Rensselaerville
Schermerhorn, J. A.: (F) Member Temple Lodge, No. 14, 1900, Albany, NY
Schermerhorn, Jacob Cornelius: (B) May 25, 1743, (CD) Jun. 17, 1743, (PB) Albany, Albany Co., NY, First Dutch Reformed Church, (D) May 5, 1822, (PD) Scodack Landing, Rensselaer Co., NY
Schermerhorn, Jacob J: (CMTS) 1790 Federal Census, Watervliet
Schermerhorn, Jacob R: (CMTS) 1790 Federal Census, Watervliet
Schermerhorn, John R: (CMTS) 1790 Federal Census, Watervliet
Schermerhorn, Johannes: (B) Aug. 31, 1718, (PB) Albany, Albany Co., NY, (PRTS) Hendrick Schmerhorn and Elsie Jan Albertse Bratt
Schermerhorn, Ryer: (OC) Printer, (CMTS) Albany 1815 City Directory
Schermerhorn, Ryer B.: (CMTS) 1790 Federal Census, Watervliet
Schermerhorn, Wm. R.: (F) Member Temple Lodge, No. 14, 1900, Albany, NY
Schermerhorne, Roeliff: (CMTS) 1790 Federal Census Rensselaerville
Scheurer, Charles T.: (F) Member Temple Lodge, No. 14, 1900, Albany, NY
Schifferdecker, Fred. A.: (F) Member Mount Vernon Lodge, No. 3, 1900, Albany, NY
Schifferdecker, Frederick: (F) Member Mount Vernon Lodge, No. 3, 1900, Albany, NY
Schimpf, Frank F.: (F) Member Mount Vernon Lodge, No. 3, 1900, Albany, NY
Schley, Evander M.: (F) Member Temple Lodge, No. 14, 1900, Albany, NY
Schoalfield, Arnold: (CMTS) 1790 Federal Census, Watervliet
Schonmaker, Charck: (CMTS) 1790 Federal Census, Watervliet
Schonmaker, Frederick: (CMTS) 1790 Federal Census Rensselaerville
Schonmaker, Henry: (CMTS) 1790 Federal Census, Watervliet

Schonmaker, Jacobus: (CMTS) 1790 Federal Census, Watervliet
Schonmaker, Peter: (CMTS) 1790 Federal Census Rensselaerville
Schoolcraft, John: (CMTS) 1790 Federal Census, Watervliet
Schoolcraft, Lawrence: (CMTS) 1790 Federal Census, Watervliet
Schoolcraft, Peter: (CMTS) 1790 Federal Census Rensselaerville
Schoon, William: (RES) 40 Fox, (CMTS) Albany 1815 City Directory
Schoonmaker, John: (CMTS) 1790 Federal Census, Watervliet
Schrider, Sebastian: (CMTS) 1790 Federal Census Rensselaerville
Schumacher, Peter: (F) Member Temple Lodge, No. 14, 1900, Albany, NY
Schumann, Henry W.: (F) Member Temple Lodge, No. 14, 1900, Albany, NY
Schuyler, Peter P.: (RES) 27 Steuben, (CMTS) Albany 1815 City Directory
Schuyler, Philip P.: (CMTS) 1790 Federal Census, Watervliet
Schuyler, Samuel: (OC) Skipper, (CMTS) Albany 1815 City Directory
Schuyler, Stephen: (CMTS) 1790 Federal Census, Watervliet
Schuyler, Stephen P.: (OC) Merchant, (CMTS) Albany 1815 City Directory
Scidmore, Isaac: (CMTS) 1790 Federal Census Rensselaerville
Scimmel, John: (CMTS) 1790 Federal Census, Watervliet
Scoby, David: (OC) Tanner, (CMTS) Albany 1815 City Directory
Scofield, Robert W.: (F) Member Temple Lodge, No. 14, 1900, Albany, NY
Scofield, Solomon: (OC) Silversmith, (CMTS) Albany 1815 City Directory
Scott, Daniel E.: (F) Member Temple Lodge, No. 14, 1900, Albany, NY
Scott, George: (OC) Pumpmaker, (CMTS) Albany 1815 City Directory
Scott, John: (CMTS) 1790 Federal Census, Watervliet
Scott, John: (OC) Millener, (CMTS) Albany 1815 City Directory
Scott, Philip: (CMTS) 1790 Federal Census, Watervliet
Scott, William: (CMTS) 1790 Federal Census Rensselaerville
Scott, William: (OC) Cartman, (CMTS) Albany 1815 City Directory
Scott, William: (OC) Grocer, (CMTS) Albany 1815 City Directory
Scovel, Hezekiah: (OC) Merchant, (CMTS) Albany 1815 City Directory
Scrippert, Charles: (CMTS) 1790 Federal Census, Watervliet
Scrymser, James: (RES) 9 Water, (CMTS) Albany 1815 City Directory
Scrymser, James: (OC) Grocer, (CMTS) Albany 1815 City Directory
Seabury, Melvin: (F) Member Temple Lodge, No. 14, 1900, Albany, NY
Seaman, Frank W.: (F) Member Temple Lodge, No. 14, 1900, Albany, NY
Seaman, Isaac: (CMTS) 1790 Federal Census, Watervliet
Seaman, Stephen: (OC) Carpenter, (CMTS) Albany 1815 City Directory

Seamen, Isaac: (OC) Ship Master, (CMTS) Albany 1815 City Directory
Sears, Charles: (RES) 71 Maiden Lane, (CMTS) Albany 1815 City
 Directory
Sears, Charles: (OC) Laborer, (CMTS) Albany 1815 City Directory
Seavers, William: (OC) Merchant, (CMTS) Albany 1815 City Directory
Sebast, Martin: (F) Member Temple Lodge, No. 14, 1900,
 Albany, NY
Seckman, Thomas: (OC) Laborer, (CMTS) Albany 1815 City Directory
Secor, Benjamin M.: (F) Member Temple Lodge, No. 14, 1900,
 Albany, NY
Sedgwick, Roderick: (OC) Merchant, (CMTS) Albany 1815 City
 Directory
Sedgwick, Theodore: (RES) 103 State, (CMTS) Albany 1815 City
 Directory
Sedlemeyer, Johannes: (CMTS) 1790 Federal Census Rensselaerville
Seeley, DavidW.: (F) Member Mount Vernon Lodge, No. 3, 1900,
 Albany, NY
Seeley, Isaac: (OC) Shoemaker, (CMTS) Albany 1815 City Directory
Segar, Alexander: (CMTS) 1790 Federal Census, Watervliet
Segar, Garret: (CMTS) 1790 Federal Census, Watervliet
Segar, Garrit: (CMTS) 1790 Federal Census, Watervliet
Seible, George: (CMTS) 1790 Federal Census Rensselaerville
Seible, Michael: (CMTS) 1790 Federal Census Rensselaerville
Selby, William: (OC) Tailor, (CMTS) Albany 1815 City Directory
Selden, Roger: (OC), (CMTS) Albany 1815 City Directory
Sely, James: (OC) Shoemaker, (CMTS) Albany 1815 City Directory
Senrick, Charles M.: (F) Member Temple Lodge, No. 14, 1900,
 Albany, NY
Seram, Clement: (CMTS) 1790 Federal Census, Watervliet
Sergeant, Frederick: (OC) Dyer, (CMTS) Albany 1815 City Directory
Sergeant, J. & G.: (OC) Merchant, (CMTS) Albany 1815 City Directory
Settle, George H.: (CMTS) 1790 Federal Census, Watervliet
Settle, Peter: (CMTS) 1790 Federal Census, Watervliet
Sever, William: (OC) Merchant, (CMTS) Albany 1815 City Directory
Severse, Johannes: (CMTS) 1790 Federal Census, Watervliet
Sewell, John: (F) Member Masters Lodge, No. 5, 1900,
 Albany, NY
Sexton, Alanson: (CMTS) 1790 Federal Census Rensselaerville
Seymour, William: (RES) 54 Lydius, (CMTS) Albany 1815 City
 Directory
Seymour, Wm.: (OC) Leather Store, (CMTS) Albany 1815 City Directory
Shadler, Jacob: (RES) 498 S. Market, (CMTS) Albany 1815 City
 Directory
Shaffer, Calvin: (F) Member Mount Vernon Lodge, No. 3, 1900,
 Albany, NY

Shaffer, Francis: (CMTS) 1790 Federal Census Rensselaerville
Shaffer, Frederick: (CMTS) 1790 Federal Census Rensselaerville
Shaffer, Yost: (CMTS) 1790 Federal Census Rensselaerville
Shanks, Seth G.: (F) Member Mount Vernon Lodge, No. 3, 1900, Albany, NY
Sharp, Abner: (CMTS) 1790 Federal Census, Watervliet
Sharp, Cornelius: (OC), (CMTS) Albany 1815 City Directory
Sharp, George C: (OC) Public Nortary, (CMTS) Albany 1815 City Directory
Sharp, George H.: (F) Member Mount Vernon Lodge, No. 3, 1900, Albany, NY
Sharp, Gilbert: (CMTS) 1790 Federal Census, Watervliet
Sharp, Jacob: (RES) 11 Columbia, (CMTS) Albany 1815 City Directory
Sharp, John: (OC) Gardener, (CMTS) Albany 1815 City Directory
Sharp, Widow of John: (RES) 279 N. Market, (CMTS) Albany 1815 City Directory
Shattuck, J. W. M.: (F) Member Temple Lodge, No. 14, 1900, Albany, NY
Shattuck, James A.: (F) Member Mount Vernon Lodge, No. 3, 1900, Albany, NY
Shave, Peter: (CMTS) 1790 Federal Census, Watervliet
Shaver, Charles: (CMTS) 1790 Federal Census, Watervliet
Shaver, John: (CMTS) 1790 Federal Census, Watervliet
Shaver, John: (CMTS) 1790 Federal Census, Watervliet
Shaw, Henry: (OC) Tanner, (CMTS) Albany 1815 City Directory
Shaw, Hugh D.: (OC) Rope Maker, (CMTS) Albany 1815 City Directory
Shaw, John: (CMTS) 1790 Federal Census, Watervliet
Shaw, John: (OC) Rope Maker, (CMTS) Albany 1815 City Directory
Shaw, John B.: (F) Member Temple Lodge, No. 14, 1900, Albany, NY
Shaw, Samuel: (OC) Bookbinder, (CMTS) Albany 1815 City Directory
Shaw, Samuel: (OC) Physician, (CMTS) Albany 1815 City Directory
Shaxby, Charles J.: (F) Member Mount Vernon Lodge, No. 3, 1900, Albany, NY
Shays, Daniel Jr: (OC) Grocer, (CMTS) Albany 1815 City Directory
Shear, Christian H.: (OC) Saddler, (CMTS) Albany 1815 City Directory
Sheffer, James H.: (F) Member Temple Lodge, No. 14, 1900, Albany, NY
Sheldon, Allanson: (OC) Merchant, (CMTS) Albany 1815 City Directory
Sheldon, James: (CMTS) 1790 Federal Census, Watervliet
Sheldon, William: (CMTS) 1790 Federal Census Rensselaerville
Shell, George: (RES) 74 Church, (CMTS) Albany 1815 City Directory
Shell, Martha: (CMTS) 1790 Federal Census, Watervliet
Shell, Philip: (CMTS) 1790 Federal Census, Watervliet
Shell, William: (CMTS) 1790 Federal Census Rensselaerville

Shelley, Charles E.: (F) Member Mount Vernon Lodge, No. 3, 1900,
    Albany, NY, (CMTS) Past Master 1885
Shelly, William: (CMTS) 1790 Federal Census, Watervliet
Shepard, Frank A.: (F) Member Temple Lodge, No. 14, 1900,
    Albany, NY
Shepheard, Edward W.: (F) Member Temple Lodge, No. 14, 1900,
    Albany, NY
Shepheard, John H.: (F) Member Temple Lodge, No. 14, 1900,
    Albany, NY
Shepherd, George: (OC) Merchant, (CMTS) Albany 1815 City Directory
Shepherd, John: (RES) Boarding House at 19 Washington, (CMTS) Albany 1815 City Directory
Shepherd, Robert: (RES) 48 Hamilton, (CMTS) Albany 1815 City
    Directory
Shepherd, Widow Catharine: (OC) Lodge, (CMTS) Albany 1815 City
    Directory
Shepherd, Widow of Thomas: (OC) Store Lane, (CMTS) Albany 1815
    City Directory
Sherer, James: (OC) Laborer, (CMTS) Albany 1815 City Directory
Sherman, A: (OC) Dentist, (CMTS) Albany 1815 City Directory
Sherman, Job: (OC) Laborer, (CMTS) Albany 1815 City Directory
Sherman, Josiah: (OC) Merchant, (CMTS) Albany 1815 City Directory
Sherman, Martha: (OC) Teacher, (CMTS) Albany 1815 City Directory
Sherman, Pardon: (OC) Laborer, (CMTS) Albany 1815 City Directory
Sherrill, Charles L.: (F) Member Temple Lodge, No. 14, 1900,
    Albany, NY
Sherwood, John E.: (F) Member Temple Lodge, No. 14, 1900,
    Albany, NY
Sherwood, Samuel B.: (RES) 9 Capitol, (CMTS) Albany 1815 City
    Directory
Sherwood, Samuel M.: (OC) Merchant, (CMTS) Albany 1815 City
    Directory
Shiffle, Adam: (CMTS) 1790 Federal Census Rensselaerville
Shippey, Paul: (OC) Shoemaker, (CMTS) Albany 1815 City Directory
Shiterly, Jacob: (CMTS) 1790 Federal Census, Watervliet
Shiterly, Johannes: (CMTS) 1790 Federal Census, Watervliet
Shiterly, Jr., John: (CMTS) 1790 Federal Census, Watervliet
Shoemaker, A. McD.: (F) Member Mount Vernon Lodge, No. 3, 1900,
    Albany, NY
Shoemaker, Jacob: (OC) Cartman, (CMTS) Albany 1815 City Directory
Shoemaker, James: (F) Member Temple Lodge, No. 14, 1900,
    Albany, NY
Shoemaker, William H.: (F) Member Mount Vernon Lodge, No. 3, 1900,
    Albany, NY, (CMTS) Past Master 1873
Shonder, John: (CMTS) 1790 Federal Census, Watervliet

Shove, William: (OC) Morocco Dresser, (CMTS) Albany 1815 City
    Directory
Shower, John: (OC) Grocer, (CMTS) Albany 1815 City Directory
Shuley, John: (CMTS) 1790 Federal Census, Watervliet
Shultis, Matthis: (B) Aug. 26, 1800, (CD) Oct. 7, 1800, (BP) Berne,
    Albany Co., NY, Beaver Dam Dutch Reformed Church
Shultus, Matthias: (CMTS) 1790 Federal Census Rensselaerville
Shultus, Matthias: (B) May 27, 1806, (CD) Jun. 22, 1806, (BP) Berne,
    Albany Co., NY, St. Paul Evangelical Lutheran Church
Shultus, William: (CMTS) 1790 Federal Census Rensselaerville
Shultz, Howard H.: (F) Member Mount Vernon Lodge, No. 3, 1900,
    Albany, NY
Shumway, Nehemiah: (OC) Grocer, (CMTS) Albany 1815 City Directory
Shutter, John: (CMTS) 1790 Federal Census, Watervliet
Sickler, Hermanus: (CMTS) 1790 Federal Census, Watervliet
Sickler, John: (CMTS) 1790 Federal Census, Watervliet
Sickles, Abraham: (OC) Police Constable, (CMTS) Albany 1815 City
    Directory
Sickles, Abram: (CMTS) 1790 Federal Census, Watervliet
Sickles, James: (OC) Runner, (CMTS) Albany 1815 City Directory
Sickles, Jane Ann: (OC) Millener, (CMTS) Albany 1815 City Directory
Sickles, John: (OC) Fisherman, (CMTS) Albany 1815 City Directory
Sickles, Lodowick: (CMTS) 1790 Federal Census, Watervliet
Sickles, Zachariah: (OC) Shoemaker, (CMTS) Albany 1815 City
    Directory
Sickman, Henry: (CMTS) 1790 Federal Census, Watervliet
Sigsby, William: (OC) Laborer, (CMTS) Albany 1815 City Directory
Simmers, Andrew: (OC) Sawyer, (CMTS) Albany 1815 City Directory
Simmons, Harry: (F) Member Temple Lodge, No. 14, 1900,
    Albany, NY
Simmons, Mrs.: (OC) Teacher, (CMTS) Albany 1815 City Directory
Simon, Michael: (CMTS) 1790 Federal Census Rensselaerville
Simons, John: (OC) Carpenter, (CMTS) Albany 1815 City Directory
Simons, Moses: (OC) Attorney, (CMTS) Albany 1815 City Directory
Simons, Widow Evelina: (OC) Lumber, (CMTS) Albany 1815 City
    Directory
Simonson, J. H.: (F) Member Washington Lodge, No. 85, 1900,
    Albany, NY, (CMTS) Past Members
Simpson, George: (OC) Laborer, (CMTS) Albany 1815 City Directory
Simpson, William: (OC) Laborer, (CMTS) Albany 1815 City Directory
Sims, Edward C.: (F) Member Temple Lodge, No. 14, 1900,
    Albany, NY
Sims, Francis: (OC) Blacksmith, (CMTS) Albany 1815 City Directory
Sims, Gardner C.: (F) Member Temple Lodge, No. 14, 1900,
    Albany, NY

Sinclair, Samuel: (OC) Cartman, (CMTS) Albany 1815 City Directory
Sipple, John: (OC) Carpenter, (CMTS) Albany 1815 City Directory
Sisco, Solomon: (CMTS) 1790 Federal Census, Watervliet
Siver, Clarkson: (CMTS) 1915, Census, District No. 4 Ward No. 12
Siver, Grace: (CMTS) 1915, Census, District No. 4 Ward No. 12
Sivers, Joseph: (OC) Mason, (CMTS) Albany 1815 City Directory
Sivert, Adam: (CMTS) 1790 Federal Census, Watervliet
Sivert, Martinus: (CMTS) 1790 Federal Census, Watervliet
Sixby, Evert: (CMTS) 1790 Federal Census, Watervliet
Sixby, John: (CMTS) 1790 Federal Census, Watervliet
Sixby, Nicholas A: (CMTS) 1790 Federal Census, Watervliet
Sixby, Nicholas E: (CMTS) 1790 Federal Census, Watervliet
Skaats, David: (OC) Coach painter, (CMTS) Albany 1815 City Directory
Skerritt, John: (RES) Rear of 174 Washington, (CMTS) Albany 1815 City Directory
Skillin, Samuel: (OC) Baker, (CMTS) Albany 1815 City Directory
Skinner, Daniel: (OC) Mrs. Shepherd's Lodge, (CMTS) Albany 1815 City Directory
Skinner, Elisha W.: (OC) Tonine Coffee House, (CMTS) Albany 1815 City Directory
Skinner, Hezekiah: (RES) 106 State, (CMTS) Albany 1815 City Directory
Skinner, Josiah: (CMTS) 1790 Federal Census Rensselaerville
Skinner, M. E.: (F) Member Mount Vernon Lodge, No. 3, 1900, Albany, NY
Skinner, Nathaniel S.: (OC) Tontine Coffee House, (CMTS) Albany 1815 City Directory
Skinner, R. C: (OC) Dentist, (CMTS) Albany 1815 City Directory
Skinner, Solomon: (CMTS) 1790 Federal Census, Watervliet
Skinner, William: (OC) Baker, (CMTS) Albany 1815 City Directory
Skinner, William A.: (F) Member Temple Lodge, No. 14, 1900, Albany, NY
Slack, John: (OC) Merchant, (CMTS) Albany 1815 City Directory
Slack, Robert F.: (OC) Shoe Store, (CMTS) Albany 1815 City Directory
Slater, Robert: (CMTS) 1790 Federal Census, Watervliet
Slater, William: (CMTS) 1790 Federal Census, Watervliet
Slingerland, Aaron: (CMTS) 1790 Federal Census, Watervliet
Slingerland, Abraham: (CMTS) 1790 Federal Census, Watervliet
Slingerland, Albert: (CMTS) 1790 Federal Census, Watervliet
Slingerland, Albert: (CMTS) 1790 Federal Census, Watervliet
Slingerland, Corn. H.: (F) Member Masters Lodge, No. 5, 1900, Albany, NY
Slingerland, Cornelius: (CMTS) 1790 Federal Census, Watervliet
Slingerland, Dauw B.: (OC) Merchant, (CMTS) Albany 1815 City Directory
Slingerland, Isaac: (CMTS) 1790 Federal Census, Watervliet

Slingerland, Storm: (CMTS) 1790 Federal Census Rensselaerville
Slingerland, Teunis: (CMTS) 1790 Federal Census, Watervliet
Slingerland, Teunis W.: (CMTS) 1790 Federal Census, Watervliet
Slingerland, Tunis: (OC) Merchant, (CMTS) Albany 1815 City Directory
Slingerland, Walter: (CMTS) 1790 Federal Census, Watervliet
Slocum, Matthew B.: (OC) Merchant, (CMTS) Albany 1815 City Directory
Sloss, Robert A.: (F) Member Temple Lodge, No. 14, 1900, Albany, NY
Smith, Abijah: (OC) Carpenter, (CMTS) Albany 1815 City Directory
Smith, Albert T.: (F) Member Temple Lodge, No. 14, 1900, Albany, NY
Smith, Andrew: (CMTS) 1790 Federal Census, Watervliet
Smith, Anthony: (RES) 18 Van Schaick, (CMTS) Albany 1815 City Directory
Smith, Augustus H.: (F) Member Temple Lodge, No. 14, 1900, Albany, NY
Smith, Barent: (CMTS) 1790 Federal Census, Watervliet
Smith, Benjamin: (CMTS) 1790 Federal Census Rensselaerville
Smith, Carroll F.: (F) Member Temple Lodge, No. 14, 1900, Albany, NY
Smith, Charles: (OC) Laborer, (CMTS) Albany 1815 City Directory
Smith, Cotton: (OC) Merchant, (CMTS) Albany 1815 City Directory
Smith, Daniel: (CMTS) 1790 Federal Census Rensselaerville
Smith, Ebenezer: (OC) Builder, (CMTS) Albany 1815 City Directory
Smith, Elias: (CMTS) 1790 Federal Census, Watervliet
Smith, Elihu R.: (F) Member Temple Lodge, No. 14, 1900, Albany, NY
Smith, George A.: (F) Member Mount Vernon Lodge, No. 3, 1900, Albany, NY
Smith, Henry: (CMTS) 1790 Federal Census, Watervliet
Smith, Henry: (OC) Merchant, (CMTS) Albany 1815 City Directory
Smith, Henry: (OC) Water, (CMTS) Albany 1815 City Directory
Smith, Henry L.: (F) Member Mount Vernon Lodge, No. 3, 1900, Albany, NY
Smith, I.: (OC) Merchant, (CMTS) Albany 1815 City Directory
Smith, Israel: (OC) Merchant, (CMTS) Albany 1815 City Directory
Smith, James P.: (F) Member Masters Lodge, No. 5, 1900, Albany, NY
Smith, James U: (OC) Merchant, (CMTS) Albany 1815 City Directory
Smith, Johannes: (CMTS) 1790 Federal Census Rensselaerville
Smith, John: (CMTS) 1790 Federal Census, Watervliet
Smith, John: (CMTS) 1790 Federal Census, Watervliet

Smith, John: (OC) Tailor, (CMTS) Albany 1815 City Directory
Smith, John D.: (OC) Shoemaker, (CMTS) Albany 1815 City Directory
Smith, Lewis C: (OC) Cabinet Maker, (CMTS) Albany 1815 City
    Directory
Smith, Martin: (CMTS) 1790 Federal Census Rensselaerville
Smith, Matthias: (CMTS) 1790 Federal Census Rensselaerville
Smith, Mrs. Schook: (RES) 13 Union, (CMTS) Albany 1815 City
    Directory
Smith, Myron S.: (F) Member Temple Lodge, No. 14, 1900,
    Albany, NY
Smith, Nathan: (CMTS) 1790 Federal Census Rensselaerville
Smith, Nathaniel: (RES) 81 Pearl, (CMTS) Albany 1815 City Directory
Smith, Nicholas: (CMTS) 1790 Federal Census, Watervliet
Smith, Obadiah: (OC) Merchant, (CMTS) Albany 1815 City Directory
Smith, Oliver: (OC) Merchant, (CMTS) Albany 1815 City Directory
Smith, Oscar: (F) Member Temple Lodge, No. 14, 1900,
    Albany, NY
Smith, Ralph: (OC) Merchant, (CMTS) Albany 1815 City Directory
Smith, Rensselaer J.: (F) Member Mount Vernon Lodge, No. 3, 1900,
    Albany, NY
Smith, Reuben: (OC) Innkeeper, (CMTS) Albany 1815 City Directory
Smith, Solomon: (OC) Druggist, (CMTS) Albany 1815 City Directory
Smith, Stephen: (CMTS) 1790 Federal Census, Watervliet
Smith, Terry: (OC) Laborer, (CMTS) Albany 1815 City Directory
Smith, Thomas: (OC) Mason, (CMTS) Albany 1815 City Directory
Smith, Widow Margaret: (RES) 28 N. Market, (CMTS) Albany 1815 City
    Directory
Smith, Wilhelmus: (CMTS) 1790 Federal Census, Watervliet
Smith, William: (CMTS) 1790 Federal Census Rensselaerville
Smith, William Henry: (F) Member Temple Lodge, No. 14, 1900,
    Albany, NY
Smith , Peter: (OC) Laborer, (CMTS) Albany 1815 City Directory
Smull, Lawrence: (OC) Painter, (CMTS) Albany 1815 City Directory
Smyley, William: (F) Member Mount Vernon Lodge, No. 3, 1900,
    Albany, NY
Smyth, Charles: (OC) Merchant, (CMTS) Albany 1815 City Directory
Smythe, Charles G.: (F) Member Temple Lodge, No. 14, 1900,
    Albany, NY
Sniper, Gustavus C.: (F) Member Temple Lodge, No. 14, 1900,
    Albany, NY
Snoke, Daniel: (OC) Laborer, (CMTS) Albany 1815 City Directory
Snow, Whiting G.: (F) Member Masters Lodge, No. 5, 1900,
    Albany, NY
Snyder, Adam: (CMTS) 1790 Federal Census Rensselaerville
Snyder, Daniel: (OC) Tiger, (CMTS) Albany 1815 City Directory

Snyder, George: (CMTS) 1790 Federal Census Rensselaerville
Snyder, Henry: (OC) Shoemaker, (CMTS) Albany 1815 City Directory
Snyder, Henry W.: (OC) Engraver, (CMTS) Albany 1815 City Directory
Snyder, Isaac: (CMTS) 1790 Federal Census Rensselaerville
Snyder, Louis G. A.: (F) Member Temple Lodge, No. 14, 1900, Albany, NY
Snyder, Martinus: (CMTS) 1790 Federal Census, Watervliet
Snyder, Peter: (OC) Laborer, (CMTS) Albany 1815 City Directory
Snyder, Peter H.: (CMTS) 1790 Federal Census Rensselaerville
Snyder, Philip: (CMTS) 1790 Federal Census Rensselaerville
Snyder, William: (CMTS) 1790 Federal Census, Watervliet
Snyder, William: (RES) 166 N. Market, (CMTS) Albany 1815 City Directory
Snyder, William: (OC) Merchant, (CMTS) Albany 1815 City Directory
Solomons, Levi: (RES) 47 State, (CMTS) Albany 1815 City Directory
Somerville, Robert: (F) Member Mount Vernon Lodge, No. 3, 1900, Albany, NY
Sottle, John: (CMTS) 1790 Federal Census, Watervliet
Soulier, Henry P.: (F) Member Masters Lodge, No. 5, 1900, Albany, NY
Souls, Jonathan: (CMTS) 1790 Federal Census, Watervliet
Southern, Samuel: (F) Member Temple Lodge, No. 14, 1900, Albany, NY
Southwick, E. M & J: (OC) Merchant, (CMTS) Albany 1815 City Directory
Southwick, Henry C: (OC) Printer, (CMTS) Albany 1815 City Directory
Southwick, Solomon: (OC) Editor Albany Register, (CMTS) Albany 1815 City Directory
Southwick, Thomas M: (OC) Merchant, (CMTS) Albany 1815 City Directory
Southwick, Wilmarth: (OC) Rope Maker, (CMTS) Albany 1815 City Directory
Southworth, William: (CMTS) 1790 Federal Census Rensselaerville
Spafford, Heratio F.: (OC) Author gazetteer, (CMTS) Albany 1815 City Directory
Sparbeck, Henry: (CMTS) 1790 Federal Census Rensselaerville
Sparbeck, Martin: (CMTS) 1790 Federal Census, Watervliet
Sparkbeck, Conradt: (CMTS) 1790 Federal Census Rensselaerville
Sparrow, James: (OC) Van Schee, (CMTS) Albany 1815 City Directory
Spawn, John: (OC) Mason, (CMTS) Albany 1815 City Directory
Spawn, Philip: (CMTS) 1790 Federal Census, Watervliet
Spawn, William H. A.: (F) Member Temple Lodge, No. 14, 1900, Albany, NY
Spearback, Andrew: (CMTS) 1790 Federal Census, Watervliet
Speck, Peter: (CMTS) 1790 Federal Census, Watervliet

Speir, Smith J.: (F) Member Masters Lodge, No. 5, 1900,
    Albany, NY
Speir, Stuart G.: (F) Member Masters Lodge, No. 5, 1900,
    Albany, NY, (CMTS) Past Master
Spemcer, Ambrose: (OC) Judge, (CMTS) Albany 1815 City Directory
Spencer, Eli: (CMTS) 1790 Federal Census Rensselaerville
Spencer, George B.: (OC) Merchant, (CMTS) Albany 1815 City Directory
Spencer, Giles: (OC) Trunk and Bandbox Maker, (CMTS) Albany 1815
    City Directory
Spencer, Israel B.: (CMTS) 1790 Federal Census Rensselaerville
Spencer, John: (OC) Merchant, (CMTS) Albany 1815 City Directory
Spencer, Thomas: (RES) 320 Washington, (CMTS) Albany 1815 City
    Directory
Spencer, Welthan: (OC) Tailoress, (CMTS) Albany 1815 City Directory
Sperry, Elisha B.: (OC) Innkeeper, (CMTS) Albany 1815 City Directory
Spierre, Alexander H.: (F) Member Temple Lodge, No. 14, 1900,
    Albany, NY
Spoo, John: (F) Member Mount Vernon Lodge, No. 3, 1900,
    Albany, NY
Spore, Abraham: (CMTS) 1790 Federal Census Rensselaerville
Spore, John: (CMTS) 1790 Federal Census Rensselaerville
Sprague, W. R.: (F) Member Masters Lodge, No. 5, 1900,
    Albany, NY
Springer, Benjamin: (CMTS) 1790 Federal Census, Watervliet
Springer, Benjamin: (B) Jan. 19, 1794, (BP) Guilderland, Albany Co.,
    NY, (PRTS) Vincent Springer and Sarah Howe
Springer, Benjamin: (CD) Jun. 14, 1740, (BP) Albany, First Dutch
    Reformed Church, (PRTS) Daniel Springer and Maria ????
Springer, Daniel: (B) Jan. 5, 1764, (BP) Albany, (PRTS) David Springer
    And Margaret Oliver
Springer, David: (CD) Mar. 11, 1798, (BP) Noormanskill, Albany Co.,
    NY, (PRTS) Vincent Springer and Sarah Howe
Springer, David: (MD) Oct. 26, 1754, (Spouse) Margaret Oliver, (PMD)
    Albany Co., NY
Springer, John: (B) Mar. 5, 1771, (BP) Albany, NY, (PRTS) David
    Springer and Margaret Oliver
Springer, Vincent: (MD) Dec. 4, 1787, (Spouse) Sarah Howe, (PMD)
    Albany Co., NY
Springer, Vincent: (CMTS) 1790 Federal Census, Watervliet
Springer, Vincent: (B) Mar. 23, 1807, (BP) Guilderland, Albany Co.,
    NY, (PRTS) Vicent Springer and Sarah Howe
Springer, Vincent: (B) Dec. 14, 1767, (CD) Jan. 16, 1768, (BP) Albany,
    First Dutch Reformed Church, (PRTS) Benjamin Springer
Springsteel, Jacob: (CMTS) 1790 Federal Census, Watervliet
Springsteel, Jeremiah: (CMTS) 1790 Federal Census, Watervliet

Springsteel, John: (CMTS) 1790 Federal Census, Watervliet
Springsteel, Joseph: (CMTS) 1790 Federal Census, Watervliet
Springsteen, Jacob F.: (CMTS) 1790 Federal Census, Watervliet
St. John, Solomon: (OC) Merchant, (CMTS) Albany 1815 City Directory
Staats, Barent: (B) Aug. 18, 1680, (BP) Albany, NY, (CD) Jan. 7, 1685, First Dutch Reformed Church, (D) Jul. 26, 1752, (PRTS) Jochem Staats and Antje Reyndertse
Staats, Barent: (MD) Mar. 25, 1789, (PMD) Albany, (Spouse) Catharine Cuyler
Staats, Barent: (B) May 16, 1762, (D) Aug. 25, 1840, (BP) Albany, NY, (PRTS) Gerret Staats and Debara Beekman
Staats, Barent: (CMTS) 1790 Federal Census, Watervliet
Staats, Barent A.: (B) Mar. 20, 1717, (D) Jul. 20, 1752, (PRTS) Abraham Staats and Maria ????
Staats, Barent G.: (OC) Merchant, (CMTS) Albany 1815 City Directory
Staats, Cornelius: (OC) Laborer, (CMTS) Albany 1815 City Directory
Staats, Edward P.: (F) Member Mount Vernon Lodge, No. 3, 1900, Albany, NY
Staats, Elizabeth: (RES) 70 S. Peark, (CMTS) Albany 1815 City Directory
Staats, I.: (OC) Apothecary, (CMTS) Albany 1815 City Directory
Staats, I. L.: (OC) Apothecary, (CMTS) Albany 1815 City Directory
Staats, Isaac W.: (OC) Merchant, (CMTS) Albany 1815 City Directory
Staats, John: (CD) Nov. 5, 1795, (BP) Albany, NY, (PRTS) Barent And Cathaerine Cuyler
Staats, John: (OC) Assistant Superintendent, (CMTS) Albany 1815 City Directory
Staats, John T.: (B) Mar. 16, 1820, (BP) Albany, (PRTS) Abraham P. Staats and Bertha Leggett
Staats, Widow of Henry: (RES) 86 State, (CMTS) Albany 1815 City Directory
Staats, William: (OC) Collector of Taxes, (CMTS) Albany 1815 City Directory
Staats, William W.: (OC) Merchant, (CMTS) Albany 1815 City Directory
Stackhouse, William: (RES) 55 Eagle, (CMTS) Albany 1815 City Directory
Stacpole, Horatio P.: (F) Member Masters Lodge, No. 5, 1900, Albany, NY
Stadder, Henry: (CMTS) 1790 Federal Census Rensselaerville
Staechia, William: (F) Member Temple Lodge, No. 14, 1900, Albany, NY
Stafford, Hallenbake: (OC) Merchant, (CMTS) Albany 1815 City Directory
Stafford, John: (OC) Merchant, (CMTS) Albany 1815 City Directory
Stafford, Spencer: (OC) Merchant, (CMTS) Albany 1815 City Directory
Stander, Nicholas: (CMTS) 1790 Federal Census Rensselaerville

Stanford, Sylvanus: (OC) Grocer, (CMTS) Albany 1815 City Directory
Stanson, Ejett: (CMTS) 1790 Federal Census, Watervliet
Stanton, Ebenezer: (CMTS) 1790 Federal Census, Watervliet
Stanton, George W.: (OC) Merchant, (CMTS) Albany 1815 City Directory
Stanton, James: (CMTS) 1790 Federal Census, Watervliet
Stanton, John: (CMTS) 1790 Federal Census, Watervliet
Stanton, Nathan: (CMTS) 1790 Federal Census, Watervliet
Stanton, Reuben: (CMTS) 1790 Federal Census, Watervliet
Stanwix, George: (OC) Grocer, (CMTS) Albany 1815 City Directory
Stark, Charles: (F) Member Mount Vernon Lodge, No. 3, 1900, Albany, NY
Starns, J. M.: (F) Member Mount Vernon Lodge, No. 3, 1900, Albany, NY
Starr, Chandler: (OC) Merchant, (CMTS) Albany 1815 City Directory
Starr, Elisha: (CMTS) 1790 Federal Census, Watervliet
Starr, P. R.: (OC) Clothing Store, (CMTS) Albany 1815 City Directory
Stearns, John: (OC) Physician, (CMTS) Albany 1815 City Directory
Stebbins, Rowland: (OC) Soda Water, (CMTS) Albany 1815 City Directory
Steel, Levi: (OC) Hairdresser, (CMTS) Albany 1815 City Directory
Steele, Daniel: (OC) Bookseller, (CMTS) Albany 1815 City Directory
Steele, Elijah: (OC) Coaler, (CMTS) Albany 1815 City Directory
Steele, Lemuel: (OC) Paperhanger, (CMTS) Albany 1815 City Directory
Steenburg, B. U.: (F) Member Mount Vernon Lodge, No. 3, 1900, Albany, NY
Stephens, Cyprin: (CMTS) 1790 Federal Census Rensselaerville
Stephens, Gershom: (CMTS) 1790 Federal Census Rensselaerville
Stephens, Jarid: (CMTS) 1790 Federal Census Rensselaerville
Stephens, Jr., Jarid: (CMTS) 1790 Federal Census Rensselaerville
Stephenson, Matthew: (F) Member Temple Lodge, No. 14, 1900, Albany, NY
Stephenson, Samuel T.: (F) Member Temple Lodge, No. 14, 1900, Albany, NY
Stern, Henry E.: (F) Member Washington Lodge, No. 85, 1900, Albany, NY, (CMTS) Past Members
Sternberg, Jacob F.: (OC), (CMTS) Albany 1815 City Directory
Sternbergh, Philip: (CMTS) 1790 Federal Census Rensselaerville
Sterns, Clifton C.: (OC) Grocer, (CMTS) Albany 1815 City Directory
Stetson, William M.: (F) Member Temple Lodge, No. 14, 1900, Albany, NY
Stevens, George T.: (F) Member Mount Vernon Lodge, No. 3, 1900, Albany, NY
Stevens, John: (CMTS) 1790 Federal Census, Watervliet
Stevens, John: (CMTS) 1790 Federal Census, Watervliet

Stevens, Joseph B.: (F) Member Temple Lodge, No. 14, 1900,
    Albany, NY, (CMTS) Past Master 1894
Stevenson, James: (OC) Counsellor, (CMTS) Albany 1815 City Directory
Stevenson, Pottam: (CMTS) 1790 Federal Census, Watervliet
Stevenson, Widow of John: (CMTS) Albany 1815 City Directory
Steward, Adam: (RES) 24 Quay, (CMTS) Albany 1815 City Directory
Stewart, David R.: (F) Member Mount Vernon Lodge, No. 3, 1900,
    Albany, NY
Stewart, Eliphilet: (CMTS) 1790 Federal Census Rensselaerville
Stewart, Gilbert: (OC) Merchant, (CMTS) Albany 1815 City Directory
Stewart, John: (OC) Grocer, (CMTS) Albany 1815 City Directory
Stewart, Lachlan: (OC) Flour Store, (CMTS) Albany 1815 City Directory
Stewart, Walter: (OC) Merchant, (CMTS) Albany 1815 City Directory
Stewart, Widow Isabel: (RES) 73 Hudson, (CMTS) Albany 1815 City
    Directory
Stickneys, Leander: (OC) Coffee & Spice Manufacturers, Bacon &
Stickneys, (CMTS) Albany 1859 City Directory
Stickneys, Moses W.: (OC) Coffee & Spice Manufacturers, Bacon &
Stickneys, (CMTS) Albany 1859 City Directory
Stiles, Samuel: (OC) Shoemaker, (CMTS) Albany 1815 City Directory
Stillman, William O.: (F) Member Masters Lodge, No. 5, 1900,
    Albany, NY
Stilwell, John: (OC) Merchant, (CMTS) Albany 1815 City Directory
Stilwell, Smith: (RES) 221 N. Market, (CMTS) Albany 1815 City
    Directory
Stilwell, Wendell: (OC) Auctioneer, (CMTS) Albany 1815 City Directory
Stilwell, William: (OC) Tobacconist, (CMTS) Albany 1815 City Directory
Stine, John V.: (F) Member Temple Lodge, No. 14, 1900,
    Albany, NY
Stockwell, U. G.: (F) Member Temple Lodge, No. 14, 1900,
    Albany, NY
Stoenman, George T.: (F) Member Temple Lodge, No. 14, 1900,
    Albany, NY, (CMTS) Life Member
Stoff, Hendreck: (CMTS) 1790 Federal Census, Watervliet
Stoker, William H.: (F) Member Temple Lodge, No. 14, 1900,
    Albany, NY
Stone, George: (CMTS) 1790 Federal Census, Watervliet
Stoner, Peter: (CMTS) 1790 Federal Census, Watervliet
Storey, Lawrence: (OC) Blacksmith, (CMTS) Albany 1815 City Directory
Storrs, Andrew: (OC) Carpenter, (CMTS) Albany 1815 City Directory
Storrs, William H.: (F) Member Temple Lodge, No. 14, 1900,
    Albany, NY
Story, James T.: (F) Member Temple Lodge, No. 14, 1900,
    Albany, NY, (CMTS) Life Member
Story, William: (F) Member Masters Lodge, No. 5, 1900,

Albany, NY, (CMTS) Past Master
Stott, Hiram W.: (F) Member Temple Lodge, No. 14, 1900,
   Albany, NY
Stoutenberg, James: (OC) Laborer, (CMTS) Albany 1815 City Directory
Stover, William: (CMTS) 1790 Federal Census Rensselaerville
Straiu, William: (OC) Laborer, (CMTS) Albany 1815 City Directory
Strange, James: (OC) Merchant, (CMTS) Albany 1815 City Directory
Strange, James: (OC) Merchant, (CMTS) Albany 1815 City
   Directory
Strange, Maxwell: (OC) Merchant, (CMTS) Albany 1815 City Directory
Strasser, Benjamin: (F) Member Mount Vernon Lodge, No. 3, 1900,
   Albany, NY, (CMTS) Past Master 1897
Strasser, Isaac M.: (F) Member Mount Vernon Lodge, No. 3, 1900,
   Albany, NY
Strasser, Solomon: (F) Member Mount Vernon Lodge, No. 3, 1900,
   Albany, NY, (CMTS) Past Master 1887
Street, Alfred W.: (F) Member Temple Lodge, No. 14, 1900,
   Albany, NY
Stremple, Anna: (CMTS) 1915, Census, District No. 1 Ward No. 10
Stremple, Catherine: (CMTS) 1915, Census, District No. 5 Ward No. 18
Stremple, Daniel: (CMTS) 1915, Census, District No. 1 Ward No. 19
Stremple, Dorothy: (CMTS) 1915, Census, District No. 1 Ward No. 19
Stremple, Frederick: (CMTS) 1915, Census, District No. 1 Ward No. 19
Stremple, J. Edward: (F) Member Temple Lodge, No. 14, 1900,
   Albany, NY
Stremple, Mary: (CMTS) 1915, Census, District No. 1 Ward No. 19
Strickland, Ralph: (F) Member Masters Lodge, No. 5, 1900,
   Albany, NY
Stringer, Samuel: (OC) Physician, (CMTS) Albany 1815 City Directory
Strong, Charles: (OC) Teacher, (CMTS) Albany 1815 City Directory
Strong, Frederick S.: (F) Member Masters Lodge, No. 5, 1900,
   Albany, NY
Strong, Joseph: (OC) Grocer, (CMTS) Albany 1815 City Directory
Strong, Michael: (OC) Laborer, (CMTS) Albany 1815 City Directory
Strong, Robert: (OC) Grocer, (CMTS) Albany 1815 City Directory
Strugess, Elnathan: (OC) Tiger, (CMTS) Albany 1815 City Directory
Stuart, J. B.: (RES) 132 State, (CMTS) Albany 1815 City Directory
Stubblebine, Daniel H.: (F) Member Temple Lodge, No. 14, 1900,
   Albany, NY
Stuckert, Abner M.: (F) Member Masters Lodge, No. 5, 1900,
   Albany, NY
Sturdivant, Mrs: (OC) Washerwoman, (CMTS) Albany 1815 City
   Directory
Sturgess, James: (OC) Shoemaker, (CMTS) Albany 1815 City Directory
Sturgess, Widow Sarah: (RES) 11 Chapel, (CMTS) Albany 1815 City

Directory
Sturtevant, Adelia U.: (CMTS) 1915, Census, District No. 3 Ward No. 14
Sturtevant, Mrs. C. T.: (CMTS) 1915, Census, District No. 3 Ward No. 14
Sturtevant, F. R.: (CMTS) 1915, Census, District No. 3 Ward No. 14
Sturtevant, Geraldine: (CMTS) 1915, Census, District No. 6 Ward No. 16
Sturtevant, Gilbert A.: (CMTS) 1915, Census, District No. 3 Ward No. 14
Sturtevant, Howard R.: (CMTS) 1915, Census, District No. 6 Ward No. 16
Sturtevant, Josephine U.: (CMTS) 1915, Census, District No. 6
   Ward No. 16
Sturtevant, Julia F.: (CMTS) 1915, Census, District No. 3 Ward No. 14
Sturtevant, Minnie L.: (CMTS) 1915, Census, District No. 6 Ward No. 16
Sturtevant, Ruppert P.: (CMTS) 1915, Census, District No. 6 Ward No. 16
Sturtevant, Jr., Ruppert P.: (CMTS) 1915, Census, District No. 6
   Ward No. 16
Sturtevant, Zebina: (OC) Grocer, (CMTS) Albany 1815 City Directory
Styner, Casper: (CMTS) 1790 Federal Census Rensselaerville
Sudgen, John R: (RES) 41 Liberty, (CMTS) Albany 1815 City Directory
Sullivan, David: (CMTS) 1790 Federal Census, Watervliet
Sullivan, David: (CMTS) 1790 Federal Census, Watervliet
Summerey, James: (CMTS) 1790 Federal Census, Watervliet
Sutherland, Charles R.: (F) Member Mount Vernon Lodge, No. 3, 1900,
   Albany, NY
Sutherland, Jacob: (OC) Counsellor, (CMTS) Albany 1815 City Directory
Sutherland, Williard J.: (F) Member Temple Lodge, No. 14, 1900,
   Albany, NY
Swain, Robert: (OC) Tailor, (CMTS) Albany 1815 City Directory
Swan, George: (CMTS) 1790 Federal Census, Watervliet
Swan, John B.: (RES) 17 Green, (CMTS) Albany 1815 City Directory
Swart, Widow: (OC) Cornelius, (CMTS) Albany 1815 City Directory
Swarthout, Adolphus: (CMTS) 1790 Federal Census Rensselaerville
Swartz, Charles L.: (F) Member Temple Lodge, No. 14, 1900,
   Albany, NY
Swartz, Conradt: (CMTS) 1790 Federal Census Rensselaerville
Swartz, Henry: (CMTS) 1790 Federal Census Rensselaerville
Syvert, Jacob: (CMTS) 1790 Federal Census, Watervliet
Syvert, Robert: (CMTS) 1790 Federal Census, Watervliet
Tabor, Carey: (RES) 10 Green, (CMTS) Albany 1815 City Directory
Tabor, Thomas: (OC) Laborer, (CMTS) Albany 1815 City Directory
Talbot, Cornelius: (OC) Shoemaker, (CMTS) Albany 1815 City Directory
Talbot, Philip: (OC) Painter, (CMTS) Albany 1815 City Directory
Talbot, William: (OC) Laborer, (CMTS) Albany 1815 City Directory
Tallcott, Edwin S.: (F) Member Temple Lodge, No. 14, 1900,
   Albany, NY
Tanner, Cyrus: (OC) Innkeeper, (CMTS) Albany 1815 City Directory
Tanner, Marvin: (F) Member Temple Lodge, No. 14, 1900,

Albany, NY
Tansel, Nicholas: (OC) Laborer, (CMTS) Albany 1815 City Directory
Tapin, Matthew: (OC) Hatter, (CMTS) Albany 1815 City Directory
Tarbell, John: (OC) Grocer, (CMTS) Albany 1815 City Directory
Tate, Joseph: (OC) Tailor, (CMTS) Albany 1815 City Directory
Tate, Thomas: (OC) Grocer, (CMTS) Albany 1815 City Directory
Tayler, John: (OC) Lieutenant Governor, (CMTS) Albany 1815 City Directory
Taylor, Edward: (CMTS) 1790 Federal Census Rensselaerville
Taylor, Edwy L.: (F) Member Masters Lodge, No. 5, 1900, Albany, NY, (CMTS) Past Master
Taylor, James: (CMTS) 1790 Federal Census, Watervliet
Taylor, James: (F) Member Mount Vernon Lodge, No. 3, 1900, Albany, NY, (CMTS) Past Master 1890
Taylor, John: (OC) Chandler, (CMTS) Albany 1815 City Directory
Taylor, Lucas: (CMTS) 1790 Federal Census, Watervliet
Taylor, Nicholas B.: (F) Member Masters Lodge, No. 5, 1900, Albany, NY
Taylor, Robert: (CMTS) 1790 Federal Census, Watervliet
Taylor, Samuel F.: (F) Member Temple Lodge, No. 14, 1900, Albany, NY
Taylor, William G.: (OC) Merchant, (CMTS) Albany 1815 City Directory
Taylor, William James: (F) Member Temple Lodge, No. 14, 1900, Albany, NY
Taylor, Z. S.: (F) Member Mount Vernon Lodge, No. 3, 1900, Albany, NY
Tearnan, Lawrence: (OC) Grocer, (CMTS) Albany 1815 City Directory
Tearpanning, Teunis: (CMTS) 1790 Federal Census, Watervliet
Tebbutt, Harry K.: (F) Member Temple Lodge, No. 14, 1900, Albany, NY
Tebbutt, Marshall W.: (F) Member Temple Lodge, No. 14, 1900, Albany, NY, (CMTS) Life Member
Teeling, George W.: (F) Member Temple Lodge, No. 14, 1900, Albany, NY
Telfair, James: (RES) 176 Washington, (CMTS) Albany 1815 City Directory
Telford, Adam: (CMTS) 1790 Federal Census, Watervliet
Teller, Isaac T.: (OC) Grocer, (CMTS) Albany 1815 City Directory
Ten Broeck, Benjamin F.: (OC) Printer, (CMTS) Albany 1815 City Directory
Ten Eyck, Abraham Jr: (RES) 368 N. Market, (CMTS) Albany 1815 City Directory
Ten Eyck, Abraham R: (OC) Bookseller, (CMTS) Albany 1815 City Directory
Ten Eyck, Andress: (CMTS) 1790 Federal Census, Watervliet

Ten Eyck, Clinton: (F) Member Temple Lodge, No. 14, 1900,
  Albany, NY
Ten Eyck, Conradt: (CMTS) 1790 Federal Census, Watervliet
Ten Eyck, Conradt A: (CMTS) 1790 Federal Census, Watervliet
Ten Eyck, Conradt T: (CMTS) 1790 Federal Census, Watervliet
Ten Eyck, Harmanus: (RES) 362 N. Market, (CMTS) Albany 1815 City
  Directory
Ten Eyck, Jacob: (OC) Merchant, (CMTS) Albany 1815 City Directory
Ten Eyck, Jacob H.: (OC) Merchant, (CMTS) Albany 1815 City Directory
Ten Eyck, James: (F) Member Masters Lodge, No. 5, 1900,
  Albany, NY, (CMTS) Past Master
Ten Eyck, James: (F) Member Temple Lodge, No. 14, 1900,
  Albany, NY, (CMTS) Honorary Member
Ten Eyck, Johannes: (CMTS) 1790 Federal Census Rensselaerville
Ten Eyck, John D. P.: (RES) 82 State, (CMTS) Albany 1815 City
  Directory
Ten Eyck, Tobias: (CMTS) 1790 Federal Census, Watervliet
Terrell, William H.: (F) Member Temple Lodge, No. 14, 1900,
  Albany, NY
Terry, David: (OC) Laborer, (CMTS) Albany 1815 City Directory
Thacher, George H.: (F) Member Masters Lodge, No. 5, 1900,
  Albany, NY
Thacher, John Boyd: (F) Member Masters Lodge, No. 5, 1900,
  Albany, NY, (CMTS) Past Master
Thacher, Ralph W.: (F) Member Masters Lodge, No. 5, 1900,
  Albany, NY
Thalhimer, Bernard: (OC) Merchant, (CMTS) Albany 1815 City Directory
Thatcher, Charles A.: (F) Member Temple Lodge, No. 14, 1900,
  Albany, NY
Thatcher, George A.: (F) Member Temple Lodge, No. 14, 1900,
  Albany, NY
Thatcher, Julian A.: (F) Member Temple Lodge, No. 14, 1900,
  Albany, NY
Thayer, Jr., Amos: (OC) Butcher, (CMTS) Albany 1815 City Directory
Thayer, Benjamin: (OC) Butcher, (CMTS) Albany 1815 City Directory
Thayer, Walter B.: (F) Member Temple Lodge, No. 14, 1900,
  Albany, NY
Thomas, John: (OC) Cooper, (CMTS) Albany 1815 City Directory
Thomas, Joseph: (CMTS) 1790 Federal Census Rensselaerville
Thomas, Richard: (OC) Cooper, (CMTS) Albany 1815 City Directory
Thomas, Thomas T: (OC) Cooper, (CMTS) Albany 1815 City Directory
Thomas, II, George L.: (F) Member Temple Lodge, No. 14, 1900,
  Albany, NY
Thompson, Aaron: (OC) Shoemaker, (CMTS) Albany 1815 City Directory
Thompson, Alexander: (CMTS) 1790 Federal Census Rensselaerville

Thompson, Andrew: (OC) Coppersimith, (CMTS) Albany 1815 City Directory
Thompson, Carmon: (OC) Carpenter, (CMTS) Albany 1815 City Directory
Thompson, Catharine B.: (OC) Young Ladies' School, (CMTS) Albany 1815 City Directory
Thompson, Charity: (RES) 63 Maiden Lane, (CMTS) Albany 1815 City Directory
Thompson, Charles W.: (F) Member Temple Lodge, No. 14, 1900, Albany, NY
Thompson, Curtiss E.: (F) Member Temple Lodge, No. 14, 1900, Albany, NY
Thompson, David A.: (F) Member Masters Lodge, No. 5, 1900, Albany, NY
Thompson, George C.: (F) Member Temple Lodge, No. 14, 1900, Albany, NY
Thompson, Jacob: (OC) Cartman, (CMTS) Albany 1815 City Directory
Thompson, John: (F) Member Mount Vernon Lodge, No. 3, 1900, Albany, NY
Thompson, John: (CMTS) 1790 Federal Census Rensselaerville
Thompson, John: (OC) Waterman, (CMTS) Albany 1815 City Directory
Thompson, Richard: (OC) Grocer, (CMTS) Albany 1815 City Directory
Thompson, Smith: (OC) Chief Justice, (CMTS) Albany 1815 City Directory
Thompson, Thomas: (OC) Shoe Black, (CMTS) Albany 1815 City Directory
Thompson, Thomas: (OC) Shoemaker, (CMTS) Albany 1815 City Directory
Thompson, Thomas: (OC) Tailor, (CMTS) Albany 1815 City Directory
Thompson, Willaim: (OC) Waterman, (CMTS) Albany 1815 City Directory
Thompson, William: (OC) Coppersimith, (CMTS) Albany 1815 City Directory
Thompson, William C: (OC) Tailor, (CMTS) Albany 1815 City Directory
Thorbes, Rebecca: (RES) Boarding House at 216 Pearl, (CMTS) Albany 1815 City Directory
Thorn, Nathaniel: (CMTS) 1790 Federal Census, Watervliet
Thorne, Jr., James: (RES) 56 State, (CMTS) Albany 1815 City Directory
Thorne, John: (OC) Clerk in M & F. bank, (CMTS) Albany 1815 City Directory
Thornton, Francis L.: (F) Member Temple Lodge, No. 14, 1900, Albany, NY
Thorp, Aaron: (OC) Stage Office, (CMTS) Albany 1815 City Directory
Thorp, Eliakim H.: (OC) Grocer, (CMTS) Albany 1815 City Directory
Tichenor, J. W.: (OC) Coach painter, (CMTS) Albany 1815 City Directory

Tiernan, Lawrence: (OC) Grocer, (CMTS) Albany 1815 City Directory
Tiffany, Widow Margaret: (RES) 107 Fox, (CMTS) Albany 1815 City Directory
Tift, Caleb: (CMTS) 1790 Federal Census Rensselaerville
Tilburn, Richard M: (OC) Planemaker, (CMTS) Albany 1815 City Directory
Tilfy, John: (OC) Laborer, (CMTS) Albany 1815 City Directory
Tillhue, Jonathan: (OC) Sawyer, (CMTS) Albany 1815 City Directory
Tillman, Richard: (CMTS) 1790 Federal Census, Watervliet
Tillman, William: (CMTS) 1790 Federal Census, Watervliet
Tillman, Jr., John: (CMTS) 1790 Federal Census, Watervliet
Tillotson, Elezer: (OC) Blacksmith, (CMTS) Albany 1815 City Directory
Tillotson, Jr., Robert: (OC) Counsellor, (CMTS) Albany 1815 City Directory
Tilman, John: (CMTS) 1790 Federal Census, Watervliet
Tilman, John R.: (OC) Rigger, (CMTS) Albany 1815 City Directory
Tilman, Margaret: (OC) Tailoress, (CMTS) Albany 1815 City Directory
Tilman, Richard: (OC) Shoemaker, (CMTS) Albany 1815 City Directory
Timeson, Elder: (CMTS) 1790 Federal Census, Watervliet
Timeson, Peter: (CMTS) 1790 Federal Census, Watervliet
Timissic, Bastian: (CMTS) 1790 Federal Census, Watervliet
Tinker, Elisha: (OC) Teamster, (CMTS) Albany 1815 City Directory
Tinker, Joshua: (OC) Teacher, (CMTS) Albany 1815 City Directory
Tinkey, John: (CMTS) 1790 Federal Census, Watervliet
Tipton, J. Benton: (F) Member Masters Lodge, No. 5, 1900, Albany, NY
Todd, Benjamin: (CMTS) 1915, Census, District No. 5 Ward No. 19
Todd, Charlotte: (CMTS) 1915, Census, District No. 2 Ward No. 14
Todd, Gail: (CMTS) 1915, Census, District No. 5 Ward No. 18
Todd, Geo.: (CMTS) 1915, Census, District No. 5 Ward No. 18
Todd, Gladis: (CMTS) 1915, Census, District No. 5 Ward No. 19
Todd, James: (OC) Carpenter, (CMTS) Albany 1815 City Directory
Todd, John: (OC) Sexton to the Episcoal church, (CMTS) Albany 1815 City Directory
Todd, Julian A.: (CMTS) 1915, Census, District No. 2 Ward No. 14
Todd, Mary: (CMTS) 1915, Census, District No. 5 Ward No. 19
Todd, Nina: (CMTS) 1915, Census, District No. 5 Ward No. 18
Todd, Paul: (CMTS) 1790 Federal Census Rensselaerville
Todd, Widow of James: (OC), (CMTS) Albany 1815 City Directory
Todd, Zella: (CMTS) 1915, Census, District No. 2 Ward No. 14
Toedt, E. B.: (F) Member Masters Lodge, No. 5, 1900, Albany, NY
Toles, Ebenezer: (CMTS) 1790 Federal Census Rensselaerville
Toles, Elijah: (CMTS) 1790 Federal Census Rensselaerville
Toles, Titus: (CMTS) 1790 Federal Census Rensselaerville

Tolle, Otto A.: (F) Member Masters Lodge, No. 5, 1900,
    Albany, NY
Tolleker, Charles: (CMTS) 1790 Federal Census, Watervliet
Tomaw, Henry: (CMTS) 1790 Federal Census, Watervliet
Tompkins, Almet: (F) Member Mount Vernon Lodge, No. 3, 1900,
    Albany, NY
Tompkins, Edmund: (CMTS) 1790 Federal Census, Watervliet
Tompkins, Daniel D.: (RES) 149 S. Pearl, (CMTS) Albany
    1815 City Directory
Top, John: (OC) Musician, (CMTS) Albany 1815 City Directory
Toppin, Sylvester: (OC) Carpenter, (CMTS) Albany 1815 City Directory
Topping, Robert R.: (F) Member Temple Lodge, No. 14, 1900,
    Albany, NY
Topping, Washington: (F) Member Temple Lodge, No. 14, 1900,
    Albany, NY
Toren, Augustus H.: (F) Member Temple Lodge, No. 14, 1900,
    Albany, NY
Totten, Samuel: (CMTS) 1790 Federal Census, Watervliet
Towneer, S. B.: (F) Member Masters Lodge, No. 5, 1900,
    Albany, NY
Townsend, Jr., Absalom: (OC) Counsellor, (CMTS) Albany 1815 City
    Directory
Townsend, Charles D.: (OC) Physician, (CMTS) Albany 1815 City
    Directory
Townsend, Isaiah: (RES) 98 N. Pearl, (CMTS) Albany 1815 City
    Directory
Townsend, John: (OC) Merchant, (CMTS) Albany 1815 City Directory
Townsend, John DeP.: (F) Member Masters Lodge, No. 5, 1900,
    Albany, NY, (CMTS) Past Master
Townsend, Joseph: (OC) Carpenter, (CMTS) Albany 1815 City Directory
Townsend, Solomon D.: (OC) Merchant, (CMTS) Albany 1815 City
    Directory
Tracy, Henry P.: (F) Member Mount Vernon Lodge, No. 3, 1900,
    Albany, NY
Tracy, Livy: (CMTS) 1790 Federal Census Rensselaerville
Tracy, Sandford: (CMTS) 1790 Federal Census Rensselaerville
Trainer, John: (CMTS) 1790 Federal Census, Watervliet
Traver, Daniel: (CMTS) 1790 Federal Census, Watervliet
Travis, John: (RES) Boarding House at 52 Hudson, (CMTS) Albany 1815
    City Directory
Treadwell, George H.: (F) Member Temple Lodge, No. 14, 1900,
    Albany, NY
Treat, Isaac: (OC) Attorney, (CMTS) Albany 1815 City Directory
Treat, Richard S.: (OC) Counsellor, (CMTS) Albany 1815 City Directory
Tredwell, Reuben: (CMTS) 1790 Federal Census Rensselaerville

Tremain, Abner: (CMTS) 1790 Federal Census Rensselaerville
Tremberlane, Joseph: (OC) Laborer, (CMTS) Albany 1815 City Directory
Trevert, Oliver: (OC) Baker, (CMTS) Albany 1815 City Directory
Trice, James: (RES) 249 Wasington
Trice, Thomas: (RES) 249 Washington, (CMTS) Albany 1815 City Directory
Tripp, Amy: (CMTS) 1915, Census, District No. 1 Ward No. 17
Tripp, Calvin: (RES) 108 Beaver, (CMTS) Albany 1815 City Directory
Tripp, Charles R.: (CMTS) 1915, Census, District No. 1 Ward No. 17
Tripp, Elisha: (OC) Shoemaker, (CMTS) Albany 1815 City Directory
Tripp, Florence N.: (CMTS) 1915, Census, District No. 5 Ward No. 12
Tripp, Francis: (CMTS) 1915, Census, District No. 5 Ward No. 12
Tripp, James: (CMTS) 1915, Census, District No. 4 Ward No. 16
Tripp, Levi L.: (CMTS) 1915, Census, District No. 5 Ward No. 7
Tripp, Mable A.: (CMTS) 1915, Census, District No. 5 Ward No. 7
Tripp, Mary M.: (CMTS) 1915, Census, District No. 5 Ward No. 12
Tripp, Mary V.: (CMTS) 1915, Census, District No. 1 Ward No. 17
Trotter, John: (OC) Merchant, (CMTS) Albany 1815 City Directory
Trotter, Mathew: (OC) Merchant, (CMTS) Albany 1815 City Directory
Trowbridge, Henry: (OC) Prop. of Museum, (CMTS) Albany 1815 City Directory
Trowbridge, Luther: (CMTS) 1790 Federal Census, Watervliet
Troy, Michael: (OC) Laborer, (CMTS) Albany 1815 City Directory
Truax, Abraham: (CMTS) 1790 Federal Census, Watervliet
Truax, Andrew: (CMTS) 1790 Federal Census, Watervliet
Truax, Carlton: (CMTS) 1915, Census, District No. 5 Ward No. 18
Truax, Christian: (CMTS) 1790 Federal Census, Watervliet
Truax, Elizabeth: (CMTS) 1915, Census, District No. 2 Ward No. 17
Truax, Henry: (OC) Merchant, (CMTS) Albany 1815 City Directory
Truax, Henry R.: (OC) Silversmith, (CMTS) Albany 1815 City Directory
Truax, Isaac: (CMTS) 1790 Federal Census, Watervliet
Truax, Jacob: (CMTS) 1790 Federal Census, Watervliet
Truax, Jacob: (CMTS) 1790 Federal Census Rensselaerville
Truax, James L.: (CMTS) 1915, Census, District No. 2 Ward No. 17
Truax, Jellis: (CMTS) 1790 Federal Census, Watervliet
Truax, Jennie: (CMTS) 1915, Census, District No. 5 Ward No. 18
Truax, Marion: (CMTS) 1915, Census, District No. 5 Ward No. 18
Truax, Mead: (CMTS) 1915, Census, District No. 1 Ward No. 12
Truax, Peter: (CMTS) 1790 Federal Census, Watervliet
Truax, William: (CMTS) 1790 Federal Census Rensselaerville
Truax, Wm.: (CMTS) 1915, Census, District No. 5 Ward No. 18
Truax, Jr., Isaac: (CMTS) 1790 Federal Census, Watervliet
Truax, Sr., John: (CMTS) 1790 Federal Census, Watervliet
Tryon, Jeremiah: (OC) Printer, (CMTS) Albany 1815 City Directory
Tryon, Williard F.: (F) Member Temple Lodge, No. 14, 1900,

Albany, NY
TTitus, Jacob: (OC) Waterman, (CMTS) Albany 1815 City Directory
Tubbs, Martin: (CMTS) 1790 Federal Census Rensselaerville
Tubbs, Samuel: (CMTS) 1790 Federal Census Rensselaerville
Tucker, Daniel: (OC) Cartman, (CMTS) Albany 1815 City Directory
Tucker, David: (OC) Gardener, (CMTS) Albany 1815 City Directory
Tucker, Samuel: (OC) Shoemaker, (CMTS) Albany 1815 City Directory
Tucker, William: (OC) Printer, (CMTS) Albany 1815 City Directory
Tucker, Willis G.: (F) Member Masters Lodge, No. 5, 1900,
    Albany, NY
Tuffs, Israel: (OC) Merchant, (CMTS) Albany 1815 City Directory
Tuffs, Joshua: (OC) Merchant, (CMTS) Albany 1815 City Directory
Tuner, John: (OC) Baker, (CMTS) Albany 1815 City Directory
Tupper, William: (CMTS) 1790 Federal Census, Watervliet
Turk, Anthony: (CMTS) 1790 Federal Census, Watervliet
Turk, Johannes: (CMTS) 1790 Federal Census, Watervliet
Turk, Thomas: (CMTS) 1790 Federal Census, Watervliet
Turner, Henry: (OC) Gunsmith, (CMTS) Albany 1815 City Directory
Turner, John: (OC) Mason, (CMTS) Albany 1815 City Directory
Turner, Peter: (CMTS) 1790 Federal Census, Watervliet
Turner, Jr., Peter: (OC) Teamster, (CMTS) Albany 1815 City Directory
Turner, Sally: (OC) Tailoress, (CMTS) Albany 1815 City Directory
Turner, Stephen: (OC) Shoemaker, (CMTS) Albany 1815 City Directory
Tuttle, Mirat: (OC) Butcher, (CMTS) Albany 1815 City Directory
Tyler, John: (OC) Cartman, (CMTS) Albany 1815 City Directory
Tymesen, Sebstian: (OC) Merchant, (CMTS) Albany 1815 City Directory
Underhill, Daniel: (F) Member Temple Lodge, No. 14, 1900,
    Albany, NY, (CMTS) Past Master 1874
Underhill, Edward H.: (F) Member Temple Lodge, No. 14, 1900,
    Albany, NY
Underhill, George R.: (F) Member Temple Lodge, No. 14, 1900,
    Albany, NY
Upfold, George: (OC) Teacher, (CMTS) Albany 1815 City Directory
Utley, Samuel W.: (F) Member Temple Lodge, No. 14, 1900,
    Albany, NY
Utter, John: (CMTS) 1790 Federal Census, Watervliet
Vadney, Albertus: (F) Member Temple Lodge, No. 14, 1900,
    Albany, NY
Vail, Samuel: (OC) Merchant, (CMTS) Albany 1815 City Directory
Valentine, James: (OC) Carpenter, (CMTS) Albany 1815 City Directory
Van Acman, Charlotte E.: (CMTS) 1915, Census, District No. 3
    Ward No. 17
Van Aerman, Cecelia: (CMTS) 1915, Census, District No. 2 Ward No. 19
Van Aernam, C. H.: (F) Member Mount Vernon Lodge, No. 3, 1900,
    Albany, NY

Van Ahon, Gilbert: (CMTS) 1915, Census, District No. 2 Ward No. 15
Van Allen, Adam: (F) Member Masters Lodge, No. 5, 1900,
    Albany, NY
Van Allen, Adam: (CMTS) 1915, Census, District No. 8 Ward No. 19
Van Allen, Beryl B.: (CMTS) 1915, Census, District No. 1 Ward No. 18
Van Allen, Charles H.: (F) Member Masters Lodge, No. 5, 1900,
    Albany, NY
Van Allen, Chas. H.: (CMTS) 1915, Census, District No. 6 Ward No. 18
Van Allen, Cynthia: (CMTS) 1915, Census, District No. 4 Ward No. 19
Van Allen, Dean F.: (CMTS) 1915, Census, District No. 1 Ward No. 18
Van Allen, Elenor: (CMTS) 1915, Census, District No. 4 Ward No. 19
Van Allen, Elizabeth: (CMTS) 1915, Census, District No. 8 Ward No. 19
Van Allen, Garret A.: (F) Member Masters Lodge, No. 5, 1900,
    Albany, NY
Van Allen, Garrit: (CMTS) 1790 Federal Census, Watervliet
Van Allen, H. Louise: (CMTS) 1915, Census, District No. 8 Ward No. 19
Van Allen, Harriett M.: (CMTS) 1915, Census, District No. 8
    Ward No. 19
Van Allen, Hazel: (CMTS) 1915, Census, District No. 5 Ward No. 12
Van Allen, James D.: (CMTS) 1915, Census, District No. 1 Ward No. 18
Van Allen, Mammie: (CMTS) 1915, Census, District No. 5 Ward No. 12
Van Allen, Mary: (CMTS) 1915, Census, District No. 6 Ward No. 18
Van Allen, Myrta: (CMTS) 1915, Census, District No. 1 Ward No. 18
Van Allen, Peter: (B) Aug. 18. 1705, (BP) Albany, Albany Co., NY
Van Allen, V.: (CMTS) 1915, Census, District No. 8 Ward No. 19
Van Allen, William: (F) Member Mount Vernon Lodge, No. 3, 1900,
    Albany, NY
Van Allen, Wm.: (CMTS) 1915, Census, District No. 4 Ward No. 19
Van Alstine, Abraham: (CMTS) 1790 Federal Census, Watervliet
Van Alstine, Andress: (CMTS) 1790 Federal Census, Watervliet
Van Alstine, Bartholemew: (CMTS) 1790 Federal Census, Watervliet
Van Alstine, Bartholemew: (CMTS) 1790 Federal Census, Watervliet
Van Alstine, Teunis: (CMTS) 1790 Federal Census, Watervliet
Van Alstyne, Adeline: (CMTS) 1915, Census, District No. 1 Ward No. 18
Van Alstyne, Alfred: (CMTS) 1915, Census, District No. 2 Ward No. 12
Van Alstyne, Bertha: (CMTS) 1915, Census, District No. 4 Ward No. 16
Van Alstyne, Buleh: (CMTS) 1915, Census, District No. 1 Ward No. 18
Van Alstyne, Elizabeth: (CMTS) 1915, Census, District No. 1
    Ward No. 18
Van Alstyne, Etta R.: (CMTS) 1915, Census, District No. 1 Ward No. 18
Van Alstyne, Florence: (CMTS) 1915, Census, District No. 4 Ward No. 12
Van Alstyne, Florence: (CMTS) 1915, Census, District No. 2 Ward No. 18
Van Alstyne, Frank P.: (F) Member Temple Lodge, No. 14, 1900,
    Albany, NY
Van Alstyne, Fred: (CMTS) 1915, Census, District No. 6 Ward No. 12

Van Alstyne, George M.: (CMTS) 1915, Census, District No. 3
    Ward No. 9
Van Alstyne, Henry: (CMTS) 1915, Census, District No. 4 Ward No. 16
Van Alstyne, Jeremiah: (CMTS) 1915, Census, District No. 2
    Ward No. 17
Van Alstyne, John: (OC) Cartman, (CMTS) Albany 1815 City Directory
Van Alstyne, Leonard J.: (CMTS) 1915, Census, District No. 6
    Ward No. 12
Van Alstyne, Lillia: (CMTS) 1915, Census, District No. 3 Ward No. 13
Van Alstyne, Marion E.: (CMTS) 1915, Census, District No. 3
    Ward No. 9
Van Alstyne, Mathew: (CMTS) 1915, Census, District No. 1 Ward No. 18
Van Alstyne, Myria: (CMTS) 1915, Census, District No. 3 Ward No. 13
Van Alstyne, P. H.: (CMTS) 1915, Census, District No. 1 Ward No. 18
Van Alstyne, R.: (CMTS) 1915, Census, District No. 1 Ward No. 12
Van Alstyne, Richard: (CMTS) 1915, Census, District No. 2 Ward No. 12
Van Alstyne, Robt. T.: (CMTS) 1915, Census, District No. 2 Ward No. 18
Van Alstyne, Sally: (CMTS) 1915, Census, District No. 2 Ward No. 18
Van Alstyne, Stonie: (CMTS) 1915, Census, District No. 4 Ward No. 12
Van Alstyne, Terresa M.: (CMTS) 1915, Census, District No. 3
    Ward No. 9
Van Alstyne, Thos. J.: (F) Member Mount Vernon Lodge, No. 3, 1900,
    Albany, NY, (CMTS) Past Master 1858
Van Alstyne, Tillie: (CMTS) 1915, Census, District No. 6 Ward No. 12
Van Alstyne, Wilbur W.: (CMTS) 1915, Census, District No. 1
    Ward No. 18
Van Alstyne, William: (F) Member Masters Lodge, No. 5, 1900,
    Albany, NY
Van Alstyne, William D.: (CMTS) 1915, Census, District No. 2
    Ward No. 18
Van Alstyne, Wm. C.: (F) Member Masters Lodge, No. 5, 1900,
    Albany, NY
Van Alter, Benjamin: (CMTS) 1790 Federal Census, Watervliet
Van Alwret, Clara A.: (CMTS) 1915, Census, District No. 1 Ward No. 16
Van Alyntire, Elizabeth: (CMTS) 1915, Census, District No. 4 Ward No. 9
Van Amberg, Alida A.: (CMTS) 1915, Census, District No. 2 Ward No. 9
Van Amberg, Clara: (CMTS) 1915, Census, District No. 5 Ward No. 19
Van Amberg, Harold J.: (CMTS) 1915, Census, District No. 2 Ward No. 9
Van Amberg, Helen: (CMTS) 1915, Census, District No. 5 Ward No. 19
Van Amberg, Henry: (CMTS) 1915, Census, District No. 5 Ward No. 19
Van Amberg, John J.: (CMTS) 1915, Census, District No. 2 Ward No. 9
Van Amberg, John S.: (CMTS) 1915, Census, District No. 2 Ward No. 9
Van Antwerp, Abraham: (CMTS) 1790 Federal Census, Watervliet
Van Antwerp, Daniel J: (CMTS) 1790 Federal Census, Watervliet
Van Antwerp, Widow: (OC) Grocer, (CMTS) Albany 1815 City Directory

Van Arnum, Evert: (CMTS) 1790 Federal Census, Watervliet
Van Arnum, Isaac: (CMTS) 1790 Federal Census, Watervliet
Van Arnum, Jacob: (CMTS) 1790 Federal Census, Watervliet
Van Arnum, John: (CMTS) 1790 Federal Census, Watervliet
Van Arnum, Jr. John: (CMTS) 1790 Federal Census, Watervliet
Van Arnum, William: (CMTS) 1790 Federal Census, Watervliet
Van Aukin, Levy: (CMTS) 1790 Federal Census, Watervliet
Van Aukin, Petrus: (CMTS) 1790 Federal Census, Watervliet
Van Aulen, John: (CMTS) 1790 Federal Census, Watervliet
Van Benthuysen, J. P.: (OC) Shoe Store, (CMTS) Albany 1815 City Directory
Van Benthousen, John: (CMTS) 1790 Federal Census, Watervliet
Van Benthuysen, Henry B.: (OC) Hairdresser, (CMTS) Albany 1815 City Directory
Van Benthuysen, Henry: (OC) Shoemaker, (CMTS) Albany 1815 City Directory
Van Benthuysen, J. P.: (OC) Shoe Store, (CMTS) Albany 1815 City Directory
Van Benthuysen, James P.: (RES) 27 Division, (CMTS) Albany 1815 City Directory
Van Benthuysen, Obadiah: (RES) 25 Division, (CMTS) Albany 1815 City Directory
Van Bergen, John: (OC) Silversmith, (CMTS) Albany 1815 City Directory
Van Bergh, Garret: (CMTS) 1790 Federal Census, Watervliet
Van Beuren, Dinah: (RES) 174 Washington, (CMTS) Albany 1815 City Directory
Van Beuren, Peter: (OC) Mason, (CMTS) Albany 1815 City Directory
Van Calkenburg, J. L.: (F) Member Temple Lodge, No. 14, 1900, Albany, NY
Van Camp, Teunis: (CMTS) 1790 Federal Census, Watervliet
Van Cot, Ebenezer: (OC) Cooper, (CMTS) Albany 1815 City Directory
Van De Carr, Charles: (F) Member Temple Lodge, No. 14, 1900, Albany, NY
Van Der Williger, Dirick: (CMTS) 1790 Federal Census, Watervliet
Van der Zee, Cornelius: (CMTS) 1790 Federal Census, Watervliet
Van Deusen, Jacob: (OC) Carpenter, (CMTS) Albany 1815 City Directory
Van Deusen, Jacob L.: (OC) Physician, (CMTS) Albany 1815 City Directory
Van Deusen, John: (OC) Laborer, (CMTS) Albany 1815 City Directory
Van Deusen, John: (OC) Rope Maker, (CMTS) Albany 1815 City Directory
Vandeusen, Widow Lydia: (RES) 90 Fox, (CMTS) Albany 1815 City Directory
Van Dolfson, John T: (CMTS) 1790 Federal Census, Watervliet

Van Dusen, John: (CMTS) 1790 Federal Census, Watervliet
Van Dyck, David: (CMTS) 1790 Federal Census, Watervliet
Van Emberg, John: (OC) Mason, (CMTS) Albany 1815 City Directory
Van Heusen, John M.: (F) Member Masters Lodge, No. 5, 1900, Albany, NY
Van Hoesen, Cornelius: (OC) Mason, (CMTS) Albany 1815 City Directory
Van Hoesen, Henry: (F) Member Washington Lodge, No. 85, 1900, Albany, NY, (CMTS) Past Members
Van Hoesen, Widow Mary: (RES) 61Hudson, (CMTS) Albany 1815 City Directory
Van Ingen, James: (OC) Clerk in Chancery, (CMTS) Albany 1815 City Directory
Van Kleeck, Lawrence L.: (RES) 35 Columbia, (CMTS) Albany 1815 City Directory
Van Loon, Barent: (OC) Merchant, (CMTS) Albany 1815 City Directory
Van Loon, Charles: (F) Member Mount Vernon Lodge, No. 3, 1900, Albany, NY
Van Loon, James: (RES) 84 do., (CMTS) Albany 1815 City Directory
Van Loon, Peter: (OC) Merchant, (CMTS) Albany 1815 City Directory
Van Loon, Samuel: (RES) 51 Columbia, (CMTS) Albany 1815 City Directory
Van Loon, William H.: (F) Member Mount Vernon Lodge, No. 3, 1900, Albany, NY
Van Loven, Peter: (CMTS) 1790 Federal Census Rensselaerville
Van Ness, Charles: (CMTS) 1790 Federal Census, Watervliet
Van Ness, Jacob: (OC) Carpenter, (CMTS) Albany 1815 City Directory
Van Ness, John: (OC) Shoemaker, (CMTS) Albany 1815 City Directory
Van Norman, Johannes: (CMTS) 1790 Federal Census, Watervliet
Van Olinda, Jacob: (CMTS) 1790 Federal Census, Watervliet
Van Olinda, Peter: (CMTS) 1790 Federal Census, Watervliet
Van Patten, Arent: (CMTS) 1790 Federal Census, Watervliet
Van Patten, Frederick: (CMTS) 1790 Federal Census, Watervliet
Van Patten, John: (OC) Blacksmith, (CMTS) Albany 1815 City Directory
Van Patten, John D.: (CMTS) 1790 Federal Census, Watervliet
Van Patten, Nicholas: (CMTS) 1790 Federal Census, Watervliet
Van Patten, Petrus: (CMTS) 1790 Federal Census, Watervliet
Van Pelt, Francis: (RES) 45 Liberty, (CMTS) Albany 1815 City Directory
Van Rensselaer, Cornelius: (RES) 62 Hamilton, (CMTS) Albany 1815 City Directory
Van Rensselaer, Henry K.: (RES) 76 N. Pearl, (CMTS) Albany 1815 City Directory
Van Rensselaer, Hon. Philip S.: (OC) Mayor, (CMTS) Albany 1815 City Directory
Van Rensselaer, John S.: (OC) Master in Chancery, (CMTS) Albany

1815 City Directory
Van Rensselaer, Philip: (CMTS) 1790 Federal Census, Watervliet
Van Rensselaer, Philip P.: (OC) Merchant, (CMTS) Albany 1815 City Directory
Van Rensselaer, Solomon: (RES) Adjutant General Office, (CMTS) Albany 1815 City Directory
Van Rensselaer, Stephen: (CMTS) 1790 Federal Census, Watervliet
Van Santford, H. S.: (F) Member Masters Lodge, No. 5, 1900, Albany, NY
Van Santvoord, Jr., A.: (OC) Grocer, (CMTS) Albany 1815 City Directory
Van Santvoord, Anthony: (OC) Merchant, (CMTS) Albany 1815 City Directory
Van Schaick, Albert: (CMTS) 1790 Federal Census Rensselaerville
Van Schaick, Egbert: (CMTS) 1790 Federal Census, Watervliet
Van Schaick, John: (OC) Merchant, (CMTS) Albany 1815 City Directory
Van Schaick, Tobias: (OC) Merchant, (CMTS) Albany 1815 City Directory
Van Schaick, Widow Mary: (RES) 251 N. Market, (CMTS) Albany 1815 City Directory
Van Schelluyye, Dirck: (RES) 46 Columbia, (CMTS) Albany 1815 City Directory
Van Schoonhaven, Dirick B.: (CMTS) 1790 Federal Census, Watervliet
Van Schoonhoven, Cornelius: (OC) Skipper, (CMTS) Albany 1815 City Directory
Van Schoonhoven, Jacobus: (B) Dec. 24, 1775, (PB) Albany, Albany Co., NY, (PRTS) Hendrick Van Schoonhoven and Aalyie Vandenburgh
Van Schoonhoven, James: (OC) Carpenter, (CMTS) Albany 1815 City Directory
Van Stanvoord, Henry: (OC) Tobacconist, (CMTS) Albany 1815 City Directory
Van Steenberg, John B.: (OC) Printer, (CMTS) Albany 1815 City Directory
Van Tassel, Peter: (RES) 92 Hudson, (CMTS) Albany 1815 City Directory
Van Valkenburgh, John: (OC) Mason, (CMTS) Albany 1815 City Directory
Van Valkenburgh, Lucas: (OC) Laborer, (CMTS) Albany 1815 City Directory
Van Valkenburgh, O. C.: (OC) Merchant, (CMTS) Albany 1815 City Directory
Van Vechen, Lucas: (CMTS) 1790 Federal Census, Watervliet
Van Vechten, Abraham: (OC) Counsellor, (CMTS) Albany 1815 City Directory
Van Vechten, John: (OC) Merchant, (CMTS) Albany 1815 City Directory
Van Vechten, Teunis: (OC) Counsellor, (CMTS) Albany 1815 City

Directory
Van Vechten, Teunis T.: (RES) 333 N. Market, (CMTS) Albany 1815 City Directory
Van Veghten, Doug K: (OC) Bookbinder, (CMTS) Albany 1815 City Directory
Van Veghten, Walter: (OC) Merchant, (CMTS) Albany 1815 City Directory
Van Voert, Willaim: (OC) Laborer, (CMTS) Albany 1815 City Directory
Van Volkenburgh, Jochum: (CMTS) 1790 Federal Census, Watervliet
Van Volkinburgh, Cornelius: (CMTS) 1790 Federal Census, Watervliet
Van Vraken, Maus R: (RES) 35 N. Market, (CMTS) Albany 1815 City Directory
Van Vrankin, Abraham: (CMTS) 1790 Federal Census, Watervliet
Van Vrankin, Cornelius: (CMTS) 1790 Federal Census, Watervliet
Van Vrankin, Direck: (CMTS) 1790 Federal Census, Watervliet
Van Vrankin, Jacob: (CMTS) 1790 Federal Census, Watervliet
Van Vrankin, Jacobus: (CMTS) 1790 Federal Census, Watervliet
Van Vrankin, John: (CMTS) 1790 Federal Census, Watervliet
Van Vrankin, Nicholas: (CMTS) 1790 Federal Census, Watervliet
Van Vrankin, Peter: (CMTS) 1790 Federal Census, Watervliet
Van Vrankin, Samuel: (CMTS) 1790 Federal Census, Watervliet
Van Vronken, Rykert: (CMTS) 1790 Federal Census, Watervliet
Van Waggoner, Barent: (CMTS) 1790 Federal Census, Watervliet
Van Waggonon, John H.: (CMTS) 1790 Federal Census Rensselaerville
Van Wee, Abigail: (CMTS) 1790 Federal Census, Watervliet
Van Wee, Abraham: (CMTS) 1790 Federal Census, Watervliet
Van Wee, Cornelius: (CMTS) 1790 Federal Census, Watervliet
Van Wee, Garrit: (CMTS) 1790 Federal Census, Watervliet
Van Wee, Hendrick: (CMTS) 1790 Federal Census, Watervliet
Van Wee, Henry H.: (CMTS) 1790 Federal Census, Watervliet
Van Wee, Isaac: (CMTS) 1790 Federal Census, Watervliet
Van Wee, Johannes: (CMTS) 1790 Federal Census, Watervliet
Van Wee, John: (CMTS) 1790 Federal Census, Watervliet
Van Wer, Casparus: (CMTS) 1790 Federal Census, Watervliet
Van West, Edna: (CMTS) 1915, Census, District No. 7 Ward No. 16
Van Wie, Benjamin: (RES) 3 Van Schaick, (CMTS) Albany 1815 City Directory
Van Wie, Casper: (RES) 99 N. Market, (CMTS) Albany 1815 City Directory
Van Wie, Garret: (OC) Saddler, (CMTS) Albany 1815 City Directory
Van Wie, Henry: (OC) Blacksmith, (CMTS) Albany 1815 City Directory
Van Wie, Isaac: (OC) Mason, (CMTS) Albany 1815 City Directory
Van Wie, William: (F) Member Temple Lodge, No. 14, 1900, Albany, NY
Van Wie, William: (OC) Carpenter, (CMTS) Albany 1815 City Directory

Van Wie, William W.: (F) Member Temple Lodge, No. 14, 1900, Albany, NY
Van Woert, Widow Catharine: (RES) 64 Hudson, (CMTS) Albany 1815 City Directory
Van Wort, Jacob J.: (CMTS) 1790 Federal Census, Watervliet
Van Wort, John: (CMTS) 1790 Federal Census, Watervliet
Van Wort, Teunis: (CMTS) 1790 Federal Census, Watervliet
Van Yorx, Widow Rebecca: (CMTS) Albany 1815 City Directory
Van Zandt, Garret R.: (OC) Carpenter, (CMTS) Albany 1815 City Directory
Van Zandt, James: (RES) 62 S. Pearl, (CMTS) Albany 1815 City Directory
Van Zandt, John: (RES) 12 S. Pearl, (CMTS) Albany 1815 City Directory
Van Zandt, John: (OC) Cashier Bank of Albany, (CMTS) Albany 1815 City Directory
Van Zandt, Joseph R.: (OC) Merchant, (CMTS) Albany 1815 City Directory
Van Zandt, Thomas: (OC) Mason, (CMTS) Albany 1815 City Directory
Van Zandt, Widow Sarah: (RES) 19 Green, (CMTS) Albany 1815 City Directory
Van Zandt, William: (OC) Mason, (CMTS) Albany 1815 City Directory
Van Zandt, William I.: (OC) Grocer, (CMTS) Albany 1815 City Directory
Van Zant, Benjamin: (CMTS) 1790 Federal Census, Watervliet
Van Zant, Garrit: (CMTS) 1790 Federal Census, Watervliet
Van Zant, Gilbert: (CMTS) 1790 Federal Census, Watervliet
Van Zant, Henry: (CMTS) 1790 Federal Census, Watervliet
Van Zant, Joseph: (CMTS) 1790 Federal Census, Watervliet
Vance, Geroge: (OC) Shoemaker, (CMTS) Albany 1815 City Directory
Vandeburgh, Vinant: (CMTS) 1790 Federal Census, Watervliet
Vandenberg, John: (OC) Joiner, (CMTS) Albany 1815 City Directory
Vandenberg, Richard: (OC) Shoemaker, (CMTS) Albany 1815 City Directory
Vandenberg, Widow Ann: (RES) 50 Orange, (CMTS) Albany 1815 City Directory
Vandenberg, William: (OC) Cabinetmaker, (CMTS) Albany 1815 City Directory
Vandenbergh, Garrit: (CMTS) 1790 Federal Census, Watervliet
Vandenbogert, John: (CMTS) 1790 Federal Census, Watervliet
Vandenburgh, Abraham: (CMTS) 1790 Federal Census, Watervliet
Vandenburgh, Cornelius: (CMTS) 1790 Federal Census, Watervliet
Vandenburgh, Garrit: (CMTS) 1790 Federal Census, Watervliet
Vandenburgh, Levinus: (CMTS) 1790 Federal Census, Watervliet
Vandenburgh, Petrus: (CMTS) 1790 Federal Census, Watervliet
Vander Heyden, Derick L: (OC) Counsellor, (CMTS) Albany 1815 City Directory

Vander Heyden, Jacob: (RES) 85 N. Pearl, (CMTS) Albany 1815 City Directory
Vander Heyden, Jacob: (RES) 86 Fox, (CMTS) Albany 1815 City Directory
Vander Heyden, John: (CMTS) 1790 Federal Census, Watervliet
Vander Ker, Barent: (CMTS) 1790 Federal Census Rensselaerville
Vander Zea, Albert: (CMTS) 1790 Federal Census, Watervliet
Vander Zee, Albert H.: (CMTS) 1790 Federal Census, Watervliet
Vander Zee, Cornelius: (CMTS) 1790 Federal Census, Watervliet
Vanderbergh, Abraham E: (CMTS) 1790 Federal Census, Watervliet
Vanderbilt, Richard: (F) Member Mount Vernon Lodge, No. 3, 1900, Albany, NY
Vanderburgh, Cornelius: (CMTS) 1790 Federal Census, Watervliet
Vanderburgh, Willhelmus: (CMTS) 1790 Federal Census, Watervliet
Vanderkirk, Dirick: (CMTS) 1790 Federal Census, Watervliet
Vanderlip, E.: (OC) Shoe Store, (CMTS) Albany 1815 City Directory
Vanderlip, Elias: (OC) Merchant, (CMTS) Albany 1815 City Directory
Vanderlip, Martha: (OC) Millener, (CMTS) Albany 1815 City Directory
Vanderlip, Philip: (OC) Coach Painter, (CMTS) Albany 1815 City Directory
Vanderlip, Philip: (OC) Milkman, (CMTS) Albany 1815 City Directory
Vanderpool, Widow: (RES) 17 Pine, (CMTS) Albany 1815 City Directory
Vandervoort, John I.: (OC) Shoemaker, (CMTS) Albany 1815 City Directory
Vanderwater, Cornelius: (CMTS) 1790 Federal Census, Watervliet
Vanderwater, Jacob: (OC) Harness Maker, (CMTS) Albany 1815 City Directory
Vandery Heyden, Isaac: (RES) 34 Orange, (CMTS) Albany 1815 City Directory
Vanderzee, Newton B.: (F) Member Masters Lodge, No. 5, 1900, Albany, NY
Vanerberg, Peter: (OC) Lumber, (CMTS) Albany 1815 City Directory
Vansandford, Anthony: (CMTS) 1790 Federal Census, Watervliet
Varbank, Abraham: (OC) Skipper, (CMTS) Albany 1815 City Directory
Varney, Amasa L.: (F) Member Temple Lodge, No. 14, 1900, Albany, NY
Vaupel, William: (F) Member Temple Lodge, No. 14, 1900, Albany, NY
Vedder, Alexander: (RES) 350 N. Market, (CMTS) Albany 1815 City Directory
Veeder, Abraham: (CMTS) 1790 Federal Census, Watervliet
Veeder, Casset: (CMTS) 1790 Federal Census, Watervliet
Veeder, Isaac: (CMTS) 1790 Federal Census, Watervliet
Veeder, Jacob: (CMTS) 1790 Federal Census, Watervliet
Veeder, Jacob: (CMTS) 1790 Federal Census, Watervliet

Veeder, Lucas W.: (CMTS) 1790 Federal Census, Watervliet
Veeder, Simon: (CMTS) 1790 Federal Census, Watervliet
Veeder, Volkirt: (CMTS) 1790 Federal Census, Watervliet
Veeley, Jacob: (CMTS) 1790 Federal Census, Watervliet
Venter, Jr., Peter: (F) Member Temple Lodge, No. 14, 1900, Albany, NY
Vernor, John: (OC) Deputy Commissary, (CMTS) Albany 1815 City Directory
Vernor, Jr., John: (OC) Grocer, (CMTS) Albany 1815 City Directory
Verplank, David: (CMTS) 1790 Federal Census, Watervliet
Verplank, Isaac D.: (CMTS) 1790 Federal Census, Watervliet
Verplank, John: (CMTS) 1790 Federal Census, Watervliet
Vervalin, Benjamin: (RES) 170 Washington, (CMTS) Albany 1815 City Directory
Vesscher, Teunis: (CMTS) 1790 Federal Census, Watervliet
Vicars, Widow Ann: (RES) 41 N. Market, (CMTS) Albany 1815 City Directory
Vickers, John: (OC) Arkell & Vickers, Grocer, (CMTS) Albany 1859 City Directory
Vine, John: (CMTS) 1790 Federal Census, Watervliet
Vineberg, Archibald: (F) Member Temple Lodge, No. 14, 1900, Albany, NY
Visscher, Bastian F.: (CMTS) 1790 Federal Census, Watervliet
Visscher, Garret: (OC) Chair Maker, (CMTS) Albany 1815 City Directory
Visscher, John: (CMTS) 1790 Federal Census, Watervliet
Visscher, John B.: (RES) 17 Van Schaick, (CMTS) Albany 1815 City Directory
Visscher, Sebastian: (OC) Clerk Court of Errors, (CMTS) Albany 1815 City Directory
Visscher, Tunis G.: (OC) Carpenter, (CMTS) Albany 1815 City Directory
Visscher, Widow: (OC) Lydis, (CMTS) Albany 1815 City Directory
Volk, Johannes: (CMTS) 1790 Federal Census, Watervliet
Volk, Mathias: (CMTS) 1790 Federal Census, Watervliet
Voorhees, John: (CMTS) 1790 Federal Census, Watervliet
Voorhees, John: (OC) Blacksmith, (CMTS) Albany 1815 City Directory
Voorhees, Willaim: (OC) Shoemaker, (CMTS) Albany 1815 City Directory
Vosburg, Peter: (OC) Wheelright, (CMTS) Albany 1815 City Directory
Vosburgh, Abraham: (OC) Laborer, (CMTS) Albany 1815 City Directory
Vosburgh, Andrew J.: (F) Member Temple Lodge, No. 14, 1900, Albany, NY
Vosburgh, Elizabeth: (CMTS) 1915, Census, District No. 2 Ward No. 11
Vosburgh, Emma: (CMTS) 1915, Census, District No. 2 Ward No. 17
Vosburgh, George: (CMTS) 1915, Census, District No. 1 Ward No. 8
Vosburgh, James: (CMTS) 1915, Census, District No. 2 Ward No. 17

Vosburgh, James: (OC) Grocer, (CMTS) Albany 1815 City Directory
Vosburgh, Louis: (CMTS) 1915, Census, District No. 2 Ward No. 11
Vosburgh, Mary M.: (CMTS) 1915, Census, District No. 1 Ward No. 16
Vosburgh, Minerd: (CMTS) 1915, Census, District No. 2 Ward No. 11
Vosburgh, Richard: (OC) Laborer, (CMTS) Albany 1815 City Directory
Vosburgh, Rollin: (CMTS) 1915, Census, District No. 2 Ward No. 17
Vosburgh, Samuel: (RES) 655 S. Market, (CMTS) Albany 1815 City Directory
Vosburgh, William: (OC) Mason, (CMTS) Albany 1815 City Directory
Vosburgh, William: (OC) Saddler, (CMTS) Albany 1815 City Directory
Vose, Charles: (CMTS) 1790 Federal Census Rensselaerville
Vossbergh, Isaac: (CMTS) 1790 Federal Census, Watervliet
Vossburgh, Abraham: (CMTS) 1790 Federal Census, Watervliet
Vossburgh, Garrit: (CMTS) 1790 Federal Census, Watervliet
Vossburgh, Jacob: (CMTS) 1790 Federal Census, Watervliet
Vossburgh, John: (CMTS) 1790 Federal Census, Watervliet
Vossburgh, John: (CMTS) 1790 Federal Census, Watervliet
Vossburgh, William: (CMTS) 1790 Federal Census, Watervliet
Vreedenburgh, Alida: (CMTS) 1790 Federal Census, Watervliet
Vrelegh, Helmus: (CMTS) 1790 Federal Census, Watervliet
Vriman, John F.: (F) Member Temple Lodge, No. 14, 1900, Albany, NY
Vrooman, Adam: (CMTS) 1790 Federal Census, Watervliet
Vrooman, Cornelius: (CMTS) 1790 Federal Census, Watervliet
Vrooman, Isaac: (CMTS) 1790 Federal Census, Watervliet
Vrooman, Jacobus: (CMTS) 1790 Federal Census, Watervliet
Vrooman, Jonathie: (CMTS) 1790 Federal Census, Watervliet
Vrooman, Nicholas: (CMTS) 1790 Federal Census, Watervliet
Vrooman, Peter: (CMTS) 1790 Federal Census, Watervliet
Vrooman, Walter: (CMTS) 1790 Federal Census, Watervliet
Wade, John: (OC) Weaver, (CMTS) Albany 1815 City Directory
Wadhams, Frederick K.: (F) Member Masters Lodge, No. 5, 1900, Albany, NY
Wadson, John: (RES) 145 S. Pearl, (CMTS) Albany 1815 City Directory
Wadsworth, Eli: (OC) plater, (CMTS) Albany 1815 City Directory
Waggoner, George: (CMTS) 1790 Federal Census, Watervliet
Waggoner, John: (CMTS) 1790 Federal Census, Watervliet
Waggoner, John I.: (OC) Grocer, (CMTS) Albany 1815 City Directory
Wagner, Robert C.: (F) Member Mount Vernon Lodge, No. 3, 1900, Albany, NY
Wagoner, Martin V. E.: (F) Member Temple Lodge, No. 14, 1900, Albany, NY
Wagoner, Richard B.: (F) Member Temple Lodge, No. 14, 1900, Albany, NY
Wakeman, Hezekiah: (OC) Saddler, (CMTS) Albany 1815 City Directory

Waldecker, Max: (F) Member Mount Vernon Lodge, No. 3, 1900, Albany, NY
Waldron, Cornelius: (CMTS) 1790 Federal Census, Watervliet
Waldron, James: (CMTS) 1790 Federal Census, Watervliet
Walker, Calvin: (OC) Merchant, (CMTS) Albany 1815 City Directory
Walker, Israel: (CMTS) 1790 Federal Census, Watervliet
Walker, James: (OC) Laborer, (CMTS) Albany 1815 City Directory
Walker, Silas: (RES) 50 State continued, (CMTS) Albany 1815 City Directory
Walker, Willard: (OC) Merchant, (CMTS) Albany 1815 City Directory
Walkins, Widow: (RES) 53 Fox, (CMTS) Albany 1815 City Directory
Wallace, Benjamin: (OC) Assist. Justice, (CMTS) Albany 1815 City Directory
Wallace, Frederick: (OC) Mason, (CMTS) Albany 1815 City Directory
Wallace, Moses: (OC) Cartman, (CMTS) Albany 1815 City Directory
Wallace, Robert A.: (F) Member Temple Lodge, No. 14, 1900, Albany, NY, (CMTS) Life Member
Wallace, Warren L.: (F) Member Temple Lodge, No. 14, 1900, Albany, NY
Wallace, William A.: (F) Member Temple Lodge, No. 14, 1900, Albany, NY
Wallace,: (OC) Fisherman, (CMTS) Albany 1815 City Directory
Wallen, Frederick: (OC) Mason, (CMTS) Albany 1815 City Directory
Walley, Francis: (OC) Grocer, (CMTS) Albany 1815 City Directory
Walley, John: (CMTS) 1790 Federal Census, Watervliet
Walls, Frederick: (CMTS) 1790 Federal Census, Watervliet
Walron, Henry: (CMTS) 1790 Federal Census, Watervliet
Walsh, Dudley: (OC) Merchant, (CMTS) Albany 1815 City Directory
Walts, John: (CMTS) 1790 Federal Census, Watervliet
Wands, Ebenezer: (CMTS) 1790 Federal Census, Watervliet
Wands, Ebenezer I.: (OC) Constable, (CMTS) Albany 1815 City Directory
Wands, Robert J.: (F) Member Temple Lodge, No. 14, 1900, Albany, NY
Wans, John: (CMTS) 1790 Federal Census, Watervliet
Ward, Andrew: (CMTS) 1790 Federal Census, Watervliet
Ward, Benjamin: (CMTS) 1790 Federal Census, Watervliet
Ward, Daniel: (OC) Tailor, (CMTS) Albany 1815 City Directory
Ward, Ebenezer: (CMTS) 1790 Federal Census, Watervliet
Ward, Jacob: (OC) Furnaceman, (CMTS) Albany 1815 City Directory
Ward, John: (CMTS) 1790 Federal Census, Watervliet
Ward, Jonathan: (CMTS) 1790 Federal Census Rensselaerville
Ward, Richard: (CMTS) 1790 Federal Census, Watervliet
Ward, Samuel: (OC) Brickmaker, (CMTS) Albany 1815 City Directory
Ward, Simeon: (CMTS) 1790 Federal Census Rensselaerville

Ward, Walter E.: (F) Member Temple Lodge, No. 14, 1900, Albany, NY
Ward, Widow: (RES) 54 Chapel, (CMTS) Albany 1815 City Directory
Ward, William: (CMTS) 1790 Federal Census, Watervliet
Ward, William: (CMTS) 1790 Federal Census Rensselaerville
Ward, William: (OC) Morocco Dresser, (CMTS) Albany 1815 City Directory
Ward, William J.: (F) Member Mount Vernon Lodge, No. 3, 1900, Albany, NY
Wareing, Jr., Thomas: (F) Member Mount Vernon Lodge, No. 3, 1900, Albany, NY, (CMTS) Past Master 1899
Waring, Richard: (OC) Counsellor, (CMTS) Albany 1815 City Directory
Warn, B.: (OC) Merchant, (CMTS) Albany 1815 City Directory
Warn, P. H.: (OC) Merchant, (CMTS) Albany 1815 City Directory
Warner, Aaron: (OC) Laborer, (CMTS) Albany 1815 City Directory
Warner, Elias: (OC) Store Lane, (CMTS) Albany 1815 City Directory
Warner, Harmon W.: (F) Member Temple Lodge, No. 14, 1900, Albany, NY
Warner, Jr., Johannes: (CMTS) 1790 Federal Census Rensselaerville
Warner, Luther C.: (F) Member Mount Vernon Lodge, No. 3, 1900, Albany, NY
Warner, Philip: (CMTS) 1790 Federal Census Rensselaerville
Warner, Widow Mary: (RES) 20 Hamilton, (CMTS) Albany 1815 City Directory
Warrant, William: (CMTS) 1790 Federal Census, Watervliet
Warren, James: (OC) Merchant, (CMTS) Albany 1815 City Directory
Warren, John W.: (OC) Merchant, (CMTS) Albany 1815 City Directory
Warren, Widow Mary: (RES) 25 Union, (CMTS) Albany 1815 City Directory
Washburn, H. L.: (F) Member Masters Lodge, No. 5, 1900, Albany, NY
Washburn, John B.: (OC) Merchant, (CMTS) Albany 1815 City Directory
Wasson, John B.: (RES) 20 Sand, (CMTS) Albany 1815 City Directory
Waterhouse, Fred A.: (F) Member Temple Lodge, No. 14, 1900, Albany, NY
Waterman, Widow: (RES) 9 Plain, (CMTS) Albany 1815 City Directory
Watkins, Seth: (OC) Grocer, (CMTS) Albany 1815 City Directory
Watley, John: (OC) Hair Dresser, (CMTS) Albany 1815 City Directory
Watson, James: (CMTS) 1790 Federal Census, Watervliet
Watson, James H.: (F) Member Masters Lodge, No. 5, 1900, Albany, NY
Watson, James H.: (F) Member Temple Lodge, No. 14, 1900, Albany, NY
Watson, Widow Lydis: (RES) 279 Washington, (CMTS) Albany 1815 City Directory

Watters, Thomas: (OC) Tailor, (CMTS) Albany 1815 City Directory
Watters, Widow Elizabeth: (RES) 245 N. Market, (CMTS) Albany 1815
    City Directory
Waugh, James: (OC) Innkeeper, (CMTS) Albany 1815 City Directory
Way, John Lewis: (F) Member Temple Lodge, No. 14, 1900,
    Albany, NY
Wayne, Anthony: (CMTS) 1790 Federal Census, Watervliet
Wayne, Benjamin P.: (F) Member Temple Lodge, No. 14, 1900,
    Albany, NY
Weatherwax, Charles: (F) Member Temple Lodge, No. 14, 1900,
    Albany, NY
Weatherwax, Frank H.: (F) Member Temple Lodge, No. 14, 1900,
    Albany, NY
Weaton, William: (CMTS) 1790 Federal Census Rensselaerville
Weaver, Abraham D.: (CMTS) 1790 Federal Census, Watervliet
Weaver, Abram H.: (F) Member Temple Lodge, No. 14, 1900,
    Albany, NY
Weaver, Francis: (CMTS) 1790 Federal Census, Watervliet
Weaver, Henry: (CMTS) 1790 Federal Census, Watervliet
Weaver, Henry: (OC) Hairdresser, (CMTS) Albany 1815 City Directory
Weaver, Jacob: (CMTS) 1790 Federal Census, Watervliet
Weaver, James: (OC) Grocer, (CMTS) Albany 1815 City Directory
Weaver, Volintine: (CMTS) 1790 Federal Census, Watervliet
Weaver, William H.: (F) Member Temple Lodge, No. 14, 1900,
    Albany, NY, (CMTS) Life Member
Weaver, Jr., Johannes: (CMTS) 1790 Federal Census, Watervliet
Webb, Alexander: (OC) Mason, (CMTS) Albany 1815 City Directory
Webb, Ella L.: (CMTS) 1915, Census, District No. 8 Ward No. 1
Webb, Ellen A.: (CMTS) 1915, Census, District No. 6 Ward No. 1
Webb, Emma: (CMTS) 1915, Census, District No. 3 Ward No. 3
Webb, Emma: (CMTS) 1915, Census, District No. 4 Ward No. 3
Webb, Emory L.: (CMTS) 1915, Census, District No. 6 Ward No. 1
Webb, H.: (CMTS) 1915, Census, District No. 1 Ward No. 5
Webb, Hazel: (CMTS) 1915, Census, District No. 2 Ward No. 15
Webb, Henry Y: (OC) maltster, (CMTS) Albany 1815 City Directory
Webb, Isaac: (OC) Flour Merchant, (CMTS) Albany 1815 City Directory
Webb, Isaac: (OC) Pastor Baptist Church, (CMTS) Albany 1815
    City Directory
Webb, John: (CMTS) 1915, Census, District No. 1 Ward No. 12
Webb, John: (CMTS) 1915, Census, District No. 7 Ward No. 16
Webb, John: (CMTS) 1915, Census, District No. 3 Ward No. 3
Webb, Joseph A.: (CMTS) 1915, Census, District No. 3 Ward No. 6
Webb, Julia: (CMTS) 1915, Census, District No. 3 Ward No. 3
Webb, L.: (CMTS) 1915, Census, District No. 1 Ward No. 5
Webb, Leo W.: (CMTS) 1915, Census, District No. 2 Ward No. 15

Webb, Margaret: (CMTS) 1915, Census, District No. 1 Ward No. 12
Webb, Margaret: (CMTS) 1915, Census, District No. 1 Ward No. 12
Webb, Robert M.: (CMTS) 1915, Census, District No. 8 Ward No. 1
Webb, Vivian: (CMTS) 1915, Census, District No. 2 Ward No. 15
Webb, William: (OC) Carpenter, (CMTS) Albany 1815 City Directory
Webb, William W.: (CMTS) 1915, Census, District No. 3 Ward No. 3
Webb, William W. Jr.: (CMTS) 1915, Census, District No. 3 Ward No. 3
Webster, Charles R: (RES) 83 State, (CMTS) Albany 1815 City Directory
Webster, George: (RES) 31 State, (CMTS) Albany 1815 City Directory
Webster, William: (OC) Mason, (CMTS) Albany 1815 City Directory
Wech, Joseph: (OC) Weaver, (CMTS) Albany 1815 City Directory
Wederman, John: (CMTS) 1790 Federal Census, Watervliet
Weed, Joseph: (OC) Justice of the Peace, (CMTS) Albany 1815
    City Directory
Weed, George: (OC) Merchant, (CMTS) Albany 1815 City Directory
Weed, Walter: (OC) Merchant, (CMTS) Albany 1815 City Directory
Weidman, John A.: (F) Member Temple Lodge, No. 14, 1900,
    Albany, NY
Weidman, Reuben L.: (F) Member Mount Vernon Lodge, No. 3, 1900,
    Albany, NY
Weight, Joseph: (CMTS) 1790 Federal Census, Watervliet
Welch, Henry: (OC) Laborer, (CMTS) Albany 1815 City Directory
Welch, Luke: (CMTS) 1790 Federal Census, Watervliet
Welch, Thomas: (OC) Grocer, (CMTS) Albany 1815 City Directory
Welch, Walter: (CMTS) 1790 Federal Census Rensselaerville
Wells, Agur: (OC) Shoe Store, (CMTS) Albany 1815 City Directory
Wells, George A.: (F) Member Masters Lodge, No. 5, 1900,
    Albany, NY
Wells, Henry: (CMTS) 1790 Federal Census, Watervliet
Wells, Lucius: (OC) Grocer, (CMTS) Albany 1815 City Directory
Wells, Teunis: (CMTS) 1790 Federal Census, Watervliet
Wells, Widow Hannah: (RES) 100 N. Pearl, (CMTS) Albany 1815 City
    Directory
Wells, William S.: (OC) Grocer, (CMTS) Albany 1815 City Directory
Welsh, John: (OC) Laborer, (CMTS) Albany 1815 City Directory
Welsh, Peter: (CMTS) 1790 Federal Census, Watervliet
Wemple, Abraham: (CMTS) 1790 Federal Census, Watervliet
Wendell, Catalina: (RES) Boarding House at 78 N. Pearl, (CMTS) Albany
    1815 City Directory
Wendell, Daniel: (OC) Skipper, (CMTS) Albany 1815 City Directory
Wendell, Garrit: (CMTS) 1790 Federal Census, Watervliet
Wendell, Harmanus: (RES) 633 S. Market, (CMTS) Albany 1815 City
    Directory
Wendell, Harmanus: (B) Jul. 2, 1693, (D) Dec. 20, 1766, (PRTS)
    Philip Wendell and Marie Visscher

Wendell, Harmanus: (CD) Jun. 6, 1743, (BP) Albany, Albany Co., NY
Wendell, Harmanus: (B) Sep. 6, 1784, (BP) Albany, NY, (PRTS) John Harmanus Wendell and Cathalyntje Van Benthuusen
Wendell, Harmanus: (B) Jan. 30, 1790, (BP) Albany, NY, (D) Jun. 11, 1810, (PRTS) John Harmanus Wendell and Cathalyntje Van Benthuusen
Wendell, Harmanus A: (OC) Sup. Of Market, (CMTS) Albany 1815 City Directory
Wendell, Jr., Harmanus: (OC) Att. & mas. in chan., (CMTS) Albany 1815 City Directory
Wendell, Hendrick: (CD) Oct. 19, 1713, (BP) Albany, NY, (PRTS) Abraham Wendell and Mayken Van Ness
Wendell, Hendrick: (CD) Jun. 5, 1730, (D) Oct. 1, 1795, (BP) Albany, NY, (PRTS) Ephraim Wendell and Anna Van Ness
Wendell, Hendrick: (CMTS) 1790 Federal Census, Watervliet
Wendell, Hendrick: (B) Mar. 16, 1729, (BP) Albany, NY, (PRTS) Issac Wendell and Catakina Van Dyke
Wendell, Isaac: (B) Nov. 5, 1688, (CD) Nov. 11, 1688, (BP) Albany, NY, (PRTS) Johannes Wendell and Elizabeth Staats
Wendell, Isaac: (MD) Nov. 18, 1717, (PMD) Albany, NY, (Spouse) Catalina Van Dyke
Wendell, Jacob: (OC) Cartman, (CMTS) Albany 1815 City Directory
Wendell, John H.: (OC) Justice of the Peace, (CMTS) Albany 1815 City Directory
Wendell, John I.: (OC) Merchant, (CMTS) Albany 1815 City Directory
Wendell, Miss: (RES) Boarding House at 22 Maiden Lane, (CMTS) Albany 1815 City Directory
Wendell, Peter: (OC) Physician, (CMTS) Albany 1815 City Directory
Wendell, Philip: (CMTS) 1790 Federal Census, Watervliet
Wendell, Widow of Philip: (RES) 112 State, (CMTS) Albany 1815 City Directory
Werley, Peter: (CMTS) 1790 Federal Census Rensselaerville
Wermer, Michael: (CMTS) 1790 Federal Census, Watervliet
Werner, Christopher: (CMTS) 1790 Federal Census Rensselaerville
Werner, Henry: (CMTS) 1790 Federal Census Rensselaerville
Werner, Matthew: (CMTS) 1790 Federal Census Rensselaerville
West, Agnes: (CMTS) 1915, Census, District No. 4 Ward No. 18
West, Aurther: (CMTS) 1915, Census, District No. 3 Ward No. 11
West, Carrie L.: (CMTS) 1915, Census, District No. 6 Ward No. 18
West, Mrs. Elenor: (CMTS) 1915, Census, District No. 4 Ward No. 19
West, Elisha: (CMTS) 1790 Federal Census Rensselaerville
West, Emma M.: (CMTS) 1915, Census, District No. 2 Ward No. 17
West, F. A.: (CMTS) 1915, Census, District No. 2 Ward No. 6
West, Florence: (CMTS) 1915, Census, District No. 4 Ward No. 8
West, Geo. H.: (CMTS) 1915, Census, District No. 6 Ward No. 18

West, Hazel: (CMTS) 1915, Census, District No. 3 Ward No. 11
West, Hazel V.: (CMTS) 1915, Census, District No. 4 Ward No. 19
West, Helen: (CMTS) 1915, Census, District No. 6 Ward No. 19
West, Henry A.: (CMTS) 1915, Census, District No. 3 Ward No. 17
West, Jennie: (CMTS) 1915, Census, District No. 3 Ward No. 6
West, Jerald: (CMTS) 1915, Census, District No. 6 Ward No. 19
West, Laura: (CMTS) 1915, Census, District No. 6 Ward No. 19
West, Leon: (CMTS) 1915, Census, District No. 8 Ward No. 19
West, Lincoln S.: (CMTS) 1915, Census, District No. 6 Ward No. 19
West, Louisa: (CMTS) 1915, Census, District No. 3 Ward No. 11
West, Martha: (CMTS) 1915, Census, District No. 2 Ward No. 18
West, Mary: (CMTS) 1915, Census, District No. 3 Ward No. 17
West, Mary: (CMTS) 1915, Census, District No. 4 Ward No. 4
West, May: (CMTS) 1915, Census, District No. 2 Ward No. 6
West, Myron: (CMTS) 1915, Census, District No. 2 Ward No. 9
West, Olive E.: (CMTS) 1915, Census, District No. 4 Ward No. 19
West, Paul D.: (CMTS) 1915, Census, District No. 2 Ward No. 17
West, Peter: (CMTS) 1790 Federal Census Rensselaerville
West, S. M.: (CMTS) 1915, Census, District No. 2 Ward No. 6
West, Samuel: (CMTS) 1915, Census, District No. 4 Ward No. 18
West, Thomas D.: (CMTS) 1915, Census, District No. 2 Ward No. 17
West, Uel: (OC) Tin Plate Worker, (CMTS) Albany 1815 City Directory
West, William T.: (CMTS) 1915, Census, District No. 2 Ward No. 17
Westcott, Henry R.: (F) Member Mount Vernon Lodge, No. 3, 1900, Albany, NY, (CMTS) Past Master 1893
Westerlo, Rensselaer: (OC) Counsellor, (CMTS) Albany 1815 City Directory
Westfall, Allice: (CMTS) 1915, Census, District No. 3 Ward No. 13
Westfall, Anna: (CMTS) 1915, Census, District No. 4 Ward No. 1
Westfall, Catherine: (CMTS) 1915, Census, District No. 3 Ward No. 13
Westfall, Charles: (CMTS) 1915, Census, District No. 5 Ward No. 18
Westfall, Charles A.: (CMTS) 1915, Census, District No. 6 Ward No. 1
Westfall, Denis: (CMTS) 1915, Census, District No. 3 Ward No. 13
Westfall, Dorothy E.: (CMTS) 1915, Census, District No. 6 Ward No. 1
Westfall, Edward: (CMTS) 1915, Census, District No. 3 Ward No. 17
Westfall, Eva: (CMTS) 1915, Census, District No. 5 Ward No. 18
Westfall, George: (CMTS) 1915, Census, District No. 3 Ward No. 13
Westfall, Harriet E.: (CMTS) 1915, Census, District No. 6 Ward No. 1
Westfall, Harry H.: (CMTS) 1915, Census, District No. 4 Ward No. 1
Westfall, Herman: (CMTS) 1915, Census, District No. 4 Ward No. 1
Westfall, James: (CMTS) 1915, Census, District No. 3 Ward No. 13
Westfall, James Jr.: (CMTS) 1915, Census, District No. 3 Ward No. 13
Westfall, James M.: (CMTS) 1915, Census, District No. 3 Ward No. 13
Westfall, Jane: (CMTS) 1915, Census, District No. 2 Ward No. 13
Westfall, Petrus: (CMTS) 1790 Federal Census, Watervliet

Westfall, Richard: (CMTS) 1915, Census, District No. 3 Ward No. 13
Westfall, Rose: (CMTS) 1915, Census, District No. 3 Ward No. 13
Westfall, Unknown: (CMTS) 1790 Federal Census, Watervliet
Westfall, Walter L.: (CMTS) 1915, Census, District No. 6 Ward No. 1
Weston, James: (CMTS) 1790 Federal Census Rensselaerville
Wetherbee, Albert C.: (F) Member Temple Lodge, No. 14, 1900,
 Albany, NY
Wetmore, Izrahiah: (OC) Innkeeper, (CMTS) Albany 1815 City Directory
Weyman, John: (CMTS) 1790 Federal Census, Watervliet
Whalen, Jeremiah: (OC) Gardener, (CMTS) Albany 1815 City Directory
Wheeler, A: (OC) Teacher, (CMTS) Albany 1815 City Directory
Wheeler, Edward J.: (F) Member Masters Lodge, No. 5, 1900,
 Albany, NY
Wheeler, Emerald: (OC) Grocer, (CMTS) Albany 1815 City Directory
Wheeler, Ephraim: (OC) Teamster, (CMTS) Albany 1815 City Directory
Wheeler, John: (CMTS) 1790 Federal Census, Watervliet
Wheeler, John: (CMTS) 1790 Federal Census Rensselaerville
Wheeler, Seth: (F) Member Temple Lodge, No. 14, 1900,
 Albany, NY
Wheeler, Silas: (CMTS) 1790 Federal Census Rensselaerville
Whiley, Samuel: (CMTS) 1790 Federal Census, Watervliet
Whipple, Barnum: (OC) Skipper, (CMTS) Albany 1815 City Directory
Whipple, Benjamin: (RES) 61 Maiden Lane, (CMTS) Albany 1815 City
 Directory
Whipple, David: (CMTS) 1790 Federal Census, Watervliet
Whipple, Griffin: (CMTS) 1790 Federal Census, Watervliet
Whish, Charles F.: (F) Member Mount Vernon Lodge, No. 3, 1900,
 Albany, NY
Whish, George W.: (F) Member Mount Vernon Lodge, No. 3, 1900,
 Albany, NY
Whish, John: (F) Member Mount Vernon Lodge, No. 3, 1900,
 Albany, NY
Whish, William C.: (F) Member Mount Vernon Lodge, No. 3, 1900,
 Albany, NY
Whish, William H.: (F) Member Mount Vernon Lodge, No. 3, 1900,
 Albany, NY, (CMTS) Past Master 1871
Whitbeck, Theodore H.: (F) Member Temple Lodge, No. 14, 1900,
 Albany, NY
Whitbeck, William H.: (F) Member Temple Lodge, No. 14, 1900,
 Albany, NY
White, Abraham: (OC) ordinary, (CMTS) Albany 1815 City Directory
White, Addison: (F) Member Temple Lodge, No. 14, 1900,
 Albany, NY
White, Andrew G.: (F) Member Masters Lodge, No. 5, 1900,
 Albany, NY

White, Elizabeth: (RES) 29 Hamilton, (CMTS) Albany 1815 City
    Directory
White, Frederick W.: (F) Member Masters Lodge, No. 5, 1900,
    Albany, NY
White, George: (OC) Printer, (CMTS) Albany 1815 City Directory
White, George A.: (F) Member Masters Lodge, No. 5, 1900,
    Albany, NY
White, Jacob: (OC) Morocco Dresser, (CMTS) Albany 1815 City
    Directory
White, James: (F) Member Temple Lodge, No. 14, 1900,
    Albany, NY
White, James: (CMTS) 1790 Federal Census Rensselaerville
White, John: (OC) Laborer, (CMTS) Albany 1815 City Directory
White, John R.: (F) Member Temple Lodge, No. 14, 1900,
    Albany, NY
White, Luther: (OC) Teamster, (CMTS) Albany 1815 City Directory
White, Matthew: (RES) 10 Chapel, (CMTS) Albany 1815 City Directory
White, Mrs. Gilbert: (RES) 52 Union, (CMTS) Albany 1815 City
    Directory
White, Shandrach: (OC) Teamster, (CMTS) Albany 1815 City Directory
White, Silas: (OC) Chair Maker, (CMTS) Albany 1815 City Directory
White, Widow Sarah: (RES) 81 Maiden Lane, (CMTS) Albany 1815 City
    Directory
Whitefield, Robert P.: (F) Member Temple Lodge, No. 14, 1900,
    Albany, NY
Whiteman, Adam: (CMTS) 1790 Federal Census Rensselaerville
Whiteman, William: (CMTS) 1790 Federal Census Rensselaerville
Whitesides, William: (OC) Laborer, (CMTS) Albany 1815 City Directory
Whiting, Elijah: (OC) Teamster, (CMTS) Albany 1815 City Directory
Whitmarsh, Zachariah: (CMTS) 1790 Federal Census, Watervliet
Whitmore, Adelbert: (F) Member Temple Lodge, No. 14, 1900,
    Albany, NY
Whitney, Charles L. A.: (F) Member Temple Lodge, No. 14, 1900,
    Albany, NY
Whitney, Selleck: (OC) Skipper, (CMTS) Albany 1815 City Directory
Whitney, Stephen W.: (F) Member Masters Lodge, No. 5, 1900,
    Albany, NY
Whittle, Daniel: (F) Member Masters Lodge, No. 5, 1900,
    Albany, NY
Wiedman, Jacob: (CMTS) 1790 Federal Census Rensselaerville
Wiedman, Jr., Jacob: (CMTS) 1790 Federal Census Rensselaerville
Wigelman, Benjamin: (CMTS) 1790 Federal Census Rensselaerville
Wilcocks, Daniel: (CMTS) 1790 Federal Census Rensselaerville
Wilcox, George B.: (F) Member Masters Lodge, No. 5, 1900,
    Albany, NY

Wilcox, Horace: (OC) Merchant, (CMTS) Albany 1815 City Directory
Wilias, James: (RES) 56 Fox, (CMTS) Albany 1815 City Directory
Wilkie, Alden: (OC) Grocer, (CMTS) Albany 1815 City Directory
Wilkinson, Franics: (OC) Grocer, (CMTS) Albany 1815 City Directory
Wilkinson, Jacob: (OC) Grocer, (CMTS) Albany 1815 City Directory
Wilkinson, John: (OC) Carpenter, (CMTS) Albany 1815 City Directory
Wilkinson, Thomas: (OC) Grocer, (CMTS) Albany 1815 City Directory
Wilkinson, Jr., George: (F) Member Temple Lodge, No. 14, 1900,
    Albany, NY
Willaims, Daniel D.: (F) Member Temple Lodge, No. 14, 1900,
    Albany, NY
Willard, Elias: (OC) Physician, (CMTS) Albany 1815 City Directory
Willard, Elias & Co.: (OC) Hatter, (CMTS) Albany 1815 City Directory
Willard, James N.: (F) Member Temple Lodge, No. 14, 1900,
    Albany, NY
Willard, John: (OC) Merchant, (CMTS) Albany 1815 City Directory
Willard, Moses: (OC) Physician, (CMTS) Albany 1815 City Directory
Willers, Jr., Diedrich: (F) Member Masters Lodge, No. 5, 1900,
    Albany, NY
Willett, Elbert: (RES) 69 Hudson, (CMTS) Albany 1815 City Directory
Willett, Widow of Edward: (RES) 18 S. Pear; (CMTS) Albany 1815
    City Directory
Williams, David: (OC) Shoemaker, (CMTS) Albany 1815 City Directory
Williams, Edward P.: (F) Member Temple Lodge, No. 14, 1900,
    Albany, NY
Williams, Enos: (OC) Laborer, (CMTS) Albany 1815 City Directory
Williams, Foster: (OC) Cartman, (CMTS) Albany 1815 City Directory
Williams, George A.: (F) Member Temple Lodge, No. 14, 1900,
    Albany, NY
Williams, George B.: (OC) porter & oyster house, (CMTS) Albany 1815
    City Directory
Williams, John: (CMTS) 1790 Federal Census Rensselaerville
Williams, John: (CMTS) 1790 Federal Census Rensselaerville
Williams, John: (CMTS) 1790 Federal Census Rensselaerville
Williams, John: (OC) Grocer, (CMTS) Albany 1815 City Directory
Williams, John C.: (CMTS) 1790 Federal Census Rensselaerville
Williams, Michael: (RES) Boarding House at 40 Green, (CMTS) Albany
    1815 City Directory
Williams, Peter: (OC) Laborer, (CMTS) Albany 1815 City Directory
Williams, Platt: (OC) Physician, (CMTS) Albany 1815 City Directory
Williams, Richard: (OC) Carpenter, (CMTS) Albany 1815 City Directory
Williams, Robert D.: (F) Member Masters Lodge, No. 5, 1900,
    Albany, NY, (CMTS) Past Master
Williams, Samuel: (OC) Printer, (CMTS) Albany 1815 City Directory
Williams, Susan: (OC) Teacher, (CMTS) Albany 1815 City Directory

Williams, Thomas: (OC) Shoemaker, (CMTS) Albany 1815 City
 Directory
Williams, Thomas J.: (F) Member Temple Lodge, No. 14, 1900,
 Albany, NY
Williams, William W.: (OC) Carpenter, (CMTS) Albany 1815 City
 Directory
Williamson, John: (OC) Butcher, (CMTS) Albany 1815 City Directory
Williamson, M. K.: (CO) L. Annesley & Co., Looking Glasses & Picture
 Frames, (CMTS) Albany 1859 City Directory
Willis, Benjamin: (CMTS) 1790 Federal Census Rensselaerville
Willis, Giddeon: (CMTS) 1790 Federal Census Rensselaerville
Willis, Ishmael L: (OC) Cartman, (CMTS) Albany 1815 City Directory
Willis, Philip: (OC) Blacksmith, (CMTS) Albany 1815 City Directory
Willis, Rowland: (OC) Cartman, (CMTS) Albany 1815 City Directory
Willoughby, Elijah: (CMTS) 1790 Federal Census Rensselaerville
Willsee, Henry: (CMTS) 1790 Federal Census Rensselaerville
Willsey, E. M.: (F) Member Temple Lodge, No. 14, 1900,
 Albany, NY
Wilmarth, Gersham: (CMTS) 1790 Federal Census Rensselaerville
Wilney, Elijah: (CMTS) 1790 Federal Census, Watervliet
Wilsey, Abraham: (CMTS) 1790 Federal Census Rensselaerville
Wilsey, Henry: (CMTS) 1790 Federal Census Rensselaerville
Wilsey, Isaac: (CMTS) 1790 Federal Census Rensselaerville
Wilsey, Jacob: (CMTS) 1790 Federal Census Rensselaerville
Wilsey, Teunis: (CMTS) 1790 Federal Census Rensselaerville
Wilson, Benjamin: (OC) Grocer, (CMTS) Albany 1815 City Directory
Wilson, James: (OC) Grocer, (CMTS) Albany 1815 City Directory
Wilson, Joesph: (RES) 49 Dock, (CMTS) Albany 1815 City Directory
Wilson, Joseph: (CMTS) 1790 Federal Census, Watervliet
Wilson, Joseph: (OC) Grocer, (CMTS) Albany 1815 City Directory
Wilson, Oren E.: (F) Member Temple Lodge, No. 14, 1900,
 Albany, NY
Wilson, Robert: (CMTS) 1790 Federal Census Rensselaerville
Wilson, Samuel: (RES) Boarding House at 34 Eagle, (CMTS) Albany
 1815 City Directory
Wilson, Stewart: (OC) Laborer, (CMTS) Albany 1815 City Directory
Wilson, Thomas: (OC) Laborer, (CMTS) Albany 1815 City Directory
Wilson, Widow Martha: (OC) Teacher, (CMTS) Albany 1815 City
 Directory
Wilson, Widow Mary: (RES) 49 Husdon, (CMTS) Albany 1815 City
 Directory
Wiltse, James W.: (F) Member Temple Lodge, No. 14, 1900,
 Albany, NY
Winchester, James: (OC) Merchant Tailor, (CMTS) Albany 1815 City
 Directory

Winder, Ashbel: (OC) Carpenter, (CMTS) Albany 1815 City Directory
Winegart, Margaret: (CMTS) 1790 Federal Census, Watervliet
Wineger, John: (CMTS) 1790 Federal Census Rensselaerville
Winess, Jeremiah: (CMTS) 1790 Federal Census Rensselaerville
Wing, J. A: (OC) Physician, (CMTS) Albany 1815 City Directory
Winhold, Louis C.: (F) Member Temple Lodge, No. 14, 1900, Albany, NY
Winne, Aaron: (CMTS) 1790 Federal Census Rensselaerville
Winne, Anthony: (CMTS) 1790 Federal Census, Watervliet
Winne, Benjamin: (OC) Mason, (CMTS) Albany 1815 City Directory
Winne, Charles: (F) Member Temple Lodge, No. 14, 1900, Albany, NY
Winne, Charles H.: (F) Member Temple Lodge, No. 14, 1900, Albany, NY
Winne, Charles V.: (F) Member Temple Lodge, No. 14, 1900, Albany, NY
Winne, Daniel: (OC) Chair Maker, (CMTS) Albany 1815 City Directory
Winne, Daniel I.: (OC) Marshal & D. Ex. officer, (CMTS) Albany 1815 City Directory
Winne, David P.: (OC) Merchant, (CMTS) Albany 1815 City Directory
Winne, Jacob L: (OC) Merchant, (CMTS) Albany 1815 City Directory
Winne, Jellis: (OC) Merchant, (CMTS) Albany 1815 City Directory
WInne, John: (F) Member Temple Lodge, No. 14, 1900, Albany, NY
Winne, John I.: (OC) Shoemaker, (CMTS) Albany 1815 City Directory
Winne, John L: (OC) Merchant, (CMTS) Albany 1815 City Directory
Winne, Lansing B.: (F) Member Temple Lodge, No. 14, 1900, Albany, NY
Winne, Levinus L: (OC) Attorney, (CMTS) Albany 1815 City Directory
Winne, Martin I.: (OC) Laborer, (CMTS) Albany 1815 City Directory
Winne, Walter M.: (F) Member Temple Lodge, No. 14, 1900, Albany, NY
Winne, William: (OC) Inspector of leather, (CMTS) Albany 1815 City Directory
Winne, William B.: (OC) Letter Carrier, (CMTS) Albany 1815 City Directory
Winney, Benjamin: (CMTS) 1790 Federal Census, Watervliet
Winney, Cornelius: (CMTS) 1790 Federal Census, Watervliet
Winney, Daniel: (CMTS) 1790 Federal Census, Watervliet
Winney, David F.: (CMTS) 1790 Federal Census, Watervliet
Winney, Francis: (CMTS) 1790 Federal Census, Watervliet
Winney, John: (CMTS) 1790 Federal Census, Watervliet
Winney, John D.: (CMTS) 1790 Federal Census, Watervliet
Winney, Jonathan: (CMTS) 1790 Federal Census, Watervliet
Winney, Levinus B.: (CMTS) 1790 Federal Census, Watervliet

Winney, Peter D.: (CMTS) 1790 Federal Census, Watervliet
Winney, Peter F.: (CMTS) 1790 Federal Census, Watervliet
Winney, William: (CMTS) 1790 Federal Census, Watervliet
Winny, Adam: (CMTS) 1790 Federal Census, Watervliet
Winslow, Richard: (RES) 656 S. Market, (CMTS) Albany 1815 City Directory
Winten, Widow Janet: (OC) Grocer, (CMTS) Albany 1815 City Directory
Winter, Michael: (CMTS) 1790 Federal Census, Watervliet
Wisegerber, Jacob: (CMTS) 1790 Federal Census Rensselaerville
Wiswall, Samuel: (OC) Captain of steamboat, (CMTS) Albany 1815 City Directory
Witaker, Gertrude: (CMTS) 1790 Federal Census, Watervliet
Witaker, Neil: (CMTS) 1790 Federal Census Rensselaerville
Witbeck, Abraham: (CMTS) 1790 Federal Census, Watervliet
Witbeck, Casparus: (CMTS) 1790 Federal Census, Watervliet
Witbeck, Garret: (CMTS) 1790 Federal Census, Watervliet
Witbeck, John J: (CMTS) 1790 Federal Census, Watervliet
Witbeck, John J: (CMTS) 1790 Federal Census, Watervliet
Witbeck, Lucas: (CMTS) 1790 Federal Census, Watervliet
Witbeck, Peter: (CMTS) 1790 Federal Census, Watervliet
Witbeck, Thomas L: (CMTS) 1790 Federal Census, Watervliet
Witbeck, Walter: (CMTS) 1790 Federal Census, Watervliet
Witcome, Simon: (CMTS) 1790 Federal Census Rensselaerville
Witman, Michael: (CMTS) 1790 Federal Census Rensselaerville
Witney, Walter: (CMTS) 1790 Federal Census, Watervliet
Witter, Park: (CMTS) 1790 Federal Census Rensselaerville
Wittiker, Joseph: (RES) 32 N. Pearl, (CMTS) Albany 1815 City Directory
Wolf, John: (CMTS) 1790 Federal Census, Watervliet
Wolf, Wilhelmus: (CMTS) 1790 Federal Census Rensselaerville
Wolfgang, F. A.: (F) Member Mount Vernon Lodge, No. 3, 1900, Albany, NY
Wolford, Jr., John: (OC) Merchant, (CMTS) Albany 1815 City Directory
Wood, A. J.: (F) Member Mount Vernon Lodge, No. 3, 1900, Albany, NY
Wood, David: (OC) Merchant, (CMTS) Albany 1815 City Directory
Wood, Jeremiah: (CMTS) 1790 Federal Census, Watervliet
Wood, Jessee: (CMTS) 1790 Federal Census, Watervliet
Wood, John B.: (F) Member Mount Vernon Lodge, No. 3, 1900, Albany, NY
Wood, Levi: (F) Member Temple Lodge, No. 14, 1900, Albany, NY
Wood, Moses: (OC) Shoemaker, (CMTS) Albany 1815 City Directory
Wood, Widow Ann: (OC) Grocer, (CMTS) Albany 1815 City Directory
Wood, Zebedy: (CMTS) 1790 Federal Census Rensselaerville
Woodford, Joseph: (CMTS) 1790 Federal Census Rensselaerville

Woodruff, Halsey: (F) Member Temple Lodge, No. 14, 1900, Albany, NY
Woodruff, Halsey: (OC) Mason, (CMTS) Albany 1815 City Directory
Woodward, James O.: (F) Member Masters Lodge, No. 5, 1900, Albany, NY
Woodward, S. G.: (OC) Austin & Co., Agents for Albany & Canal Line, (CMTS) Albany 1859 City Directory
Woodward, Walter M.: (F) Member Masters Lodge, No. 5, 1900, Albany, NY
Woodworth, Benjamin: (CMTS) 1790 Federal Census Rensselaerville
Woodworth, David: (OC) Grocer, (CMTS) Albany 1815 City Directory
Woodworth, John: (OC) Counsellor, (CMTS) Albany 1815 City Directory
Woodworth, Robert: (OC) Cartman, (CMTS) Albany 1815 City Directory
Woolcock, William: (OC) Tinplate Worker, (CMTS) Albany 1815 City Directory
Wooley, Jesse B.: (F) Member Mount Vernon Lodge, No. 3, 1900, Albany, NY
Wooster, Samuel C.: (F) Member Temple Lodge, No. 14, 1900, Albany, NY
Worchester, Edwin D.: (F) Member Masters Lodge, No. 5, 1900, Albany, NY
Wordon, Nathaniel: (CMTS) 1790 Federal Census, Watervliet
Wormer, Abraham: (CMTS) 1790 Federal Census, Watervliet
Wormer, Arent: (CMTS) 1790 Federal Census, Watervliet
Wormer, Frederick: (OC) Innkeeper, (CMTS) Albany 1815 City Directory
Wormer, Isaac: (CMTS) 1790 Federal Census Rensselaerville
Wormer, Petrus: (CMTS) 1790 Federal Census, Watervliet
Wormer, Jr., Frederick: (CMTS) 1790 Federal Census Rensselaerville
Worth, Gerham A: (OC) Cashier of M & F. bank, (CMTS) Albany 1815 City Directory
Worthington, Daniel: (RES) 184 S. Pearl, (CMTS) Albany 1815 City Directory
Wright, Alfred W.: (F) Member Temple Lodge, No. 14, 1900, Albany, NY
Wright, Frank L.: (F) Member Temple Lodge, No. 14, 1900, Albany, NY
Wright, Jobe: (CMTS) 1790 Federal Census, Watervliet
Wynants, William: (CMTS) 1790 Federal Census Rensselaerville
Wyncoop, Harmen G.: (OC) Druggist, (CMTS) Albany 1815 City Directory
Wyncoop, James: (OC) Merchant, (CMTS) Albany 1815 City Directory
Wynkoop, Evert: (CMTS) 1790 Federal Census, Watervliet
Yager, John: (CMTS) 1790 Federal Census Rensselaerville
Yates, Christoper A.: (CMTS) 1790 Federal Census, Watervliet
Yates, Christopher C.: (OC) Physician & Surrogate, (CMTS) Albany 1815

City Directory
Yates, John V. N.: (OC) Recorder, (CMTS) Albany 1815 City Directory
Yates, John W.: (OC) Cashier New York State Bank, (CMTS) Albany 1815 City Directory
Yates, Widow Rachel: (RES) 22 Green, (CMTS) Albany 1815 City Directory
Yeomans, Miss: (OC) Teacher, (CMTS) Albany 1815 City Directory
Yorke, Joseph W.: (F) Member Mount Vernon Lodge, No. 3, 1900, Albany, NY
Youdell, Leoni: (CMTS) 1790 Federal Census Rensselaerville
Youdell, William: (CMTS) 1790 Federal Census Rensselaerville
Yound, William: (OC) Teacher, (CMTS) Albany 1815 City Directory
Young, Abraham: (CMTS) 1790 Federal Census Rensselaerville
Young, Hays: (F) Member Temple Lodge, No. 14, 1900, Albany, NY
Young, Henry: (CMTS) 1790 Federal Census Rensselaerville
Young, James: (F) Member Temple Lodge, No. 14, 1900, Albany, NY, (CMTS) Past Master 1870
Young, James: (OC) Cooper, (CMTS) Albany 1815 City Directory
Young, Jeremiah: (CMTS) 1790 Federal Census Rensselaerville
Young, John: (CMTS) 1790 Federal Census, Watervliet
Young, John: (CMTS) 1790 Federal Census Rensselaerville
Young, John: (OC) Laborer, (CMTS) Albany 1815 City Directory
Young, John H.: (F) Member Temple Lodge, No. 14, 1900, Albany, NY
Young, Peter: (CMTS) 1790 Federal Census Rensselaerville
Young, Philip B.: (F) Member Temple Lodge, No. 14, 1900, Albany, NY
Young, Robert: (F) Member Mount Vernon Lodge, No. 3, 1900, Albany, NY
Young, Widow: (RES) 36 Columbia, (CMTS) Albany 1815 City Directory
Young, Samuel: (CMTS) 1790 Federal Census Rensselaerville
Young, Thomas: (OC) Comedian, (CMTS) Albany 1815 City Directory
Zautner, George: (F) Member Mount Vernon Lodge, No. 3, 1900, Albany, NY
Zeddle, Jacob: (CMTS) 1790 Federal Census Rensselaerville
Zeeman, Dirk: (RES) 37 Chapel street, (CMTS) Albany 1815 City Directory
Zeh, Adam: (CMTS) 1790 Federal Census Rensselaerville
Zeh, Charles: (F) Member Temple Lodge, No. 14, 1900, Albany, NY
Zeh, Hendrick: (CMTS) 1790 Federal Census Rensselaerville
Zeh, Johannes: (CMTS) 1790 Federal Census Rensselaerville
Zeh, Jost: (CMTS) 1790 Federal Census Rensselaerville

Zimmer, Peter: (CMTS) 1790 Federal Census Rensselaerville
Zoe, Nicholas: (CMTS) 1790 Federal Census, Watervliet

Heritage Books by Sherida K. Eddlemon:

Missouri Genealogical Records and Abstracts:
  Volume 1: 1766–1839
  Volume 2: 1752–1839
  Volume 3: 1787–1839
  Volume 4: 1741–1839
  Volume 5: 1755–1839
  Volume 6: 1621–1839
  Volume 7: 1535–1839

Missouri Genealogical Gleanings 1840 and Beyond, Volumes 1–9

1890 Genealogical Census Reconstruction: Mississippi, Volumes 1 and 2

1890 Genealogical Census Reconstruction: Missouri, Volumes 1–3

1890 Genealogical Census Reconstruction: Ohio, Volume 1
(with Patricia P. Nelson)

1890 Genealogical Census Reconstruction: Tennessee, Volume 1

A Genealogical Collection of Kentucky Birth and Death Records

Butler County, Missouri Genealogical Tidbits

Callaway County, Missouri, Marriage Records: 1821 to 1871

Cumberland Presbyterian Church, Volume One: 1836 and Beyond

Dickson County, Tennessee Marriage Records, 1817–1879

Genealogical Abstracts from Missouri Church Records and Other Religious Sources, Volume 1

Genealogical Abstracts from Tennessee Newspapers, 1791–1808

Genealogical Abstracts from Tennessee Newspapers, 1803–1812

Genealogical Abstracts from Tennessee Newspapers, 1821–1828

Tennessee Genealogical Records and Abstracts, Volume 1: 1787–1839

Genealogical Gleanings from New York Fraternal Organizations Volumes 1 and 2

Index to the Arkansas General Land Office, 1820–1907 Volumes 1–10

Kentucky Genealogical Records and Abstracts, Volume 1: 1781–1839

Kentucky Genealogical Records and Abstracts, Volume 2: 1796–1839

Lewis County, Missouri Index to Circuit Court Records, Volume 1, 1833–1841

Missouri Birth and Death Records, Volumes 1–4

Morgan County, Missouri Marriage Records, 1833–1893

Our Ancestors of Albany County, New York, Volumes 1 and 2

Our Ancestors of Cuyahoga County, Ohio, Volume 1
(with Patricia P. Nelson)

Ralls County, Missouri Settlement Records, 1832–1853

Records of Randolph County, Missouri, 1833–1964

Ten Thousand Missouri Taxpayers

The "Show–Me" Guide to Missouri: Sources for Genealogical and Historical Research

CD: Dickson County, Tennessee Marriage Records, 1817–1879

CD: Index to the Arkansas General Land Office, 1820–1907 Volumes 1–10

CD: Missouri, Volume 3

CD: Tennessee Genealogical Records

CD: Tennessee Genealogical Records, Volumes 1–3

www.ingramcontent.com/pod-product-compliance
Lightning Source LLC
Chambersburg PA
CBHW050802160426
43192CB00010B/1608